BEST PRACTICE

BEST PRACTICE

IDEAS AND INSIGHTS FROM THE WORLD'S FOREMOST BUSINESS THINKERS

PERSEUS
PUBLISHING

A Member of the Perseus Books Group

Many of the designations used by manufacturers and sellers to distinguish their products are claimed as trademarks. Where those designations appear in this book and Perseus Publishing was aware of a trademark claim, the designations have been printed in initial capital letters.

ISBN 0–7382–0822–1
Perseus Publishing is a member of the Perseus Books Group.
Find us on the World Wide Web at
http://www.perseuspublishing.com

Perseus Publishing books are available at special discounts for bulk purchases in the U.S. by corporations, institutions, and other organizations. For more information, please contact the Special Markets Department at the Perseus Books Group, 11 Cambridge Center, Cambridge, MA 02142, or call (800) 255-1514 or (617) 252-5298, or e-mail j.mccrary@perseusbooks.com.

Text design by Fiona Pike, Pike Design, Winchester, U.K.
Typeset by RefineCatch Limited, Bungay, Suffolk, U.K.

First printing, May 2003
1 2 3 4 5 6 7 8 9 10-

For more information about *Business: The Ultimate Resource* and related titles, and to register for your free electronic upgrades, please visit: www.ultimatebusinessresource.com. At the subscriber registration page enter your name, e-mail address, and your password: mybiz

CONTENTS

INTRODUCTION:
Getting the Best from Best Practices
Rosabeth Moss Kanter

Some of the best innovators I know are borrowers.

Intel borrowed marketing techniques to sell computer chips like potato chips. Chapparal Steel, one of the new breed of successful steel mini-mills, discovered ideas about better ways to produce molds for casting from a Mexican company. A large hospital system sent administrators and physicians to Disney World to learn about guest relations. Japan modeled its post office after that of Great Britain. The Singapore government routinely sends delegations to study how the best private and public sector organizations handle new issues. When Robert Saldich was C.E.O. of Raychem, he instituted a Not-Invented-Here Award for the person or group that did the best job of adapting an idea from somewhere else. The founders of City Year, the large multi-city urban youth corps that became the model for national service in the United States and South Africa, took best practices from the military (disciplines, uniforms, boot camps), the Olympics (corporate-branded team sponsorships), education (graduation requirements and commencement ceremonies), and business (performance measurement).

All great borrowers—perhaps all visionary leaders—know the best practice secret. Stretching to learn from the best of the best in any sector can make a big vision more likely to succeed. Of course, reaching for excellence requires learning what excellence is. High performers open their minds to new ideas, challenge their assumptions, and scrutinize their performance practice by practice.

This kind of rapid adaptation is essential in a global information economy that seems to throw curve balls as often as winning pitches, one that brings terror along with technology. Organizations and leaders must be adept at learning, adept at change, always striving to perform at their peak.

WHY BEST PRACTICE?

Lurking behind "best practice" is a simple concept: measurable standards.

The idea of benchmarking, one aspect of the search for best practices, started pragmatically, with the curiosity and precision of scientists. Benchmarks are measurements done in a laboratory, at a workbench, that are so precise they can be used to set the standard. The idea has traveled from yardsticks to business management. In the early days of the Total Quality Management movement in the 1980s, Xerox—which then desperately needed improvement, as it did again 20 years later—brought the idea of competitive benchmarking from Japan to the United States. Somewhere along the way, absolute standards—such as zero defects—became relative standards—who's doing the best job of reducing defects? "Best" became "better" or, in some cases, simply good enough.

Performance of anything—a product line, a business unit, a hospital, a school, or anything—can be measured against three different standards: the past, a set of peers, or potential that could be achieved. Think about the differences in terms of how much learning and change occurs.

For starters, you can measure performance against the past, against your own record—the stuff of corporate annual reports. How are you doing compared to last year, last quarter, last month? If the trend is up, you feel pretty good. You decide to keep on going with whatever it is that's already underway. Not much learning there. If the trend is down, you feel dissatisfied. You look for something to blame, or you vow to do better. The emphasis is on what went wrong and how to fix it. Not much learning there either.

You can go one step further and start looking outside your own experience to measure performance against peers. How are you doing compared to those who are similar entities, whether competitors or counterparts? If you're beating them, good for you—look no further. If you're behind, then you work harder to catch up. Sometimes, but not always, you decide to learn from them. The emphasis is on staying close enough to industry standards that you're a little ahead, but not too far ahead. All you have to do to win is beat someone else, then relax. Some companies set compensation just above industry average. Football and baseball teams send in relief players toward the end of the game when they're enough ahead to afford to use the second string.

Peer comparisons emphasize getting ahead, not achieving excellence. This is expressed well in an old joke about the two campers who wake up at their campsite in the woods to find a bear near their tent. One immediately puts on his running shoes. His companion, observing this, admonishes him, "That's foolish; you can't outrun a bear." "That's right," the first camper replies over his shoulder as he starts moving, "but all I have to do is outrun you." There's some learning and change involved in peer comparisons, but not all that much.

Most businesses, indeed most people, are content with the first two kinds of assessments, against the past and against peers. *Am I better off today than I was five years ago? Is my team winning?* But that's not enough to lay the foundations for success in a world of rapid change, of demanding competition, of new technologies, of empowered customers and consumers. Looking backwards or looking at peers doesn't provide sufficient impetus for finding better approaches.

Leaders who want to achieve sustained success reach for a higher standard. They want to be not just good or better, but best. They imagine greater heights to be attained. They envision an even better world and encourage themselves and others to achieve it. They use best practices to challenge themselves in a third way.

This third way to measure performance is against potential, against all that could be achieved, against all that's possible. The C.E.O. of a food company wanted more innovation and bigger ideas because he saw people settling for small gains and small profits when total market size was so much bigger. In bagged cereals, for example, his company had increased sales by 15% in the last year, which the product manager reported proudly; but a small, previously ignored competitor was up 50% and had sales volume three times as high as the food giant. To the C.E.O., the measurement system that rewarded people for small gains and making their numbers, and bench-marked only against similar peers, stifled innovation and restricted growth. Similarly, Gateway founder Ted Waitt returned as C.E.O. to lead a turnaround premised on the untapped potential of Gateway stores to grab a much larger market share, if only timid managers could look beyond merely making incremental gains over last year. To Waitt, settling for good enough isn't good enough.

It's not only business leaders that see the need to reach for higher standards. Donald Berwick, founder of the Institute for Healthcare Improvement, had focused his advocacy for many years on improving quality and reducing errors. Recently, he charted a new course and set a new standard: the pursuit of perfection. He wants every single encounter with the healthcare system to be as good as it can possibly be.

Perfection! How many C.E.O.s urge their people to set such a high aspiration? Instead, many companies settle for less than they could achieve.

The search for excellence involves an attitude that goes beyond marketplace goals to cover every aspect of an organization's performance, process by process, practice by fine-grained practice. The corporate ethics scandals in the United States raise questions of relative ("everybody else is doing it") versus absolute standards. If you have reduced accounting errors to below industry average, is that good enough, or is there a higher standard for financial reporting? Embracing best practices, not just better practices, leads companies to set new standards and come closer to full potential, if not perfection.

Of course, the decision to go for the best practice has to be grounded in reality and informed by priorities. An organization can't necessarily be best at everything without exorbitant cost. Under new C.E.O. Jim Kilts, Gillette established a best practices benchmarking initiative to see where its functions stand on hundreds of processes and practices. But then managers assessed each result against the benefits to customers, weighed against the costs of achieving the highest standard. Sometimes excellence on everything isn't worth it. Still, Gillette finds even the scrutiny a spur to improvement.

The next challenge is acting on higher standards. High aspirations must be translated into high performance. Standard-setting leadership at the top must be reflected in standard-actualizing behavior throughout the organization.

COMMUNITIES OF (BEST) PRACTICE:
EVERYONE A PROFESSIONAL

High-performing, change-adept organizations make striving for excellence a way of life, embedded in organizational culture. They do this by trying to turn everyone, at every level, into a professional.

When my husband needed repairs to a torn rotator cuff in his shoulder, we wanted a state-of-the-art surgeon, so we did some searching and found a sports medicine clinic in San Diego, 3,000 miles from our home in Boston. That's one indication of how far some of us will go to find a consummate professional.

Medicine, law, engineering, and many other high-skill professions are widely regarded as beacons of best practice. But why stop there? Why can't other workers strive to be best in class, whatever the form their contributions take? Servicemaster, a contractor for janitorial services in hospitals, turns low-skill tasks into professional jobs, developing the best wall scrubbers and the best floor cleaners, characterized by carefully researched disciplines, excellent tools, abundant training, and a feeling of professional pride on the part of people who feel that they, too, are contributing to the medical mission. Closer to home, Home Depot wants to take pride in running the best paint departments, with knowledgeable associates schooled in paint techniques.

Professionals are known by their knowledge. All professionals use their instincts, listen to their gut, and exercise judgment, but they do it based on thorough grounding in best practices. Armed with best practice knowledge, anyone and everyone can act like a professional, exhibiting the key characteristics that distinguish mere amateurs from committed professionals:

- high performance standards
- mastery of common ways of doing things that meet those standards
- belief in a mission apart from financial success
- career progress through an increase in skills and the respect of peers
- a shared language and knowledge base
- participation in networks and events to exchange knowledge
- self-management and autonomous decisions on the job
- peer review of performance

In an information economy populated by knowledge workers, organizations run less like hierarchies and more like communities of practice, knit together by professional standards. In my recent book, *Evolve!*, I suggest that the digital age makes it both necessary and possible for organizations to become connected communities where ideas spread quickly and parts can pull together in the interests of the whole. Shared communication platforms, tools, and disciplines provide helpful structure for guiding autonomous decisions; without structure, empowerment produces chaos. Shared standards of practice provide common approaches and vocabulary to help people from diverse backgrounds or places work together smoothly. Any team crossing functions or geographies to tackle a new task has a common starting point.

If people are treated like empowered professionals, they do not wait to be told what to do, they just do it. This changes the work of managers. To restate a cliché, managers must become leaders. As leaders, they must be engaged in coaching: teaching people how to do the job autonomously, how to exercise judgment, and how to customize solutions for unique customers or clients. In short, they guide people not through rules and over-the-shoulder supervision but through knowledge of standards.

Think of this as a new kind of control system, one emanating from identification and dissemination of best practices. It guides empowered individuals toward achieving organizational objectives through shared values, standards, and priorities. People are informed about how their tasks fit into overall goals and strategy, so they can contribute to alignment. They get ongoing process measures and feedback given directly to people to help them judge and guide their own performance. Professional rewards, recognition, and future opportunities build commitment. And, of course, systematic transfer of best practices helps people to learn from what works elsewhere.

Professionalism requires continuous upgrading of skills. It has become fashionable for companies to articulate a desire to become "learning organizations." But sometimes they fail in practice because of under investment in occasions for learning, coupled with that other legacy of large bureaucracies, the politics of rank. More senior hierarchical positions often allow managers to surround themselves with sycophants and flatterers or to insulate themselves from challenge and criticism.

In the digital age, learning takes place in all directions, not just from the top down or from headquarters out. The Internet ensures this, whether managers like it or not. Before the era of PCs on every desktop and handhelds on the factory floor, the conventional wisdom in management theory was that networks were underground rumor mills. They were part of the so-called informal organization that thwarted officials and their policies, by producing illicit understandings about how to break rules or organize workers against management. Now companies encourage networks to form, realizing that they perform knowledge-transfer tasks important to the organization.

Communities of practice are networks that exchange knowledge—with or without the help of computers—and create the infrastructure for learning that characterizes high performing, change-adept organizations. Or perhaps it is more accurate to call it an infrastructure for *teaching* and learning. Professionals not only learn from best practices, they teach each other. What's important is not that individuals have images of excellence locked in their heads, but that they communicate with others, creating a foundation for collective action.

Professionalism is a dynamic capability that produces its own demand. Once people have been treated like professionals and have been encouraged to use their judgment, they want more of this treatment. Once people have earned the respect of peers by staying at the cutting edge, they recognize that they must continue to learn about the newest and best, or that respect will erode. Standards thus continue to rise, generating demand for still more knowledge of new developments and best practices.

The next question is where to look for best practices. My answer is: everywhere.

FROM BEST IN CLASS TO WORLD CLASS: BEST PRACTICES ARE EVERYWHERE

When top leaders at the BBC (British Broadcasting Corporation) decided that their organization's culture needed to change, they visited seven North American companies known for excellent cultures, including Southwest Airlines, Cisco Systems, and the Container Store. They described what they found to executive committee colleagues, to stretch thinking about how to achieve the BBC's goal of becoming "the world's best creative organization." This openness to learning was encouraged by a visionary new C.E.O. from commercial television, Gregory Dyke, who took the helm in early 2000.

Too many other companies give lip service to learning from global best practice. A large North American telecom company offers an annual quality award to the factories and facilities exhibiting the highest standards, announced at a strategy conference for the top 200-plus executives. The year I participated in the conference, the quality award went to the company's subsidiary in Istanbul, Turkey. I was intrigued. It's one thing to go to Cisco in California, but I wondered whether managers would hop on a plane for Istanbul. I asked for a show of hands: how many planned to go to Turkey to see first-hand how they did it? No hands went up. "We bring them to headquarters," an executive explained. So much for learning from international best practice.

What a long way we've come. What a long way still to go.

The global information economy continues to make world standards the highest standard—despite terrorist attacks, global recessions, anti-free-trade protestors, and protectionist moves to limit the flow of capital or goods (or even to block access to Web sites in particular countries). The backlash against globalization will serve to improve it, but I do not doubt that the flows across borders, especially of people and their ideas, will continue, and they will continue to make world standards the standards for business.

A major force behind this trend is the buying habits of giant companies themselves. Large companies have changed their purchasing patterns dramatically, consolidating their supply base and making it a global supply chain. The benefits of technology, the ease of travel, and the ubiquity and convenience of an international infrastructure such as over-night package delivery services, mean that large international companies no longer have to buy from those suppliers in the places where they are producing or selling. They shop the world. They seek fewer suppliers who can supply them everywhere at the highest standards of performance. Companies as diverse as IBM and McDonald's from the United States or L'Oréal from France have consolidated world purchasing of goods and services, finding component makers or advertising agencies that meet world standards and serve them in every part of the world.

Even if not geographically ambitious, local companies can no longer succeed by being the best in their neighborhood. Small as well as large organizations increasingly must meet the standards of the best in the world even to hold the business in their local neighborhood, as I show in my book, *World Class: Thriving Locally in the Global Economy*. This truth holds even for global giants themselves, who must ensure that their units in every country are globally competitive. The head of Gillette Asia-Pacific, headquartered in Singapore, felt that his challenge in 2002 was to raise standards continually; to be really good for Asia but not ready for the rest of the world was unacceptable.

So many vehicles spread best practices: standard-setting organizations, report cards and certifications, awards and prizes. The ISO 9000 series of European quality standards (which became de facto world standards) are now spreading all over the world; U.S. companies ask Latin American suppliers to meet these European standards. In border-crossing industries such as air transportation or telecommunications, the need for global connectivity tends to be accompanied by world standards set by international agreement. When companies form cross-border alliances to further connectivity, such as the airlines' code-sharing consortia, they try to spread best practices among their members to serve customers seamlessly as they transfer from one airline to another. It is likely that world standards will become more prevalent in more sectors—for drug or food safety, for environmental protection, or for mathematical literacy.

In a global information economy, it seems that anybody can know instantaneously what's the best and the latest—or the worst. In my book, *Evolve!*, I identified a growing number of watchdog sites ready to pounce on bad behavior. Web sites offer detailed data and comparisons of organizations; the U.S. government advertised its site comparing nursing home performance on national television. The Internet contributes to a flow of information about what's available at what price in any market. While bus tours take U.S. senior citizens across the border to fill their prescriptions at Canadian pharmacies offering the same drugs but at lower prices, some Americans buy those drugs from the comfort of their homes through Canadian e-commerce Web sites.

World best practice standards are also pushed by professions that increasingly operate in world labor markets. Scientists, engineers, accountants, lawyers, and management consultants are educated disproportionately in the United States, recruited to work anywhere, and carry desire for best practices with them across borders. Professional firms compete locally on the premise that they meet world standards. This is true even for the helping professions such as medicine.

An emerging generation of global consumers reinforces the spread of world standards. Young people use the Internet, know the same popular culture, like the same products, and speak the same second language, English. Even in fundamentalist Muslim-led Iran, international pop music stars have a teenage audience. Globe-trotting European and American teenagers are already exchange-rate savvy and can distinguish levels of quality. The teenage son of a Dutch executive, who traveled frequently for his global company, asked his father to bring him Levi's blue jeans when he returned from business trips. But, the son advised his father, "Don't buy those blue jeans at the Levi's store in London, buy them at the store in New York, because they have the same numbers on the price tags, but in London that's in pounds and in New York it's in dollars."

Ethnicity and national identity still matter greatly to people—witness the Kosovo tragedy or the fierce devotion of Palestinians to their cause—but it is portable, as ethnic groups and nationalities spread throughout the world. Overseas Chinese are at the helm of businesses in Muslim Malaysia and Indonesia. There are nearly as many Muslims in Detroit as in Baghdad, and more French-speaking people in Montreal than in any other city outside of Paris. When global variety appears everywhere, the best in the world becomes a standard for what people find at home—for example, standards for good Japanese sushi in Brazil or Boston. Local differences have not been eliminated; climates still shape business practices despite air conditioning, to pick just one driver of difference. Nor have local preferences given way to homogenized tastes. But the entire range of tastes might be found in cosmopolitan cities in every major country.

The search for best practices must be broad and comprehensive. Virtuosos and standard-setters are not the monopoly of any particular place, although some places might do more to cultivate excellence. If you want to know about lean production, go to Japan, home of Toyota—or to Toyota plants around the world. If you want to know about mobile telephony, go to Finland, home of Nokia—or to Nokia outposts everywhere. If you want to know about computer-controlled containerized shipping, go to Denmark, home of Maersk—or follow Maersk ships to major ports anywhere.

Even problem-ridden places can be sources of best practices. Fleet's inner-city banks, in run-down American neighborhoods populated by immigrants, have become sources of best practices in retail banking, because they had to innovate to deal with multilingual customers from diverse backgrounds. Brazil is a center of excellence in cash management techniques, because high inflation made it necessary for financial firms to find better ways to close transactions fast.

Best practices are anywhere and everywhere.

THE BEST PRACTICE HABIT

I started by praising the virtues of borrowing. Visionary leaders treat borrowing as the foundation for much more creative acts of learning and change. They understand that they not only must improve on their own past and do well against peers, but they must also venture beyond their own boundaries to find the best and use it to become the best. They find the underlying principle behind why a best practice works, apply it to new circumstances, and improve on it. This is not mindless copying, it is intelligent adaptation.

Let me suggest an exercise regime for enlightened leaders and those who want to join their ranks:

1. Reach high. Stretch. Raise standards and aspirations. Find the best of the best and then use it as inspiration for reaching full potential.

2. Help everyone in your organization become a professional. Empower people to manage themselves through benchmarks and standards based on best practice exchange.

3. Look everywhere. Go far afield. Think of the whole world as your laboratory for learning.

Now, please turn the page. Read this book to absorb some of today's state-of-the-art ideas. Then use it to get into the best practice habit.

Rosabeth Moss Kanter is an internationally known business leader, best-selling author, and expert on strategy, innovation, and leadership for change. She is the Ernest L. Arbuckle Professor of Business Administration at Harvard Business School. She advises major corporations and governments worldwide, and is the author or co-author of 15 books, including her latest book, *Evolve!: Succeeding in the Digital Culture of Tomorrow*. Other award-winning bestsellers include *Men & Women of the Corporation, The Change Masters, When Giants Learn to Dance,* and *World Class: Thriving Locally in the Global Economy*. In 2001 she received the Academy of Management's Distinguished Career Award (the association's highest annual award) for her contributions to management, and in 2002 received the World Teleport Association's Intelligent Community Visionary of the Year Award. Considered one of the most prominent business thought leaders in the world and well-known as a dynamic speaker, she has shared the platform at major events with prime ministers and presidents as well as C.E.O.s in many countries, and she appears often on radio and television. In addition to serving on company boards, she cofounded Goodmeasure Inc., whose consulting clients have included some of the world's best companies; Goodmeasure is currently developing electronic Web-based versions of Kanter's leadership and change tools, to help embed them in the daily work of organizations everywhere. Dr. Kanter's current research is on the development of new leadership for the digital age—how to guide the transformation of large corporations, small and mid-sized businesses, health care, government, and education as they incorporate new technology, create new kinds of alliances and partnerships, work across boundaries and borders, and take on new social responsibilities. In 1997 and 1998 she conceived and led the Business Leadership in the Social Sector (BLSS) project, under the auspices of the Harvard Business School's Initiative on Social Enterprise, which involved national leaders, including C.E.O.s, senators, governors, and the First Lady, in dialog about public-private partnerships for change, the launch of a BLSS video series, and a national call to action in collaboration with business associations, an activity she continues as Senior Adviser to IBM's Reinventing Education program. From 1989 to1992 she also served as Editor of the *Harvard Business Review*, which was a finalist for a National Magazine Award for General Excellence in 1991. She joined the Harvard Business School faculty in 1986 from Yale University, where she held a tenured professorship from 1977 to 1986. She has received 21 honorary doctoral degrees and over a dozen leadership awards, and has been named in lists of the "50 most influential business thinkers in the world" (ranked #11), the "100 most important women in America", and the "50 most powerful women in the world." She serves on many civic and nonprofit boards, including City Year, the 14-city national service program that was the model for Americorps. Her public service activities span local and global interests. She has been a judge for the Ron Brown Award for Corporate Leadership given at the White House, a member of the Board of Overseers for the Malcolm Baldrige National Quality Award, is a Fellow of the World Economic Forum, served on the Massachusetts Governor's Economic Council (for which she cochaired the International Trade Task Force), and led the effort to establish a Year 2000 Commission for legacy projects for Boston. She currently serves on U.S. Secretary of Labor Elaine Chao's task force on the skills gap for the 21st Century Work Force Council.

Management in the 21st Century

Tom Brown

> ... [F]rom the commencement of my management I viewed the population, with the mechanism and every other part of the establishment, as a system composed of many parts, and which it was my duty and interest so to combine, as that every hand, as well as every spring, lever, and wheel, should effectually cooperate to produce the greatest pecuniary gain to the proprietors.
>
> Robert Owen, *"Address to the Superintendants of Manufactories"*

MANAGEMENT, *THEN*

In the beginning—well, it was complex then, too.

To "manage" resources effectively is a concept, says Daniel Wren in *The Evolution of Management Thought*, which can be traced back to the Babylonian King, Hammurabi. That ancient manager, if you will, issued "a code of 282 laws, which governed business dealings, personal behavior, interpersonal relations, wages, punishments, and a host of other societal matters," says Wren. He points out that "Law 104, for example, was the first historical mention of accounting." Consider it very early B2B thinking, which dealt "with the handling of receipts and established an agency relationship between the merchant and the agent." Another law, amazingly, provided very early consumer protection. Hammurabi prescribed a clear-cut consequence for any builder of a house that collapses on the owner and kills him: "[T]hat builder should be put to death."

As Wren expands the evolution of management to more familiar names (Chris Argyris, Henry Ford, John Kotter, Elton Mayo, William Whyte), it's interesting to note that Wren's analyses, in many ways, reveal the same complex skein of critical factors that challenge anyone today who has tried to convert resources into results. The Chinese general, Sun Tzu, really *was* struggling with the principles of managing a 600 B.C. army; and he wasn't planning to start a consultancy or go on a speaking tour. He wanted to get things done. Simply. Effectively. Correctly. *Now.*

In its familiar definition, management is "getting work done through others." Yet anyone who has tried to manage knows that management is never simple, is only sometimes effective, may or may not be done right the first time, and can never happen fast enough. Management may not be rocket science, but it *is* complex. "Management thought did not develop in a cultural vacuum;" says Wren, "managers have always found their jobs affected by the existing culture." Given the elements of any culture (economic variables, social norms, politics, and so on), managers have always had to think first about current norms—*and only then*—move forward.

The *Oxford English Dictionary* starts its derivative history of *management*, the word as it would be used today, with a 1598 citation; *manager*, it says, was actually in use some 10 years before. It makes more sense to jump to 1813 and to Robert Owen, the first authority cited in *Classics in Management*, a collection of excerpts from the thinkers who most influenced the profession during its formative years. Owen, a Scottish textile manufacturer, was consciously managing in the Industrial Age. His address to his fellow manufacturing magnates shows that he well understood how "inanimate machines" had altered the workscape permanently. "Many of you have long experienced in your manufacturing operations the advantages of substantial, well-contrived, and well-executed machinery," wrote Owen. He talked excitedly about the wonders of a well-oiled manufacturing machine in the way we might boast of the power and beauty of a pulsing new personal computer. He was also well aware of the potential profits from an investment in new technology, "money expended," he says, "for the chance of increased gain."

His 1813 address was far from a paean to technology and profits alone, however; he spent most of his attention on the numerous advantages of managing *people*. "[W]ill you not afford some of your attention," Owen implores, "to consider whether a portion of your time and capital would not be more advantageously applied to improve your living machines?" He argued that a healthy synergy of workplace conditions (including state-of-the-art technology) and workplace humanism ("care and attention to the living instruments") would yield unheard-of profits. Owen promised his fellow manufacturers that, by following his advice, they too would see returns of "not five, ten, or fifteen per cent, for your capital so expended, but often fifty and in many cases a hundred per cent."

Among the many management gurus who followed, Frederick Winslow Taylor (*The Principles of Scientific Management*), Henri Fayol (*General Principles of Management*), Mary Parker Follett (*Freedom and Co-ordination*), and Elton Mayo (*The Social Problems of an Industrial Civilization*) are forebears to the autograph-signing management stars of today. But Owen, even though he knew that management had always operated in the context of economic variables, social norms, and politics, set the essential challenge for all managers thereafter with his elevation of three distinct issues: technology, people, and profits. How do we balance these three elements into the best combination, the most productive combination, the longest sustainable combination: in short, a *winning* combination?

> . . . [I]n 1981, . . . I said I wanted GE to become "the most competitive enterprise on earth." . . . In the end, I believe we created the greatest people factory in the world, a learning enterprise, with a boundaryless culture.
>
> *Jack Welch, Jack: Straight from the Gut*

MANAGEMENT, *NOW*

The thousands of management books proffered over the last decade can be easily divided into two stacks. On one side are the numerous best-selling management authors (from thinker Rosabeth Moss Kanter to real-life manager Jack Welch) who often present an overall picture of corporate management doing things exceedingly right. Stellar managers, as presented in some books, have balanced the complexities of technology, people, and profit into distilled and potent commercial certainty. Bookstore racks teem with such tomes; the more cynical readers consider such works "fad books," designed to spawn yet another *program du jour* inside the corporate world. The excellent enterprise may be named General Electric, though it just as well could be called Camelot Inc. Often the same companies and managers are heralded in multiple books by different authors. And those who offer management wisdom gleaned from such paragons seem convinced that managers in any company need follow only a few nicely jotted bullet points to guarantee success.

But amidst the thunderous accolades accorded those few companies and executives that have earned widespread public adulation, many serious observers talk about working and managing with voices pitched harsh, even doleful. In the July 22, 2001, issue of the *New York Times*, Margo Jefferson, focusing on the drama world, posed an interesting question: "How Can the Theater Make Itself Matter Again?" Her answer, in part, was this: "Theater needs new work. It has to catch something of the way we live here and now: take in the facts and the sensations, show us our minds and bodies as they react and realign themselves. And theater needs to take more risks." Change the word *theater* to *management*, and many would argue that Ms. Jefferson's thoughts apply equally to the complex meshing of technology and people to produce profits.

Throughout *The Working Life*, her eminent study of the history of work, Joanne Ciulla also raises some tough issues; she comments that too many people "can't choose when to go to work and what to do at work. They do not deliberate on management policies or decide how to do the task at hand. Worst of all, many still can't plan for the future because they don't know if they will have a job." Richard Donkin spent six years researching the same subject, work, and reached comparable conclusions in *Blood, Sweat & Tears*. "The more I write," he says about the world of work, "the more I ask myself this recurring question: Why on earth do we do it?" Donkin points out, as do others, that management has become such a prized profession that, with salaries and bonuses, some top executives now easily earn "150 times more than their lowest paid employees." But it's not excessive money making that seems to disturb Donkin the most. His introduction relates how he once sat beside "a FTSE 100 company chief, fishing by the riverbank . . . listening to him giving instructions [to his office] on his mobile phone." Says Donkin: "The craziness is that some of these highly paid individuals are working such long hours they rarely have the opportunity to step outside their jobs and enjoy a moment's leisure."

Christina Maslach and Michael Leiter believe that burnout affects far more than tired top execs. When their book on burnout was published (just a few years ago), they offered this challenging thought: "Burnout is reaching epidemic proportions among North American workers today. It's not so much that something has gone wrong with us but rather that there have been fundamental changes in the workplace and the nature of our jobs. The workplace today is a cold, hostile, demanding environment, both economically and psychologically . . . People are becoming cynical, keeping their distance, trying not to let themselves get too involved." There's perhaps good reason not to be too attached to one's job. Citing statistics collected by Challenger, Gray & Christmas, the Associated Press reported at the end of 2001 that job cuts in the United States were the highest in almost a decade. For too many management teams, has strategic planning now been permanently reduced to an exercise in subtraction?

Bill Jensen is actively trying to capture the difference between what the workplace is like and what it *should* be like. He speaks and writes about *Work 2.0*, where people (and managers) need to stop thinking about organizational productivity and start thinking about personal productivity. He says we all need to stop focusing on things like operational excellence and tune into "radical simplicity," an awareness of what people really need to get their work done. In a Work 2.0 world, he stresses that people are "business units of one." Another vanguard management thinker on how organizations should be is Thomas Stewart, of *Fortune*, who wrote in *The Wealth of Knowledge*: "The modern corporation, like modern art, is over. The postmodern corporation is different." He argues that one of the chief differences lies in how management defines employment. "It's more accurate—and more useful—to think of employees in a new way: not as assets but as investors. Shareholders invest money in our companies; employees invest time, energy, and intelligence."

Arie de Geus, drawing on his long career at Royal Dutch/Shell, argues in *Business Minds* that management may be suffering a crisis of vocabulary. "[C]ompanies have become trapped in the prison of economic language, which is why so many companies suffer premature deaths . . . [C]ompanies tend to die early because their leaders and executives concentrate on production and profit, and forget that the corporation is an institution . . . a community of human beings." In that same work, Fons Trompenaars argues that, since "culture" today must be defined globally, the basic job of a manager is overdue for a radical redesign. "Just because people speak English does not mean they think alike," he argues. "The international manager needs to go beyond aware-ness of cultural differences. He or she needs to respect these differences and take advantage of diversity through reconciling cross-cultural dilemmas."

How could modern management, almost 200 years after Robert Owen, be so div-ided? On the one hand, the biggest bestsellers in management are tied to a daily cartoon strip named "Dilbert" that chronicles the work strife of a high-tech laborer who seemingly debases management for a living. On the other hand, another simple storybook features a cartoon mouse who can't seem to manage a block of cheese. And such contrarian views get even starker. Anita Roddick, founder of The Body Shop chain of stores and a former C.E.O. who has also generated considerable controversy, has written two books about both her trade and her views on management. Her latest work acknowledges that, for many, management has made business "a jungle where only the vicious survive." She laments that, for too many, managing a business is about sitting "in front of computer screens, moving millions of dollars from Japan to New York." She yearns for "a new view of business as a community where only the responsible will lead."

Margaret Wheatley is today more a social philosopher than a management guru. Yet by looking at management practices through the lens of modern physics, her early-1990s book, *Leadership and the New Science*, took "scientific management" to a depth that Frederick Winslow Taylor could never have imagined. Today, she says management is *stuck*. "If we don't change the way we manage business in the next ten years," she says bluntly, "we're dead." A chorus of management thinkers, writers, and managers is there to back her up. W. Chan Kim and Renée Mauborgne, talking about the difficulties of managing strategy in a knowledge economy, believe that a quantum leap in management will come only when "fair process" comes to the modern work world, something that involves "major changes in [behavior] and working practices" which "will not be achieved without people willingly co-operating with the innovation process and making their skills and experience available to a company." It should come as little surprise that Richard Leider these days asks every top exec he meets to answer just one question: *Why would the best people in the world want to work for your company?*

Two Stanford University professors, Jeffrey Pfeffer and Robert Sutton, looking at the corporate world at large, found that, despite all the gleeful chirps by proud executives about their companies being elite learning organizations, there were plenty of organizational examples of the polar opposite. They subsequently wrote *The Knowing-Doing Gap*. Its very first sentence is an indictment of the profession of management today—or, at least, a diagnosis of serious managerial schizophrenia. "We wrote this book because we wanted to understand why so many managers know so much about organizational performance, say so many smart things about how to achieve performance, and work so hard, yet are trapped in firms that do so many things they know will undermine performance." It's as if too few managers (and management thinkers!) had ever read, bothered to think about, act upon, or even recall Douglas McGregor's mournful challenge to the management profession in the closing paragraph of his landmark 1960 work, *The Human Side of Enterprise*. Forty years before Pfeffer and Sutton's research, McGregor had already concluded: "Fads will come and go. The fundamental fact of man's capacity to collaborate with his fellows in the face-to-face group will survive the fads and one day be recognized. Then, and only then, will management discover how seriously it has underestimated the true potential of its human resources."

> As we learn more about life ... Mendel, Darwin, Watson, Crick, Venter ... Will be figures every bit as important as Edison, Einstein, Ford, the Wright brothers ... What they have taught us and produced is changing each of our lives ... How we work, live, and think. You can stand on the sidelines and assume fate will guide things ... (God willing ... Si Dios Quiere ... Insha'Allah ... Shikatta ga nai ...) Or you can help yourself, your family, your company and country navigate ... This wondrous and scary adventure.
>
> *Juan Enriquez, As the Future Catches You*

MANAGEMENT, *TOMORROW*

E-mail and the Internet are two of the technological forces that have altered the job of a manager. Whether the concern be how to manage "virtual employees" who work from home (are they *really* working?) or how to decide who should be able to access the megabytes of intimate corporate data that now course through any modern company, technology is as daunting today as it was for Robert Owen in 1813—with a commensurate impact on people and profits. Yet, for managers, there's an even bigger horizon to glimpse and ponder.

In his role as director of the Life Sciences Project at Harvard Business School, Juan Enriquez has thought deeply about the personal and fiscal import of such society-shaking developments as the recent mapping of the human genome. That may seem like a too-distant subject for someone managing a steel mill, grocery, or factory—or even a software development company. Enriquez thinks otherwise. Referring to the work of Robert Fleishmann and Craig Venter, work that produced "the first genetic map of a living organism," Enriquez reflected that such scientific breakthroughs raise questions that people never even thought they would be able to ask. Robert Owen fretted over how best to control the capital assets and human resources of his manufacturing plant; now people are starting to fret over how, as Enriquez says in his book, "To control ... Directly and deliberately ... The evolution of our species ... and that of every other species on the planet." It's a big jump. Can management, as a profession, make it?

We don't know. What we do know is that every manager today has both new *and* old questions to answer. Andrea Gabor probed the lives of ten individuals (whom she called *The Capitalist Philosophers*) who were management heavyweights of the last century, people like Chester Barnard, Abraham Maslow, and W. Edwards Deming. She concluded that management tomorrow has to find an answer to the question that, at heart, also bothered Owen. Says Gabor: "At the root of the conflict between the humanistic and the scientific are two warring images of the business organization and its purpose in ... society: One sees the corporation as a pivotal institution of democracy with complex responsibilities to a host of constituencies, including its employees, its customer, and the community. The other, much more utilitarian, view recognizes one primary corporate constituent—the shareholder—and a single purpose—profit making."

Technology is now proceeding at a pace that may quickly outstretch management's (and, perhaps, mankind's) ability to decide *what* to do with what we are so rapidly learning *how* to do. The very real prospect arises that many will simply conclude that life and business, both, are irrefutably un-manageable. Owen feared that technology would overpower the human being; Deming feared that human myopia about issues like quality would overpower an organization's technological capability to deliver excellent products. Today, some fear that the push for profit could throttle both technology and humanity. Even a sober thinker like Charles Handy (who calls himself "a reluctant capitalist") talks about "elephants" (large companies) and "fleas" (individuals or small groups with innovative ideas), conceding that "[M]any observers think that the big corporations are now both richer and more powerful than many nation states .... The elephants, people feel, may be out of anyone's control."

AND YET—

And yet one can safely assert that the hundreds of years of management debate have not been without value—that the hundreds of management treatises, the hundreds of management theories, the hundreds of management gurus, the hundreds of management "solutions" (from Theories X and Y to the Managerial Grid to the Eight Principles of Excellence to Business Process Reengineering)—all of this management commotion has not been without a constructive role in society. For the study of management, during the centuries in which it has been active and accepted as a discipline, has always served as the testing ground for how we could and should work, individually and collectively. Management thinking has served as the closest thing to a laboratory where the "genetic code" of human enterprise can be mapped, to see if there are new ways to pool the resources tied to every human endeavor into new vistas of human possibilities. As Robert Heller and Tim Hindle note in their illuminating *Essential Manager's Manual*, "A full understanding of what makes people perform well and of the problems that may affect performance in the workplace is therefore essential for any manager. He or she will need to employ a wide range of skills, both interpersonal and professional, in order to resolve these problems."

The practice of management, through both its scientific standards and its artistic renderings, remains the best way yet to channel the raw energy of human minds, the brute force of vast capital, and the quixotic capability of new technology to transform people by reshaping their perceptions of what's possible on this planet, and ultimately, even beyond. The marketplace of ideas about management has always been a free market. Accounting, information, logistics, marketing, manufacturing, organizational culture, research and development, sales, social policy—pick *any* discipline within the profession of management, and you'll find intense debate about the questions that matter most to each particular realm of the corporate world. It is as it always was. It is as it should be.

Thus, whenever a large collection of management thinkers are assembled under one roof, one book, or one Web site, the last thing one should expect is congruence. Management, as it has evolved and is evolving, is a battle of ideas and ideals. Management thinkers and practitioners only align with others when they share common views of how technology can be deployed, how humans can best interact with the machines and systems they have created, and how, when combined, these forces can create new wealth. But wealth follows achievement. Businesses do not prosper because of their strategic planning; they succeed because of their strategic execution and because of the extent to which they can attract both investors and customers to share their strategic purpose. And achievement is very much an exercise in managing for the future.

There are still many questions about management that have not been asked or answered.

The greatest debates about how to manage ourselves and our companies have yet to be staged. The most salient ideas about how to manage both the workplace (and the world!) have yet to be widely disseminated, considered, and tested. Even the largest collection of management information and ideas is simply a mental cake mix until students and practitioners stir themselves into the blend and begin to practice new forms of management—to become, in essence, new kinds of managers.

Management and human enterprise have brought mankind a long way. We travel fast, communicate easily, shop globally, and learn rapidly. Yet, judging mainly by what management has accomplished in the past (and what it hasn't), we can be quite sure that its study will never become passé. The word will never be pulled from the dictionaries because it has become archaic. We need not quake over the prospect that the study of management will no longer be needed because its best practices have accomplished everything that needs to be done. We need not fear terminal success. Whenever enormous problems involving work, people, and organizations crop up, this question will imminently bubble up too: how do we *manage* this problem? The list is endless but undoubtedly starts with . . .

- Some executives do achieve long-term business success. Yet we really don't know how to replace that executive with one just as capable in order to keep the good corporate times going—nor do we know how to transfer an excellent manager's expertise to another company or another industry. We in management own that problem.

- The power of large corporations rivals many nations; their top managers are often more widely known than presidents or prime ministers. Yet corporations don't really know how to wield that power in ways that do not devastate some communities while disproportionately blessing others. We in management own that problem.

- E-commerce is an increasing force in the buying and selling of goods, both between businesses and between companies/customers. Yet we really don't know how to e-replicate the relationships and loyalty that used to be the greatest asset of any business: customer goodwill. We in management own that problem.

- Corporations no longer have to be mega in size to leverage global connections; 24/7 workdays and Internet communications make it probable, not just possible, that for many, the worker "in the next cubicle" will be thousands of miles away. Yet few companies have meshed the unique cultural perspectives of a multi-national workforce into a coherent, collaborative team. We in management own that problem.

- Advanced technology has made it possible to fly to outer space and return safely. Yet, all over the globe, people today are struggling with how to fly or drive millions of miles without facing overt terrorism or risking the less obvious terror of enviro-toxic byproducts corrupting the atmosphere permanently. We in management own that problem.

- Even in the most heralded companies boasting a badge of merit that says they are "wonderful" places to work, employees and managers slink to work each day uninspired, even desperate—incapable of connecting the mission of the company with their own mission in life. We in management own that problem.

Management in the 21st century is incomplete, imperfect, and quite often insufficient to meet pressing needs. That makes management tomorrow as exciting as ever, an exhilarating subject to study and a dynamic profession to practice. In almost any corner of your life, your workplace, your community, or your global marketplace, there are problems that simply won't be addressed unless *someone* in management owns them.

Therefore today—right now!—the most important unanswered question in management comes down to four words: *Might that be you?*

———◦•◦———

Thomas Brown is the author of the first online book on leadership, *The Anatomy of Fire: Sparking a New Spirit of Enterprise.* He has written more than 400 articles for major journals such as *Across the Board,* Harvard's *Management Update,* and the *Wall Street Journal.* He has been the keynote speaker at major meetings (including the International Association of Management), presented his ideas to many corporations, and lectured at several universities. He recently helped to establish BrownHerron LLC, a company providing information worldwide about leading-edge management and leadership via electronic documents (e-docs).

Create, Connect, Evolve

Stan Davis and Christopher Meyer

Stan Davis and Christopher Meyer have coauthored three books, *Blur*, *Future Wealth*, and *It's Alive*, as well as numerous articles. Stan Davis is an independent author, speaker, and consultant and Senior Research Fellow at the Center for Business Innovation in Cambridge, Massachusetts. Christopher Meyer is Director of the Center for Business Innovation. Standing on the given—the present—and using the perspective of the past, the two authors leap into a future that is challenging and exhilarating.

Comparing the four phases of the life cycle (of plants, people, industries, or civilizations) to the development of economies, they predict the creation, connection, and evolution of the next economy: a boundary-crossing mix of science and technology. What will the next economy be like? What will be its core products?

Anyone who can discern the answer to those questions will have a measurable head start on the competition. Say Davis and Meyer about the next economy's core product: "Whatever it is, and wherever and whenever it emerges, it will not grow from design or from chance. Rather, it will evolve . . . "

Something unprecedented is about to happen: the next economy is already in the wings waiting to come on stage before the information economy is fully mature. The ideas and technologies of these two economies will affect one another during the coming decades, creating a rapidly evolving climate for business and management. This is our take on what's next, what it will it be like, what's driving it, and where it is in its life cycle.

In the life cycles of economies, we've seen a succession: from hunting and gathering economies lasting hundreds of thousands of years, to agrarian economies lasting ten thousand years, to the industrial period dominating for slightly less than two hundred years (1760s–1950s), and now the information era. The first half of the information economy was dominated by computers, as free-standing boxes whose importance was measured by their crunching power. The connecting power of networked computers, which began with the explosion of the Internet in the early 1990s, is nowhere near complete and is dominating the second half. We're already five decades into the current information economy, which will likely last only another three—at most.

Everything that has a beginning has an ending, and therefore a life cycle. Plants, planets, and people all have life cycles. So do products, businesses, industries, economies, and civilizations. They all have life cycles, and the cycles seem to follow some basic principles.

Cycles, for example, go through distinct periods or quarters: gestation (Q1), growth (Q2), maturity (Q3), and decline (Q4). The first quarters of economies are dominated by science, the second quarters by technologies that bridge between science and the businesses that mature in Q3s. The fourth quarter focuses on organizational innovation. Thermodynamics led to the steam engine, for example, which led to railroads and the industrial economy, and to top-down rational bureaucratic management models. Solid-state physics led to semiconductors, which led to computers and the information-based businesses of the information economy, whose network-centered organizational form is just beginning to come into focus as we near Q4.

Cycles also overlap, with the next one already gestating while the previous one grows and matures. People may live to their eighties, but most have children in their twenties and thirties. What's new is an economic teenage pregnancy. The next economy has already begun its growth phase before the information economy is mature—two economic generations are increasingly living side by side. The next economy will be marked by three drivers: the creation of value at the molecular level, the connection of infotech and biotech, and an economic environment in which evolution replaces engineering as the dominant source of management and economic ideas. The mindset for the decades ahead is simply this: create, connect, evolve.

CREATE

The clues for the next economy are in the sciences that are becoming technologies, and these increasingly involve the mastery of molecules. This mastery will likely play out in three successive waves: first in organic (bio)technology, then in inorganic composite materials, and ultimately in nanotechnologies.

In the first wave, the appropriate beginning marker is probably Crick and Watson's 1953 discovery of the double helix structure of DNA. Almost five decades later, the completion of the Human Genome Project in 2001 is probably a convenient marker for the start of the second quarter. Q2 will last for at least the next two or three decades, during which we will see the commercialization of many biotech products, and meaningful overlap between biotech and infotech.

Biology operates at distinct nested levels, scaling up through connections among elements at smaller levels: molecules (including DNA) /organisms /species /ecologies. In other words, ecology is derivative of molecules, and not vice versa unless you are a creationist. The design principle of building from the small and scaling up operates in economics as well as in biology. Semiconductors led to computers and then to the Internet, not vice versa. Like biology, economy will also be derivative of molecules—quite literally, not simply as metaphor, which was the case with the social Darwinists a century ago and still is with many management gurus today.

Recombinant DNA, the first biotech ripple (mid-1980s to mid-1990s), used an engineered economic model that was akin to big pharma: big money, big mixing vats, and big risks because the molecular structure of the targets for these drugs was poorly understood. The management model was still top-down control. Genomics, the current ripple, by contrast, uses techniques akin to molecular biology and genetic engineering. The business model has more in common with infotech startups than with big pharma, and the management model shifts to control from the bottom up.

The second and third waves in the next economy will also involve large-scale commercializing of molecules, but they lie a bit further in the future. There we'll likely see major advances in inorganic composite materials and in nanotechnologies, creating product by programming and self-assembling matter. A new class of ceramics, for example, has heat-tolerant properties that could reduce gasoline consumption by a million barrels a day. New structures based on nanotubes are already being exploited to detect environmental toxins. During the next decades we'll also see a smaller and more efficient computing platform emerge. There are currently four candidates: molecular electronics, photonics, quantum computing, and DNA computing.

Whether you're an entrepreneur or an executive, if you've got an eye for the future during the coming decade you should be asking: "How can I deliver value in my business through molecular technologies?"

CONNECT

In 1998 we wrote a book, *Blur*, that said connectivity was changing the rules of business. There, we focused on the information economy. The really big blur, however, is likely to occur as the current and next economies rub up against each other more and more in the decade ahead. That's when economics will borrow more from biology. And that's when we will see the blurring between the organic and inorganic, the natural and artificial, the living and non-living.

Connections between seemingly distinct worlds are clearest at the most basic levels, in their fundamental codes. Codes derived from science create the same world in different ways, just as do codes from religion and from art. They're all different interpretive truths of the same universe. In science, whether we're dealing with material code (based on the 92 elements), genetic code (based on A, C, G, and T), or information code (based on 0 and 1), at the molecular level, code is code. Code crossings, connections, are easier within these worlds than between them, but that's never stopped mankind from seeking connections at all nested levels.

In science we've reached the point where biotech and infotech can literally be translated into each other. The elements in each code scale up through successive layers, branching over micromoments or millennia, until you have enterprises and organisms, industries and species, and ultimately economies and ecosystems. Literally, the world is built on code from the bottom up, and so are the economies that populate it. Still, in its essential and elemental form, code is code. Conceptually, therefore, it can be treated interchangeably, and today's cutting-edge technologies are working to make this interchange practical in the world of business. Thus models created by molecular biologists and ecologists are becoming useful for managing business strategies and processes.

Molecules now are regularly moved from one code to another in laboratories, and the results of this R&D are beginning to move into production. Yesterday's science fiction will be tomorrow's over-the-counter home healthcare products. Entire artificial hearts controlled by microchips are already a reality. Blending the organic and inorganic at molecular levels will blur the distinction even more. Nerve cells of a leech have been connected to a silicon transistor and an artificial neuron has been implanted in a lobster.

Boundary crossing between different species is also becoming commonplace. Two decades ago, genetic engineering came closer and jumped a code across species, implanting human interferon, for example, into rapidly replicating bacteria and creating pharmaceutical proteins in a factory that is literally alive. And we already grow human elements in mice because they share so much of our genome. More adventurous still, spiders' silk glands and goats' mammary glands share enough similarity that, after isolating the gene that codes for silk protein in spiders, scientists inserted it into the mammary glands of goats. The silk protein comes out in the transgenic goats' milk.

The next step will be to remove it and use it to mass-produce "extreme performance fibers" that might one day result in bio-steel. Yes, manipulating codes predates Mendel and selective breeding is certainly an ancient art, but understanding and connecting the molecular codes and building technologies to manipulate them will produce far more powerful and wide-reaching results. Similarly, the nascent field of bioplastics is at the crossroads of petrochemicals and agriculture, and its intentions are to do things like growing plastics in corn. Plastics come from oil, which is often expensive, unclean, and geopolitically unstable. In the future they may grow locally, cheaply, and green. A polystyrene substitute has already been produced by genetically modified corn plants. Biopharming, or molecular farming, is a potential new industry at the boundary between medicine and food. Genetically modified organisms (GMOs) and therapeutic cloning are some controversial results of such code-crossing activities.

Computer software follows the same rules as molecules, "create, connect, evolve." The rapidly growing field of bioinformatics marries infotech and biotech. Evolving systems create simulated, virtual worlds that "self-organize" on the basis of a few simple rules. Digital immune systems work the way mammalian ones do. Genetic algorithms exist only in computers but work by biologics. Silicon retinas may soon be implanted in human eyes. Worlds are connecting, and boundaries are indeed blurring. From the new connections of chemical, biological, and informational codes are emerging new technologies with commercial applications that we have never before considered. We are merely at the point of beginning to know what we don't know.

EVOLVE

When creative elements like molecules or business ideas connect, they begin to evolve. As our economy becomes more connected both within and across codes, the management wisdom of the next decades will come more from evolution than from engineering.

Things are definitely speeding up, so much so that a simple linear extrapolation might lead us to predict that the next era will be a one-minute economy. We think, to the contrary, that it will be much longer lived than the current one. One simple reason is that, while generations of new product occur annually or faster, new generations of living things don't speed up the same way. Virtual simulations give us a glimpse of what might be, but actual results in people and society will take more time.

Also, every economy has its core product and the molecular era will be no different. But it is still a way off, in what we like to call the adjacent possible. Looking backwards, the railroad, using the steam engine, was core to the infrastructure of the industrial economy and, using the combustion engine, the car became the consumerized version of this industrial core. The mainframe computer then the PC, and the Internet then the World Wide Web, held similar importance in the information era.

There's a good chance the next economy's core product will emerge from health care, because it is the economy's largest sector. The reading of the human genome and advances in stem cell research provide a strong platform for commercial products to arise. Alternatively, it may appear in the next largest sector and apply to education, intellectual property, and human capital, but the science here is much less precise.

Whatever it is, and wherever and whenever it emerges, it will not grow from design or from chance. Rather, it will evolve, and it will do so from the bottom up, and quite possibly by using more than one code and connecting across what currently we know as very different worlds. Any environment creating things that connect with each other, whether through microbial soup or through microchips, will evolve. More specifically, we should expect the coevolution of the born and the made software will breed its own new generations, and new kinds of organisms will be manufactured in mechanical wet labs.

These recombinations are nothing less than directed evolutionary engineering. For this, we have to remove ourselves from the center of things, much as Copernicus had to "stand on the sun" to comprehend the solar system. Then we might marvel at an extraordinary participation in our own evolutionary futures, to say nothing of the artifacts and devices that our imaginations and future factories will create and evolve. Of course, this evolutionary process won't stop with economy.

Above, we said the big blur will be between the organic and inorganic. Many balk at the notion of blurring carbon and non-carbon life. They ask: How can cold code be infused with warm, wet life? How can the ineffable qualities of humans be passed on into computers? In return, however, we must ask: How can we accept evolution yet believe that it stops with us?

If it does not stop with us, and we accept the evolution of beings more intelligent than ourselves, where do they come from? Species do not spring into existence *de novo*. They emerge first as mutations and recombinations of codes, creating innovative organisms and differentiated species, ultimately coevolving in even less understood ecologies. And if they evolve from earlier forms, then might not humans evolve forms more intelligent than themselves? We seem to think the apes did it. Aren't we at least as capable as they were of such creative, connective evolution?

Scientific developments in the past decade offer encouraging support for the line of reasoning we've spelled out above. The further reaches of our argument, by contrast, take us into speculative worlds beyond our current life spans. In the middle distance between molecules and magic, in that adjacent possible, we can see outlines of new products, new businesses, new industries, and the next economy.

The Case for Business Criticism

Christopher Locke

What's unique about Chris Locke rapidly comes through when visiting one of the numerous Web site pages dedicated to his work. In a short bio, the first sentence says that he is "Chairman of The Titanic Deck Chair Rearrangement Corporation (NASDAQ: TDCRC)." And, somehow, this is exactly what one might expect from the popular coauthor of *The Cluetrain Manifesto* and author of *Gonzo Marketing: Winning through Worst Practices* and *The Bombast Transcripts: Rants and Screeds of RageBoy.*

What is one to make of someone with a point of view that diverges so strongly from standard wisdom? That, Locke would probably point out immediately, is not the most salient question to ask. Rather, Locke puts forth a more fundamental query: Why is it that the business world has not developed its own form of rigorous business criticism? Says Locke about the "logic" of business: it "has become toxic, a dysfunctional complex of neurotic behaviors and primitive defense mechanisms." Thus, he urges us to establish a new genre of business writing, one "that recognizes the profound connections between commerce and culture . . ."

Business and society often seem worlds apart, each operating under a separate set of principles that have little to do with the interests of the other. As business becomes more global in scope, and global networks underscore its world-spanning effects, the results of this radical disintegration are approaching a critical pass. Yet where are the critics to explore, contextualize, and make sense of the changing relations between business and the human societies it both depends upon and shapes?

Any mature field of knowledge has developed a critical community that looks at its history, schools of thought, concepts, categories, language, and practices. Substantial bodies of criticism focus on art, literature, music, and media. Why not business criticism? The counter-intuitive answer seems to be: because we don't take business seriously.

A Web search for "business critic[ism]" returns mostly pages denigrating business as a whole. This is not so for other types of criticism. Art critics may deeply dislike particular artists, but few are anti-art. Anthropologists may argue about what "culture" means, but none is anti-culture. Such critics share the basic aims and interests of both practitioners and their audiences. However, most "business critics" are unabashedly anti-business. As a result, they are largely preaching to the choir. Because such criticism is unaligned with the assumptions of business, business tends to ignore it altogether.

The lack of business criticism constitutes a glaring gap in our understanding of today's world. We have data reporting on the financial markets, economic treatises, and business journalism of the who-what-when-where-why variety. However, unlike other forms of criticism, which situate their subjects within an historical context, this sort of business writing typically does not take history into account. It tends to focus almost exclusively on current events, ignoring the larger context that shaped the present business environment. We need to begin thinking critically about business—not to deny its place in the world, but to consider that placement more thoughtfully.

Art, music, and literature date back millennia. While trade and commerce have similarly long histories, the business we know today is barely 150 years old. When it first emerged in the middle of the 19th century, it had no pedigree whatsoever. The period after Reconstruction saw the establishment of the form of legal incorporation currently recognized in the U.S., and the rise of so-called robber barons such as Andrew Carnegie, John D. Rockefeller, Cornelius Vanderbilt, and Jay Gould. Many of these proto-capitalists were subjected to intense ostracism—not just because they were unschooled, but because they were unlanded. The derogatory label *nouveau riche* implied that they lacked "culture" and "cultivation"—terms rooted in an earthier sense of culture: agriculture.

Unlike the powerful titans of industry portrayed in high school civics classes, the first capitalists of the modern era were embittered, embattled, defensive, and paranoid. Business was not only rejected by society, it made the rejection mutual. Unhappy with the reception it had received, business began to develop a long-term strategy for revenge.

In short, business realized it could buy the status it had been denied. What conferred the most status in the 19th century was science, which, since the European enlightenment, had overturned ecclesiastical authority and made mankind (women, non-whites, and the "lower classes" excepted) the center of a suddenly knowable universe. The power of science lay in abstraction. Scientific method used hypothesis, observation, and repeatable experiment to establish facts, then employed mathematics and logic to arrive at first principles. Suddenly, the "laws of nature" could be expressed as powerful mathematical abstractions—which also conferred prestige and legitimacy. Even better, the application of such principles enabled companies to survey rail lines, pump oil, smelt ore, charge interest. Business favored this practical approach over the sort of liberal education fostered by the old agrarian elite. Andrew Carnegie wrote: "While the college student has been learning a little about the barbarous and petty squabbles of a far-distant past, or trying to master languages which are dead, such knowledge as seems adapted for life upon another planet than this as far as business affairs are concerned, the future captain of industry is hotly engaged in the school of experience, obtaining the very knowledge required for his future triumphs ... College education as it exists is fatal to success in that domain." (Quoted in Laurence R. Veysey, *The Emergence of the American University*, University of Chicago Press, 1965, p. 14.)

Following this sentiment, Carnegie, Cornelius Vanderbilt, Leland Stanford, and others founded their own business schools (the Rockefeller and Ford Foundations later influenced education as a whole). Beginning with Wharton in 1898, business schools grew and prospered through the largesse of wealthy industrialists who wanted to pass along their hard-won knowledge to future generations. The current cachet of the MBA degree, once a humble technical certificate, has made their revenge complete.

In 1911, Frederick W. Taylor claimed to have developed scientific principles. His "scientific management"—with its clipboards, stopwatches, graphs, and charts—reduced complex work to just two abstract dimensions: time and motion. This later became know as "industrial engineering." To leverage the power such abstraction provided, it was necessary to ignore "human factors." Any area of study that involved human beings was folded into an overarching category called social science. However, the social sciences were far less prestigious, and increasingly came to be considered "soft." Economics was once a social science, typified by economists like Thorstein Veblen, who wrote about "conspicuous consumption" and railed against the degradation of university education at the hands of business administrators, and Max Weber, who warned of the "iron cage" inevitably created by corporate bureaucracy. For these sins of softness, they have since been reclassified as sociologists.

Science introduced a new level of mathematical abstraction, and this kind of abstraction was powerful for business because it supported equations, formulae from which it was possible to construct standard procedures. All the intractable, uncountable stuff about workers and customers—the human factors—get factored out. Business became a paint-by-numbers, puzzle-solving exercise; operations experts and bean-counters came into the corporate ascendant, and a mountain of stuff got mass-produced and mass marketed. This form of applied scientific abstraction worked like a charm.

Ironically, in turning toward such abstraction, business was only following in the footsteps of the society that had previously ostracized it. "High culture"—the cultured and cultivated cadre who delighted in looking down on business—was doing exactly the same thing at the same time. This was called modernism, a reaction against the Enlightenment's goals of rationality and progress filtered through the darker aspects of early industrialism and World War I.

This proscription of social context—often expressed by the slogan "Art for art's sake"—was no less strange than the attitude business adopted toward another kind of abstraction at roughly the same time. "The business of America is business," said president Calvin Coolidge in 1925. In other words: business for business's sake. Through "scientific management," business could ignore those ultimately soft "human factors": people. In the hands of business, abstraction became infinitely more powerful than it did in the world of art. It enabled repeatable procedures, and grounded command and control on powerful principles, equations, formulae, and finally algorithms—the "recipes" underlying computer software.

Like modernist art, business convinced itself it could ignore everything outside the frame—in the case of business: maximize profit. But fixed categories don't work any more. There is no world of art, no world of business—nor of science, politics, religion, music, literature. These "worlds" never existed. They are abstractions. In partial evidence of this, the interdisciplinary field of "economic sociology"—which Max Weber founded many years ago—is enjoying a remarkable resurgence. Trying to understand human beings as strictly economic, non-social entities doesn't work any better than trying to understand them in strictly social, non-economic terms.

While many fixed categories—sociology, economics, anthropology, business—long ago outlived their usefulness as stand-alone disciplines, much of business continues to depend on their rigid segregation. This "logic" of business as usual has become toxic, a dysfunctional complex of neurotic behaviors and primitive defense mechanisms. In a global economy held together by global networks, it is a fatal mistake for business to isolate itself from society.

Understanding the impact and importance of such errors requires a form of business criticism that is largely lacking today. Half a century ago, we had better examples of what such criticism might look like: *The Lonely Crowd* by David Riesman (1950), *White Collar* by C. Wright Mills (1951), *The Organization Man* by William H. Whyte, Jr. (1956). These works appealed to broad audiences, not just to microscopic specialist readerships. They showed how business and society constitute context to each other. Business is embedded within a deeply social and historical context. The societies in which we live are deeply influenced by corporate actions with respect to physical, psychological, and spiritual environments.

Business depends on both workers and markets, both of which are invisible to abstract algorithms and formulaic procedures. Without a business criticism that recognizes the profound connections between commerce and culture, such blindness will continue, and we will never accomplish the increasingly urgent task of reintegrating business and society.

Changing the Workplace Into a Meaningful Community

John Seely Brown

John Seely Brown is not your typical scientist, but rather a blend of scientist, artist, and strategist. Combining the worlds of digital culture, ubiquitous computing, and organizational learning, he serves as chief scientist for the Xerox Corporation and was director of the Xerox Palo Alto Research Center (PARC) from 1990 to 2000. His acclaimed *Social Life of Information*, a book he coauthored, is transforming the way people think about information. Offering a rare perspective on the human contexts in which technologies operate, he maintains change does not always represent genuine progress.

What is the most important thing and who is the most important person to have influenced your thinking on business and management?
Actually, two people come to mind—each operating in different domains from the other and both radically distinct in their views.

The first is Elizabeth Teisberg, now at the University of Virginia's Darden Graduate School of Business Administration. Taking "real options evaluation" theory from the world of finance and capital management, she demonstrated how options thinking could be applied to the funding and evaluation of research and development initiatives. The concept is very dynamic and, truthfully, there's nothing I do any day that is not influenced by her model.

Real options analysis represents a merging of *investment* decision making with *strategy*. It enables us in effect to value two sources of *learning*: learning by *doing*, which allows us to determine if there are any unexpected problems with an undertaking; and learning by *waiting*—to see how the market develops and learn what customers really want.

By using these techniques companies can take calculated R&D risks, in the form of options on the future, without "betting the farm" or making full-scale strategic commitments initially. Indeed, it encourages the creation and exploration of opportunities, while providing a discipline for continuously assessing whether the options being created are *real*—having potential for significant returns and being worthy, therefore, of further investment. Most importantly, real options thinking strongly implies that viewing risk-taking as "betting" is a mistake!

As we begin to incorporate options thinking, we're continuously *staging* and *gating*—creating opportunities and determining checkpoints for making "go" and "no-go" decisions. This is a very useful concept in the world of R&D, particularly when you're concerned with cash flow. It establishes a dynamic system for scaling an investment as well as exiting a project altogether. The process effectively shapes conversation around managed risk-taking and the reserving of options for the future. It also favors a bias for innovative thinking, while eliminating much of the politics underlying the innovator's dilemma.

In a world of accelerating change and dynamic tension, we need disciplines in which we can be playful—frameworks for choreographing the delicate dances of opportunity and commitment. For me, the appeal has been in my being able to take the world of research management to a new plane—allowing for a sort of *creative abrasion* between acts of creation and evaluation.

The second person is Professor Lucy Suchman of Lancaster University's department of sociology. An anthropologist, ethnomethodologist, and author, Professor Suchman completely blew away a corner stone of artificial intelligence with her analyses of situated action. She elaborates on these findings in her book *Plans and Situated Actions: The Problem of Human-machine Communications*.

Drawing on ethnomethodological studies of all types of work, from the seemingly mundane to the most complex and intellectually demanding, she successfully uncovered the specific culturally and materially embodied identities, knowledge, and practices that make up technical systems. Her research helps us to understand how work gets done and to honor the context and situations in which workers find themselves. For example, at Xerox we were interested in the role and importance of business processes. Professor Suchman conducted analyses as a participant observer and then returned to ask that community of practice if certain office procedures were helpful. They affirmed they were. But she found the procedures were not being used as originally intended. Workers did not follow the step-by-step instructions; instead, they improvised around the "unexpected," while ensuring the ensemble of improvisations created a result that looked like what they would have gotten had they followed the overall procedure.

I came to the conclusion that many practices in which employees are engaged in the workscape today are driven by improvisation and can't be reduced to written procedures—simply because workers are continuously problem solving, improvising, and dynamically interpreting what is going on in the contexts of their environment. That realization moved me to appreciate the inherent creativity of people "at work" and to conclude that *practice makes process* and not the converse.

What will business need to do differently in the 21st century?

We will need to transform the workscape into a place of *meaning*. It will be incumbent upon managers to view the work environment as "communities of practice." They must recognize their existence, understand them, and build environments that are genuinely supportive of continuous learning and identity formation. *Their challenge will be to architect the workscape of the future utilizing the triadic elements of social, physical, and informational space.* Those who understand will come to lead organizations that are enormously successful and truly beneficial to all stakeholders.

I believe the pathway to the future will require "looking around"—managers will need to eschew the sort of tunnel vision that "sees" only *one* system or solution for getting there. Let's be frank! Real innovation is not born of logic, but of aesthetics based on a sort of playfulness and constant interpreting of the world in which we operate.

Creating joy, innovation, and meaning in the workscape requires that managers see and think contextually. They will have to unlearn old styles of managing and create, instead, workscapes that foster emergent communities of learning by honoring worker improvisation and knowledge formation.

What new skills will be needed to cope with these changes?

One's ability to unlearn is constrained by *tacit beliefs*. Successful managers must not assume they know someone else's frame of operation. Instead, they will have to appreciate the profound significance of seeing the environment through the eyes of the other person—whether employee, customer, or resource provider. They will have to determine what matters most to others and move to satisfy their needs.

As in sailing, it's a matter of "triangulation." When navigating through unfamiliar waters, managers need to reference various points continuously to get their bearings. Dead reckoning and triangulation are principal methods by which we can learn, but doing this is almost an art form. To be sure, in the corporate world there's a thin line between joy and terror, and it takes a skilled navigator to keep from going over the edge.

Managers must move increasingly to the mode of win-win. Consider Li & Fung Limited in Asia, a highly successful global sourcing company, that orchestrates an entire network of some 6,500 shops in 100 countries to produce goods for their corporate clients. They can take an order from a retail customer and determine the best source according to craft skills, materials used, product quality, and turnaround times. Li & Fung have mastered a deep knowledge of their producer communities. By playing to individual strengths rather than forcing each to a uniform standard or to a least-cost basis, Li & Fung foster an environment where everyone wins and learns. Successful managers will need to become proficient in this regard and emulate the skills of orchestrators like Li & Fung, rather than controllers of work practices.

Are there new management questions we should be considering?

Two questions relate to how well an organization is managing its own "periphery"—both *within* and *outside of* its own walls. The first periphery deals with finding the "radicals" who live on the fringes of the organization—customer contact people, for example, who make discoveries every day. Good ideas come from lots of different places. Managers need to honor those on the margins of the enterprise and centralize their knowledge for the sake of the business.

The second periphery has to do with looking and listening to the marketplace—looking at competitors, especially new entrants. It's so easy to discount the smaller players, but often they're only "small" relative to one's interpretation of the market.

A third consideration relates to how effectively managers challenge one another to think about strategic surprises they can launch at their competitors and, in turn, surprises the competition may be planning for them. This line of questioning is an effective way of getting people to think out of the box.

How can companies best promote enterprises that are both profitable and good places for people to work?

The answer relates again to the idea of creating a learning milieu. By paying serious attention to *people* in an organization—on the fringes, serving customers, in the trenches—roles get reversed, as potentially marginalized ideas and competencies become central. Work becomes meaningful for everyone, and both individual and corporate intelligence grows. By understanding the contextual aspects of work, honoring the creative abilities of employees, and reserving opportunities for the future, managers can produce enterprises that are highly successful and enormously satisfying. Of course, the icing on the cake comes with building information systems that facilitate the flow of ideas and nurture the social capital of the enterprise.

On Booms, Busts, and the Value of Good Judgment

Robert Hormats

Robert Hormats is vice chair of Goldman Sachs (International). Before joining Goldman Sachs, he was a presidential advisor, an assistant secretary for economic and business affairs in the U.S. State Department, and a staff member of the National Security Council. He has been a member of the Trilateral Commission and is on the board of directors of the U.S.-Russian Enterprise Fund, the Human Genome Sciences Corporation, Englehard Hanovia, and the Council on Foreign Relations. In this piece, he writes about the instability of financial markets and their influence on the future.

In the first part of the 1890s, the United States financed and built 70,000 miles of rail track. In the second part of the 1890s, companies that had built 40,000 miles of that track went bankrupt. Competition to build rail track got way ahead of demand; there wasn't enough stuff to put over those rails, so companies went bankrupt. The similarity between rail track then and fiber optics now (and other components of the telecom and information infrastructure as well) are striking. But there is also a hopeful side to the analogy. Despite the bankruptcies, the rails are still there. Someone bought them and consolidated them—the Harrimans and others. They knew how to manage a continental rail system, so they bought cheap properties from bankrupt companies and put them together to make money. Now we have a well-developed telecommunications and IT infrastructure, plus a lot of very talented engineers, scientists, and programmers who can be mobilized—at prices a lot lower than a few years ago. They will sustain the technology boom—but on a more realistic basis, with less hype, less debt, and less "irrational exuberance" in the stock market. The rail industry did not end with the bankruptcies of the 1890s; it got stronger with consolidations and good management. The telecommunications/Internet industry will not end with the crash of the last couple of years; it will thrive with new configurations, new management, and new business opportunities.

One of the key points of a transformative technology is not that the individual people who develop the technology make the money. Some do, many don't. The key point is that transformative technology enables other people in other sectors to become more productive and to make money. In other words, it is a technology that has broad productive uses for a large portion of the economy. Often it's not the first mover who profits most; it's those who use the technology most effectively to improve their own existing business models or to develop new ones. For instance, AOL was not the first of the online companies. We don't even remember what the first companies were; they're mostly forgotten.

One of the big mistakes people make is to think of financial markets as highly efficient. While they can be efficient over the long term, they can be very inefficient for sustained periods of time. They experience big booms and big busts—and are rarely at equilibrium. Money is often allocated for very inefficient uses or to finance excess. But markets are generally good at enabling people to allocate risk. If you are starting a company, you can then take that company public or to venture capitalists and spread the risk around instead of taking all or most of the risk yourself.

This is part of the entrepreneurial process. Is it an efficient way of allocating capital? No, not always. But it is a critical part of the way capitalism works and technology evolves. If you could not spread the risk, you probably wouldn't have made the initial investment to begin with or developed the company as rapidly. If you are Bill Gates, you couldn't finance the rapid rise of Microsoft all on your own. You have to have others participate in the equity.

In the 1990s the public equity market became, in effect, a venture capital market. In the history of American capital markets, most companies don't come to the public market until they are making money or are about to make money. They get money from banks before that. Generally speaking, very few companies come to the public market without some sort of track record. After Amazon and Netscape, though, many high-tech companies came to the public market with no profits and only the vaguest expectation or hope that they had short-term or medium-term or even long-term prospects for making profits. So the high-tech, overly exuberant investors, in effect, became venture capitalists, buying companies at a much earlier stage than they would have 10 to 15 years ago. A lot of people regarded this as a get-rich-quick approach, and really didn't have sufficient appreciation of the high risks involved. They were becoming venture capitalists without the sophistication—or very deep pockets.

Most people have learned their lesson and won't go back to buying those kinds of stocks very soon. Average investors will steer clear of start ups for a long time to come. In the future investors will be more cautious and they'll have much more diversification in their portfolios among categories of stocks, and between stocks and bonds. It will slow the whole capital-raising process down. I think it will make equity capital raising for many companies much more difficult in the next ten years.

THE ECONOMY WILL LIKELY GROW AGAIN, BUT AT A SLOWER PACE

If you go back to the railroad and electricity booms, the economy did build on these technologies quite successfully. We are in, and will continue to experience, a period of very substantial technological progress. But for a while it will be harder to raise equity capital, except for extremely good technology companies with good business plans and good management. There will be a continued dynamism in many sectors of the economy. The "new economy" wasn't just about technology; it was about better management practices, better business models, more efficiency, globalization, more immigration. It was about combining many factors to achieve high productivity. That progress will continue. And the U.S. economy will grow thanks to the remarkable resilience of its people and an attitude that accepts that risk is part of economics—and that in the long run taking risks may produce some dislocations and failures but over time it also produces dynamic growth.

The knowledge we have gained from financing these new technologies, as well as from the technologies themselves, has been dramatic. Someone said to Thomas Edison: "Mr. Edison, you have done 50 experiments and haven't developed a light bulb. Are you concerned about these failures?" Edison replied: "What failures? We have learned 50 different ways not to make a light bulb." This is a great part of the American entrepreneurial spirit. Try, fail, learn from mistakes, and then do it better.

A NEW LEVEL OF TRANSPARENCY IS EVOLVING BETWEEN COMPANIES AND THEIR CUSTOMERS

The corporate sector will become much more responsive to the concerns of its stakeholders and will, in its own right and through governmental lobbying pressure, make changes. If you are a corporation, you're operating in an environment today where you have to be more environmentally minded because more and more consumers are environmentally minded. The Internet exposes any indiscretions, any violations, and any polluting that is being done around the world. It also exposes the way you treat your workers, or conduct your human-rights policies. The bright light of exposure on corporate policies and the growing numbers of people—particularly younger people—who are socially minded and obtain information in real time off the Internet will make a difference to the way corporations act. It will place them under continuous pressure to adhere to high standards of social responsibility.

You don't have to wait until the government tells you to do it. Look at BP. It has been a very progressive company on environmental practices. Toyota developed the Prias, a hybrid car that is very gas-efficient and very cool. And it is working on fuel cells for the next generation of cars with high environmental standards. I think you will see a lot of companies doing this.

Companies are also under pressure to improve workplace standards. The notion put about by the antiglobalization forces that foreign investment brings down workplace, environmental, or other standards is a myth. Generally these companies introduce higher standards than are commonly found in local companies. Moreover, if workers are treated badly in, say, a factory run by an American company in Guatemala, kids all over the United States know about it in minutes, because it is on the Internet. They talk about it in school, and they won't buy the company's products.

I think transparency is here to stay. The Internet is just a sliver on the information timeline. The church and the king dominated books until Gutenberg, and then books were developed for large numbers of people. More and more people learned to read because there were more books. And more and more writers came forth to write books that interested large portions of the population. Magazines and pamphlets were instrumental in getting support for the American Revolution. Television and radio exponentially increased the number of people exposed to information—and helped win the Cold War by penetrating the Iron Curtain. King and church controlled information for the first half of the last millennium. Once moveable type was developed, they couldn't do that anymore. I think the Internet is the latest stage in that process of democratizing information—and it has had its effect quickly and globally. It provides individuals with access to others around the world—and no one, no country, no group can control it.

MAINTAINING A SENSE OF PERSPECTIVE

I think what happens is that when things start looking good, too many people downplay and disregard risk. It always happens when you get a boom. That is why there are busts—people borrow too much and invest too much in high-risk enterprises with the expectation that the boom will continue indefinitely.

Some argued that more information would prevent this from happening, because it would enable investors to assess the prospects of companies better or shift out of bad investments more quickly, thus cutting their losses. But information is not a substitute for good judgment. Tom Friedman has made the point that there should be a warning label attached to information technology that says, "Judgment not included." He is right. There is a lot of information available—and the key now is to exercise good judgment in evaluating it and deciding how to act on the basis of it.

So far we haven't found the substitute for human judgment. Investors and companies made a lot of mistakes. They got greedy and careless—and a lot of people lost perspective about risk. For many it was a financial tragedy. If you had $1 million and put $100,000 into the dot-coms or other technology companies and lost much of it, that was unfortunate but probably not catastrophic. That was risk money. The real problem is that people who had $100,000 put $90,000 into these kinds of stocks, which is really where the human tragedies occurred. That's where you get the heartrending stories of this period. Things were going so well they thought they could afford to take that kind of risk. And they not only lost their money, but also in many cases—in light of the Enron and WorldCom abuses—concluded that the deck was stacked against them. One casualty of this period has been investor faith that markets are fair; to many, the C.E.O.s of the companies in which they invested treated them with contempt, and so did many of the so-called gatekeepers. Restoring confidence will not be done by legislation or pronouncements by committees; it must be done one C.E.O. at a time, one company at a time, one audit at a time, one analyst at a time.

The lesson is that the potential for loss is often forgotten when everything is going well. You need to be very diversified. Don't invest more than you can afford to lose, and recognize that there are real risks. And demand that corporations, accountants, bankers, and government regulators adhere to high standards of ethics, transparency, and corporate conduct. The problem is that most companies did adhere to these standards—but the few that did not tarnished the overall image of corporations and corporate governance. For the small investor especially, that image will take some time to recover. And for everybody there is a risk that overregulation could stifle risk taking and entrepreneurialism.

This essay was adapted from an interview undertaken with Mr. Hormats by Peter Leyden, Knowledge Developer at Global Business Network (www.gbn.com). The publishers gratefully acknowledge the support of Global Business Network in making these ideas and insights available.

Setting the Agenda for the Next Generation of Leaders

Michael Hammer

Michael Hammer is the originator of both the concept of "reengineering" and of "the process enterprise." Through his teaching and research, he works with the management teams of leading companies to bring about fundamental change in their organizations. He is the coauthor of *Reengineering the Corporation* (with James Champy; revised ed., HarperCollins, 2001) and author of *Beyond Reengineering* (HarperCollins, 1996) and *The Agenda* (Crown, 2001).

A company can have brilliant leadership and an effective strategy, but these don't guarantee success. What's too often missing—and, therefore, what has always interested me the most—is operations: getting things done. I'm on an eternal quest for more effective ways of executing. The domain in which I specialize is different from that of most other management thinkers. I often refer to myself as "a plumber." I'm concerned with how companies do and should operate, how best to get work done, and how to organize an enterprise so that work will be done that way. Specifically, I am a believer in process: that it's better for a company to develop a system that will produce an unending stream of results, rather than hope for brilliant ideas and individual heroics.

While many of my colleagues are professors, consultants, or inspirational speakers, I think of myself as mostly a teacher. Trying to discover and communicate the best ways to get work done is what drives me, and is what underlies the educational programs that I present to thousands of managers each year. Instead of selling fish, I teach fishing.

I owe a lot to someone I've never met but respect immensely. David Halberstam and his milestone book *The Reckoning* moved me greatly. I still quote from that book, even though I first read it in the mid 1980s when I was a technology consultant.

At that time, I had recently left my MIT faculty position, and I was working with companies to help them use automation and technology more effectively. I ultimately concluded that technology utilization was only a fraction of the real problem, and that the best technology could not help a company that was organized ineffectively and had poorly designed processes. Without rethinking the basics, we would end up paving the cow paths. That's why *The Reckoning* grabbed me so strongly. What Halberstam did in that book was to track the parallel histories of Nissan and Ford. As he looked at the two companies over a long period (roughly 1947 to 1983), his chapters on Ford were a damning indictment of what was (and is) wrong with many enterprises.

The book was a revelation to me: it confirmed and elaborated my worst fears about large organizations. In the book Ford was depicted as a company more focused on financial issues rather than operational ones. How to design, make, and sell cars was less important than how to manage a balance sheet. Halberstam's insights made me face up to the fact that my technology advice would do little good unless companies rethought their priorities. I still have my copy with my marginal notations; some of the anecdotes in *The Reckoning* are burned into my memory.

However, we can't be too critical of companies like Ford (whom I have worked with and, hopefully, helped since reading that book). After all, we still haven't had that much experience with large enterprises, and it is not surprising that we are still trying to figure out how they should be run.

The modern corporation as we know it is a very recent phenomenon, a creation of the 20th century. We're still just beginning to understand how to operate and manage these large enterprises. Furthermore, the world we face today is very different from the world in which the modern corporation was born. Therefore, nothing in conventional business practice should be regarded as set in stone. Indeed, the very identity of the corporation is now being called into question. Looking forward, the issue of enterprise boundaries will dominate much of our discourse.

Today most companies still try to be self-contained enterprises. Today's typical corporation believes, as companies have done for the last 100 years, that it needs to do everything required to provide its product or service—and do it all inside the corporation. But that point of view is evaporating, and it will evaporate faster and faster as we move into the new century.

In other words, the question "What is a business?" is now in question.

As products have ever shorter lifetimes, we need to define our companies not in terms of what they produce, but in terms of what they do, focusing on process rather than product. To explain that distinction, let's think about a company that today considers itself in the jet aircraft business. Right now, that company does just about everything required to design, make, and sell jet aircraft. In the future, however, I can envision the managers in that company defining it as being in the business of assembling complex systems (for instance). They would assemble the components of a jet aircraft, but would work closely with other companies who would specialize in selling aircraft, or maintaining aircraft, or financing aircraft purchases by major airlines. In the past this idea was not very practical because of what economists call "transaction costs," the overhead of interfacing and coordinating with other companies. But with the advent of the Internet it is not much harder to work with others than it is to work with yourself—and the advantages of focus make doing so very worthwhile.

As this trend develops, it will change people's perspective of what a business is and what it should be doing. Businesses become parts of systems rather than whole systems in themselves. More than that, it also says that the process by which you do business is the most important part of the business. In other words, your process is your business.

All that this means is that two management skills that today are largely absent will jump to the very top of the leadership agenda. Managers will have to be proficient in designing and instrumenting systems and processes and have an enormous capacity for teamwork and collaboration.

Managers will have to get a whole lot better at looking holistically at operational processes and systems, at designing ones that operate at maximum efficiency, at measuring system performance, and at improving a system once it's up and running. This is a very different emphasis from today's; management takes on much more of an engineering flavor, rather than a financial focus. I see this already starting to take place, as phrases like "business systems engineering" and "process management" enter the parlance and organizational charts of more and more companies. I also see an indicator of this shift in the increasing number of executives with engineering backgrounds. I don't think it is an accident that the most influential executive of modern times, Jack Welch, has a background in chemical engineering.

Managers have to shake off once and for all the sense that they are independent actors responsible for a self-contained unit. It used to be that the grade-school child who came home with a report card that had an unsatisfactory grade in "playing well with others" was marked as one with executive potential. No longer. Companies can't afford the infighting and suboptimization that results from giving managers individual fiefdoms and letting them fight it out. Just as people on the front lines need to work collaboratively, so do their leaders. Nor can this collaboration end at company boundaries. As companies integrate their processes with each other, their managers will need to work together closely. To return to our jet aircraft example, the managers of the various companies that design, make, and sell the plane all need to work together.

We need to invoke new questions to guide our thinking. We should all be asking, every day, not only "What should I do?", but also "How can I do it better?" and "What should I not do?"

The way to shake off past traditions that are no longer relevant to tomorrow's business world is to make some hard choices. If your company is to move forward, which customers should you no longer serve? Which products should you discontinue? What things that your enterprise now does should be done instead by some other company?

This line of questioning will force companies to think of themselves in new ways. And it will also promote an environment in which everyone in the enterprise is thinking hard about how to sustain profitability and make the company the best possible place to work. Ultimately, good management tomorrow will come down to giving everyone in the corporation an understanding of the business, its customers and processes, and where each employee and manager fits. Good management tomorrow will give everyone a sense of connection and a real view of the opportunities that can be seized to generate success.

Globalization and the Really Long View

Stewart Brand

The insight that first made Stewart Brand famous was: take the far view. If you look at something from really, really far away, then not only your view changes, but also your understanding—the shift in your vision will prompt a shift in your mind. Back in 1966, when he was a photographer in San Francisco, Brand started musing one day about what would happen if you pulled your view back from the city so far that you could see the whole Earth from space. That prompted him to ask the question why, ten years after Sputnik, the public had not yet seen a photograph of the entire Earth? And that, in turn, immediately prompted him to launch a campaign (complete with buttons) calling for the image. Thus, some people credit Brand with nudging NASA to release the famous photos taken on Apollo 8.

Today Brand's overarching insight has shifted from "take the far view" to "take the long view"—the really, really long view. When Brand talks about long, he doesn't just mean a five to ten year perspective, which is unusual enough in business circles, he means thinking in centuries, millennia, even in 10,000-year stretches of time . . .

THE LONG VIEW SHOWS THAT ACCELERATING CHANGE MATTERS, AND THAT TOTAL COLLAPSE IS PLAUSIBLE

The long view makes the prospect of total collapse seem thinkable. Every now and then, civilizations decline steadily or come to relatively sudden ends. It's normal. In the perspective of centuries, there is nothing special about it. The sense that "that's something those poor fools in history did" goes away, because you realize that, in their way, they were just as smart about what was going on as we are about our times. The fragility of things becomes interesting.

Another thing that emerges by taking the long view is Ray Kurzweil's idea of the self-acceleration of technology and, thereby, of the pace of history. There has been a pretty circular trend of logarithmic increase for many centuries. There is no reason to expect that acceleration to suddenly turn into an S curve that levels off on its own terms. Technology accelerates itself and is accelerating itself more and more, and that singularity offers a way to think about the present that is clear and productive. A whole bunch of technologies accelerate each other to the point where, basically, it's a new world every week.

There are countervailing intelligent, and sometimes not-so-intelligent, forces working against the pace of change. As technology pioneer Jaron Lanier said at a *Fortune* magazine conference in Aspen in 2001, all of the rhetoric of the hyperacceleration of technology absolutely freaks people out. People feel that engineers are messing with their essence, and they're not going to stand for it. They think: "I've got to protect my children. I've got to protect my family. I've got to protect my church. I've got to protect all of these things against the nitwits who think they'll just give us a pill so we can live forever."

They've got a point. The rhetoric is overwrought. Nevertheless, the argument made by Institute for the Future director Paul Saffo and others that we *overestimate* how rapidly change is coming in the short term, and *underestimate* how much change is coming in the long term, continues to be valid. While the United States is focused on stem cells, eight other things are swarming ahead with no attention paid at all. Somebody creates an advanced birth control pill without asking anyone's permission, and it changes the world. Doom is plausible when you take a long-term view, and acceleration matters when you take a long-term view.

They were actually called megatrends once upon a time; they're large trends with sudden manifestations. A major acceleration of everything in ten years' time is a sudden manifestation. There's a mild form of that going on in Japan at the present. They fell out of their bubble economy into a place where they can't pick themselves up. Israel has fallen down and can't get up.

There's a malaise of progress going on that I think is somewhat part of the long view. It was in a way predicted by cyberpunk science fiction writers. The Bruce Sterlings and the Bill Gibsons saw it coming—that there would be a *noir* version of high-tech that was not going to be glossy, it was going to be ugly; it was not going to be freeing, it was going to be enslaving; it wasn't going to make everybody rich, it was going to make some people rich.

All these are ways of saying that technology acceleration goes on and that contaminant things go with it: the deepening of fundamentalism; liberal resistance; conservative resistance. Liberal resistance takes the form of building preservation. Conservative resistance is to stop stem cell research or cloning or whatever. It's unlikely that the bioethicists are going to solve all of the problems and that there won't be any new ones. People who say that this is a resistance to Darwinism are absolutely accurate. Darwin knew that he was basically saying, "God is not only dead, he never existed." Humans weren't designed by a great designer; they emerged from 3.5 billion years of mindless mistakes and successes.

WE'VE GOT A GLOBAL ECONOMY; NOW WE NEED A GLOBAL SOCIETY

I think we are, in fact, in a long boom. The opportunities of globalization drastically outweigh the downside. It is going ahead and can't be stopped. There will be other avenues that will emerge for managing it. That's what people like former president Bill Clinton and former secretary of state Madeleine Albright are basically bearing down on: How to make a global system that can progress pretty rapidly without breaking.

I'm talking about civilization. We've had a century of a global economy without a global body politic. At least a third of this present century—maybe half, maybe the whole thing—will be spent sorting out the global society in terms of global governance, global civilization, the global frame of reference. We may have one big currency or just a few big currencies. We may all see the same entertainment—or not. What things are increasingly unique? How fine-grained can uniqueness go?

I think one of the interesting things is going to be which states are permitted to fail and which are not. States in central Africa are permitted to fail; Argentina is not. The most hardcore Republicans, holding their noses the whole way and trying to do it almost in secret, will come to the rescue of Argentina when it's in trouble. The system simply will not tolerate it. That's pretty interesting.

It's a centuries-scale project, building a global society. In the past, when civilizations have failed, other civilizations have taken up the slack. When Europe is in a dark age, Islam is having its own renaissance and helps the European renaissance. Once it's an all-encompassing thing, all your eggs are in one basket. If you drop the basket, all of your eggs are broken. You have to build in the comeback capabilities internally. There's a certain rent you have to pay to have a relatively safe global civilization, and we don't know what that is yet.

SCIENCE AND THE LONG-TERM PERSPECTIVE

Scientific knowledge is increasing and archeology never stops. We know more and more about everything. Science is increasingly able to tell us things like global warming is real, methane at the bottom of the ocean is released or not released and has this effect. These are multicentury, deeply important trends. As soon as you take seriously the idea of the oceans rising x feet in your lifetime, or the Gulf Stream turning off over a period of a couple of years and freezing Europe in your lifetime, it's a different story.

I think that science is giving us this long-term perspective, and it gets out there through the media, through the schools. Kids care about it. That starts to yield a long-term frame of reference in terms of responsibility, in terms of things that are going on for which you can't buy a solution. One nation alone can't unilaterally fix it, or be ignored by the others if it's part of the problem. There's a globalization of concern, and you've reason to think in century terms because science gives you both the need and the tools to do that.

I think part of the increased awareness in long-term thinking is the increasing life span of some people. If an eight-year-old in a couple of years starts to assume that 150 to 200 years is a plausible lifespan for him or her personally, that's going to change thinking and probably behavior. People never used to know their great-grandparents. Now everybody does. That will go on to great-great-grandparents. In turn, they're going to know their own great-great-grandkids. What's life going to be like for them? What will I do now about that? I think that that, in addition to science, creates a personal lengthening of the frame of reference. The "now" of one's life is extending. Things will change around that.

This essay was adapted from an interview undertaken with Mr. Brand by Peter Leyden, Knowledge Developer at Global Business Network (www.gbn.com). The publishers gratefully acknowledge the support of Global Business Network in making these ideas and insights available.

Human Capital

Edward E. Gordon

The high performance workplace over the past two decades has been driven by two titanic forces: globalization and an increasing pace of technological change.

At the beginning of the 21st century these factors have combined to demand a new kind of well-educated knowledge worker, as profound a change as that wrought by the early Industrial Revolution on the role of manual labor in the 1800s.

In this environment, harnessing the human capital—the accumulated skills, experience, wisdom, and capabilities of all of the people employed in the organization—is fundamental to success. This may seem obvious—after all, why pay for the most expensive resource in terms of results than any other, without using it to the full? However, at a time when skills are more complex and transferable, traditional loyalty is reducing, and the significance and value of knowledge is rising, there is a premium and renewed focus on managing human capital.

The U.S. departments of labor and education now estimate that 80% of all jobs in the high-tech workplace require at least 13th-grade reading, math comprehension, and applications skill levels. Unfortunately, the National Adult Literacy Survey (NALS) reported that 48% of U.S. adults fail to meet these criteria.

Though this problem can be found in many countries, it is most acute in the United States. The international Organisation for Economic Co-operation and Development (OECD) ranked the United States 15th out of 47 major industrial nations in the education and training levels of its citizens. This study showed about half of the U.S. adults reading below eighth-grade level, with much of the population performing below sixth-grade level.

In another comparative study of 18 nations, the OECD found that of U.S. high-school graduates who do not go on to acquire further education, nearly 60% perform below a literacy level that international experts consider necessary to cope with the complex demands of the modern workplace. That percentage was the highest among the nations studied, with Finland the lowest at 10% and other countries falling in between—20% in Germany, 35% in the United Kingdom, 50% in Poland. Instead of becoming knowledge workers, it would seem that many members of the current U.S. workforce, as well as students about to emerge from school, are in danger of becoming the new techno-peasants. "Investment in human capital is necessary for any nation to reap the benefits from information technology," says John Martin, director of education for the OECD. In this section, we will assess the importance of human capital: what it is, where it is, and how it can be managed to best effect.

WHERE ARE THE KNOWLEDGE WORKERS?

As the world economy has grown during the past ten years, a demographic time bomb is in the making. The U.S. Census Bureau, Department of Labor, and Immigration and Naturalization Service concur that the population younger than 34 is declining.

Increasing retirements will combine with this shrinking labor pool to produce a dramatic knowledge-worker shortfall until 2020. The same trends hold true throughout Western Europe and Japan. In some countries the total population may even decline.

With skilled workers in such high demand, U.S. companies have repositioned operations overseas, and they now lure up to 600,000 skilled workers to the United States on temporary H-1B visas.

The United States projects a shortfall of 2 million IT workers by 2005, while the European Union (EU) forecasts a 1.5 million worker labor gap. The United States and the EU share the same human-capital strategy—import the workers. But there aren't enough IT workers worldwide to fill the knowledge-worker gap. A so-called skill war is now starting, one that will see nations bidding up salaries just to attract these workers from a diminishing world supply.

To create real value, businesses must better leverage their human capital by helping develop larger numbers of their employees into better-educated workers, who will then be able to create more high-value-added products and services at extremely low cost.

DEVELOPING HUMAN CAPITAL: AVOIDING THE PITFALLS

The learning organization has largely failed in the boardroom for two reasons. First, presidents, C.E.O.s, and small-business owners still see no connection between company profit and investing in their human capital, because they believe you can't measure it. Second, training programs often don't improve employee performance, because they aren't based on the most recent advances in teaching critical-competency and problem-solving skills.

Complex and multilayered workplace performance issues need to be stated in a language and format that will move more business leaders to give them their personal support. Poll after poll shows that people in the United States support the concept of better education in general, but it is in realizing the concept that support falls apart.

Many of the world's leading industrial powers are beating the United States at its own game simply by understanding that knowledge equals profit. Rather than ignoring the relationships, they are acting on the critical interactions among technology, smarter employees, and return on investment (ROI). They invest extensively in student career education and employee-retraining programs—and reap the short- and long-term profits.

The key is high-quality reeducation programs that motivate employees to use their own learning by applying innovative thinking on the job. This strategy will increase personal performance, better their lifetime careers, and in turn give business a high ROI in human capital.

TAKING RESPONSIBILITY FOR HUMAN CAPITAL DEVELOPMENT

Many organizations are abrogating the responsibility for human-capital development by empowering people to figure out what new knowledge they need and encouraging them just to go and get it. However, this do-it-yourself approach to training is a naive management strategy; for most people it's too scattered for any meaningful buildup of new personal skills.

Too many executives have followed the questionable supposition that Web- and video-based training can do it all. This confuses the delivery system with the content. It's a huge mistake to think of e-learning simply as a cheaper way to distribute knowledge, without taking into account the factors that really motivate people to learn. First comes acquiring new information; second, trying it out by applying it; third, reaching personal understanding. The social aspect of learning is vital for most people. A relationship needs to exist between a good teacher and learner. Web- and video-based training are important components of most well-rounded training programs, but they're not always the best teaching methods. The teacher/trainer remains central to a successful learning experience, with the latest electronic teaching aids serving as supplemental tools, not a total system solution.

Trident Precision Manufacturing of Webster, New York, is one of the smallest companies ever to win a Malcolm Baldrige National Quality Award (in 1996). Over a period of six years, Trident invested 4.7% of the payroll in educating its employees. This custom-product sheet-metal company taught workers blueprint reading, trigonometry, and English as a second language (ESL). Product defect rates improved from 3% to 99.994% defect-free, annual revenue rose from $5 million to $19 million, and revenue per employee shot up by 73%.

Equimeter, based in the United Kingdom, invested its human capital in its Pennsylvania operations by providing a group of engineers with a *kaizen*-team-training program in order to improve the quality and productivity of a gas-meter assembly line. The company achieved a 16% productivity improvement and 22% space savings, reduced the work in process by 10%, and solved three safety issues. The estimated ROI of this training program was 31.6%.

Human-capital investment by thousands of other organizations, including Allied Signal, Elco Industries, Hampden Papers, Hardy Industries, Lumonics, MacLean-Fogg, the Northeast Illinois Metropolitan Transit Railroad Authority (METRA), Warner-Lambert, and Will-Burt, more clearly demonstrated the direct correlation of skills, training, and education with increased productivity and profit.

FedEx has established learning and growth as one of its four key business strategies. FedEx Quality University is a global learning system. More than 140,000 employees worldwide have access to its content. When FedEx employees can't find a suitable e-learning course in the Quality University, they can take classroom courses from outside sources that are paid for by the $2,500 annual Personal Learning Fund that FedEx offers every employee. By offering these career development opportunities, FedEx has been better able to retain valuable employees and leverage its available human capital.

MAKING IT HAPPEN

Investing in human capital produces better business returns; it provides cost savings and efficiencies, maximizes the use of available resources, and addresses specific performance and productivity issues. To succeed, it can help if:

- **Investments in human capital are measured in cash** — clearly highlighting the benefits of acting, and the perils of inaction.

- **The personal knowledge of employees across the organized is assessed**: this gives managers benchmarks for understanding its human capital strengths and weaknesses.
- **Relevant and appropriate performance development programs in skills, education, and training areas are selected.** These should be directly linked to productivity improvement needs and the strategy of the business—what skills are needed to progress towards the desired destination?
- **A human capital measurement system is applied,** so that the best return on investment is achieved in the short and long terms.

Such management strategies for human-capital investment encourage business innovation by leveraging structural capital and human capital in new combinations. The company benefits from a steeper learning curve at its critical cutting edge: the friction points where people grapple with operational productivity issues. Critical competencies are generated in-house that encourage people to create new procedures, services, products, and intellectual properties—the competitive ideas of business success that generate real profit.

Unless businesses invest in people to reverse the dangerous trend of discounting the value of human capital, both technology and management systems will fail as they become more complex and require more people who can think for themselves and adapt information. By investing in their most critical intangible—human capital—businesses will rise to the challenges of technology and globalization and speed up the process of building a knowledge economy in their own communities and across the world.

Edward E. Gordon is a consultant, writer, speaker, academician, and president of Imperial Consulting, a firm specializing in human capital development (www.imperialcorp.com). He has taught at three Chicago-based universities, appeared on television and radio, and is the author or coauthor of ten books, including *Skill Wars: Winning the Battle for Productivity and Profit* (Butterworth/Heinemann, 2000) and *FutureWork: The Revolution Reshaping American Business* (Praeger, 1994).

Finding and Keeping the Best Talent in the World

Richard J. Leider

The era of talent has shifted power to talented people. As the world moves towards an information economy, talented people will be able to demand purpose-driven work environments where they are free to contribute their gifts and talents.

IS TALENT ONE OF YOUR TOP THREE PRIORITIES?

Recently I listened to a powerful presentation on a company's new vision. The persuasive executive presenting it painted an inspiring picture of the operating model that she saw the company needed to execute the new vision. It was brilliant. But there was one thing missing: she never discussed talent. Talent is the make-or-break element the company needs to build the new vision. I see this often, and it perplexes me. Great vision requires great talent, but the pool of talent is shrinking. To create competitive advantage, the company needs to attract talent, and to attract the best talent in the world the company will need to be seen as a great place to work.

When I coach executives most of them can articulate their business vision with great passion. Then I ask, "What keeps you awake at night?" They all tell me the same thing: "How are we going to find the best talent to execute our vision?" Yet there's rarely a talent strategy to address the cause of their sleeplessness. For these executives to sleep soundly, talent must be one of their top three strategic priorities.

WHAT DO EMPLOYEES WANT TO KNOW?

To attract talent, you must recognize the need for an engagement strategy. You have to engage employees emotionally if you want them to deliver big. In workshop discussions with employees from many companies, a major frustration they often cite is: Why should I go above and beyond what's required? Companies just want to get more and more and give less and less.

To address employees' frustration you need to answer the four core questions that everyone wants clarified:

1 Where are we going?
2 What are we doing to get there?
3 What do you want me to do?
4 What's in it for me when I do?

These are the common concerns on talented people's minds. What company, regardless of size, industry, or country, wouldn't benefit from clearly answering these four questions for their best employees? When it comes to answering them, there's one basic you can't afford to overlook: a feeling of purpose in the workplace. If you can create a culture of purpose you can attract the best talent to work at your company, even when talent is in short supply.

DOES MONEY MATTER?

Money matters. But competing for talent primarily by offering more money has rarely been enough to attract or retain the best people. Good pay is essential, but after a while the best people look for more from their work than just money. Talented people demand purposeful, challenging work, and they want the chance to express and develop their strongest talents.

The best people want to be part of something they can believe in—something that brings meaning to their work and their lives; something that involves a purpose bigger than themselves and their individual success. They want work that challenges them to make a difference. A powerful purpose is a magnet for attracting powerful people.

WHAT IS THE POWER OF PURPOSE?

The purpose I'm describing creates a psychological bond between employees and the company. This attachment is essential for you to execute your vision. Nancy Hutson knows that Pfizer's research pipeline depends on attracting and retaining the best talent in the world. As senior vice president and site head for the pharmaceutical company's 5,000-person Groton Research Laboratories in Connecticut, she also knows that great people can go anywhere today. That means her biggest competitive headache isn't companies like Merck or Johnson & Johnson. Her biggest worry is holding onto great people. "There's nothing more important than helping people succeed," she says. "That's my number one job."

Nancy is one of the company's leading advocates and models for creating a culture of purpose. She says, "I'm passionate about building an organization that allows people to be all that they can be and that exemplifies the Pfizer values. Helping others succeed is in my DNA!" Nancy knows it's a seller's market for talent. People with the right combination of talents, passions, and values can afford to shop for places to work. For example, the baby boomers, the largest and most significant part of the North American and European working population, are attracted to work that provides purpose and meaning. During this phase of their life they start to look inward and ask, "Was it worth it? Did what I do make a difference?"

In earlier eras meaning came from company identity. Today purposeful work has replaced company identity. What's important now is a source of meaning in the work itself. The intrinsic purpose of the work has to be powerful enough to make up for the eroding employer–employee identity of the past.

ARE YOU WORKING ON PURPOSE?

Several years ago Tom Schultz, a corporate vice president and director of financial planning for Motorola, issued a couple of simple questions to 25 of his colleagues: "How do you see me? What's my legacy?" He requested frank, honest responses from others about how they thought he might be remembered. Within 48 hours, 19 people responded. Tom was surprised by the feedback. Hardly anyone mentioned his "hard" skills, his financial accomplishments. Everyone talked about his "soft" skills, his interpersonal contributions. Tom was, without knowing it, building a legacy.

"Today I always ask myself what impact this decision will have ten years from now." His answers help Tom manifest his purpose, which he defines as *making a difference with one person a day.* These days Tom also works to make a difference with his daughter, Kelly, who faces daily the challenges of spina bifida. Kelly's illness has at times tested Tom's resolve to keep making a difference at work. Exhausted by the pressures of caring for Kelly, he was ready to call it quits at Motorola. A senior executive shocked him by saying, "Don't do it! You need us and we need you right now."

Tom stayed and has taken the lead in creating a world-class leadership development process. Fueled by his interest in the long-term direction of people's lives, he's creating a role for himself in which he can make a difference in not just one life, but many people's lives each day. He says, "I love getting up in the morning to open up growth possibilities for people."

Picture the working lives of two people who do the same work. One has a job that pays the bills, while the other, like Tom Schultz, has a life's work that makes a positive difference in the lives of others. One drags out of bed most mornings feeling purposeless, tired, and stressed out. Tom has a reason to get up in the morning and feels a sense of purpose and energy most days. The difference is that Tom is *working on purpose* and the other person is not. Are you working on purpose? Are you creating a work culture in which the best people can work on purpose? (See the Working on Purpose Quiz on the next page.)

Purpose is a deep concept. It is not a simple management or employee development technique. It's an issue reserved for the best talent in the world, those who are willing to engage the bigger questions that our work eventually presents to all of us. It's an issue for people who are not going to be sitting at their own retirement party wondering what it all added up to, why they worked so hard, and whether it was really worth it.

MAKING IT HAPPEN
The following steps can help you get top talent to work for your company.
- Develop an *on-purpose* work culture in your company by first clarifying your own purpose and vision. Is it compelling? Are you passionate about doing that work?
- Create an engagement strategy by answering the four key questions that employees want to know.
- Communicate your answers to the four key questions relentlessly. Keep in mind that with every change, no matter how large or small, people start asking these questions all over again. Does your top talent know the answers to these key questions?
- Invite dialog with your talent. What challenges them? What are their purposes and passions? What do they want out of their work? A key to retaining your top talent is the relationship that you as a leader develop with them.

Working on Purpose Quiz. Are you working on purpose?
Does your current work feel like purposeful work?
Check the appropriate box in the table below.
The more Yes answers you have, the more purposeful you feel your work is. If you have fewer than five Yes answers, it becomes important to clarify what you believe your purpose is.

	YES	NO
1. I wake up most work days and feel energized to go to work.	–	–
2. I have a deep energy—feel a personal calling—for my work.	–	–
3. I am clear about how I measure my success as a person.	–	–
4. I use my gifts to add real value to people's lives.	–	–
5. I work with people who hold the same values I do.	–	–
6. I speak my truth at work.	–	–
7. I am experiencing true joy in my work.	–	–
8. I am making a living doing what I most love to do.	–	–
9. I can speak my purpose in one clear sentence.	–	–
10. I go to sleep most nights feeling "This was a well-lived day."	–	–
Total Yes responses		
Total No responses		

It's a revolutionary notion: the most talented people are attracted to places where they can work on purpose. Purpose inspires creativity and innovation—the fundamental qualities of the successful company of the 21st century. The innovation economy is your invitation to create a company where people can work on purpose. That's what the best people want.

————◆————

Richard Leider is founding partner of The Inventure Group, a firm that designs workshops, tools, and processes for organizations in the areas of life planning, leadership, team building, and career coaching. He is also an internationally respected author, speaker, and career coach. He has written five books, including *Whistle While You Work* (with David Shapiro; Berrett-Koehler, 2001) and *The Power of Purpose* (Berrett-Koehler, 1997). He is also a contributing columnist to *Fast Company*'s Web site.

Driving Fear from the Workplace

Dick Richards

In the early 1980s management guru W. Edwards Deming admonished managers to "drive out fear so that everyone may work effectively for the company." He was referring to fear that causes people to distort or ignore unpleasant results. Deming held that such fear stifles learning. Despite Deming's admonishment, fear still stalks workplaces and remains a potent force. The Discovery Group, an opinion survey organization, concluded that "half of all employees do not feel free to voice their opinions openly."

Fear takes many more forms than the one Deming described. It is apparent when we retreat from speaking to someone who does not listen, or when we recoil from saying difficult things to people who are known to shoot messengers. Fear is present whenever we suspect a hidden agenda, or when we are summoned to find a better way of working. It shows up as job insecurity and as dread that our positions might be usurped. It is close by when we feel unwilling to take risks or do what we know is right, and whenever we masquerade as someone other than who we are. Startup companies frequently have an entirely distinct set of fears such as raising capital and making payroll.

Fear originates from different sources: as a consequence of the world we live in; or induced by people who want us to feel fearful; or self-generated in response to a challenge. Whatever its form or source, the effects of fear are insidious and pervasive; it corrupts learning, improvement, innovation, measurement, and relationships. However, fear itself is not the lone culprit. Disallowed or disowned fear, which I refer to as "unacknowledged fear," is another, perhaps more insidious, danger.

FEAR AND PASSION

While it seems that fear ought to have no home in our workplaces, we do want passion. We want excitement about visions. We want enthusiasm for strategic plans. We want the energy that people bring to work when they feel those emotions. It's obvious that emotions are sources of energy that compel action. That's why we welcome passion, excitement, and enthusiasm. When people experience those emotions things get done.

It's less obvious that emotions are inextricably connected to each other. We cannot readily isolate just one emotion. We cannot drive out fear, or any other so-called negative emotion, without the risk of driving out the energy we want—excitement and enthusiasm. Daniel Goleman, author of *Working with Emotional Intelligence*, writes, "When the dictates of a boss determine the emotions a person must express, the result is an estrangement from one's own emotions." For example, when a manager suggests, either directly or subtly, that he or she wants everyone to feel part of one big happy team, but never fearful, angry, or sad, people are likely to shut their genuine emotions down altogether and put on a happy face. Goleman calls this "emotional tyranny." When we fail to acknowledge fear, we also extinguish passion. The result is a robotic workplace.

ENGAGING EMOTIONAL ENERGY

A fundamental task of management is engaging human energy and connecting it with organizational purpose. One popular model posits four kinds of human energy. *Physical* energy is the energy of the body. Engaging physical energy involves deciding who does how much of what work and when. *Intellectual* energy is of the mind. Engaging it involves such activities as making sense of problems and finding creative solutions. *Spiritual* energy arises from feeling connected to something larger than the self—an idea, a cause, a place, a deity. Engaging spiritual energy is seen in attempts to gain commitment to a vision or mission; these are endeavors to enlist people in a higher calling.

Our concern is with the fourth of these—*emotional energy*, and specifically fear. Engaging emotional energy means, first, mobilizing the passion and commitment that spurs people into action and, second, dealing effectively with emotions that create barriers to such action. George Davis, cofounder of Davis & Dean, a global project-management education company, believes that our prevailing model of management fails when we deal with fear. Davis says, "We reward managers who are warriors. The warrior's orientation is toward short-term goals: win today's battle, take that hill." With such a mentality, Davis believes, induced fear becomes useful because it's a good short-term motivator. "The problem is," says Davis, "if you use it again and again the fear becomes replaced by a sense of helplessness. This is typical of many corporate cultures. It is what employees of large organizations express when they resist change, dismiss change efforts, or become passive and cynical. Induced fear, which seems to work great in the short term, eventually creates apathy, a sense of oppression, and hopelessness."

When induced fear loses its impact, the warrior's impulse is to induce more fear. In the hands of a warrior, Deming's injunction to drive out fear may become a license to make people afraid to be afraid, or at least afraid to admit to being afraid. Rather than engaging emotional energy, warrior managers are likely to kill it.

SELF-GENERATED FEAR

There is little human progress without fear. Psychologist Susan Jeffers said it this way: "The fear will never go away as long as I continue to grow." This is a different kind of fear from the induced fear used to threaten people. This fear is the self-generated consequence of accepting a meaningful challenge. It can be a friend, a harbinger of an important opportunity. It is stimulating rather than paralyzing and can provide energy to meet the challenge.

Erik Sprotte, former director of human resources for Sears, accepted the challenge of helping to start a Web enterprise called FreeSamples.com. Self-generated fear arises from the challenge of "going where others haven't gone." Sprotte says, "I used to fear making a mistake like not having the facts at a meeting. This new kind of fear is good. It creates discipline and helps me focus on the important things that I really need to do."

THE ART OF ENGAGING FEAR

While fear is an individual phenomenon, people collude with one another in order to allow it to remain unacknowledged. They agree, if only tacitly, that fear should be disallowed or disowned, that "we just don't talk about those things around here." Disallowing and disowning fear thus becomes a cultural norm. Managers can and should take the lead in encouraging people to allow and own their fear. Today's business environment is soaked in challenge. Managers need all the energy they can muster from themselves and from people they manage. They cannot afford to ignore or destroy emotional energy, even when it arrives in an uncomfortable form.

Management, like any other work, is part science and part art. Engaging emotional energy is an aspect of the art of managing. As painters engage the energy of paint and poets engage the energy of words, managers' artistic medium is the energy of the people they manage. So managers must be acquainted with human energy in the same way that a painter is acquainted with how paint behaves, or a poet with the rhythm of words.

Many organizations are reluctant to have outsiders know they are fearful, so best practices aren't freely shared. However, Pfeffer and Sutton mention three companies that manage fear successfully:

- PSS/World Medical, where managers work to get problems raised faster than they would be in a fearful environment, gives everyone the opportunity to communicate with others and does not punish honest mistakes.
- SAS Institute, where David Russo, vice president of human resources said, "We punish nothing."
- Men's Wearhouse, where senior managers believe so strongly in eliminating fear that a transgression such as stealing is often viewed as a signal that development is needed rather than that the transgressor ought to be fired.

MAKING IT HAPPEN

Mastery of any art depends on developing certain skills and techniques. Consider the following:

- **Befriend your own fear.** There are three skills involved in befriending fear (or any other emotion): recognizing how it feels physically, putting it into words, and engaging it productively. None is easy in a work context, because most organizations discourage any emotion that seems negative. Find the people around you who are competent at managing their emotions. They are not those who overcontrol, but those who express emotions well and use them to create productive actions. Learn from those people.
- **Facilitate honest dialog about fears of all kinds.** This requires developing a high level of trust. People won't talk about their fears if there are negative consequences for doing so. Once fear is in the open, treat it as a gift. Treat induced fear as a signal that someone must learn to challenge rather than threaten. Treat self-generated fear as a signal that growth is at hand. It is important to listen and cope with uncomfortable situations.

- **Challenge rather than threaten.** Drive out induced fear and befriend self-generated fear. George Davis argues: "It is far more valuable to challenge people than to induce fear. The person will then create his or her own basket of fears that will spawn creativity."
- **Connect people with purpose.** Erik Sprotte is convinced that people need to believe in what their organization is doing and need to know how their contributions make a difference. He says, "Good managers help others understand their role in keeping the boat afloat. When we know we have a common goal, and have owned our fear, we can keep each other inspired every day."

Mastering the art of management requires developing skills and learning techniques for engaging human energy, including fear. And it requires something more. In *The Art Spirit*, artist and art teacher Robert Henri wrote, "The technique learned without a purpose is a formula which, when used, knocks the life out of any ideas to which it is applied." If we employ skills and techniques to engage the energy of fear, they will work only when coupled with a heartfelt purpose to value the full spectrum of emotional energy. When this is accomplished, your team will have the motivation, discipline, and cooperation required to reach ever more demanding organizational activities.

Dick Richards is a consultant, coach, speaker, writer, and ghostwriter who guides people, teams, and organizations in pursuit of their aspirations. He has contributed to over 50 organizations of all sizes, in business, social service, health care, government, and education. He has worked in more than a dozen countries to develop leadership, teamwork, and customer service, and to implement strategy. He is the author of *Artful Work: Awakening Joy, Meaning and Commitment in the Workplace* (Berkley, 1997), which won a Benjamin Franklin Award for best business book, and *Setting Your Genius Free: How to Discover Your Spirit and Calling* (Berkley, 1998). He contributes frequently to professional and business magazines and electronic publishing, appears in the media and at conferences, and leads public workshops.

Improving Company Performance with an Older Work Force

Beverly Goldberg

The months before the collapse of so many dot-coms in 2001 were marked by the influx of senior executives into a once totally youthful culture. These new companies, usually started by twenty-somethings with brilliant, innovative ideas, suddenly brought in older business managers to help them weather what seemed like bumps on the fast road to success. For all too many it turned out to be too little, too late. The lesson of the dot-coms is clear: experience counts. The world's industrial societies remain youth-oriented, even though the so-called baby boomers, the group that brought about this orientation, are now in their mid-fifties.

The aging of the baby boomers, born between the end of World War II and 1964, will bring a dramatic change in the age makeup of both the general population of the industrialized countries and the workplace. For example, in 2025, more Italians will be over than under 50 years old. In 2010, in the United Kingdom there will be 25% more workers aged between 45 and 49 than aged 25 to 29. The median age of the U.S. workforce will reach 40 in 2005, and in 2010 50% of all prime-age workers will be over 45.

Moreover, people in the industrialized nations have been retiring well before the usual retirement age. According to the Organization for Economic Cooperation and Development, workforce participation by people over 55 will have to increase by about 25% to maintain a constant employment-to-population ratio from 2005 onward. The message: companies that don't retain and recruit older workers won't be able to meet demand, let alone grow.

Older workers, however, are not just bodies to fill vacancies. Companies need older workers for their experience, institutional memories, work ethic, and, perhaps surprisingly, their ability to accommodate change and to focus—moreover, they're likely to remain with an organization longer than younger workers.

A VALUE-ADDED PROPOSITION

Many beliefs about older workers result in companies deciding that younger workers are a better-value proposition when it comes to hiring, training, and retention—these beliefs are patently false.

Older workers cost more. While the actual salaries of new, younger replacements may be lower, there are hidden costs of replacing older workers, for example, severance pay and agency fees for replacements. Corning Glass spends around $40,000 replacing each lost worker. Merck estimates that retraining a successor costs about one-and-a-half times the new person's average salary.

Older workers are less creative. While younger workers may come up with a larger number of ideas in meetings, fewer of those ideas prove to have value. Some have already been tried and failed, others don't work in the company's culture. Measuring the ultimate value of new ideas is more important than measuring their number.

Older workers don't learn as well as younger workers.   Surveys show that the ratings of older workers increased between 1985 and 1994: the percentage of older workers rated excellent for flexibility rose almost 20%; the percentage of older workers who are comfortable with new technology rose almost 15%. One problem may be that the average age of trainers is 33, also people learn differently depending on their age. For example, older workers unfamiliar with a classroom setting may do better learning one-on-one or on the shop floor.

Older workers aren't worth retraining, because they won't be around for long.   Today younger workers move from job to job quickly, because they haven't been raised in an environment in which corporate loyalty is a part of their thinking or tradition. Older workers remain longer, partly because they are more concerned about finding a new job if there is an economic slowdown.

Older workers have poorer attendance records.   Human resource managers report that older workers are less likely to be late or absent than younger workers. Also, workers over 55 account for 13.6% of the workforce, but only 9.7% of on-the-job injuries, and workers over 50 file far fewer worker compensation claims than younger workers.

Older workers are resistant to change.   False. The fastest-growing group of Internet users is people over 50. When training programs are made available to older workers, such as the programs offered by Microsoft Skills 2000, the Green Thumb, Inc., and the federal government, the number of applicants is far greater than the number of openings. More than 350,000 people between the ages of 50 and 64 were full- or part-time students pursuing degrees in the United States in 1998.

Older workers have less to contribute.   Not only do older workers contribute, but when organizations are concerned about maintaining their institutional history and values—and maintaining skills and techniques when those remain constant—they turn to older workers. Older workers can train new workers by working side by side with them and passing on the expertise and experience accumulated over long years, often reducing formal training time. Moreover, it takes an institutional memory to answer such questions as: Why were certain decisions about processes made? Why don't we do business with company X? These are things that don't get captured in memos or expert systems; they're the stuff of history, stored in memory, and they're invaluable.

ATTRACTING OLDER WORKERS

No matter how much companies may want to keep older workers, however, they are likely to discover that many such workers don't want to stay—at least, not under the same conditions they had in the past. Many no longer want to devote their lives to work. Even though life expectancy has increased dramatically so that people are no longer afraid they'll never have time to do the things they've always wanted to if they put off retirement, the urge to enjoy life while they're fit and hearty is strong. People want to take that exotic vacation, spend time with grandchildren, take courses, or pursue hobbies now. And often work has become tedious and dull, partly because companies don't offer older workers training opportunities, leaving them bored and interested in any form of change.

This is where companies need to be imaginative. We've been hearing about the new flexible organization for a decade, and now it's time for companies to apply the concept of flexibility to employment, to wake up to the fact that they can hold on to valuable older workers by being creative. Some companies have adapted, and they're better positioned to take advantage when the baby boomers consider retiring. Flexible arrangements include:

- part-time permanent work, sometimes known as "bridge retirement"—these jobs are scheduled for less than 40 hours a week, whether fewer hours a day or fewer days a week. For those of actual retirement age, it might involve a contract reducing the number of workdays by one day a week for the first three months, two days for the next three, and so on until full retirement is reached.
- full-time and part-time temporary work—an interesting development is the creation of in-house temporary agencies for workers who have retired from the company. Travelers Corporation set up an agency two decades ago and has enjoyed considerable success, encouraging other companies to adopt similar programs.
- contract work or consulting—this covers temporary assignments on specific projects rather than temporary work for different companies on an as-needed basis. Companies looking for workers for specific assignments often entice retired workers to return for the life of the project because they understand the corporate culture.
- telecommuting—working at home at least part of the time. For older employees, at-home work can make life easier, but it doesn't provide the social interaction that can make work attractive.
- on-call work—this arrangement, found most often in organizations such as hospitals that must be fully staffed at all times, involves a guaranteed minimum number of hours. It usually involves varying shifts, so is ideal for older workers who have few specific demands on their time.
- special assignments—these include temporary assignments, for example, serving on a disaster recovery project, representing the company in a community project, or working abroad. Whirlpool finds it less expensive to hire retired workers for short-term assignments abroad than to relocate full-time workers, while Quaker Oats has used retirees for a project in Shanghai. GTE has also tested this approach and plans to expand it.

MAKING IT HAPPEN

Three underlying principles are at the heart of any company's approach to investing in an older workforce.

- **Train older workers.** Kevin Doran, vice president of human resources and government and public affairs at Philips in Somerset, New Jersey, says that the company has not found it necessary to take age into account when it comes to retraining. For example, when Philips adopted new enterprise software companywide, everyone received "equal training regardless of their demographics. We don't see any difference in the ability to learn by age."

- **Take advantage of experience and institutional memory.** Texas Refinery Corporation, based in Fort Worth, Texas, hires older workers as independent contractors (as well as full-time employees). In 1995, 500 members of its 3,000-person sales force were past retirement age. The independent contractors who work for the company receive commissions and benefits on the basis of their sales. The company likes these arrangements because it believes that older salespeople have a distinct advantage when it comes to client relationships and that they are inclined to be self-starters.
- **Be flexible.** Neuville Industries of Hildebrand, North Carolina, set up a job-sharing program for employees over the age of 62. The program, which was initiated in the early 1990s, is aimed at employees with at least five years of experience. It provides for job-sharing with younger employees and allows employees to continue working for as long as they want to.

Over the next three decades the workforce in general will become older, and the baby boomers will begin to think strongly about retiring. Experience, people skills, focus, a strong work ethic, and the desire and ability to learn make these older workers extremely valuable. Attracting and then finding ways to hold onto the best and brightest is going to be the key to success. Organizations must begin to address misconceptions about older workers and put in place programs to address their needs and aspirations.

Beverly Goldberg is a management consultant and vice president of The Century Foundation, an 80-year-old nonprofit think tank in New York City that examines the United States' economic, political, and social policies. Before coming to the foundation some 20 years ago, Goldberg had worked in publishing and administration. She also is the cofounder and principal of Siberg Associates, a management consulting firm. She has written four books, her most recent being *Age Works: What Corporate America Must Do to Survive the Graying of the Workforce* (Free Press, 2000) and *Overcoming High-tech Anxiety* (Jossey-Bass, 1999).

Making Recognition and Rewards a "Whole-person" Experience

R. Brayton Bowen

Managing people is increasingly complex. Markets expand globally. Labor forces grow invisible and offices are virtual. People are less committed to organizations emotionally. And running a successful enterprise has become more difficult and competitive. What are the best ways to engage, activate, and motivate employees?

From hourly wages to piece rates, and profit sharing to gain sharing, the number of incentive programs and pay packages is legion. But why do some employees check out—operationally, emotionally, even physically—while others tune in? Why are some organizations confounded by poor returns from reward systems while others rocket ahead? The answer lies in a *whole-person* approach to recognizing and rewarding employees.

Effective systems of recognition and reward engage an individual's entire being. They encourage employees to unleash stores of productive energy while exhibiting regenerative qualities that foster creativity, emotional reserves that translate into passion, and even spiritual attributes that result in the inspired performance needed to achieve a larger vision.

Successful managers respect both people and processes. Abandoning command-and-control management, they emphasize relationships. These managers regard employees as part of their customer base, continuously looking for ways to satisfy and retain employee commitment while ultimately inspiring them to peak performance.

THE NEW MILLENNIUM WORKPLACE

Today's labor force is diverse: boomers, generation Xers, generation Y, former welfare recipients, the Net generation. Add multicultural and multiracial labor pools and the management challenge becomes enormous. Compensation experts and professional managers have realized that a one-size approach to human resources won't fit all. Different people have different values, needs, wants, and expectations, and unless these conditions can be addressed satisfactorily the outcomes can prove disastrous.

Employees are increasingly knowledge workers. No longer can the workplace house all employees under one roof under the watchful eye of a supervisor; workers often telecommute. Furthermore, individual contributors are joining teams, with perhaps team members scattered around the globe, prompting the need for yet more varied performance management systems and reward programs.

Given this diversity, an appropriate blend of recognition and rewards that meet individual requirements must be available.

THE TRUTH ABOUT CARROTS, STICKS, MOTIVATION, AND REWARDS

Some experts have determined that incentives and alternative pay packages can have a positive influence on employee performance—short-term. Others claim that such packages actually have a negative influence, especially over the long term. Almost all agree it's essential to pay people fairly and competitively. Some experts are wrong, however, in arguing that pay is the chief motivator. For the welfare-to-work employee and minimum-wage earners, money is a basic need, not a motivator. In reality, motivation is an inside job; money may influence behavior, but it's no substitute for motivation. People require a greater sense of achievement and self-actualization.

Enlightened managers use total reward systems that link direct and indirect payments to performance requirements tied to the organization's success. Such an approach is far more effective than simpler, more restrictive, linear systems that function on a quid pro quo: produce this widget and you get x. But, even total reward packages fall short of achieving everything that's possible if they fail to engage the whole person. Leading systems are holistic.

HOLISTIC SYSTEMS OF REWARD AND RECOGNITION

Southwest Airlines has a superb record of satisfied customers and upbeat employees. Moreover, while competitors have succumbed to the downturns and upswings of economic cycles, only Southwest has been consistently profitable. The carrier lavishes attention on its employees (who also hold company stock), displaying plaques honoring those who have achieved outstanding performance and promoting a fun-filled culture.

Toyota encourages employees worldwide to generate new ideas at a rate of some 40,000 *per plant* annually, and each is recognized and rewarded according to its operational impact. Moreover, so imbued is Toyota's culture with concepts of quality, teamwork, and empowerment that a single employee can literally stop production for the good of the ultimate customer, without supervisory approval. Indeed, turning the organizational pyramid upside down is nothing new at Toyota, where managers are viewed as resources for team members and an "office" is simply a desk on the production floor readily accessible to the team.

Mary Kay Cosmetics may reward outstanding performers with pink Cadillacs, but the organization is focused on enhancing the self-esteem and economic independence of women, especially those who represent the company. Moreover, Mary Kay rewards and recognizes women while having fun. The combination of economic opportunity and psychic income has propelled the organization to phenomenal levels of growth.

Many other organizations, including Federal Express, the Body Shop, Hewlett-Packard, and Disney, have created environments and traditions that have appealed to the emotional, professional, and economic interests of employees. They use holistic systems of reward and recognition via:
- job design
- decision-making processes

- pay equity
- performance planning and management systems
- self-direction
- communication
- organizational culture
- leadership styles
- professional development

A holistic system is open to incorporating anything that influences employees to unleash their motivation and passion. Holistic systems are especially valuable with free agents.

THE RISE OF THE FREE AGENT

For some time companies have been downsizing—essentially, firing large numbers of employees wholesale—to ensure profitability, even survival, during harsh economic times. Many redundancies have been of middle managers. People that remain, managers and nonmanagers alike, have had to demonstrate their value to their organization to stay employed. Gone is the old-style psychological contract for lifelong employment for performing employees. As one manager expressed it, "Loyalty is dead. We can no longer afford it."

The bad news: While companies have been getting meaner and leaner, worker commitment has been lost. The good news: Employees have become more resourceful at finding ways to demonstrate and increase their worth to current and prospective employers. Smart employees see themselves as free agents and are continuously looking for ways to improve their skills, competencies, reputation, and marketability.

IN SEARCH OF NEW CURRENCY

Smart managers recognize the needs of free agents by engaging in practices that say: "I'll meet your needs; I expect you to meet mine. Let's work together!" Free agents want flexibility to move through organizational systems without being locked in to one department. They want to be recognized and valued for the talents they bring and for results achieved. They prefer teams in which they can realize a more self-directed environment than they can in a single job reporting to a supervisor. While rewards are important, so, too, are responsibility, respect, recognition, and relationships. Moreover, because of their concern for independence and marketability, they have a critical need to protect their reputation; they gravitate to assignments that enhance their standing in the estimation of others.

The new currency that managers must use in today's workplace has respect as its underlying value. Even in situations in which organizations are known to or intend to downsize, smart managers understand the importance of respecting people's intelligence and telling it like it is. They work collaboratively with employees. They make conscious decisions to join forces instead of subordinating or dominating. And as newer systems such as skill-based pay, total-reward programs, pay-for-performance plans, and open-book management become more mainstream, the challenge for management will be to avoid any suggestion that they are manipulative or disrespectful. In fact, placing too much emphasis on pay and pay systems will detract from the intrinsic value of work itself.

WORK AS ITS OWN REWARD

Recognizing the short-term nature of employment and the need to influence peak performance, organizations have generated elaborate programs to motivate employees, including informal awards (spontaneous shows of appreciation, thank-you gifts for special services) and formal awards (bonuses, prizes, trophies, service awards).

These are all extrinsic awards, providing recognition by means of factors external to the work itself; other examples include:

- base-pay packages
- variable pay plans
- incentives
- cash and cash equivalents
- benefits
- gain-sharing plans
- profit-sharing plans
- commissions
- stock options
- alternative pay programs

Intrinsic rewards, by contrast, are inherent to the nature of the work itself and the context or environment in which it is performed. They are innately energizing and satisfying, either because the work is pleasurable or because it fulfills individuals' desire to support the organization's mission or value system or their own relationships with colleagues. Enlightened managers know the importance of responsibility, respect, recognition, and relationships; these are intrinsically rewarding (and may ultimately result in extrinsic rewards). In the rush to motivate employees, any number of managers have invested heavily in extrinsic rewards, overlooking the enormous value of intrinsic rewards.

Indeed, one intrinsic value of work is that at some level it is a creative expression of self. That's why some people "love" their work. It helps them feel a sense of mission in their life. Consequently, by aligning personal needs, desires, and expectations with the needs of the enterprise, work can be performed, analyzed, and redesigned continuously to create a win-win situation for employer and employee.

The hard reality, however, is that it takes willingness on the part of managers and involvement on the part of employees to construct work assignments and processes that add value for all stakeholders. Indeed, in the new workplace employees will require more respect—and that means more recognition—to feel passionate about their work and motivated to excel. The shared objective for both managers and employees must be to find work that employees can come to love and that they feel valued in doing.

MAKING IT HAPPEN

- Begin with a mindset that's passionate about making a difference in people's lives, not just the bottom line.
- Design an environment that encourages people to give their best—because they want to, not because they have to.
- Think big picture! Integrate rewards, benefits, and recognition with the entire work experience.
- Unless you've done it before, get professional help. This is no time to be thrifty at the expense of the company's future.
- Involve employees in the redesign process. Inclusion is the quintessential form of recognition.

True recognition is a whole-person experience. Said one employee, "I appreciate that my manager asks how I *feel* about a situation, then what I *think* about it, and lastly, what I want to *do*." The approach is holistic. It begins with feelings. Smart managers know they may engage the head, but they must also engage the heart of every employee. It's the only way to recognize and reward employees in the workplace of the new millennium.

R. Brayton Bowen is author of *Recognizing and Rewarding Employees* (McGraw-Hill, 2000). As well as being a former senior executive with five major corporations, an author, speaker, and columnist, he is president and senior consultant of The Howland Group (www.howlandgroup.com), a management consulting firm based in Louisville, Kentucky, which specializes in organizational strategy, structure, and systematic change initiatives.

Boosting Business Success through Diversity

Debbe Kennedy

Regardless of your business, organizational goals, or where you live and work in the world, we share two undeniable areas of common ground as leaders. We all have a mission and we all have an increasingly diverse set of "customers" to serve, both inside and outside our organizations. Whether your goals are bringing new product and service innovations to the marketplace, serving communities or nations, creating new wealth, or just getting better and better at your brand of excellence in any endeavor, it is clear that our leadership calling across industries, sectors, and geographies is to forge new paths—to lead the way, embracing new faces, cultures, and a broad array of differences in order to fully participate in the opportunities of the 21st century.

Interestingly, we have been talking about such realities all over the world as if they were some new phenomenon. In fact, this leadership calling is not new. Great leaders have always been able to tap into the best in people. You can see examples in the history and success stories of enduring global corporations like Hewlett-Packard, IBM, and General Electric of the United States, Kyocera Corporation of Japan, and Siemens of Germany, just to name a few. Each of them in their own unique way built success upon deeply held beliefs and values about people, striving to create an environment of mutual respect.

Today, leading corporations are expanding their focus on diversity and inclusion worldwide. Their purpose is one that touches every organization today: to attract and retain multicultural, multitalented workforces. The aim is to enable them to connect and serve a multitude of new *customers* in emerging unexplored *markets,* reaching people, places, and potential that will nourish them and ensure their continued business success.

The next generation of bold steps into a more richly diverse world rests with leaders like you. So, what is the link between diversity and business success? What can you learn from what others are doing to make diversity a competitive advantage? What diversity leadership disciplines are essential? These are the important questions we will explore.

THE BUSINESS CASE FOR DIVERSITY

Don't make the mistake of seeing diversity and inclusion as "nice to do" moral issues, nor quickly dismiss them as North American problems. Not today. It is true that across the world we may need to deal with unique issues of difference in our workplaces, marketplaces, and communities. Additionally, our specific issues about creating an inclusive environment may also be unique, but in principle a *culture of inclusion* operates in a similar way anywhere. *No one is left out.* More importantly, there is increasing evidence that the business case for diversity and inclusion is one that transcends geographic boundaries.

One of the most compelling presentations of the new business thinking surrounding the topics of diversity and inclusion comes from the research of futurist Joel A. Barker in his landmark film, *Wealth, Innovation, & Diversity*. In his research on innovation and creating new wealth he discovered some startling evidence in history, science, and industry that proves that innovation is driven by diversity and creates new wealth through:

- sustainability
- variety
- innovations
- efficient resource utilization
- new thinking
- lowered risks
- increased predictability
- improved productivity
- economic wealth

Leading companies are recognizing these truths and acting on them to position themselves for success.

DIVERSITY BUSINESS LEADERSHIP BEST PRACTICES

Below are four companies that serve as examples for all of us. Each has a history of leadership in valuing people, reflected in their beliefs, policies, and practices. Each is positioning itself for leadership in the 21st century, translating their enduring values into a new level of commitment to diversity and inclusion. Here is a sampling from their efforts.

Hewlett-Packard (Corporate H.Q. U.S.). Hewlett-Packard have strengthened their long-held commitment to diversity by establishing diversity and inclusion as key business priorities for HP's reinvention. Their expanded business focus incorporates diversity and inclusion in the marketplace, workplace, and the community, maximizing the opportunity for creativity, invention, and profitability, and fulfilling their vision of being "a winning e-company with a shining soul."

> Our goal is to integrate diversity into the fabric of HP—into all our processes, into day-to-day business practices—creating a mindset within every employee and manager so they think about diversity and inclusion in everything they do.
> *Emily Duncan, Director, Global Diversity*

IBM (Corporate H.Q. U.S.). As IBM worked to reinforce the link between the marketplace and the workplace, they developed a Global Diversity Council that established six global challenges to guide their actions:

- the global marketplace
- multicultural awareness and acceptance
- diversity of the management team
- advancement of women

- work/life balance: dependent care and work flexibility
- integration of people with disabilities within IBM

General managers from the Americas, Asia-Pacific, and EMEA (Europe, Middle East, Africa) and our Global Industry team, come in once a year to present their results and their strategies to address these challenges the next year. Leadership for diversity at the top remains an IBM tradition.

J. T. (Ted) Childs, Jr., Vice President, Global Workforce Diversity

Kyocera Corporation (Global H.Q. Japan). The "Kyocera philosophy," based on a strong belief in people, led to global expansion, serving a diverse set of customers, and a legacy of business success.

Respect the divine and love people. Preserve the spirit to work fairly and honorably, respecting people, our work, our company, and our global community.

As a leader, you must clearly indicate your unselfish stand. You should set a meaningful goal for your group and follow it yourself.

Kazuo Inamori, Founder and Chairman Emeritus, Kyocera Corporation

MAKING IT HAPPEN
We are what we repeatedly do. Excellence then, is not an act, but a habit.

Aristotle

To make embracing differences and mastery of creating an inclusive environment a *habit* of your excellence requires developing a conviction to a few leadership disciplines. The rationale is best illustrated with a story.

Some years back, I visited Sue Swenson, president and C.O.O., Leap Wireless International, to discuss her approach to diversity and inclusion. "As a practice, I don't do disconnected programs and separate launches of initiatives," she told me. "I have been on the receiving end of such headquarters-driven programs. As a young manager, I was continuously asked to put energy into new programs. If I had responded to every one, I would have done none of them well. As a leader, I've personally taken responsibility for finding ways to engage the organization—integrating fairness, openness, diversity, and inclusion into our business strategies, measures, recruiting practices, new hire orientation, management training, employee development, recognition programs, and our common protocol of behaviors and expectations for everybody. What has convinced me that this approach works are the results."

So, what can you do to take such an integrated approach? Below are three leadership disciplines that when practiced can become *habits of excellence*.

- **Create a culture of inclusion, trust, and mutual respect**. Start by internalizing company values and beliefs that support a culture of inclusion. Learn to express what they mean to you. Set expectations for everyone's behavior by example and through your messages. Guarantee that everyone who does business with you, or who works for you, will experience a culture of inclusion, trust, and mutual respect. Tolerate nothing less.

How to practice: Let your beliefs and values become part of your day-to-day dialog. Develop your own style of integrating them, perhaps subtly, into your messages, conversations, business planning considerations, and interactions to keep beliefs, values, and expectations in the forefront.

- **Lead by example every day.** See every day as an opportunity to set an example for others in building a culture of inclusion. Develop a genuine interest in your employees and customers. Look for the good in others. Appreciate their differences. Model inclusiveness more by your actions than your words. As Gandhi said, "Be the change you want to see in the world."

  How to practice: Make a habit of reviewing your behavior and actions at the end of each day. Evaluate your effectiveness as a role model for the culture of inclusion you are working to create.

- **Make diversity and inclusion organizational *habits* in all work.** Integrating diversity and inclusion considerations into your mainstream business procedures, practices, programs, and protocol of behavior starts with thinking and questioning. Keep it simple. Begin by asking questions that cause you to consider diversity and inclusion implications in such practices as hires, job assignments, promotions, development opportunities, meetings, recognition and awards, pay, who you invite into your inner circle, who you talk with, spend time with, and get to know. Your attention will communicate the importance you place on creating a culture of inclusion. It will also help others in the organization develop their own discipline of thinking about considerations of diversity and inclusion in all their work.

  How to practice: Help yourself develop your own diversity and inclusion thinking and questioning *habits*. Create a reminder on the back of a business card. Keep it where you can see it as you work through your day. Commit to practicing for two weeks to develop your skill and make it a habit.

The great leaders of the 21st century will be those who incorporate considerations of diversity and inclusion into their *habits of excellence* as leaders and into the mainstream of their organizations. It is essential to participate fully in the opportunities of the 21st century.

Debbe Kennedy is president of the Leadership Solutions Companies, a consulting firm which provides custom leadership communications and development products and services. Prior to this, she spent over 15 years in management at IBM, and has served as a strategic business partner in Hewlett-Packard's worldwide diversity initiative since 1995. She is a problem solver, change leader, speaker, group facilitator, and author of several books, including *Breakthrough!* (Leadership Solutions, 1998). Her latest contribution is the *Diversity Breakthrough!® Strategic Action Series*, seven books and tools published by Berrett-Koehler.

Managing Today's Angry Workforce

Florence M. Stone

Conflict isn't new in the workplace—indeed, disagreements can help select the best among good ideas—but today's offices seem prone to excessive conflict. Studies by Integra Realty Resources of more than 1,000 office workers in the United States and the United Kingdom revealed growing numbers of overworked, overwrought employees. The surveys showed a worldwide pattern of endless complaints, put-downs, angry outbursts, trashed office equipment, and gave a name to the behavioral pattern—"desk rage." The U.S./U.K. findings and subsequent surveys have found anger at work to be pervasive, taking not only the forms of yelling, verbal abuse, and damage to office technology, but of fistfights among office colleagues. One in ten respondents in the Integra survey said they worked in an office where physical violence had occurred.

TICKED OFF . . . AND TICKING

These survey results should not cause surprise. After all, the phrase "going postal," derived from early incidents of employee violence in U.S. post offices, has become part of our vernacular. Although some may see workplace anger as a U.S. phenomenon, it is a worldwide trend.

According to a report from the Geneva-based International Labour Organization in 1997, *Violence at Work* by Duncan Chappell and Vittorio Di Martino, the issue "transcends the boundaries of a particular country, work setting, or occupational group." Because the initial survey on anger was sponsored by a real estate firm considering among other factors office working conditions, particularly the "Dilbertization" of the workplace—the accommodation of employees in cubicles barely bigger than their desks—its results were belittled in some quarters. But interviews with security experts have supported the findings. They all point to the same situations in our workplaces: more work, less time, much change in how the work is done, continuous demand for greater productivity.

According to R. Brayton Bowen, anger is often triggered by the threatened loss of something greatly valued. Translate this to the workplace, and I'd rank these three factors as the biggest causes of anger:

- downsizing, or the threat of job loss
- the pressure to do more with less, or the loss of existing resources
- disempowerment, or the loss of control over the work to be done

The high-stress conditions in today's offices make it difficult to achieve teamwork or creativity, but the bigger problem is that they set the stage for unstable people to act out their anger, pushing them over the edge to violent behavior. Circumstances ranging from an unresolved conflict with a coworker or supervisor to a bad performance evaluation or a major change in work procedures can contribute to heightened anxiety and, in turn, to raw anger. If an individual has a predisposition to aggressive-ness and perceives the workplace as a hostile environment, experiencing stress can trigger violent behavior, according to Anthony Baron, C.E.O. of Baron Center, a California-based organization of trainers specializing in workplace and school violence protection.

The number of homicides is already disturbing: "boss-icide" has doubled in a little more than ten years. In 1999, 856 homicides were reported in the workplace, more than twice the number reported a dozen years before. On average, workers murder three to four supervisors a month, or double the number a little more than a decade ago. A study by the American Management Association in 1994 found more than half of 500 human resources managers had had to contend with threats of violence in their companies in the previous four years. Multiple occurrences were reported by 30% of respondents.

Security experts contend that most violence-prevention programs are initiated after an incident, not beforehand. As the labor shortage has made it more difficult to find qualified employees, some organizations have forgone reference checks thereby increasing the potential for negligent hiring. Threats to coworkers or managers are ignored because there is no zero-tolerance policy that covers them. Many supervisors aren't trained to handle on-the-job conflicts, and consequently conflicts are allowed to fester. Employee-assistance programs (EAPs) that exist to help identify and address personal and work-related problems may be not mandatory or not accessible.

DEFUSING AN ANGRY WORKPLACE

On the assumption that intervention by an EAP may come too late, the Purdue Employees Credit Union in West Lafayette, Indiana, also trains its own managers to identify and advise employees on stress-related behaviors that could evolve into threats or violent behavior. Training updates, provided quarterly, keep managers alert to the issue and abreast of the latest need-to-know information.

As we see an increase in desk rage, it's evident that companies should not wait for anger to grow into violent behavior. Yet too often that is exactly what has happened. Employees at U.S. Foodservice in East Allentown, Pennsylvania have not forgotten the day three years ago when a troubled and angry employee shot three managers, killing one, before fatally shooting himself. Repetition of the incident is unlikely: security has increased since the shootings. U.S. Foodservice has been training man-agers in its 38 branches about violence in the workplace and how to spot the warning signs of a violent employee, according to Bonna Walker, vice president of marketing and public relations. Managers, in turn, teach their employees. The company has also instituted zero-tolerance guidelines on violence in the workplace. A policy on vio-lence existed before the shootings, but has since been rewritten, says Walker, in "plainer language so there is no misunderstanding of what that policy is."

According to Larry Chavez, founder of Critical Incidents Associates, an organiza-tion that conducts training seminars on preventing workplace violence, companies should go beyond spelling out policies. Top management should be quick and stern in dealing with violations. Indeed, there should be zero tolerance.

Applied Materials' lawsuit to obtain a restraining order is an example of the way businesses should respond to threats, even when offenders state that they meant nothing by a threatening remark. In the case of Applied Materials, an employee allegedly complained to fellow workers about a potential job reassignment, saying that he would "bring an Uzi and start mowing people down." Concerned not only with the threat but with the man's aggressive nature, a colleague reported the remark to a manager. As a consequence, the worker was placed on administrative leave while an investigation was undertaken. The company's response to the verbal threat illustrates the zero-tolerance policy that is spreading across the country.

Steve Kaufer, cofounder of the Workplace Violence Research Institute, compares corporate response to the heightened use of metal detectors in airports. "You can't joke about guns and bombs," he says. "Employees are being trained to understand that those threats aren't appropriate and will be dealt with very seriously." Employees can be placed on unpaid leave or fired if found guilty of making remarks perceived as threatening, since they challenge a company's responsibility to secure the workplace and protect the other employees.

Besides a no-threat policy and supervisory and employee training in violence prevention, a means should be established whereby employees and their family members can anonymously report potential threats. Special consideration should be given to procedures to address involuntary separations and disciplinary actions. These two kinds of incidents trigger almost half of the violent incidents in the workplace.

Airlines all have EAPs, but the Association of Flight Attendants (AFA) has an additional support system, the Member Assistance Program (MAP). This program provides AFA's 47,000 members, representing 26 airlines, with peer support for work-related or personal problems and referral to professional resources. Volunteer employees receive special training on how to counsel their peers, and to date the AFA has more than 170 peer counselors worldwide. The peer program is considered superior to traditional management-sponsored EAPs in that employees don't have to wait until the problem intrudes on their job performance.

In 1999 Pfizer launched its Vista Rx program, which allows salespeople to cut back to a 60% work schedule while retaining 100% of their full-time benefits. The program alleviates a major source of stress—difficulty balancing work and family demands. According to Bruce Fleischmann, national sales director of Vista Rx, the program meets Pfizer's need to have 100+ salespeople calling on physicians, yet also allows the participants to balance work–life issues. For some salespeople, Vista Rx is a short-term solution to a family situation; for others, it's a permanent career change. The company limits participation to around 130 employees, and there's currently a waiting list.

MAKING IT HAPPEN
Companies need a tandem effort of prevention and protection to defuse and protect against workplace tension.
- Review hiring processes, including background checks, reference verifications, and applicant screening for propensity toward violence.

- Review and implement policies and procedures that ensure that under the worst of circumstances employees are treated with dignity. Many of those who exhibit violent behavior attribute it to actions they say stripped them of their dignity in some way.
- Institute handgun policies covering the carrying of concealed firearms on the premises.
- Institute training programs to educate managers on early-warning signs and emergency procedures.
- Create a safe environment by establishing workplace violence policies, including a zero-tolerance policy on threats of harm. Provide for an employee assistance or counseling program for workers who threaten or harass fellow employees.
- Create a threat management team to detail a specific plan of action to be taken every time a threat is reported, with participants from human resources, security, the EAP, and legal counsel.

Companies need to take the issue of growing anger and uncivil behavior among colleagues seriously. Left unchecked, in certain individuals it can trigger violent incidents that can be costly beyond the safety of coworkers and customers. Businesses are facing recent judicial trends that find employers liable for acts of violence due to negligence in hiring, supervision, or retention. Aside from instituting violence prevention/protection programs, companies need to look more closely at surveys that show pervasive anger within their rank and file. Anger in the workplace is a signal that there's something wrong in the system. It's management's responsibility to investigate the corporate climate and culture, identify the causes, and, with its workforce, collaboratively and collectively seek effective solutions.

Florence M. Stone has worked with the American Management Association (AMA) for 30 years in numerous management positions, and was most recently promoted to editorial director with responsibility for Web, e-newsletters, and print. She has written nine business books on numerous supervisory and management issues, from coaching to team building, communications and leadership, and her more recent books include *Coaching, Counseling and Mentoring* (AMACOM, 1998). She has also been published under the pseudonym Rebecca Saunders.

Raising the Bar: Setting Effective Targets

Matthew Budman

We want more productivity from workers; indeed, we often need more productivity. Often, as managers we have no choice—we must continue to raise the bar under pressure from all sides: enforced cost-cutting, tetchy labor markets, fresh competition from developing nations, increasingly in-charge customers, and so on.

And we have to do it with fewer people and less leverage. Downsizing has led to fewer people being forced to do more work and to permanently heightened expectations of what employees are capable of.

But in asking for more from workers, we frequently make mistakes.

- We fail to understand adequately what workers are already doing, either during or outside the 9-to-5 routine.
- We ask for more while at the same time we undermine trust and commitment through paternalistic electronic supervision and demoralizing layoffs.
- We don't put the necessary thought and effort into managing people and the challenges of the 21st-century workplace.

SCORING WITH GOALS

It's a well-established fact that setting concrete objectives raises workplace productivity; moving the bar upward is practically guaranteed to produce higher returns. People respond to targets by striving to reach them.

But moving goals is a double-edged sword. Workers who fail to meet their objectives are likely to suffer disappointment and frustration, particularly if office mates have reached their respective targets. Yet if the goal is met before the specified date, an employee may slacken the pace since the pressure is off. Either case requires managerial attention.

With many jobs it's not easy to shift annual target numbers higher. Despite a post-reengineering emphasis on accountability and verifiability, knowledge-economy work is not readily measurable. (The Taylorist ideal of timing workers with stopwatches is often irrelevant in the modern office; work is now usually too complex to isolate tasks and measure efficiency in completing them.) Targets must be qualitative, and therefore somewhat subjective, rather than strictly numerical.

Goal setting must be considered regularly. Generally, the subject of new objectives is only raised annually, at performance appraisals—usually dreaded by all participants. Typically there's a space labeled "Goals for Next Year" that must be filled in, an automatic demand for more work.

It's important that new goals don't appear arbitrary or seem to take precedence over quotidian core tasks. They should be produced collaboratively, through manager–employee discussions. Incremental targets, or subgoals, are more effective than distant goals, which may seem daunting.

Setting goals constructively is a tall order. You don't want good people to stagnate; realistically there is no point at which you can tell anyone, "You're doing enough."

LONGER DAYS, LONGER TO-DO LISTS

Don't consider asking more from your people until you understand how much they're already giving you. Many corporations have become "white-collar sweat-shops." Your department or company may not fit this pattern, but it might, and you may simply be unaware of it. There's no question that a general culture of overwork has arisen, with Silicon Valley entrepreneurs sleeping on cots and working around the clock. U.K. workers report high levels of stress stemming from increasing demands and hours. Some have estimated that one-third of the working population in Japan suffers from chronic fatigue, and thousands of white-collar workers have died from *karoshi* (death from overwork) in the last two decades.

Why are so many people working so hard? Firstly, under the aegis of empowerment, companies have shifted much of the burden of management to workers themselves.

Secondly, there are fewer people to do the work, and not all of them are top performers. Even after all the downsizings and reengineerings there's plenty of dead wood. Companies announcing layoffs obviously hope to prune only the worst performers, but invariably good people depart as well, partly because they dread the inevitable increase in workload.

Thirdly employees cite management's tolerance of below-par work as a cause of overwork. Managers' endless patience with mediocrity is easy to explain: it's difficult and unpleasant to fire individuals and expensive to hire and train new people. But unequal distribution of work is a crucial issue for managers to address.

Finally there is the issue of trust. Don't expect people to embrace new demands and goals while the company installs new electronic tools as a result of managerial suspicion. Workers aren't primed to give their all to the company when they know their bosses are reading their e-mail, logging their lunch-hour minutes, counting their keystrokes, watching their Web site use, and recording their voice mail.

TAKING WORK HOME

Technology has allowed both employers and employees to blur the distinctions between work and life; people are working more even as they're enjoying new freedom and flexibility. At the office people surf the Net for sports scores and make personal telephone calls without feeling as though they're exploiting the company.

But in return, they're accountable to the demands of work. They stay at the office later; on the commute home they return phone calls and study spreadsheets on their laptops; they block out time after dinner to read memos and prepare presentations; they check and reply to work-related e-mail and voice mail at all hours.

Managers know whether projects are completed by deadline, and whether people are physically in the office, but it's hard to look over an employee's shoulder and gauge how much work the person is actually getting done. It's especially difficult when that employee is working from home two or three days a week.

Some see this work/home trend as bad for employees, who find themselves not only carrying heavier workloads but, with beepers and electronic desk calendars, taking on work responsibilities around the clock. Others insist that workers don't necessarily resent the encroachment of the office on their personal lives, and that many people find more fulfillment and fun in the office than they do outside of it.

Either way, these shifts augur more challenges for managers. In conjunction with your input and in line with overall company policies, each worker can arrive at an individual best balance of efficiency and fulfillment. The more options, support, and coaching you can offer, the more productivity you'll get.

PLAYING FAIR

Each worker performs at a particular level and a particular speed. Some thrive under heightened expectations; others grow sullen, believing their supervisor to be impossible to satisfy. The bottom line is that both want to be treated fairly.

What does *fairness* mean? Simply, fair treatment means something different to everyone. Some want special breaks, others no special breaks. For parents, allowing flexible scheduling to deal with children; for singles, ensuring that their workload doesn't rise disproportionately to compensate for the missing parents. Some demand that work be shared equally, others only that they don't have more than they can handle.

For U.S. workers in many industries, heavy workloads used to be an issue handled by union representatives, whose job it was to protect them from unreasonable demands. Today, as machinery takes more and more manual labor out of workers' hands, the strength of unions—both in numbers and by moral weight—continues to decline. This is a trend likely to continue even in countries with traditionally strong organized labor. In France, for instance, trade union membership has fallen below 10%, lagging behind even the U.S. figure of 14%.

And for white-collar workers, technology has rendered union-driven job protections less relevant than ever: productivity is usually measured not by piecework standards but by more intangible and individual methods. Even the issue of working conditions is fuzzy, since work often spills into out-of-office hours, and workspaces sometimes include commuter-train seats and living-room coffee tables.

Without the help of the unions, workers have little official bargaining power when it comes to telling their employers what they will or won't do; often their only defense against increasing demands is to threaten to resign. Obviously, it is best to avoid reaching that point.

MAKING IT HAPPEN

Is it acceptable and productive to raise the bar through new targets? Empirically, the evidence suggests that where new targets are discussed and set in a realistic, achievable and trusting manner, these targets will be effective. Increasing targets requires greater effort from management; it's your responsibility to put that additional work in context. You can't simply raise the bar and assume everyone will rise to meet the new standards. No size fits all; pushing up standards in a knowledge-economy era of amorphous jobs requires more than cookie-cutter solutions.

- Familiarize yourself with current workloads and employees' feelings about their responsibilities. It is important to avoid burnout and resentment, especially as your most conscientious people are the ones likely to burn out first.
- Set goals, but be aware of the attendant complications. Collaborate with individual workers on their goals, keeping targets reachable but challenging enough to be interesting.
- In expanding responsibilities for employees, don't overemphasize tasks that aren't directly job-related. If the core fails, the rest doesn't matter.
- Don't assume that slogans or, worse, motivational posters or insincere rah-rah rallies will produce any effect other than cynicism.
- Through coaching and rewards, make it clear that slacking is unacceptable and that you're concerned about all employees feeling that they are treated fairly.
- Work with your staff to arrive at mutually beneficial schedules and workloads that satisfactorily balance work and home lives. A telecommuting option may be ideal for some; others need the structure of a 9-to-5 office.
- Don't ask for more without making it worth your people's while, either financially or through other means such as a job assignment or, when convenient for all, extra time off work.

The key to setting effective targets is to understand the needs of the team, the individual, and the tasks involved. Managers need to ensure that targets are both realistic and challenging. Nothing de-motivates like failure to meet expectations, while success in meeting targets will generate further confidence and productivity. Reinforcing a positive attitude to abilities will promote future success and a flexibility to engage new and more challenging targets. Setting a clear, unambiguous direction, ensuring that people are ready to meet the new challenges and that they remain on course is not easy. It requires a great deal of attention and keen leadership skills.

This necessitates leadership, not only by example, but also by making a real commitment to keeping staff engaged, productive, and flexible. You'll have to balance what is possible with how much of your people's lives you can legitimately ask for. No small task, but then no one ever said managing was easy.

Matthew Budman has worked in journalism for 15 years, the last several as managing editor of a Manhattan-based bimonthly business magazine, The Conference Board's *Across the Board*. The Conference Board is a global, independent membership organization that conducts research, convenes conferences, makes forecasts, assesses trends, publishes information and analysis, and brings executives together to learn from one another.

SQ: Investing in Spiritual Capital

Danah Zohar

We've all heard of the Midas touch. Most of us wish we had it. But the original King Midas's ability to turn everything that he touched into gold was a curse placed on him for his greed. When Midas touched his wife and children, they turned to gold. When Midas touched his food, *it* turned to gold, and the cursed king starved to death.

Today, all of us in business or who are *touched* by the ethic of business, are under a Midas curse, put upon us not by the gods but by the dictates of capitalism and business-as-usual. Present-day assumptions of capitalism are (1) that humans are primarily economic beings who thrive in an environment dominated by money and (2) that humans are selfish beings who will always act rationally to improve their own financial best interests. Greed and a justification of greed are built into our capitalistic system. But if everything we have and are is turned to gold, we too, like Midas, will starve to death—emotionally, spiritually, and ultimately even physically.

To lift the curse of contemporary capitalism, we must envision a broader and deeper view of what it means to be human and what motivates human beings. We are not primarily economic beings; we are fundamentally creatures of *meaning*. Our brains are designed to ask deep, existential questions such as *What is the meaning of life? Why was I born? What am I here for? Why must I die?* We are designed to seek an overarching "story" about ourselves that gives meaning, value, and a sense of purpose to our lives.

A MATTER OF INTELLIGENCE

Intelligence is meant to be the tool with which we cultivate our lives and win control over or cooperation with our environment. But IQ alone won't access meaning, value, and purpose: it measures rational, logical, linear intelligence designed to solve practical or abstract problems. EQ (emotional intelligence) enables us to use feelings to boost and complement our IQ. But SQ (spiritual intelligence) allows us to tap into and use our most fundamental needs. To transcend the crisis created by modern capitalism, business has to use its *whole* brain—IQ, EQ, and especially SQ. Spiritual intelligence is the ultimate intelligence needed to elevate the corporate soul.

WHY TODAY'S CAPITALISM IS UNSUSTAINABLE

Bolstered by Newtonian science and its accompanying technology and by Darwinian "survival of the fittest," capitalism's own "laws of motion" (competition, profit maximization, capital accumulation) have locked business-as-usual into a ruthless pursuit of competitive advantage in a world whose resources its own practices are constantly diminishing. This is not sustainable. Like a monster eating its own flesh, business is destined to consume first its own resources, then itself.

Why is business-as-usual unsustainable? Six major reasons explain why:

- **Finite resources.** The Western ethic has been that the earth and its resources are there for human use and control. But the earth's resources are finite, while the assumption of business-as-usual is that they are infinite. We arrogantly assume continued and constant growth using our present practices.
- **Environmental damage.** Global warming, floods, holes in the ozone layer, air pollution and its attendant side effects on health, and extreme weather patterns are the result of our reliance on technologies that pollute our own nest.
- **Inequality.** The assumption that human beings are primarily consumers favors the big consumers over the small, those who can pay over those who can't. This deepens inequality between rich and poor nations and between rich and poor groups within nations. Such inequality breeds crime, family breakdown, political instability, and mass, illegal immigration. These things are all bad for business.
- **Leadership crisis.** Making ever more money is not in itself high on the list of what motivates people. The best, most thoughtful, most idealistic people, the best leaders, want to serve something greater than themselves, want their lives to *mean* something—they become doctors, teachers, heads of international aid organizations, go into politics or research. They are seldom found guiding private organizations; there is a critical shortage of great leaders in business today.
- **Short-term thinking.** Concern with maximizing short-term shareholder value deprives business of long-term perspective. It doesn't plan ahead or look at the "big picture." Time comes in quarterly chunks, severely limiting consideration of research needs, long-time viability, and future growth.
- **Human factor.** The mistaken notion that humans are primarily economic creatures increases the stress and exhaustion of the "winners" who serve the existing system. Other values—time with family, time to relax, to nourish inner needs, to enjoy accumulated wealth, to find fulfillment or a sense of fundamental purpose—are all sacrificed to the fast buck. Stressed and exhausted people miss work, suffer disease and premature death. They have reduced creativity and productivity. Stress is bad for business.

DEVELOPING SPIRITUAL CAPITAL

If challenged about the prime motive of profit maximization, most business people look dumbfounded, saying, "It has always been that way!" But business as we know it today is only 200 years old. Today's capitalism was conceived by a small handful of 18th century Enlightenment philosophers inspired by Newtonian mechanism. Their idea of capital was solely *material capital*—measured in money.

According to the *Oxford English Dictionary*, capital is "that which confers wealth, profit, advantage, or power." This lends itself to broader interpretation. Today we hear a great deal about "social capital." Here, writers mean both the material wealth and social benefit gained by a society that has, for example, low crime, low divorce, and low illiteracy. I want to extend this further by introducing the concept of spiritual capital.

Spiritual capital challenges capitalism's assumption that we are primarily economic creatures and argues instead that human beings are essentially creatures of meaning and purpose. The spiritual qualities of a business or a life are those that show a need for dialog with meaning, vision, fundamental values, and deep purpose. Spiritual capital takes these as the crucial commodities of exchange. A company or a person who acts in accordance with meaning, vision, purpose, and fundamental values— *while making a profit*—is invested with spiritual capital. Its primary assumption is that companies can make *more* profit by doing more good. We act on this assumption by using our spiritual intelligence.

Here is a small set of companies whose manufacturing or trading behavior elevates the corporate soul.

- Amul markets the Indian state of Gujarat's 10,000 milk cooperatives. A peasant with only one bucket of milk to sell per day can earn his vital 20 rupees, competing in his own right, and regardless of caste, with larger dairy farmers. An embodiment of Mahatma Gandhi's social and economic principles, Amul sales are $516 million annually.
- Van City, Vancouver's largest credit union, channels lending funds to customers and causes marginalized by mainstream banks—inner city development, risky small business ventures, environmental protection projects, disadvantaged women, and investment funds for the developing world—and has a commitment to corporate social responsibility, with $6.4 billion annual turnover and $39 million profit.
- Coca-Cola has put its distribution network in India at the service of the Indian national government to distribute polio vaccine to remote rural areas. It has a similar project in Africa to distribute AIDS medication, providing, at no extra cost, enormous gain in spiritual capital.
- BP/British Petroleum has adopted a new motto, "Beyond Petroleum," making it an energy company instead of an oil company. Its heavy investment in developing hydrogen and other alternative energy technologies that both reduce dependence on scarce and damaging hydrocarbon fuels and provide energy for the post-petroleum future, keeps its profits high *by way* of reducing environmental damage.

CRITERIA FOR A HIGH SQ

We are all (if healthy) born with a potential for high SQ. It is a basic, innate capacity of our brain; but like all our innate capacities, it needs nurture and development. To encourage the further development of the spiritual intelligence and build the means for companies to commit more deeply to it, we can identify ten criteria for high SQ. The criteria are:

- self-awareness (awareness that we have a "deep" self);
- spontaneity (emergence, self-organization);
- leading from vision and fundamental values;
- holism (seeing the web, the system, the connections);
- compassion (sense of community, sense of belonging to the flow of life);

- celebration of diversity;
- field-independence (standing against the crowd);
- asking fundamental "Why?" questions;
- reframing (seeing the whole, or big picture);
- using, and thriving on, adversity.

SPIRITUAL LEADERSHIP IN THE FUTURE OF BUSINESS

Does business today need "spiritual" leaders? Definitely yes! Those who managed old-style capitalist systems, with their sterile assumptions about human nature and narrow reliance on mechanistic philosophies, cannot lead us through the human and global challenges facing business today. We need a new kind of leader for a new kind of "servant capitalism."

Taking for granted that global business has the money and the real power to make a significant difference in today's troubled world, elevating the corporate soul envisages business raising its sights above the "bottom line," becoming more service- and value-oriented (largely eliminating the assumed distinction between private enterprise and public institutions), and having a higher proportion of "servant leaders" — leaders who serve not just colleagues, employees, products, and customers, but the community, the planet, humanity, the future, and life itself.

The bottom-line criterion for business will always be material solvency and a decent profit. Business *is* society's engine of wealth creation. But wealth is broader than *mere* money. Solvency and profit leave room for maximizing meaning, service, quality of life, health, enjoyment of work, for amassing not merely material but also social and spiritual capital, and thereby contributing hugely to the common well-being and self-organizing creativity of life on earth. That, I believe, is the true purpose of business.

Physicist and philosopher Danah Zohar is the author of *The Quantum Self* (reprint, Quill, 1991), *Rewiring the Corporate Brain* (Berrett-Koehler, 1997), and world bestseller *SQ: Spiritual Intelligence* (Bloomsbury, 2001), which has been translated into more than 20 languages. She is a visiting fellow at the Cranfield School of Management.

Helping Managers to Assess the Value of Human Capital

Christopher Bartlett

A long-standing faculty member at Harvard Business School, serving as Chair of the school's Program for Global Leadership, the Australian Christopher Bartlett is best known for his ground-breaking work with Sumantra Ghoshal of the London Business School. Their 20-year writing partnership—a rarity in academe—has produced a steady stream of highly influential articles and books based on in-depth research among practicing managers. These include *Managing Across Borders* (Harvard Business School Press, reissue 1998) and *The Individualized Corporation* (HarperBusiness, 1997).

In their most recent work Bartlett and Ghoshal argue that the old corporate model oriented around strategy, structure, and systems is now undergoing a process of rebirth. As human capital usurps financial capital as the key strategic resource, the new model, they say, will be built around purpose, people, and process.

What has had the greatest influence on your thinking on management?

Before I became an academic I used to work for an honest living as a line manager. That evolved into working as a consultant with McKinsey & Company. But the experience as a line manager has had the biggest influence on my thinking. That gave me a frame of reference and a great respect for where the learning really occurs in organizations—in the trenches. It has informed my work. My academic career has been based on clinical field-based research: going into companies, talking to practicing managers. I think sometimes there is an arrogance in business books: the authors imply that they know best. I have the opposite view: that we learn most about management from the people who are making it work on a daily basis.

Who has influenced me most? I'd have to say the hundreds of managers I've interviewed. There is so much I've learned from them. People like Jack Welch, Percy Barnevik, and Bill Gates are the Alfred P. Sloans and Pierre Du Ponts of their generation. I use them as examples because they are icons that people know, but there are many others whose names are less well known from whom I have learned.

How will business be different in the 21st century?

In *The Individualized Corporation*, my last book with Sumantra Ghoshal, we wrote about a management revolution that's in its early stages. Behind the turmoil of restructuring and reengineering, we argued, is the corporate model that is in rebirth. The fundamental shift is that companies are trying to reorganize themselves around what is now the scarce resource—human capital.

Traditionally, there has been an assumption that financial capital is the scarce resource and that companies should be organized around its effective use. That is reflected in the way that companies have been managed in the past. Return on investment, earnings per share—all the measures we've got are about controlling and managing financial capital. Companies used to create sophisticated systems designed to haul the information to the top of the organization so that senior managers could make decisions about the allocation of financial capital.

It's not that financial capital is no longer important; it's that it is no longer *the* constraining resource. The constraining resources, and therefore the strategic resources, are information, knowledge, and expertise. And unlike financial capital, which you can allocate, measure, and control, the knowledge and expertise reside deep down in the organization, in the minds of individuals and in the relationships between people who are closest to the customers, the competitors, the technology, and the regulatory environment. That is what companies are trying to capture, use, embed, and diffuse through the organization—and that's a very different task.

The company of the 21st century will have to learn how to manage human capital rather than financial capital as a strategic resource. This shifts our whole mindset from one that is about appropriating value to one that is about creating value. Creating value is about generating ideas and innovation, and capturing and leveraging the scarce knowledge, expertise, and best practices that reside inside the organization.

The old strategic models were about the external market. Michael Porter's "Five Forces," which dominated strategic thinking for years, were about industry structure and competitive dynamics. That was the model that was embedded in the 1970s and dominated through the 1980s. But by the time we got into the 1990s, we started to think about a very different model of strategy laid on top of that external strategy, and that was looking at organizational capability—core competencies if you like.

That new strategic framework was about looking internally to examine how to build sustainable competitive advantage through hard-to-imitate organizational capabilities, and not just about the external environment. I think it is now becoming clear that these internal processes depend on the ability to attract, motivate, and retain individuals with the requisite knowledge and expertise.

What new skills will be needed to cope with these changes?

The old model of the hierarchical bureaucracy was all about measuring, allocating, and controlling financial capital. The skills required were very much about having accountability for things that were put under your direct control. As we move toward this very different model of organization—and very different sources of competitive advantage—managers will require different skills from those needed for vertical control processes.

There are three core internal processes that they will have to be able to manage. First, they will need to create a process to elicit entrepreneurial initiative—not just top-down internal directives—although those will remain in terms of the direction and objectives. In the past directives often extinguished the ability for bottom-up initiatives. In the future we will have to create organizations that enable entrepreneurial initiators on the front line.

The second management skill is being able to link and elicit knowledge and expertise in such a way as to diffuse them, and to develop people and relationships as a source of organizational capability. That's very different from the vertical, financially-driven control processes.

The third skill is the ability to self-obsolete. Traditionally, what managers have done is to drive their organizations up the learning curve, to get better and better at what they've always done. In future it will be much more about jumping learning curves and being willing to constantly redefine the business, the product and processes, and to self-renew.

Are there new management questions that we should be asking?

There's a fundamental question that faces corporations and management. Today the assumption is that corporations are primarily responsible to their shareholders, and legitimately so, because shareholders have historically been the providers of the financial capital that was the scarce strategic resource. Companies had to compete for it and justify their use of it to the shareholders. But as we shift the primary way of gaining competitive advantage from appropriating value to creating value through intellectual capital, the constraining resource becomes people rather than financial capital. Then the question becomes what does this mean for the distribution of the value created?

The assumption at the moment is that the value should be distributed to the owners of the scarce capital resource. But, increasingly, that assumption is starting to fray at the edges. Companies are asking: if the people are so important for the creation of value, then don't we need to find ways to distribute more of the value to them? But we're still measuring, evaluating, and rewarding them by the old rules. Increasingly, companies are using stock options and making their people shareholders. And that's legitimate. But I think the real question is: is the balance moving to the point where we need to think about the distribution of the value to them not as a secondary responsibility but as a primary responsibility—a byproduct of maximizing shareholder returns—and an objective of the organization? I think it is.

That's what sole proprietors do; that's what partnerships do; that's what small start-ups do. It's what the large corporations haven't done. They are stumbling toward it with options. But they are a pretty blunt instrument, with lots of risks attached, as the 2000 "tech wreck" demonstrated.

How can companies best promote enterprises that are a) profitable and b) good places to work?

Companies will *only* be profitable if they are good places to work. Talented people will be attracted to places that engage them and give them meaning and development; that, in turn, will allow those companies to be profitable. How they distribute that financial profit is a question we've already talked about.

Working from the Outside In

Bill Jensen

Shortly after the September 11, 2001 attacks on New York's twin towers, I had a gut-wrenching conversation with a fellow airline passenger. She was angry and frustrated at having to be on the plane. Even though she is one of the most senior execs at a *Fortune 50* company, she felt like she didn't have control of her own life. She was traveling 3,000 miles just because the C.E.O. said she had to. "What if something happens on this plane?" she said. "I don't want to leave my two girls believing that life is about sucking up and doing the right thing just for a paycheck or a career. This company just doesn't get that."

That same conversation is rippling across every workplace, in every sector, at every level of the organization. A lot of people are asking with new urgency, "Why am I doing this? Am I really making a difference? Is this what I want out of life? Out of my career?"

The events and aftermath of September 11 have altered forever the public conversation about how companies and individuals serve each other. The very covenant and rules of engagement between employee and employer are being questioned. However, the new rules were emerging long before we got that tragic wake-up call.

During the past decade I have studied how about a thousand companies get work done. And a startling shift and major inequity have occurred during that time. The people most companies want to attract and retain are bringing with them never-before-seen levels of sophistication and insights about the design of knowledge work. They know more than most leaders about how to collaborate, how to organize information, what they need to get stuff done, how to communicate, and how decision making really works. Technology, marketplace, and social changes have trained, enticed, and forced them to hone these skills.

Yet, for more and more employees, *the more they invest in their company, the more they lose control of their own destiny*. They have focused on customers. They have drunk the corporate Kool-aid, and they have worked hard. But the overwhelming majority of the tools, structures, and support they get are *still* designed to ensure corporate success—not necessarily theirs.

A NEW CONTRACT EMERGES

This inequity is forcing a new covenant. Under the new work contract, employees see themselves as investors. Every day, they invest scarce and precious assets—their time, attention, ideas, knowledge, passion, energy, and social networks—to make our companies go. They watch today's leaders wasting these assets and, like Wall Street, they want better returns.

Decent pay, appropriate benefits, feeling appreciated, being treated and rewarded fairly, and being part of a great team will always be important. But our best employees are moving beyond entitlements and nurturing. They know that they have to be more productive, more efficient, and deliver more better and faster every day. They also know that each day contains only 1,440 minutes with which they can make a difference.

So, in return for those minutes, they're looking at:

- how easy it is to make a big impact;
- how much of their time is spent doing great and important work;
- how much and how fast they can learn;
- how challenging, rewarding, and exciting their work remains;
- how much personal success and balance they achieve—however they choose to define these things;
- how well, or poorly, your company uses their 1,440 minutes;
- how much control they have over their own destiny.

Since there are no guarantees with any employer, employees are beginning to see your firm as a middleman between them, their team mates, customers, and the marketplace. Your company is a tool to connect all these constituencies. And the new contract says it's time for you to start acting like an elegant tool.

Whoa, does this add a new dimension to the basic covenant! There is a great and grave difference between employee satisfaction and satisfying employees' work needs. The new contract is about that difference.

Wrenching uncertainty and tough economic times have not disguised the fact that— especially as you slash budgets and reduce headcount—you are using employees' time, attention, and energy as working capital to meet your company's short-term obligations. They know it. And your best talent is seeking more in return than just a job, a paycheck, or benefits—all of which may be yanked from them without notice.

People are seeking more in return for their time . . . because life is just too short. More to the point, it's just too damn precious.

THE WAR FOR TALENT CHANGES

If we begin to think about our employees as investors, many efforts to attract and retain talent come up short.

Do you waste any of your talent's time, attention, ideas, knowledge, passion, energy, or social networks? What is the daily/weekly/monthly return your talent gets for investing their assets in your firm? The new war for talent will be fought over who provides the best returns on life's precious assets. Among the coming changes:

Employees Are Seeking to Participate in Infrastructure Specs. Your technology, processes, information flows, and everything that connects your employees and organizes their work are being examined from the user's perspective. Sun Microsystems is one company where this is happening. They formed a Workplace Effectiveness group to track how their workspaces and tools are viewed by the people who use them. Every six months, Sun surveys up to 6,000 employees worldwide on issues such as the factors behind personal productivity.

Employees Are Seeking More Input into Who Manages Them. IBM's Extreme Blue student interns have made it clear they won't tolerate "loser managers." And some companies, like PepsiCo, are allowing high-potential talent to select their own managers. Smart companies are beginning to change the rules of how managers and employees are paired and developed.

Employees Are Seeking More Input into How They Collaborate. Companies also understand that new standards are being set daily for what is valued in work exchanges—for example, what content is most valuable, and what social connections, timing, tips, and tools are needed, and what type of coaching would be most helpful. Companies like Cisco and Dell are designing entire learning structures based upon workforce feedback on what they say they need.

EXTREME LEADERSHIP

A new war for talent is emerging through tougher examination of work itself. For years, our companies have operated on the premise that there's *work* and there's *life* and it's up to employees to balance the two. Since September 11, it has become clear that this view is no longer acceptable. The very act of using someone's time assigns new accountabilities to each of us.

This creates new rules in how you fight the war for talent. Among them:

Great workplaces respect life's precious assets. Smart companies are beginning to attract and retain people with an amazingly simple idea: improve business results and create a great place to work by improving how they use employees' time and energy. This means embracing a bottom-up asset revolution.

Great workplaces get better results by giving people better control over their own destiny. Business must focus on personal, not just organizational, productivity. The future of work is increasingly customized, personalized, and tailored to each individual.

This means the future war for talent will be anchored by My Work My Way—delivering business success by customizing more and more information, work tools, and experiences to individual needs. As long as the future includes heavy knowledge work, where personal choices are integral to success, My-Way approaches will be critical.

Great workplaces get more out of collaboration by putting more into it. Today's centralized, top-down approaches to planning collaboration infrastructure and tools are simply not keeping up with the rate of change in how peers want and need to collaborate with each other. If you are going to add value to peer-to-peer exchanges, you must be willing to design budgets and strategies around what the people doing the work find most valuable. You need to focus a lot more on how you deliver peer-to-peer value.

The leaders of great workplaces accept accountability for life's precious assets. Those whom we will follow in the war for talent are "extreme leaders." What makes leadership "extreme" is greater accountability for performance through greater willingness to be challenged on, and address, work-level details. It is about partnering with employees who have no fear about pushing upward. Extreme leaders acknowledge that the route to corporate success includes changing the path employees must take for their personal success.

NEW METRICS FOR GREAT PLACES TO WORK

The SimplerWork Index™ tracks six new dimensions of great places to work. Beyond being nice to your employees, this index tracks what it takes to do great work in a knowledge-based economy. Each measure focuses on how well you enable people to work smarter and faster *while also* giving each employee greater control over his or her own destiny. Unfortunately, the percentages below* illustrate how much today's companies must still improve.

- **Competing on clarity 45%** — evaluates manager's effectiveness in helping individual employees work smarter and faster;
- **Navigation 25%** — evaluates company's effectiveness in helping individual employees find who or what they need to work smarter and faster;
- **Fulfillment of basics 25%** — evaluates company's effectiveness in work-oriented communication and knowledge management;
- **Usability 15%** — evaluates company's effectiveness in all that it designs to help people get tasks done (tools, technology, training, instructions, and so on);
- **Speed 12%** — evaluates company's effectiveness in enabling employees to work in a 24/7, ever-faster world;
- **Time 10%** — evaluates company's respect for employees' time as an asset to be invested.

No one has a crystal ball. Nobody knows perfectly how to juggle shareholder needs, customer needs, employee needs, and corporate strategies. And certainly, the whole story of the war for talent is far more complex than space here allows.

Yet one signpost on the path ahead is undeniable. Our best employees will no longer tie themselves to any organization that doesn't give them greater control over their own destiny, or respect all of life's precious assets that they put to use each and every day.

The future of business success is tied to every individual's success. We win together, or not at all.

———————

Bill Jensen is an information architect with over 20 years experience in communication and change consulting. He is C.E.O. of The Jensen Group (www.work2.com), a consulting group whose mission is to "help clients succeed simply by changing how they organize and deliver what they know." As well as speaking and teaching in well-known organizations, he regularly contributes articles to magazines and journals and has written two books, *Simplicity* (Perseus, 2001) and *Work 2.0: Rewriting the Contract* (Perseus, 2002). He is currently working on his third book, *The Simplicity Survival Handbook* (2003).

---

* 2001 survey of 7,500 individuals in 180 companies

Keeping Control in Nonhierarchical Organizations

Karin Klenke

Nonhierarchical organizations have many advantages over their conventional, stratified counterparts. For example, experience and expertise are often shared; creativity and new ideas are fostered, tested, and discussed. The organization is more cohesive; empowerment is a key feature; and it can be highly supportive.

However, there are several potential pitfalls. "Group think" or the herd mentality can prevail; implementing decisions can be difficult; and exercising control and bringing focus can be a significant challenge.

UNDERSTAND THE VALUE OF FLATTER ORGANIZATIONS

Control is achieved through a number of classical management principles, including *division of labor*, *formalization* (the extent to which work rules are specified, written, and enforced), and *centralization* (the decision-making authority in the hierarchy of the organization). Centralization for the purpose of tight control provides stability, continuity, and predictable career paths and reward systems. In addition, each manager has a clear, unambiguous span of control (the number of employees they can effectively supervise), which creates a set of obligations and role differentiation, with the manager as the brain and the worker the hand. Control is reinforced by a dictatorial top-down, command-and-control leadership style.

The sheer size of the hierarchies in large traditional organizations, coupled with top management's distance from the market, makes this type of structure unresponsive. Many of the reasons for the failures of old-economy leaders in the steel, automotive, and consumer-electronics industries can be directly traced to the structure of fat organizations. Similarly, much of the renaissance of companies such as Xerox, Ford, and Hewlett-Packard can be attributed to throwing off the shackles of vertical integration.

In the new economy speed is of the essence and the time frame for decision making has been dramatically reduced. Hence, bureaucratic hierarchies are being deconstructed. What will tomorrow's organizations look like? What radical surgery may be necessary to transform the vertically integrated structures of the industrial paradigm into designs of the future? How can organizations learn today the skills they need for tomorrow? Answers to some of these questions are found in flat, or nonhierarchical, organizations.

BUILD NONHIERARCHICAL ORGANIZATIONS

21st-century organizations tend to adopt the flatter structures that have become possible as more and more information within an organization comes online. Instead of a managerial hierarchy with seven to ten or more layers of fat, flat organizations have three or four levels. Flat organizations are a cross between a spider's web (interconnected networks) and a leaping frog able to jump into innovations, reinvention, and renewal.

Flat organizations have been called boundaryless, networked, lattice, ameba, and virtual organizations or global heterarchies (the opposite of hierarchies). They are structured around self-directed or self-managed, multidisciplinary, cross-functional work teams in which power flows from expertise, not position. In flat organizations, a decentralized approach to management is emphasized, as is high employee involvement in decision making. Flat organizations are structured around customers, teams, problems and opportunities, adaptiveness, horizontal connections, and networking. They decentralize authority, share information, diffuse and distribute competency, and use reward systems that are primarily team-based. Their strategies consistently emphasize growth, innovation, product customization, and technological leverage, rather than cost containment and operating efficiency.

EXPLOIT THE BENEFITS OF NETWORKED ORGANIZATIONS

Worldwide networking within and across organizations, linking companies, suppliers, customers, designers, and sometimes even competitors, is common in building collaborative advantage and global connectivity. Although by definition competitors are fighting over the same bone, your competitors are probably the only people who know as much about your business as you do. Take Pomarfin, a Finnish shoe manufacturer that markets the Ten Toes brand. The linked company consists of five competitors that share their hidden knowledge in a way that strengthens their ability to compete. Such partnerships and strategic alliances blur traditional hierarchies.

The joint ventures and partnerships established through interorganizational networks are less formal, nonhierarchical, less permanent, and more opportunistic, since the companies within a network band together to meet a specific market opportunity. AOL Time Warner, Wal-Mart, Procter & Gamble, and Disney's Celebration City have created conglomerates with fluid boundaries between the participating organizations for the purpose of sharing resources (financial, intellectual, and human) or inventing new businesses.

DEVOLVE RESPONSIBILITY AND SET PARAMETERS FOR ACTION

Control in flat organizations lies in the mutual agreements that establish the parameters of discretion and performance expectations. Control is dispersed throughout the organization, with emphasis on self-control and problem solving. People own their work—they are self-managing, self-organizing, self-designing. They take personal responsibility for work outcomes, continuously monitor their own performance, seek corrective action when necessary, and take the initiative to help others improve their performance. They also design and control their careers by defining the social contract with the organization, as opposed to having the organization determine individual career paths and progress. In short, in nonhierarchical organizations the main incentive of work is work itself.

Leadership in flat organizations constantly espouses the values of collaboration. It is shared, lateral (as opposed to top-down), and dispersed among organization members. It is a reciprocal investment process between leaders and collaborators. Through the processes of leadership making and team making, individual employees are integrated into cohesive adaptive units at the work level and larger competence networks at organization level. People take responsibility for the development of their leadership and collaborative skills, facilitate the leadership of others, and cultivate leadership processes, functions, and roles that maximize team performance. Leaders as designers, coaches, collaborators, and catalysts influence the workflow through coalition building and value consensus. In flat organizations, the larger-than-life, omnipotent individual leader is often replaced by executive teams, which form a key mechanism for managing the organization of the future.

BE CAREFUL, CAUTIOUS, AND REALISTIC WHEN BUILDING THE ORGANIZATION

Managers must design effective organizations and create superstructures within which the company's work takes place. In today's flatter companies trust is the glue that holds organizations together. Trust is important, because decentralized discretion implies that managers can no longer maintain the level of control they have been accustomed to in the past. When management does not control, but only monitors, it needs the trust of the workers, especially when they are geographically dispersed without face-to-face contact.

In both fat and flat organizations managers, as designers, must understand their industries' dominant technologies, economic prospects, and degree of organizational uncertainty. They must be capable of navigating in the fog, as Hewlett-Packard C.E.O. Carly Fiorina put it, in order to make effective choices about organizational design. Effective organizational structures are aimed at enhancing and maximizing the firm's capacity for innovation and change. Although the Internet is provoking companies to dynamically restructure their infrastructures, don't expect technology alone to radically change organizations and managerial practice.

Put simply, there's no such thing as a one-size-fits-all organizational design. Organizations must instead be in tune with their environments. A hierarchical organization will not work in a creative, rapidly changing e-commerce environment, although it may work in a standard business-as-usual environment. Similarly, large hierarchical organizations can be managed as if they were small, while mature conglomerates like General Electric can grow like startups. Organizational structures must change to facilitate growth.

Consider the following examples. In the 1990s General Motors (GM), the world's largest automobile manufacturer, laid off 74,000 workers, closed 21 plants, and suffered from a staff bureaucracy that was in many places redundant. GM came to symbolize the bloated inefficiency of a contemporary hierarchical organization.

Before restructuring, Motorola had 12 layers of management. Even when the company decided to cut some of the fat by reducing the levels of management, top management was concerned with how such efforts would affect the organization's core values, such as protecting employees who had served the company well in the past.

Saturn plants consist of semiautonomous teams of between 6 and 15 people, each of which is responsible for every aspect of its area. Showrooms guarantee no-pressure sales and eliminate haggling.

Edward Jones financial services has an organizational structure that has been called a confederation of highly autonomous entrepreneurial units bound together by a highly centralized core of values and services. The company is a network of thousands of brokers, each of whom works from a wired office.

MAKING IT HAPPEN
- Learn everything there is to learn about organizational forms; as organizational designers managers must know their design options and the full range of probable and possible structures, from the centrally controlled hierarchy to a totally flat organization with no control at all.
- Build strategic relationships and nurture them through collaborative efforts to compete in global markets.
- Learn the basic skills of collaboration—in your family, team, within and across organizations, and in your community.
- Develop an innovation culture.
- Don't let the old dinosaur eat you up.

Even the aging dinosaurs have to change and adjust to the rugged landscape of the global economy. Businesses can do so by decentralizing and splitting into smaller and smaller configurations and more adaptable units. Organizations of the future must innovate, therefore they must take risks. One of those risks is reinventing themselves when necessary. Leaders and managers must be able to create organizational environments that encourage out-of-the-box and contrarian thinking, cultural dexterity, knowledge sharing, and diffusion of ideas.

———

Karin Klenke is a research professor at the Center for Leadership Studies at Regent University, Virginia, senior principal of the Leadership Development Institute (LDI) International, and chairperson of the board of directors of the Association of Management/International Association of Management. She has published widely in management and leadership journals, founded and edited several journals including *Journal of Management Systems*, and is author of the award-winning book, *Women in Leadership: A Contextual Perspective* (Springer, 1996).

Making the Workplace Flex, Not Break

Ken Murrell

Never in history has business played such a central role and been such a globally competitive endeavor. It's also very likely that what we are experiencing today is an easier time for business compared with what is projected to occur in this new century. Dee Hock, founder of Visa International and C.E.O., is correct when he says, "Fasten your seat belts, the turbulence has barely begun."

Staying competitive isn't just about hiring and developing the very best people you can. It's much more than that. It's about building the workplace that allows for these talented individuals to create a sustainable organization that has the capacity to learn and to stay a step ahead.

The roadsides of business growth will be littered with the husks of organizations that once enjoyed success but then couldn't change. Often the failure will have occurred because in the process of building success the organizations broke their people. In the past this breakage was most often a matter of physical breakdown; now more often the breakdown is in the spirit of the work force. Sadly, this also creates a disintegration of the workplace community often to an irrevocable degree.

How to create flexible and highly competitive workplaces is challenging the best minds in business and the applied behavioral sciences. The Center for Effective Organizations at the University of Southern California, the London School of Economics, the Swedish School of Economics, and countless research universities and consulting firms around the world are grappling with the challenge of creating new forms of organization for the business environment of the 21st century.

WHAT'S NEW? MAYBE OUR WAYS OF RESPONDING
What is the problem? It's the same problem as always! Competitive organizations depend upon people for everything but short-term successes. Market forces and monopolistic positions can generate success for a quarter or even a year, but a healthy workplace is needed for long-term growth. Simple enough to say. Not so easy to do. The challenge is in thinking beyond the current pressures and building the effective workplace as a community in which empowerment occurs naturally. Also needed is a place in which the soul and spirit of the work force are nourished as they produce the excellence that is required of them.

All of this carries with it an obligation to recreate the meaning of work and to base that recreation on the wisdom developed from the knowledge and experimentation among some of the world's most successful organizations. In today's competitive environment, it is essential to transform the workplace. This will necessarily involve a departure from many previous assumptions. Being creative and taking risks produces the learning needed to help drive the change process.

SETTINGS THAT EMPOWER BRING OUT A
FLEXIBLE LABOR FORCE

Being competitive requires the full engagement of the workforce. If an organization has to hire and pay management to continually instruct workers, the game is lost: the cost alone would prohibit successful competition with companies in countries in which the wage scale is a fraction of its own. Efficiencies must be found everywhere; managerial overhead costs that do not add value to the product or service must be reduced.

Jim Collins and Jerry Porras have identified 18 "built-to-last" companies that have done all these things well over the years. One such company is GE, whose "workout" system brings the work force directly into the organizing process. Workouts are offsite sessions at which facilitators help management and workers to look deeply into issues and jointly arrive at new solutions and workable plans of action. Motorola does much the same thing in getting enhanced employee involvement and building ownership for its Six Sigma quality initiatives. Although costly, the investment has a high return.

Companies that become great often have a culture that promotes flexibility. Fad programs are ineffectual: empowerment comes from employees who are able to pursue organizational goals that they're aligned with. In doing this they develop their own work spirit and create a community of others who believe in what everyone—together—is doing. Flexibility comes from people free to do right, with an agreed value base to help guide them. Real settings where this has been created can be found around the world.

The principles in all successful empowerment cases seem to be the same: there must be sincere respect for the people who work for a company, and management must request that people offer their voices as well as their labor. To create such a flexible workplace is possible; and when it is working well the stressfulness of each job is balanced by a shared desire on everyone's part to provide a performance level that guarantees the success of the company overall.

The Toyota facility in Ontario, Canada (along with its sister sites in many other countries) represents some of the best examples not only of this flexibility but also of the power of *kaizen*, the practice of continuous improvement. Dozens of countries are represented in the plant. The spirit of creating a new way of work and a culture that shows full appreciation for the gifts of each worker has won the facility many awards for learning how to flex and change as each of the company's models requires. The workers understand and adapt without stringent supervision; Toyota has learned to be both flexible and supportive of its workforce.

Similar studies of empowerment success can be found in Asia. Nicholas Kristoff and Sheryl Wu Dunn have reported on a Thai sandwich shop that has succeeded in becoming a major competitor to McDonalds. It achieved this by giving its existing employees support and direct help in feeding their families and in creating a new enterprise that would allow them back into the economic game. It's an amazing story of dedication of leadership and a model of how an organization can recreate itself by leveraging maximum flexibility in the workforce.

In Europe, numerous Scandinavian experiments in worker democracy have created the flexible yet empowering work environments that regularly attract study teams from around the world. A work research institute in Norway is also a leading center for such experimentation and change.

CREATING MORE EFFECTIVE AND EFFICIENT SELF-ORGANIZING SYSTEMS

Creating a workplace and a workforce that have the capacity to change via flexible self-management requires fundamentally new working principles for a new work environment. The following issues need to be addressed:

- Work force environments built on command-and-control assumptions must yield to the higher performance potential of workplace communities. Research indicates there is no one best model; what's needed is a commitment to discover the ideal form that fits the unique culture and work performance.
- Spirit and soul of work are not just interesting phrases but are also necessary conditions for the full investment of the workforce in its work. Work that does not have meaning or cannot give something back to the worker is counter-productive. Work that inspires through meaning and in relationships with others is effective. Inspirational work is a competitive force. Deadening work leads to a broken workforce.
- Work itself is being redefined. As work increasingly depends on knowledge, the place it plays in people's lives is becoming more complex. The whole person must be considered in order to build effective knowledge work. Balance of work and life is the goal.
- The wisdom to know how to lead a new workforce requires careful study and a great deal of self-awareness. Knowing others first requires insight into self.
- The changing global economy demands transformational thinking and outside-the-box ways of creating new work environments. These are best created as partnerships in which both workers and managers are expected to change.

MAKING IT HAPPEN

Putting these principles into action requires the following:

- Align work priorities with a clear vision.
- Involve everyone in deciding those priorities.
- Define and publicly state how people will work with one another.
- Promote the idea of the whole person at work.
- Reward risk-taking to enhance experimentation and discovery.
- Boost performance by boosting learning.

These are not simple or easy principles, but within them lie the answers to the questions that each organization will have to address in the future. Leadership is key to facilitating and guiding the process, but a commitment to creating an empowering workplace is necessary to start the process. Following these key principles will insure success.

Moreover, as a manager you must:

- share information and educate employees about corporate goals;
- develop a guiding structure, not a controlling one;
- lead with others and invite many to join in creating leadership at all levels;
- support and encourage involvement;
- be sure the process is adequately resourced in terms of time, money, and team development.

Finally, be sure you have employees who can rise to the occasion. Assume they can meet these challenges; if it appears they can't, address that as the first challenge. Get whatever help you need for the whole system to move forward.

Although the task might appear daunting, there is much help available. The emergent global economy is forcing all organizations to move in this direction. The best are already moving quickly, and they represent potential resources for benchmarking or comparing notes. Since new work structures and cultures are in high demand, the path around the problems created by inflexible and damaging environments is well trodden. Finally, it is essential that workplaces have the capacity to create and recreate themselves. This work will always be important; in essence, this is true job security. It is also the work that creates in the leader a spirit and a potential for finding personally satisfying work. When the only constant in business is change, building a flexible workplace that can adapt to and thrive in the rapidly changing business environment will be the cornerstone of successful companies in the future. To build long-term competitive advantage, the whole company needs to move in the right direction. Successful organizations are characterized by a flexible culture; brittle ones will break and be left by the roadside.

Ken Murrell is professor of management at the University of West Florida; president of Empowerment Leadership Systems, and in the process of developing new doctoral programs on the subject of organizational change at Pepperdine University. He has worked around the world helping global organizations improve their effectiveness, and published extensively on the nature of empowerment and the future of work organizations.

Intrapreneurial Warriors Versus Traditional Managers

Gifford Pinchot

As we leave the industrial era, work is increasingly about innovation and doing something different for customers. Dull repetitive jobs are being eliminated by machines and computers, leaving only the more human work of dealing with the shifting desires and needs of people in a world of rapidly emerging technical possibilities.

Almost all the good jobs now require imagination and getting things done in new ways. Traditional bureaucratic expertise is not enough to achieve the rate of innovation needed to compete. What is needed is the skill of the intrapreneurial warrior.

TECHNIQUES FOR GETTING RESOURCES: THE QUIZ

Your project has come to a screeching halt, because the people in another department don't understand its importance. You know the ROI for the company would be great. You need their help or their permission, but they are too busy to help. *What can you do?*

Which of these seven options would you select? Pick the top three, then let's score the effectiveness of each choice.

1 Plead with your boss to lobby the resource owners for what you need.
2 Explain all the glorious implications of the idea so that resource owners recognize how important it is.
3 Ask resource owners for advice on your project before asking them for resources.
4 Express gratitude for whatever help you get.
5 Broadcast your idea and see who steps forward to help.
6 Build a network of friends and colleagues.
7 Seek out another project with more powerful sponsors.

Plead with your boss?

Well, you've probably tried asking your boss already. If it worked, fine, but before you ask your boss to spend precious political capital on your behalf, ask yourself if you have made the job as easy as possible.

When your boss requests project resources from someone in another area, it's going to be easier if you have pre-sold the idea to the people who will do the work. Have you converted those people to your cause—are they supportive? Getting someone to lobby others on your behalf may be part of the solution, but it is not the place to begin.

Intrapreneurial Warrior Score: 0 points

Explain the glorious implications?

It's tempting, when visualizing the positive impact of your project, to tell the world about it, but the effect of your excitement may be to scare people. If, in its fully realized form, the implications of your project will change everything—their department, their job, and the comfort of familiar ways of doing things—you cannot blame them for being cautious. If you make your project seem too world-changing, they will respond with delaying tactics and requests for more information, not action or help.

Intrapreneurial Warrior Score: –3 points

Ask resource owners for advice?

The danger of premature glorification is neatly matched by the danger of premature requests for resources. Ask too soon and there is a good chance that you will get some version of "No!" Once someone has denied you resources, rationalization sets in: if they refused to provide resources, then your idea must be bad. If it was good, then they, a good manager, would have found a way to help.

This vicious cycle of rejection can easily be turned around. Simply ask for some form of help that will not be refused. *The request for help least likely to be refused is a request for advice.* When someone gives you advice, they are contributing to your project. If they contribute to your project one of two things must be true:

1 Your project is worthwhile, so their helping makes them good managers.
2 Your project is worthless or destructive, in which case helping is a poor use of time, and therefore they are a poor manager.

The attraction of seeing oneself as good manager will win out almost every time. Keep asking for things they will agree to and be careful not to ask for too much too soon. The more someone contributes, the more the project becomes their own. So start with advice and build your requests gradually until you can ask for resources. The intrapreneurial warrior gets people involved before asking them for anything of significance.

Intrapreneurial Warrior Score: +5 points

Express gratitude?

Gratitude cements the value of whatever help you have been given, and can even dissolve overt hostility to a project. When someone in a position of power criticizes the project of an intrapreneurial warrior, the intrapreneur takes careful notes. After some time to cool off and a bit of checking, the warrior finds truth in some of the criticisms. In some small way the plan is changed.

The intrapreneur then goes back to the critic and thanks him or her for picking up on a problem that could have sunk the project: "Without your help, we might have . . . " Your critic may have tried to define himself or herself as your enemy, but you have reframed the criticism as a form of support. To balance things out they rationalize that there must be good in your project. Few can resist the praise, *if it is delivered with total sincerity.* Thanking critics for their contribution sincerely requires the generosity of spirit to genuinely forgive and appreciate. Don't try it until you have done so.

Intrapreneurial Warrior Score: +4 points

Broadcast your idea?

It seems smart to "run your idea up the flagpole and see who salutes." It makes sense, but it doesn't work. Every innovation involves a bit of creative destruction; the new way replaces the old. Those who will benefit from the new order don't really get the implications of the change; and those whose privileged positions will be challenged by the new order recognize it at once and come forward with spears sharpened. The lesson is this: premature promotion of your idea triggers the immune system. The grander you make your idea sound and the more widely you distribute it, the more people it will frighten.

Intrapreneurial Warrior Score: –4 points

Build a network?

Gone is the era of the lonely innovator. The intrapreneurial warrior knows that when you are not in charge of everything you need, your success hinges on the quality of your relationships with the other players (and the referees). The warrior is alert to the feelings of others. He distributes credit widely. (The more you give away, the more comes back in the long run.)

The intrapreneurial warrior keeps everyone in the coalition fully informed, takes time to check up on everyone, and keeps relationships alive even when there is no immediate need for help. Building a network of friends and colleagues is "Innovation 101."

Intrapreneurial Warrior Score: +3 points

Seek out another project?

Every innovation passes through dark and discouraging days. Intrapreneurial warriors don't give up easily. They find ways around obstacles; they don't knuckle under to them.

There are fake intrapreneurs who only want to head large projects with an impressive staff roster. They jump from project to project depending on what is in favor. If the project hits a political snag, they blame others and move on. This may be a good career strategy in some companies, but it will not lead to effective innovation.

Intrapreneurial Warrior Score: –5

Points Scoring.   Add the points from your three choices; if the total is

–4 or less: *Bureaucrat:* Stay in safe bureaucratic jobs or break out by starting a whole new career outside of large organizations.

–3 to 1: *In transition to the 21st century:* Take more time off from work and spend time learning to build relationships.

1 to 7: *Emerging Intrapreneurial Warrior:* Get an intrapreneurial mentor. Build your network. Get smart about handling the immune system.

7 or more: *Intrapreneurial Warrior:* Keep up the good work!

The Intrapreneurial Warrior.   To be an intrapreneurial warrior, one must have:

- an inspiring vision
- integrity, trustworthiness
- an inner compass guiding one toward the vision
- the courage to follow this compass
- the emotional intelligence to understand others
- the wisdom to use diplomacy
- the stealth and cunning to avoid organizational backlash
- the generosity of spirit to make and keep allies across bureaucratic lines
- the business judgment to make good use of resources

It Can Be Done!

DuPont's Medical Products department sold equipment to test for HIV. One of its customers, the New York Blood Bank, asked for help. If HIV were found, the source of the blood must be located. The Blood Bank needed a massive database to track all blood from collection to transfusion—and they wanted it in 90 days!

The department sought help from information technology and from corporate staff. Neither could meet the deadline. However, the medical products' account executive had heard of a special intrapreneurial team in DuPont's fibers department. Traditionally, a staff group from one division does not do major jobs for another division. But, since this was considered an emergency, IEA got the job. It provided the blood-tracking database within deadline, and Medical Products solved its customer's problem successfully.

Furthermore, as IEA's reputation spread, the group found itself working with many other departments to solve their information problems. Ultimately, IEA became an intraprise (an independent enterprise within the corporation); it went on to provide new and better information technology services for every division of DuPont and spread learning across the organization.

MAKING IT HAPPEN

The intrapreneurial warrior makes it happen by building relationships across the boundaries of the organization.

1 Build your network across organizational boundaries. Keep up with old friends when jobs change, and be curious about others' work; interest is a key currency.
2 Give credit widely: express gratitude, and give others credit.
3 Always gauge requests for help so the answer you get is yes. Ask for advice before asking for resources, and build collaborative relationships gradually.
4 Be trustworthy, and make sure your partners come out winners too.

Getting help and resources for your project is more about relationships and trust than it is about the quality of your ideas. The intrapreneurial warrior treasures a reputation for integrity, for without trust innovation is impossible. The intrapreneurial warrior is somewhat modest about the idea and its potential, lest others be scared by it. The intrapreneurial warrior asks for advice before resources, because advice is the form of help that people are most willing to give.

Gifford Pinchot is widely considered the father of the intrapreneuring movement and is the author of *Intrapreneuring: Why You Don't Have to Leave the Corporation to Become an Entrepreneur* (Harper & Row, 1985) and *The Intelligent Organization* (with Elizabeth Pinchot; Berrett-Koehler, 1994). Pinchot & Company, the firm he leads, helps companies to reduce bureaucratic obstacles and to design and implement more effective and sustainable business practices. He is a worldwide speaker and consultant. For more information, visit www.pinchot.com.

Preventing Corporate Systems from Holding You Back

Leslie L. Kossoff

"**N**o. We can't do that." Far too frequently managers return the ever-present and usually nonsensical "No" without thinking of the real consequences for the organization. This unarguable negative is based on policies, procedures, management, and other organizational systems that were designed by someone else at some other time for an organization that may no longer exist.

Ultimately, that negative response can mark the beginning of the end of the enterprise. However, a modern organization that recognizes and values initiative and market change, avoiding yesterday's rules to govern today's challenges, is much more likely to succeed.

ASSESSING THE IMPACT OF ORGANIZATIONAL SYSTEMS

Living in the technology era as we do, we have a tendency to equate organizational systems with information systems. In fact, there's a great deal of difference between the two. Information systems are those technological marvels that allow us to access and communicate information in ways never before possible. Organizational systems, on the other hand, develop in a patchwork over time. They constitute the regulatory infrastructure of the organization—the skeleton of policy, procedure, rules, and regulations that each employee is to follow.

The intent of these systems is positive; they're designed to protect the organization and its employees from harm and to create as fair, smooth running, and positive a workplace as possible.

Organizational systems run the gamut from security and disclosure edicts to dicta on compensation, attendance, vacation, and retirement programs. They address law and legal precedent as well as homegrown instructions on how things are done. They create a thinking process that allows management and employees to know the parameters within which they need to work.

The problem is that the systems are rarely correlated with the needs of the business. In the worst cases, they determine and direct how you are to operate, as determined by someone in the organization who probably has no idea what you actually do and possibly does not even work there any more.

Eventually organizational systems become embedded—and invisible—to almost everyone except those who are being adversely affected. It's conceivable that if all current employees were removed from an organization and replaced with people not at all familiar with the enterprise—but instructed to follow the same policies, procedures, rules, regulations, and instructions—the organization would continue to operate in exactly the same way.

Such is the unrecognized impact of organizational systems.

TECHNIQUES FOR IMPROVING CORPORATE SYSTEMS
This situation leads to the questions all executives and managers should be asking themselves:

- Is my organization operating the way I want it to and the way it must for us to succeed?
- Which policies, procedures, rules, regulations, and instructions within the organizational systems infrastructure support the organization's real goals? Which do not?
- Which systems cannot be changed, for example, because of laws or government regulations?
- Of those systems that can be changed, what must we do to make sure that the systems that direct and drive the organization are designed to help us succeed?
- Which systems have been unintentionally imposed or supported?

1 Understand the impact of organizational systems: in the form of rules, policies and procedures, systems give people a sense of security. Those same systems form a connection with the past for longer-term employees, who learned specific policies and procedures from people long gone from the organization. The rules represent the good old days.

Don't suppose that new organizations are immune from this syndrome. By the time a new organization has been in business a week or so, any new employee is likely to be instructed on "how we do business here."

As the organization grows and becomes more complex, more structure and systematization are necessary, to establish continuity and predictability across and between functions, departments, and employee activities. It's not that systems are bad, nor are they developed with ill intent. It's simply that they grow without consideration of their impact unless management takes an active role in seeing that the systems are designed for success.

Hence organizational systems should be treated organically as a reflection of the changing needs of the business.

2 Review your metrics: take a look at the various measures you use to track and monitor your organization. Determine where you see progress and where your performance doesn't meet the needs or expected goals for your area. Identify new measures needed to fully understand your performance and impact.

3 Assess your impact: using those same metrics as well as those of other departments or areas, look at how your organization is doing in supporting your internal customers and suppliers—as well as how it is forwarding ultimate organizational goals.

Wherever possible apply monetary figures to the processes and impact of your area—including its impact on the real and potential profitability of the larger organization.

4 Establish a systems dialogue within your organization: at scheduled staff, team, or communication meetings ask employees whether the policies, procedures, rules, and instructions they follow make sense to them. Also ask how the systems requirements of other departments affect their performance.

5 Make every employee a C.F.O.: using the data you've collected and reviewed, incorporate the measures and their monetary impact into the ongoing dialogue. Explain how the financials of your particular department—and employees' individual jobs—affect the greater organization. Use this as a means of describing each employee's importance and contribution to the greater good and goals of the enterprise. Begin developing employees' financial understanding of their own jobs and garner their input on how those financials can be improved. (Do not use this as a means of berating any department's or individual's performance.)

6 Create an active systems redesign process: ask employees to discuss how they might be better able to perform—initially, with specific reference to changes they see as necessary to established organizational systems. Use existing teams, or form a team, to review current organizational systems, gain input from employees about their performance and financial impact, and recommend improvements.

Most important of all, implement the changes and continue the dialogue to address other embedded issues within the organization.

AVOIDING SYSTEM IMPLOSION

Because system implosion is usually invisible to the organization until it's too late, managers and executives need to look for signs that things aren't working as they should. Some examples of system implosions:

When Hughes Aircraft Company exclusively contracted with the government, its accounting departments had a policy that suppliers were paid 90 days after invoice. Even knowing that this policy was putting small businesses out of business (one department even posted a tally of the companies it had destroyed), it never occurred to anyone to consider the impact on Hughes' own manufacturing floor. Ultimately, because so few suppliers either could or wanted to continue doing business with Hughes, the line workers were constantly working with differing parts; supplier certification was overwhelmed and unable to adequately oversee and monitor suppliers. The quality of the product—and company profits—suffered.

Even a function as simple as newspaper circulation demonstrates how the system can affect customer retention. The *Financial Times* circulation department assures its customers that the paper can be delivered anywhere. However, customers based in the United States but wanting the paper delivered in the United Kingdom, where the *FT* has its headquarters, are informed that it can't be done. Even in this world of globalization, the *FT*'s circulation system doesn't cross the Atlantic. This leaves the subscribing customers with broken promises—and a potential preference for competing publications.

Cisco Systems got caught in its own trap of cornering the market on supplied products to ensure that manufacturing could go forward without delays. While the technology sector was waning, Cisco continued to order supplied parts as if there were no foreseeable changes to production volume or scheduling. The technology downturn finally affected the company with the result that suppliers were paid late, orders were cancelled, and the company had to take a write-off for excess inventory.

These problems could have been avoided if managers had reviewed whether their systems were designed to support the organization's present needs and future goals especially in the context of market change. Taking that closer look could have avoided or addressed the existing system pitfalls before they adversely affected the enterprise.

MAKING IT HAPPEN

Organizational systems are owned by management—which means that only management can do anything about them.

However, it really isn't difficult to ensure that the systems are in alignment with the organization's goals. The bad news is that this is a time-consuming process. This process is straightforward, whether applied on a cross-organizational or department-specific basis. The following measures can help to improve the situation:

- Understand the current position: the scope of the rules, why they are there, and the impact they have. Is the net effect of each rule positive?
- Consider how to mitigate the effects of necessary rules or systems which may have some challenging or potentially frustrating consequences.
- Involve people: systems are devised by people for people, so don't ignore them.
- Keep the process of reviewing, replacing, and enforcing rules dynamic. It is not an advantage simply to review the changes once and then leave well alone. Times change; so do systems.

The greatest win for the organization occurs when the initial systems review is complete and the less-structured systems become the center of management's and employees' attention.

An ongoing dialogue within and between departments will keep the organization a living, growing entity focused on health, welfare, and profitability for all stakeholders. Whether it is communication systems and information movement or how departments coordinate with others, no part of the organization should remain unexamined over time. Every department should be subject to modernization.

Through this ongoing and expanding process management will ultimately create an organization designed to succeed, one that never rests on its laurels.

———

Leslie L. Kossoff is a leading international executive advisor. For over 15 years she has worked with clients from companies of all sizes and sectors in the United States, Europe, and Japan helping them to focus on the business of their business. Her award winning book, *Executive Thinking* (Davies-Black, 1999), has been translated into multiple languages while her first book, *Managing for Quality* (Kossof Management Consulting, 1998), is in its third edition. She spent three years as an assistant to Dr. W. Edwards Deming.

Project Management

Robert Buttrick

Today, managers may spend as much time in interdisciplinary, cross-functional project teams as they do in their normal posts—project management has now become a core competence for all managers. This applies not only to projects undertaken for customers (external projects), but also to those undertaken for the development of the organization itself (internal projects).

Many factors have contributed to this. Among them is speed, coupled with the increased complexity of organizations and the closer relationships within and between companies, their customers, and suppliers. We now need evolutionary change at revolutionary speed, necessitating skillful project management.

As a vehicle of change, project management is well suited to meet these needs. However, it is too often perceived as a necessary technical discipline rather than the powerful business tool it really is.

THE CHALLENGES TO BE FACED

All organizations have problems with the ways they tackle change within their businesses—these may be related to technology, people, processes, systems, or structure. During the late 20th century, there has been a variety of techniques and offerings available to managers to enable them to do this, most notably total quality management and business process reengineering.

Unfortunately, not all organizations secure the enduring benefits initially promised by these techniques. The initiatives often fail because they cost too much, take too long, are inadequately thought out and specified, or simply don't deliver the expected benefits.

This amounts to failure on a grand scale, costing billions every year, and results in the demise of some organizations. For two reasons. Organizations don't know *how* to tackle these initiatives: there's no company-wide way of organizing this. Also they don't know *what* they should be doing: there's no clear strategy driving decision making.

PRINCIPLES OF PROJECT MANAGEMENT

Project management gives you the environment to solve the first of these root causes, and by its proper implementation will prompt you to think about the second.

Make Sure Your Projects Are Driven by Your Strategy. You should be able to demonstrate explicitly how each project you undertake fits your business strategy. The screening out of unwanted projects as soon as possible is essential. The less clear the strategy, the more likely unsuitable projects are to pass the screening: hence there will be more projects competing for scarce resources, resulting in the company losing focus and risking its overall performance.

Use a Staged Approach. Rarely is it possible to plan a project in its entirety. You should, however, be able to plan the next stage in detail and to the end of the project in outline. As you progress through the project you gather more information, reduce uncertainty, and increase confidence. The typical framework comprises the following progressive steps, or stages:

- *Proposal*—identifying the idea or need.
- *Initial investigation*—a brief overview of the possible requirements and solutions.
- *Detailed investigation*—undertaking a feasibility study of the options and defining the chosen solution.
- *Development and testing*—building the solution.
- *Trial*—piloting the solution with real people.
- *Operation and closure*—putting it into practice and closing the project.

You should use the same generic stages for all types of project. This makes the use and understanding of the process familiar and easier, avoiding the need to learn different processes for various types of project. What differs is the content of each project, the level of activity, the nature of the activity, the resources required, and the stakeholders and decision makers needed within each use of the framework. The *gates* are entry points to each stage, and are the key checkpoints for revalidating a project and committing resources and funding.

Placing high emphasis on the early stages of the project might mean that between 30% and 50% of the project's life cycle is devoted to investigative stages before any final deliverable is physically built. Research clearly demonstrates that placing heavy emphasis up front significantly decreases the time to market/completion. Good investigative work means clearer objectives and plans. Decisions taken at the early stages of a project have a far-reaching effect and set the tone for the remainder. In the early stages, creative solutions can slash delivery times in half or cut costs dramatically. Once development is underway, changes can be very costly.

Engage Your Stakeholders. A stakeholder is any person involved in or affected by a project. The involvement of stakeholders such as users and customers adds considerable value at all stages of the project. Engaging them is a powerful mover for change; ignoring them can lead to failure. When viewed from a stakeholder perspective, your project may be just one more problem they have to cope with in addition to fulfilling their usual duties; it may appear irrelevant to them, or even regressive. If their consent is required to make things happen, it is unwise to ignore them.

Be sure to encourage teamwork and commitment at all times. The need for many projects to draw on people from a range of functions means a cross-functional team approach is essential. The more closely people work and the more open the management style, the better they perform. Although this is not always practical, closeness can be achieved by frequent meetings and good communication, often through Web tools or videoconferencing.

Ensure Success by Planning for It. The more functionally structured a company, the more difficult it is to implement effective project management: project management by its nature crosses functional boundaries. To make projects succeed, the balance of power usually needs to be tipped toward the project and away from line management.

Monitor Against the Plan. There must be guidance, training, and support for all staff related to projects, including senior managers who sponsor projects or make project-related decisions.

Core control techniques include planning, managing risk, issues, scope change, schedule, cost, and reviews. Planning as a discipline is essential. If you have no definition of the project and no plan, it will be virtually impossible to communicate your intentions to the project team and stakeholders, and terms such as "early," "late," and "within budget" have no real meaning.

Risk management is key: using a staged approach is itself a risk management technique, with the gates acting as formal review points. It is essential to analyze the project, determine which are the inherently risky parts, and take action to reduce, avoid, or, in some cases, insure against those risks while looking to exploit any opportunities that arise.

Monitoring and forecasting against the agreed plan ensures that events do not take those involved in the project by surprise. This is best illustrated by the "project control cycle," the frequency of which depends on the project, its stage of development, and the inherent risk. Monitoring should focus more on the future than on what has actually been completed. Completion of activities is not sufficient to predict whether milestones will continue to be met. The project manager should continually check that the plan is still fit for the purpose and likely to deliver the business benefits on time.

Manage the Project Control Cycle. Monitoring should focus more on the future than on what has actually been completed. Completion of activities is not sufficient to predict whether milestones will continue to be met. The project manager should continually check that the plan is still fit for the purpose and likely to deliver the business benefits on time.

Many projects are late or never even get completed. One of the reasons for this is "scope creep": more and more ideas are incorporated into the project, resulting in higher costs and late delivery. Changes, even beneficial ones, must be managed to guarantee that only those enabling the project benefits to be realized are accepted; you must communicate this to the team and stakeholders so they are absolutely clear what the current project comprises.

Formally Close the Project. Finally, every project must be closed, either because it has completed its work or because it has been terminated early. By explicitly closing a project you make sure that all work ceases, lessons are learned, and any remaining assets, funding, or resources can be released for other purposes.

One company that has a product leadership strategy terminated a new product before launch because a competitor had just released a superior product. It was better to abort the launch and work on the next generation product, than to continue working toward the release of a new product that could be seen by the market as inferior. If they had done so, their strategy of product leadership would have been seriously compromised.

MAKING IT HAPPEN

The success of an organization rests on its ability to manage projects effectively and efficiently. Common mistakes include:

- intrafunctional thinking—not having a company-wide view;
- having too many rules—the more project rules you make, the more people will break them;
- disappearing and changing sponsors—continual changing of the driver will cause you to lose focus and forget why you are undertaking the project at all;
- ignoring the risks—risks don't go away, so acknowledge and manage them;
- rushing in prematurely to get something going—resist the temptation to confuse activity with progress;
- analysis paralysis—you need to investigate, but only enough to gain the confidence to move on;
- untested assumptions—all assumptions are risks, so treat them as such;
- executive's pet projects—make no exceptions. If an executive's idea is really so good, it should stand up to the scrutiny all the others go through.

Your project will run much more smoothly if you focus on a few basics:

- define strategies clearly so you're better able to eliminate low-leverage, low-value projects;
- plan through progressive stages: proposal, initial investigation, detailed investigation, development and testing, trial, operation, and closure;
- concentrate on the early stages of the project, when the decisions taken have a far-reaching effect on the outcome;
- analyze the project to reduce, avoid, or insure against the risks;
- to make projects succeed, tip the balance of power toward the project and away from line management;
- focus progress monitoring more on the future than on completion of activities, which doesn't predict that future milestones will be met.

The interdisciplinary nature of project teams combined with the significance and sensitivity of their impact places considerable demands on management. Acquiring key skills will ensure that the process runs smoothly, minimizing costs and maximizing benefits, while securing stakeholder involvement and commitment. Responsiveness is an increasingly significant source of competitive advantage, and a fast, flexible and focused project management capability is essential for every organization. Tomorrow's successful corporations will reflect the efforts those organizations make in the way they research, plan, and execute new initiatives and projects.

Robert Buttrick is known for his refreshing and practical insight into business-led project management. His best-selling book, *The Project Workout* (Prentice Hall/ Financial Times, 2000), is widely adopted by major corporations and business schools alike, both in the United Kingdom and around the world. He is also a key speaker at conferences as well as in-company events. Buttrick has lived and worked in countries as diverse as the United States, Yemen, Sudan, Senegal, Mauritius, Bahrain, and Japan.

Outsourcing

Ronan McIvor

One of the key issues for many organizations has been the growing importance of outsourcing. The potential for outsourcing has moved on from those activities that are normally regarded as peripheral, such as cleaning, catering, and security, to include critical areas such as design, manufacture, marketing, distribution, and information systems, with almost the entire value chain open to the use of outside supply (Jennings 1997). Within organizations the outsourcing decision is being given more consideration because of its strategic implications.

However, there is evidence to suggest that organizations are not achieving the desired benefits from outsourcing. Research carried out by Lonsdale and Cox ("Outsourcing: Risks and Rewards." *Supply Management*, July 3, 1997) has revealed that outsourcing decisions are rarely taken within a thoroughly strategic perspective, with many firms adopting a short-term perspective and being motivated primarily by the search for short-term cost reductions. Also, some commentators have expressed serious concerns over companies that have embarked upon extensive outsourcing without fully understanding the concept (Alexander and Young, "Outsourcing: Where's the Value?" *Long Range Planning*, May 29, 1996).

THE DECISION TO OUTSOURCE

The conceptual basis for outsourcing is Williamson's (*Markets and Hierarchies.* Free Press, 1975) theory of *transaction cost analysis*. This combines economic theory with management theory to determine the best type of relationship a firm should develop in the marketplace. The central theme of transaction costs theory is that the properties of the transaction determine the governance structure. Asset specificity refers to the nontrivial investment in transaction-specific assets. For example, the level of customized equipment or materials involved in the transaction relates to the degree of asset specificity. When asset specificity and uncertainty are low and transactions are relatively frequent, transactions will be governed by markets. High asset specificity and uncertainty lead to transactional difficulties, with transaction held internally within the firm—vertical integration. Medium levels of asset specificity lead to bilateral relations in the form of cooperative alliances between the organizations.

A term that is frequently used in connection with outsourcing is "core competence." The ideas of core competence and its relationship to outsourcing have evolved from the work of Prahalad and Hamel ("The Core Competence of the Corporation." *HBR*, July–August 1990). Prahalad and Hamel argue that the real sources of competitive advantage are to be found in management's ability to consolidate corporate-wide technologies and production skills into competencies that empower individual businesses to adapt rapidly to changing business opportunities. Canon's core competencies in optics, imaging, and microprocessor controls have allowed it to be a significant player in markets as diverse as photocopiers, laser printers, cameras, and image scanners. These core competencies underpin the ability of the organization to outperform the competition, and therefore must be defended and nurtured.

KEY PROBLEMS WITH THE OUTSOURCING PROCESS

Many companies have failed to take a strategic view of outsourcing decisions, deciding to outsource for short-term reasons such as cost reduction and capacity constraints. A number of problems encountered by companies in their efforts to formulate an effective outsourcing decision are as follows:

- **No formal outsourcing process.** Many companies have no firm basis for evaluating the outsourcing decision. In many instances, the decision about which parts of the business to outsource is made by ascertaining what will save most on immediate overhead costs, rather than on what makes the most long-term business sense.
- **A fragmented piecemeal approach.** Many companies have failed to integrate outsourcing decisions into their overall corporate strategy. This has led to a fragmented and piecemeal approach with no coherent strategy on how outsourcing should contribute to strategic objectives.
- **Limited cost analysis.** Cost analysis of the outsourcing decision involves comparing the important costs associated with internal work and outsourcing. However, in many cases these calculations tend to focus primarily on manufacturing costs and do not provide a true reflection of the total costs involved. Also, other more qualitative factors, such as the long-term strategic implications and the workforce reaction to outsourcing, may have a greater impact on the decision.
- **Core business definition.** The embedded skills that give rise to the next generation of competitive products cannot be "rented-in" by outsourcing. Too many companies have unknowingly relinquished their core competencies by cutting internal investment in what they mistakenly thought were "cost centers" in favor of outside suppliers. Outsourcing may provide a shortcut to a more competitive product, but it typically contributes little to build the people-embodied skills that are needed to sustain future product leadership.

KEY REQUIREMENTS FOR EFFECTIVE OUTSOURCING

Any successful outsourcing strategy should include the following elements.

Core Activity Definition. Companies must identify their core and noncore activities. A core activity is central to the company successfully serving the needs of potential customers in each market. The activity is perceived by the customers as adding value, and therefore being a major determinant of competitive advantage. Distinguishing between core and noncore activities is a complex task, and care must be taken to ensure the long-term strategic considerations and true benefits are assessed. This process of identifying the core activities should be carried out by top management with inputs from teams at lower levels in the organization. Each team should encompass a broad section of members—functionally, divisionally, and hierarchically. Noncore activities for which the company has neither a critical strategic need nor special capabilities should be outsourced. Companies adopting this approach, such as Honda and Nortel, build their strategies around their core activities and outsource as much of the rest as possible.

Core Activity Capability Analysis. Each core activity must be benchmarked against the capabilities of all potential external providers (both suppliers and competitors) of that activity. This will enable the identification of the relative performance for each core activity along a number of selected measures. Resources should be focused on the activities where pre-eminence can be achieved and unique customer-perceived value can be delivered. For example, Eastman Kodak has world leadership in two of its core activities—chemical and electronic imaging. Thus, these activities are held within the company in order to maintain and build upon this leadership. A key strategic issue in the outsourcing decision is whether a company can achieve a sustainable competitive advantage by performing a core activity internally on an ongoing basis. Many companies assume that because they have always performed the activity internally, then it should remain that way. In many cases, closer analysis may reveal a significant disparity between their capabilities and those of the world's best suppliers. For example, Ford found that many of its internal quality and cost performance indicators were significantly lower than those of suppliers when it carried out a benchmarking exercise across a range of processes for one of its models (Quinn and Hilmer, "Strategic Outsourcing." *Sloan Management Review*, Summer 1994).

Cost Analysis. All the actual and potential costs involved in sourcing the activity, either internally or externally, must be measured. This encompasses all the costs associated with the acquisition of the activity throughout the entire supply chain and not just the purchase price. It is important to consider costs right from idea conception, as in collaborating with a supplier in the design phase of the component, through to any costs (for example, warranty claims) associated with the component once the completed product is being used by the final customer. The data requirements for this stage are quite formidable. Management must break down the company's functional cost accounting data into the costs of performing specific activities. The appropriate degree of disaggregation depends upon the economics of the activities and how valuable it is to develop cross-company comparisons for narrowly defined activities as opposed to broadly defined activities.

Supply Management. As a result of increased outsourcing, companies have become more dependent upon their suppliers, thus making supply management a key success factor. Many companies have been attempting to develop collaborative relationships with suppliers as they seek to reduce the risks associated with outsourcing. Companies may establish a collaborative relationship with a supplier in order to exploit their capabilities. For example, a company may wish to maintain the knowledge (design skills, management skills, manufacturing, etc.) that enables the technology of the activity to be exploited, even when another partner is providing it. Also, it is possible for a company to develop a core competency by learning from partners. For example, NEC top management determined that semiconductors would be the company's most important "core product." Hence, it entered into strategic alliances aimed at building competencies quickly and at low cost. Alternatively, in some circumstances it may be more beneficial to pursue a relationship where the company holds the balance of power rather than pursuing a relationship based upon equality and the mutual sharing of benefits. For example, a company may use its influence to obtain reductions in inventory and cost, which in turn have a positive impact on the achievement of its own competitive position. Also, this may ensure greater flexibility in that the company will not get locked into a long-term relationship with a supplier whose technology or processes may become uncompetitive.

MAKING IT HAPPEN

First, take a strategic view of outsourcing decisions—don't act on short-term factors such as cost reduction and capacity constraints.

Second, outsource what makes the most long-term business sense, not what for will save most on overhead costs.

Third, identify core activities by supporting top management with lower-level teams with broad functional, divisional, and hierarchical membership.

Fourth, benchmark each core activity against the capabilities of all potential external providers (both suppliers and competitors).

Fifth, keep a core activity internally on a continuing basis only if you can achieve a sustainable competitive advantage by doing so.

Finally, measure all the actual and potential costs involved in outsourcing the activity—not just the purchase price.

Ronan McIvor is a senior lecturer at the School of International Business, University of Ulster. He has conducted extensive research in supply chain management and information systems. He is currently researching in the areas of outsourcing and the application of electronic commerce at the buyer-supplier interface.

Lean Manufacturing

Daniel T. Jones

Although the terms "lean production" and "lean manufacturing" have only been in circulation since the publication of *The Machine That Changed the World* in 1990, the concepts and practices have a much longer history. Indeed, the core idea of lining production steps in process sequence can be traced back to Colt's armory in Hartford, Connecticut, in 1855. What Henry Ford later called "flow production" reached its peak at his plant in Highland Park in 1915, where every machine making parts and every step toward assembling them were lined up in single-piece flow, so that it took a matter of hours from raw casting to the finished product.

This system could not offer customers enough choice. So when Ford built his next plant at River Rouge in 1931, it was organized quite differently. Large machines able to make large batches of different parts were grouped together in separate departments, maximizing efficiency by ensuring there was always work waiting to be done. Batches of products wandered from department to department and throughput times stretched from several hours to several months. Long lead times entailed making to forecast and selling from several months' stock of finished cars in dealer lots. Thus the world of mass "production" was born and became the dominant model as long as producers could sell everything they made.

DISCOVERING LEAN PRODUCTION

Across the Pacific the founders of Toyota, Sakichi Toyoda and his son Kiichiro, were working on their own version of flow production in the 1930s. They formulated the two key pillars of what later became the Toyota Production System (TPS): automatic machine and line stopping whenever a mistake is made so that no bad parts are passed forward to interrupt the downstream flow (a system they called *Jidoka*), and a pull system in which only parts that are actually needed are made (called *just-in-time*). Later on the third pillar, involving leveling the workload in a mixed model production flow, was added (called *Heijunka*).

It was not until after World War II that Taiichi Ohno, the production chief at Toyota, implemented these principles. Ohno was determined to overcome all the obstacles to producing a range of products in low volumes, using simple equipment laid out in process sequence. His 20-year experiment started in the engine plant before extending to pressing, body welding, and assembly. Only when Ohno needed to extend the TPS to the supply base in the early 1970s was it written down for the first time, though it was another decade before it was published in books and articles.

Toyota's steady and continuing rise to become the third largest carmaker in the world led others to try to follow its example. This could only be done by understanding the principles behind TPS and then selecting the right tools in the right sequence. Lean production is the generic version of TPS and lean thinking describes the principles behind not just TPS but the whole Toyota business system, including product development, supplier coordination, and customer management. These principles are based on five key insights.

1 Specify value from the standpoint of the end customer.
2 Identify the value stream for each product family.
3 Link value-creating steps so the product can flow.
4 Enable your customers to pull what they need.
5 Manage toward perfection—where every action and asset creates value.

If you define value from the standpoint of the end customer, you realize that only a tiny fraction of actions and time actually create value. In a typical factory this might be 5% and in a whole value stream (from raw material to end customer) it is usually less than 1%. The rest of the steps are only necessary because of the way firms are currently organized and because of past decisions about assets and technologies. So the greatest opportunity for performance improvement is to reconfigure operations across the value stream to remove these wasted steps.

1 Overproduction
2 Inventories
3 Defects
4 Waiting
5 Excess Transport
6 Excess Movement
7 Excess Processing

If you identify the whole value stream for a given product (both the flow of orders upstream and the flow of products downstream) you see that optimizing each asset and activity in isolation creates huge amounts of waste elsewhere. It is only by optimizing the product value stream that you can identify ways of eliminating these interface wastes and can begin to rethink the appropriate equipment, technologies, and locations for the future.

The ideal way to organize waste-free production is to line up the value-creating steps so the product flows through them in the shortest possible time. This, in turn, means that every activity must be standardized and repeatable, and that every machine must be fully capable of delivering exactly what is needed and fully available to operate when needed. Where machines cannot be colocated and serve several product flows, then products need to be pulled directly as required from the upstream step. Time compression of every step is the only way to maintain these disciplines and to ensure that waste does not creep back when attention shifts elsewhere.

Multiple decision points and time lags in processing orders lead to amplification of the variance in orders passed upstream, which in turn requires larger inventories and excess capacity to cover demand spikes. Time compression and direct pull systems are the key to eliminating this amplification and to being able to move away from make-to-forecast and sell-from-stock toward true build-to-order systems able to deliver what customers want within the time available.

The final insight is that reconfiguring the value stream to eliminate waste is a step-by-step process: the more waste you remove, the more you can see to remove next time. It starts by understanding the current state of your operations and defining an achievable future state in a short space of time, which then becomes the current state of the next improvement cycle. However, this cyclical process also needs to be guided by a vision of the perfect state to which you should be headed, in which every action and asset creates value for the end customer.

IMPLEMENTING LEAN PRODUCTION

Lean production is by no means widespread, even in Japan. Indeed, it was only after 1973 that the rest of the Japanese auto industry recognized that Toyota was following a different path. By 1987 the first companies in the United States began to make serious progress with the help of several of Ohno's disciples, who had by then left to become consultants. The early lean conversion stories of Pratt & Whitney, Wiremold, and Lantech are described in *Lean Thinking*. Since then lean production has spread across the automotive, aerospace, and engineering industries and, following Alcoa's example, to raw material processing.

Many firms began implementing lean by involving the workforce in team-based problem-solving and *kaizen*, or continuous improvement activities. Putting the spotlight on operations should certainly lead to the removal of the most obvious wastes in the organization. However, lean production only really begins when you use value-stream mapping to learn to see the product flow from door to door, and when you give someone the responsibility for reconfiguring operations into continuous flow cells linked by leveled pull systems.

Once progress has been made within the plant then it is time to involve your suppliers by linking plants using simple pull systems and your customers by linking them directly to production using build-to-order systems. Beyond this it is possible to envisage rethinking and compressing the value stream using different technologies and right-sized tools colocated close to the point of use. We have in truth only just begun to realize the full potential of lean production.

MAKING IT HAPPEN
- Putting the spotlight on all of your operations should eliminate the most obvious wastes and deficiencies in the value chain—from the start of the process to the customer.
- For a more comprehensive assessment of the areas where your organization's processes may improve, use value stream mapping to clearly show product flows.
- Ensure that there is one person with overall responsibility for reconfiguring operations into continuous flow cells, linked by leveled "pull" systems.
- Knit together different parts of your value stream using build-to-order mechanisms.
- Compress your value stream through the development of new and ongoing strategies, and the application of new technologies, to eliminate wastage and continuously improve efficiency.

- Regularly review your activities—ideally from a customer or end user perspective—to make sure that they are delivered in an effective and profit-centered way.

Managing lean value streams is harder than managing individual operations. However, the gains are substantial, particularly when replicated across the whole value stream. First, your customers get defect-free products on time. Second, your suppliers get leveled orders and can deliver to you on time. Third, inventories at every point down the value stream can be cut in half. Fourth, you free up a lot of resources—people, machines, and space—that will not appear on the bottom line until they are used. The challenge in sustaining progress towards lean is to grow the throughput and bring operations in house as you free up those assets.

Daniel T. Jones is a world expert on supply chain management and coauthor of the bestseller *The Machine That Changed the World* (with James P. Womack and Daniel Roos; reprint, HarperCollins, 1991). His main interest has been understanding the differences in industrial performance and the transfer of a set of ideas called lean thinking, from the Japanese auto industry, to a wide range of other industries across the globe. He has led a series of pioneering benchmarking and action research programs, articulating and carrying lean thinking through to pilot implementation. Appointed professor of manufacturing management at Cardiff University Business School, Wales, in 1989, he established the Lean Enterprise Research Center in 1994. Jones is currently a member of the STI Automotive Innovation and Growth Team and the grocery industry's Efficient Consumer Response (ECR) European Academic Advisory Panel, and editor of the *ECR* journal.

The True Total Quality

Masaaki Imai

The differences between Knowledge and Wisdom are very important to our thinking about Total Quality Management. Knowledge is something we can buy. We can gain knowledge by reading books and attending seminars and classroom lectures. Knowledge remains just knowledge until we put it into action. On the other hand, wisdom is something we learn by doing. Practice is the best way of learning, and wisdom emerges from practice.

I have observed that Western management has tended to stress teaching knowledge in the classroom over wisdom through doing, whereas the Japanese approach for quality management has been to provide both knowledge and wisdom to employees. This latter approach is particularly effective in solving quality problems in "gemba" (shop floor).

GEMBA KAIZEN

"Gemba" means the place where real action occurs. In manufacturing, "gemba" means the shop floor. In my book *Gemba Kaizen: A Common-sense, Low-cost Approach to Management* (McGraw-Hill, 1997), I pointed out the three major activities to support good gemba management, namely: standardization, good housekeeping, and "muda" (waste) elimination. Let me explain the difference between wisdom and knowledge, citing an example from the housekeeping activities.

One of the five steps of housekeeping in gemba is "seiso," or cleaning, meaning the involvement of operators in cleaning the machines they work with. As they do so, operators often discover oil leaks or loosening of bolts on the machine. This gives them the opportunity to take corrective actions and eventually develop maintenance standards. This is learning by doing, and the operators gain valuable wisdom about machine maintenance, which is an important step for quality improvement.

I have observed that many managers often neglect these three foundations of good gemba management and are interested in pursuing sophisticated approaches instead.

There are five Golden Rules of gemba management:

- when a problem (abnormality) arises, go to gemba first;
- check with "gembutsu" (relevant objects);
- take temporary counter-measures on the spot;
- find the root cause;
- standardize to prevent recurrence.

Fabricated Data.   In managing gemba, the most critical part is for managers to go to gemba and have a good look. Managers who stay away from gemba, and seldom take the trouble of going there, are in contact with the reality of gemba only through indirect means, such as reports and conferences. In such cases, managers are making decisions based on fabricated data.

When you go to gemba where an abnormality occurred, you do not need any data, because what you see there is the reality. A manager on the shop floor is right in the midst of reality, and chances are that the problem may be solved on the spot and in real time by following the five golden rules.

Collect and Analyze Data. Another effective approach for problem solving in gemba has been to collect and analyze data.

Generally speaking, when these down-to-earth activities in gemba are carried out, the reject rates should go down to a tenth of their original levels. And yet, I find most Western managers do not take advantage of these effective gemba practices and pursue more academic and sophisticated approaches for quality improvement.

CONVERSION FROM BATCH TO JIT/LEAN PRODUCTION

The second and perhaps more acute issue facing most manufacturing companies today is the fact that their current production systems are the biggest hindrance to achieving quality management.

Today, most manufacturing companies subscribe to the traditional batch-production system. I define batch production as an antiquated paradigm patterned after agriculture. In agriculture, farm products are sewn, grown, harvested, and stored in batches. The more grain you have in the warehouse, the better. Agriculture must take into account the shifting seasons, and it is taken for granted that the lead time of growing and harvesting grain must be long.

When modern manufacturing emerged, it was patterned after this agricultural mentality. Raw materials were bought, processed, and stored in batches. Not much consideration was given to establishing a flow of work, and no effort was made to shorten the lead-time of production. Keeping a large inventory was taken for granted as a way of doing business. Even today, good inventory means high inventory to some managers.

As long as the varieties of products offered to customers were small in number, this type of production did not pose many problems. As customers have come to demand diversified products to be delivered on time and in different volumes, it has become increasingly difficult to develop flexibility to meet such demands in the context of the batch production system.

To cope with the new demand, efforts have been made by management in such areas as shortening set-up time, quality improvement, adding more lines, and even building new plants.

Unfortunately, even to this day, more than 90% of all manufacturing companies in the world still subscribe to batch production, a system that is one of the biggest obstacles to establishing good quality management.

The Drawbacks of Batch Production. The following features of the batch-production system stand in the way of quality management:

- **Large inventory.** As the name batch production suggests, the system is based on producing large batches of inventory at every production process. As a result, 100% quality-control inspection is nearly impossible. Even if quality defects are found at a later stage, it is almost impossible to go back to the previous process which produced the defects, seek out the root cause, and take corrective actions, since such rejects were made several days earlier. Also, the quality of products or parts deteriorates over time when stored in inventory, the only exceptions to this, of course, being red wine and whisky.

- **Long lead time.** The long lead time required by the batch-production system makes it difficult to take prompt and flexible action to meet the customer requirements for quality and delivery. For instance, the batch-production system is far less flexible when design changes are called for.
- **Isolated islands.** Batch production is necessitated because each manufacturing process is separated from the others—each on its own isolated island. This necessitates transport between processes, causing damage. Again, the isolated islands make it difficult to diagnose quality problems in real time. When operators do their jobs surrounded by inventory, housekeeping is difficult to maintain, which in turn leads to lower morale and less self-discipline of employees.

It becomes clear from the reasons given above that no matter how much effort management may make towards improving quality, batch production destroys those efforts.

JUST-IN-TIME PRODUCTION SYSTEM

The JIT production system was developed as an antithesis to batch production by Taiichi Ohno at the Toyota Motor Corporation and, along with many other practical tools like kanban (a card system that monitors and controls workflow), poka-yoke (fail-safe device) and jidohka (automation), is supported by the following three pillars of production:

- takt time versus cycle time (theoretical time versus actual time for processing one work piece);
- pull production versus push production (producing only as many items as the next process needs versus producing as many as can be produced);
- establishing production flow (rearranging equipment layout and processes according to the work sequence).

Just-in-time is really a revolutionary production system, and is in every sense just the opposite of the batch production. It employs minimum materials, equipment, manpower, utility, space, time, and money. It produces products within the shortest possible lead time, meets the diversified demand of customers, and delivers the products just-in-time.

Quality is ensured by keeping small inventories and through the use of flow production. Small inventories eventually lead to one-piece flow, namely one work piece moving from process to process. This enables operators to make a 100% inspection of each piece. In flow production, unlike in the isolated islands approach of batch production, processes are arranged in a flow, and any quality reject created in one process can be identified in the next process immediately.

MAKING IT HAPPEN

How many quality managers and engineers realize that the production system of their own company is a major cause for many quality problems they have to deal with? A review of the production system currently in use should be the first action taken by those engaged in quality improvement.

To solve quality problems, help employees to gain wisdom, as well as knowledge. Base total quality on good "gemba" (shop floor) management—meaning standardization, excellent housekeeping and effective elimination of "muda" (waste). When a problem (or abnormality) arises, always go to "gemba" first, and never rely on secondary information—reports, meetings, etc. When at "gemba," check with "gembutsu" (relevant objects), take temporary counter measures on the spot, find the root cause, and standardize to stop problems recurring. Recognize that batch production itself is one of the biggest obstacles to good quality management. Replace the batch system with Just-in-time production, arranging processes in a flow, so that any quality reject created in one process can be immediately identified in the next.

Masaaki Imai is one of the most widely acknowledged theorists on incremental change. As well as being a lecturer and consultant, he is founder and chairman of the international Kaizen Institute, an organization that helps Western companies introduce kaizen concepts, systems and tools. As one of the leaders of the quality movement and a champion of the kaizen philosophy, he has written several best-selling books on the subject.

The Critical Factors That Build or Break Teams

Meredith Belbin

The problem about the word "teamwork" is that it has become too popular and has therefore lost its meaning. A person deemed good at teamwork is all too often someone who fits into a group and keeps out of trouble. Ideal behavior is often judged to mean complying with majority decisions and being willing to do anything that's required. Yet if everyone behaved like that, you'd have good reason to doubt that the team would function effectively. A flock of sheep may hang together well, but their only accomplishment is to eat grass.

For anyone interested in productive teamwork, it's often better to start with the work rather than the team. First of all, does the work call for a team? There are many types of repetitive operation, unskilled work, and specialist activities that are best performed by loners. Rounding up such people and making them members of a team risks producing a double disadvantage: their personal productivity falls and their privacy is invaded. Such social engineering may accord with the prevailing culture, but it's difficult to see any other benefit. Of course, it may be argued that isolated workers need a social dimension to their work. If this is true it implies that individuals engaged on such jobs have been wrongly placed. Introverts need work suitable for introverts, while extroverts need work appropriate to extroverts.

DESIGNING WORK TO FIT THE PERSON

It is important to make sure that people have the right fit in the organization, if not, difficulties may arise. The example below provides an illustration of this.

Introverts and extroverts look for different things in a job. Lighthouse-keeping and leading tour groups are contrasting jobs calling for different personalities. In the case of most jobs, of course, the relationship between work demands and personal characteristics is less pronounced. The reality is that most jobs entail some degree of individual work and responsibility along with a degree of liaison activity and some shared responsibilities. Such a mixture of demands not only makes it difficult to find candidates with the ideal profile, but there are intrinsic problems in setting up jobs encompassing such different constituents. Most employers make few attempts to define the boundaries, and even if they are laid down in advance, people who work in close association are inclined to move them at will. That's why colleagues are often cited as the biggest aggravation at work. When conflicts result, one party or another will be blamed as a poor team player.

The best starting point for establishing good teamwork is to begin with the principal demands of a broad work area. What are its structural characteristics? Do some responsibilities need to be shared? If so, which responsibilities, and with whom? Which responsibilities can be assigned to individuals and made subject to personal accountability? Which tasks are critical in their timing and mode of treatment and require a prescriptive approach based on best practice? These are all basic questions. They can either be asked and answered with the manager as the sole decision maker, or such decision making can be carried out in consultation with others. Either way, there's a risk that a busy manager will cut corners and make hasty decisions that are out of touch with operational realities. That's why it is often better to assign a group of workers to address these basic questions and seek to find answers. Those at the sharp end will be most familiar with the demands and pressures of the work. They are often better placed to decide how work should be shared out.

I was engaged on a project to facilitate the introduction of a cargo-handling computer system at a large airport. The perceived problem was that the workers whose jobs were to be converted were both computer-illiterate and highly unionized. Devising a suitable form of training proved a challenge, but once this had been accomplished the introduction went without a hitch. The main problem arose in the way in which the design engineers had devised the work itself. The physical arrangement required these sociable workers to sit in isolation at consoles. They soon tired of it and chose instead to bypass the information system by riding on the mechanical handling equipment in order to conduct personal inspections of the cargo bays. Such bravado may have been exhilarating, but it was also dangerous practice.

Clearly, it is not only vitally important to understand the nature of the work being undertaken, but also the skills, experience, and approach of those doing the work. Taking account of people's strengths and motivations can certainly help to build or break teams.

TEAMS NEED TO BE GIVEN SCOPE

The team approach for organizing work depends on empowerment; it relies on trust, the confidence that a manager places in the qualities and caliber of the work force. It also depends on how well members of a group have developed an understanding of each other's strengths and weaknesses. That's why training in teamwork is so important and why it helps to understand the language of team roles. People make different contributions to teams, and it's important that every team plays to the best strengths of its individual players. Diversity in the range of available team roles lays the foundation for a balanced team. But diversity does not automatically produce harmony or balance. It can just as well produce conflict as different individuals strive to do their own thing. This is where the manager becomes so important, in creating the vision and the ethos. The role of the manager is to turn a potentially balanced team into a mature team.

Mature teams have the capacity to make local decisions in distributing the overall workload and its various elements appropriately. This is impossible unless the manager has set the stage, believes in empowerment, and knows how to put it into effect. The key to success lies in managing the interface between team roles and work roles. The manager has to understand this before the team can be expected to respond with appropriate action. Managers sometimes fear that workers will lack the will to take tough decisions, for example, when one person is not up to a particular aspect of the job. The surprise is often that workers prove more intolerant of a slacker or a poor performer than the manager. The group builds up a body of opinion that's a powerful force in its own right. Such a force can operate against the interests of management, but it can equally well reinforce the policies and strategies that management favors. The more autocratic the management, the greater the likelihood that the group will combine to become a counterforce. The greater the level of empowerment, the more likely will be the team's sense of ownership and pride, and the greater its commitment to the responsibilities undertaken. Without empowerment, balanced groups cannot be developed into mature teams.

REWARDING TEAMS APPROPRIATELY

All teams need to be assessed. The question is, how should it be done so that it is positive and constructive? One way is to set objectives for teams and judge how well these have been met. Such a view prevails in the top-down school of management and is given added impetus by performance-related bonuses. The argument put forward is that teams need fixed incentives to perform well, an assumption linked with the converse view that without such an incentive the team will not perform satisfactorily. This mechanistic view of human motivation is mistaken and is likely to backfire. Success in meeting given criteria depends partly on circumstances and contingencies. Success may not be commensurate with effort or skill. Objectives may be too easy to reach or too difficult. In the end, people may focus more on the shortcomings of the incentive than on the sense and purpose of their work. Retrospective awards for teams performing well are better received than prospective rewards for teams given set targets.

MAKING IT HAPPEN

- Start with the work, not the team. Ask first whether the work calls for a team at all.
- If a team is required, determine which responsibilities need to be shared and by whom.
- Decide which remaining responsibilities can be assigned to individuals, and make them subject to personal accountability.
- Use training in teamwork and team roles to ensure that every team plays to the best strengths of its individual players.
- Understand the team's strengths, weaknesses, and sense of "self-awareness" to improve.
- Maximize empowerment to develop ownership, pride, and maximum commitment to the team's responsibilities.
- Delegate work efficiently, and enable people to succeed.
- Understand what motivates the team, providing impetus and momentum.
- Give retrospective rewards for teams performing well rather than incentive rewards linked to set targets.

In recent years we have developed an approach to work that hinges on understanding and mastering two languages: the language of contributors to team effort—team roles—and the language of the work demands themselves—work roles. Essentially this approach offers a framework for deciding who does what. Unless people decide for themselves, or at least share in that decision making, there will be no commitment to the work itself.

———••———

Meredith Belbin is a consultant to the European Commission, the U.S. Department of Labor, and the OECD, and is senior associate professor at Cambridge University. He is a partner in Belbin Associates, a company known principally as the producer of Interplace—a company-based, team-role advice system, used internationally. He has written several successful business books, including the European bestseller, *Management Teams* (Butterworth-Heinemann, 1996) and, most recently, *Managing Without Power* (Butterworth-Heinemann, 2001).

Reorganizing the Firm Without Destroying It

Colin Price

We all know that reorganizations have a bad history, not just at McKinsey and not just recently. A 1990 study found that more than 50% of firms reported stagnant or reduced productivity after downsizing. In 1995 a study by INSEAD Business School reported that only 46% of 1,005 downsized firms surveyed had actually cut expenses, and fewer had increased profits or productivity. In 1996 *The Economist* reported research by Monitor looking at firms that had outperformed their industry over a ten-year period. Researchers found that nine out of ten had stable structures with no more than one reorganization.

Despite these failures, the imperative to change is still with us. We need to transform the corporation without losing the things that made it work. I'll discuss the mental traps that I believe cause these failures and the elements you need to consider. The goal is to achieve a transformation that fundamentally shifts an organization's strategy, business system, and culture to deliver measurable and sustainable improvements.

THE AWFUL LAW OF UNINTENDED CONSEQUENCES

The law of unintended consequences states that any change will be accompanied by a set of consequences that cannot be accurately predicted. The reason this law is awful is that the consequences have a strong tendency to destroy all the value of your planned change.

The problem stems from two sources: the objectives of the change and the process. Major programs of change are often begun for unpopular reasons—downsizing, business process reengineering, and takeovers all seem unattractive and threatening to staff. The process is often unpopular because it disenfranchises people within their own organization. Morale sinks, productivity drops, people lose their trust in management, and the value of the change is lost. If we're going to avoid these problems in our own programs, we need to understand the underlying causes and design our own process so that we can reorganize the firm without destroying its soul. This essay outlines four mental traps we need to avoid and ten rules we need to follow to avoid the awful law of unintended consequences.

FOUR MENTAL TRAPS

There are four common mental traps that can prevent any change program from being successful.

People vs. Performance.   Many change programs are stuck in the old paradigm of improving despite people. Successful companies recognize that you can only improve *through* people. This recognition comes from two main forces. First, the move toward a service economy and the growth in the value of intangible assets mean that these days the people *are* the organization—you can't change without changing them. Jack Welch said of the merger with Honeywell that GE would be bringing its "social architecture" to bear in driving the integration. This is a real acknowledgement that the people and the program are inseparable in creating effective change.

Structure vs. System. Many change programs are overly focused on rearranging the formal organizational structure. The change will only be effective if the structure is part of a broader systemic transformation. In our ten-year survey of companies, structure was only one of several levers (with strategy, execution, culture, talent management, leadership, innovation, and growth through successfully managed mergers and acquisitions) that led to dramatic performance improvements.

Us vs. Them. The role of the leader in crafting a transformational process is to create an environment in which people can take leadership of the changes wherever they are able. Talented people are motivated by freedom, autonomy, and the opportunity to rise to challenges. They can bring your transformation to life, particularly if you have a strong story they can dramatize. This is more engaging and compelling than their simply rolling out your program for you.

Concurrent vs. Consecutive. Because the elements of the transformation program are complementary, you cannot achieve successful change by tackling them one at a time. Improvements to leadership, culture, and management processes will reinforce the changes you make to customer management, operational processes, and organizational design. Effective transformations work simultaneously on more than one element of the change to unfold a sequence of related chapters in the program.

WHAT MOTIVATES TALENTED PEOPLE?
(Percentage of top 200 executives rating factor absolutely essential)

GREAT COMPANY	%	COMPENSATION AND LIFESTYLE	%	GREAT JOBS	%
Values and culture	58	Differentiated compensation	29	Freedom and autonomy	56
Well managed	50	High total compensation	23	Job has exciting challenges	51
Company has exciting challenges	38	Geographical location	19	Career advancement and growth	38
Strong performance	29	Respect for lifestyle	14	Fit with boss I admire	29
Industry leader	21	Acceptable pace	1		
Many talented people	20				
Good at development	17				
Inspiring mission	16				
Fun with colleagues	11				
Job security	8				

TEN GOLDEN RULES
Although every transformation is different, from our experience we have abstracted ten basic principles that you should observe in transforming performance.

1 **Confront the facts continuously.** Make sure you understand the reasons for your current situation, however good or bad. Take time and be open-minded in

analyzing the organization's current performance. Remember the world doesn't stop to wait for your transformation.

2 **Build a coherent and compelling transformation story.** Staff, customers, analysts, and investors need to see for themselves why the organization needs to change, where it is going, and how you plan to get there. Successful transformations are built on compelling stories that confront the existing facts, bring alive the point of inflection, threat, or opportunity that the company faces, and chart a clear course toward a new reality.

3 **Use the collective wisdom of the organization.** Transformation is far more effective when people discover a new reality for themselves and adopt new ways of working. No matter how convinced you are of the superiority of your business model, think carefully before imposing your views on the company—ultimately your transformation will take only if it taps into the organization's collective energies and insights. This isn't just a matter of buying in, it's one of genuine discovery.

4 **You can hold a few elements of your transformation sacrosanct, but be flexible about the rest.** As the organization changes its final form won't be clear. The process of revelation is a necessary part of change, and your design must be flexible enough to accommodate it; interim developments often reflect the changing reality of the business. But you need to be clear about the few elements that are nonnegotiable, and see that they're not compromised by any element of the transformation.

5 **Work through leaders at all levels.** Leadership is critical, but this is not just about your role as C.E.O. The transformation needs leaders throughout the organization, building commitment to the new possibilities that emerge and engaging people in the story of the change.

6 **Get the right balance between action and reflection.** Action and reflection are both vital elements of the transformation process. Without sufficient action the process will lose momentum and fail, but you also need reflection to furnish renewal, check that the change continues to respond to the reality of the situation, and make sure that lessons are learned. Overemphasis on one or the other leads to failure.

7 **Demonstrate early success.** It's not enough to talk about change—people need to experience it. Inertia can often be overcome by demonstrating early progress in microworlds that deliver visible improvements in operating and financial performance, increase customer satisfaction, and spark enjoyment and motivation in employees participating in them.

8 **Make the change process unique.** Your organization is unique, your people are unique, and your transformation is unique. This means that you must follow a tailored, dynamic change process that meets your needs and responds to events as they unfold. You need to design the change process so that it works for your situation, leveraging the leaders available and the balance of action and reflection to allow you to learn and develop on the journey.

9 **Expect resistance—listen constantly, but be clear about the boundaries.** It's clear from this memo that transformation is not easy. People, probably including some members of the leadership team, will almost certainly undermine the process, either through active opposition or through passive but visible lack of support. Many transformations fail because top management refuses to listen to these people. Nonetheless, it's up to you to limit the space in which people explore and the degree of resistance that's acceptable. Ultimately people who refuse to join the process must be moved aside.

10 **Measure progress at every stage.** To be effective in your role as leader of the change, you need access to real information about how things are going. Constantly and rigorously measure progress against specific milestones, changes in organizational energy and alignment, operational performance, and financial performance. Make all of these results widely visible in the organization.

These principles are based on observation of organizational changes; they encapsulate lessons learned from the successes and failures of others. For the whole of the last century we were collectively stuck in the paradigm that insisted the role of leadership is to drive hard for performance and brush aside resistance. The time has come to abandon this limiting model. Our research on motivation and performance is conclusive: the best people are turned on by a strong performance ethic and an open, trusting, and supportive culture. A performance orientation and a people orientation are not opposites. They aren't even choices. Instead they're the two components that will enable us to achieve outstanding and sustainable results.

Colin Price is a partner of McKinsey & Company and the coauthor of several books including the bestseller *Straight from the C.E.O.* (reissue; Nicholas Brealey, 1998) and *Wisdom of the C.E.O.* (Simon & Schuster, 2000). Price was formerly global head of the Strategic Change consulting practice at PricewaterhouseCoopers and is a regular speaker at international conferences.

Downsizing with Dignity

Alan Downs

Make no mistake: downsizing is extremely difficult. It taxes all of a management team's resources, including both business acumen and humanity. No one looks forward to downsizing.

Perhaps this is why so many otherwise first-rate executives downsize so poorly. They ignore all the signs pointing to a layoff until it's too late to plan adequately; then action must be taken immediately to reduce the financial drain of excess staff. The extremely difficult decisions of who must be laid off, how much notice they will be given, the amount of severance pay, and how far the company will go to help the laid-off employee find another job are given less than adequate attention. These are critical decisions that have as much to do with the future of the organization as they do with the future of the laid-off employees, so they must be considered carefully.

So what happens? These decisions are handed to the legal department, whose primary objective is to reduce the risk of litigation, not to protect the morale and intellectual capital of the organization. Consequently downsizing is often executed with a brisk, compassionless efficiency that leaves laid-off employees angry and surviving employees feeling helpless, demotivated, and poorly prepared to start rebuilding the business.

Helplessness is the enemy of high achievement. It produces a work environment of withdrawal, risk-averse decisions, severely impaired morale, and excessive blaming. All of these put a stranglehold upon an organization that now desperately needs to excel. In this situation, downsizing becomes a contributor to an organization's downfall rather than a catalyst for growth and profitability.

AVOIDING THE PITFALLS OF DOWNSIZING

Ineffective methods of downsizing abound. Downsizing malpractices such as those that follow are common; they are also inefficient and very dangerous.

Allowing Legal Concerns to Design the Layoff. Most corporate attorneys will advise laying off employees on a last-hired, first-fired basis across all departments. The method for downsizing that is most clearly defensible in a court of law, for example, is to lay off 10% of employees across all departments on a seniority-only basis. This way no employee can claim that he or she was dismissed for discriminatory reasons. Furthermore, attorneys advise against saying anything more than what's absolutely necessary to either the departing employees or the survivors. This caution is designed to protect the company from making any implied or explicit promises that aren't then kept. By strictly scripting what is said about the layoffs, the company is protecting itself from verbal slips by managers who are themselves stressed at having to release valued employees.

This approach may succeed from a legal perspective, but not necessarily from the larger and more important concern of organizational health. First, laying off employees by a flat percentage across different departments is irrational. How can it be that accounting can do with the same proportion fewer employees as human resources? Could it be that one department can be externalized and the other left intact? The decision of how many employees to lay off from each department should be based on an analysis of business needs, not an arbitrary statistic.

The concept of laying off employees strictly on the basis of seniority is also irrational. The choice of employees for a layoff should be based on a redistribution of the work, not the date the individual employee was hired. Sometimes an employee of 18 months has a skill far more valuable than one with 18 years' seniority.

Giving As Little Notice As Possible. Out of fear and guilt many executives choose to give employees as little forewarning as possible about an upcoming layoff. Managers fear that if employees know their fate ahead of time, they might become demoralized and unproductive—they may even sabotage the business. However, there is no documented evidence that advance notice of a layoff increases the incidence of employee sabotage.

The lack of advance notice, however, does dramatically increase mistrust of management among surviving workers. Trust is based on mutual respect. When employees discover what has been brewing without their knowledge or input (and they will when the first person is let go), they see a blatant disrespect for their integrity, destroying trust. By not giving employees information that could be enormously helpful to them in planning their own lives, management initiates a cycle of mistrust and helplessness that can be very destructive and require years to correct.

Afterward, Acting As If Nothing Happened. Many managers believe that after a layoff, the less said about it the better. With luck, everyone will just forget and move on. Why keep the past alive? The reality is that surviving employees will talk about what's happened whether the management team does or doesn't. The more the company tries to suppress these discussions and act as if nothing has happened, the more subversive the discussion becomes. Remaining employees will act as a consequence of what has happened regardless of whether the management does.

Recovery from a layoff is greatly hastened if managers and employees are allowed to speak their minds freely about what's happened. In fact, it can be a great opportunity for the team of surviving employees to pull together and renew ties. When management refuses to acknowledge what has really taken place, it appears emphatically heartless, feeding the employees' sense of helplessness. If management won't talk about it even after the fact, what else is it hiding?

DOWNSIZING EFFECTIVELY

When faced with an organization that isn't functioning at optimal efficiency and thinking that a layoff is needed, there are a few key principles to keep in mind. Observing these principles won't completely eliminate the dangers of downsizing, but they will help to avoid the common pitfalls of a poorly planned layoff.

Is the problem too many people or too little profit? The critical first question to ask before any layoff is: Is the need for this layoff driven by having too many employees or too little profit? If it's too little profit, this is the first warning sign that your company isn't ready for a layoff. Using a layoff solely as a cost-cutting measure is utterly foolish: throwing away valuable talent and organizational learning by dumping employees only makes a bad situation worse. When your business lacks revenue, annihilating intellectual capital and thus reducing the efficiency of remaining resources as well as the potential for future growth is not the solution.

If the answer is too many employees, then you've begun the process of a well-thought-out strategy for change. To legitimately determine if you have too many employees, look at the organization's business plan, not its head count. What product and services will you be offering? Which of these products and services is likely to be profitable? What talent will you need to run the new organization? These questions will help you plan for the post-layoff future. These issues will enable a quick turn-around from the inevitably negative effects of downsizing to positive growth in value and efficiency.

What will the post-layoff company look like? Having a clear, well-defined vision of the new company is imperative *before the layoff is executed*. Management should know what it wants to accomplish, where the emphasis will be in the new organization, and what staff will be needed.

Without being directed according to a clear vision of the future, the new organization is likely to carry forward some of the same problems that initially created the need for the layoff. Unfortunately, many managers underestimate the momentum of the old organization to recreate the same problems anew. Unless there is a clearly defined, shared vision of the new company among the entire management team, the past will be likely to sabotage the future and create a cycle of repeated layoffs with little improvement in organizational efficiency.

Always respect people's dignity. The methods employed in many poorly executed layoffs treat employees like children. Information is withheld and doled out. Managers' control over their employees is violated. Human resource representatives scurry around from one hush-hush meeting to another. How management treats laid-off employees is how it vicariously treats remaining employees—everything you do in a layoff is done in the arena, with everyone observing. How laid-off employees are treated is how surviving employees assume they may be treated.

Why does this matter? Because successfully planning for the new organization will keep it going and improve its results. You must keep exceptional talent, who are also the employees most marketable to other organizations. When they see the company treating laid-off employees poorly, they'll start looking for a better place to work, fearing their heads will be next to roll.

Respect the law. While it's important not to allow the legal department to design a layoff, it's nevertheless important that you respect the employment laws. In different countries such laws include entitlements tied to civil rights, age discrimination, disabilities, worked adjustment, and retraining. These laws are important and should be respected for what they intend as well as what they prescribe—or proscribe. If you have planned your layoff according to business needs, and not on head count or seniority, you should have no problem upholding the law. You will almost always find yourself in legal trouble when you base your layoff on factors other than business needs.

MAKING IT HAPPEN

Downsizing successfully is immensely difficult. The following ideas can help to focus thinking for anyone considering such a move:

- Plan for the future, including a shared vision of the company post-layoff. Consider how best to motivate and reward employees after downsizing and how to retain the most talented and valuable employees.
- Treat all employees with dignity and respect. Communicate too much rather than withholding information.
- Research applicable laws and follow the spirit of the legislation.
- Afterward, give employees the psychological space to accept and discuss what has happened.
- Understand what the downsizing process must achieve—and what it must avoid.

There are two important factors to keep in mind when planning a layoff: respecting employee dignity, and business planning. No one, from the mailroom to the board-room, enjoys downsizing; but when the need for a reduction in staff is unavoidable, a layoff can be accomplished in such a way that the problem is fixed and the organization excels.

Alan Downs, Ph.D., is a management psychologist and consultant who specializes in strategic human resources planning and helping business executives reach their maximum potential. He has written several books, including *Corporate Executions* (AMACOM, 1995), the much-acclaimed exposé on downsizing, *The Seven Miracles of Management* (Prentice Hall, 1998), and *The Fearless Executive* (AMACOM, 2000). He has also written on management topics for numerous national newspapers and trade publications, including *Management Review* and *Across the Board*.

Becoming a Market-driven Organization

George S. Day

Today we experience a much higher level of uncertainty than ever before on three fundamental levels—technology, markets and market response, and competition. How do we absorb and process this uncertainty? The question for organizations in general—regardless of what they produce—is, how can they align themselves better with their markets so they can deal with this uncertainty instead of getting trapped into rigid organizations that are not responsive?

The first thing companies need to understand is that there is a fundamental distinction between: (a) make-and-sell organizations (they look at their markets, make a forecast, build their product, and hope to hell they can sell it), and (b) sense-and-respond organizations (those that are very close to their market, sense changes and requirements among their customers, deal with them in real time, and then respond with superior value—literally a build-to-order model).

Beyond this distinction is another, more subtle, distinction—between a *market-driven strategy* and a *market-driven organization*. They are highly complementary, but not identical. Take strategy: you have some very distinct choices about how to position yourself in the market. One of those choices is whether you're going to be principally a make-and-sell operation (build as much as possible at lowest cost) *or* a sense-and-respond organization. That is a very profound strategic choice. But there are other choices:

- Do you want to compete just on superior technology and performance?
- Do you want to compete on the basis of being the best at building total solutions for companies?

For example, consider GE Aircraft Engines' strategy of "power by the hour." The company is no longer in the engine business; it takes over the provision of "deliverable thrust" to airlines. GE manufactures *and* maintains the engines; it leases them to the airlines and runs the maintenance facility. What it guarantees to its customers is that it is going to deliver a contracted amount of power at the gate. This is an example of a company offering total solutions, not just a superior product.

SETTING STRATEGIC CHOICES

Where does the market-driven organization come into this? It informs the choices and helps a firm anticipate market opportunities earlier than the competition does. Being a market-driven organization helps you make better choices because you are better aligned with your market (and you can more clearly see the impact of these choices)—and it helps you get to market faster. Designing the market-driven organization requires superior skills in understanding, attracting, and keeping valuable customers.

Since uncertainty drives strategic choices, how does the market-driven organization help you make and implement better choices? Often people say, "Well, we're really a tech company. We win by giving companies the best performance; that's our strategy." I argue in those cases that you'll implement that strategy better if you're market orientated—that is, you engage in how your customers make choices and tradeoffs, and you have much better insight into how you can deliver superior value to them. It's not about being a tech company, or even delivering the best performance; it's about sensing your customers' needs so you can provide superior value to them.

The market-driven organization is simply better at executing a market-driven strategy.

COMMUNICATING COMMITMENT

How do we improve our market orientation? This comes down to questions of accountability and prioritizing decisions. Companies that want to become more market driven—and do it successfully—really demonstrate consistent leadership commitment. Everybody in the organization has to understand *why* you're doing it. Let's say your company is headed in a sense-and-respond direction. Does everybody from the executive suite to the call center to the shop floor understand why this is going to deliver more customer value? You want everyone who is affected by this decision to buy into it.

How does this commitment get communicated successfully? How does everybody come to understand, appreciate, and become enthusiastic about it? Certainly with the top management team, the process includes getting them out talking and living with customers, doing competitive role playing. All sorts of research can help support the decision, but experience will have the most profound impact. One technique that seems to be most powerfully persuasive is what I call "hothouse experiments"—you take a part of the organization and really do everything right. You build a structure that is highly accountable (such as organizing around markets or customers) and then do a fast-paced experiment that serves as a model. A good example is Tesco, the chain of grocery stores in the United Kingdom. Tesco consistently outperforms everyone else. It will give five stores to a team of managers, who are told, "You have carte blanche to do what you think best; we'll give you support." They may radically transform these stores; then they'll run them for six months, often seeing 15–20% improvements in profitability and efficiency. Then managers and employees from the other 550 stores come around and have a look. This is the power of persuasiveness from an effective demonstration.

So you've got commitment, you've persuaded the staff, you've demonstrated success, and people now have a vision of how superior value will be created. The last piece of making this transformation is to get alignment of capabilities and configuration (incentives, organizational structure, and systems). That's when we start thinking about organizing around customer groups or segments. Who is accountable for solving problems and satisfying the requirements of customers with very distinct needs?

To address this issue, you need to recognize that there is a difference between *loyal* customers and *profitable* customers. You want to avoid those who are loyal on the surface (though it's hard to quantify); you have a better chance of figuring out whether they are profitable. Many companies emphasize reducing the customer turnover rate, the rate of defections. However, this can be a faulty strategy; you *want* unprofitable customers to defect. Here's an example: the wireless phone industry. Businesses experience defection rates of 35–40% a year, so just to keep their revenue base more or less constant in a period of declining prices, they need to find 35% new customers annually. In fact, it's much cheaper to keep existing customers than it is to wrestle them away from competitors. Here's an industry that has a lot of bad habits, such as price promotions designed to lure customers who only defect the following year. The only way to get out of this cycle is to offer a better *value proposition*. This means you need to understand your customers well, and you can't do that by being all things to all people. The U.K. wireless industry is a case in point. You cannot win in that market by trying to appeal to every segment simultaneously, as British Telecom is trying to do. The winners are those who are sharply positioned to the segment(s) they best understand; they stick with their target market and give it everything they've got.

BEYOND CUSTOMER FOCUS

How do you orientate people to see things clearly? You can't beat living with your customers! If you look at Hewlett-Packard, you'll notice it has made a centerpiece of its market-driven strategy—it requires all its new product development teams to visit customers as teams, not one-person filtering. They live out there. They visit plants, spending days or weeks. They try to understand how their customers use their instruments and systems. For every hour with a customer, it takes them an hour to figure out what they've heard. There will be marketing, manufacturing, R&D, and finance people on the team—and they all hear different things. This is part of the process, to help people develop shared mindsets. They become the experts on the customer, and, more accurately, experts on the market.

My key argument is this: being market-driven is much more than being customer-focused. Customer focus is a crucial element, but being market-driven also requires that you be expert and have insight into your competitors and your channel members. You can be very good at understanding the market without being on a par with competitors; think about how disastrous copycat strategies can be in driving down prices or eroding customer respect. You then have to look for ways to get an edge in a competitive environment. You have to embed customer focus as a dimension or facet of being market-driven, while getting close to your customers and staying ahead of your competitors. Remember that channel members (suppliers and distributors) are potential competitors and potential collaborators.

Of course, any company risks paralysis in the face of all of this uncertainty. One of the ways to survive is to say: let's create an organization with strong central values that is at the same time very, very flexible. To what degree will values manifest themselves in strong processes and systems?

You can't change cultures directly. The way to do it is to immerse the organization in understanding its customers, and then you make changes in processes, structures, and incentives that reflect and reinforce this orientation (I say "orientation" to capture the broader sense of culture—mindset, beliefs, values). Trying to change the culture head on is not going to work. You have to create conditions where people see that it is in their interest to change. The culture will change in order to make sense out of a successful experiment. People see something successful, and if it challenges their assumptions or expectations, they will adapt to make sense of the success; this, in turn, will help to change underlying values.

It's still not very easy! Because one definition of culture is "this is the way we do things here," how do you get a large organization with multiple units and multiple geographies to accept deep-level change? Again, I point to the power of example: studies of best practice in large organizations have demonstrated that the difference between best and worst can be a on a scale of 4:1.

Becoming a market-driven organization may require profound changes in your organization's leadership, culture, processes, and systems, but it is ultimately more likely to produce best rather than worst practices.

———

George S. Day is the Geoffrey T. Boisi Professor of Marketing at the Wharton School, University of Pennsylvania, where he also serves as codirector of the Mack Center for Technological Innovation and director of the Emerging Technologies Management Research Program. The recipient of numerous research and teaching awards and a member of the editorial boards of several distinguished publications—including the *Journal of Marketing, Strategic Management Journal, Strategy and Leadership*, and the *Journal of Product Innovation and Management*—Day consults to a wide variety of business, government, and research organizations on issues of marketing management, strategic planning, and competitive strategies. He is the author or coauthor of dozens of articles and several books, the most recent being *Wharton on Managing Emerging Technologies* (ed., with Paul J. H. Schoemaker, John Wiley, 2000).

Marketing: The Importance of Being First

Al Ries and Laura Ries

Who has the best rent-a-car service? The best cola? The best ketchup? If you are thinking Hertz, Coca-Cola, and Heinz, you agree with most customers who make these three companies the leaders in their fields. In fact, there is a strong axiom, or belief, in the minds of consumers that "the best product or service wins in the marketplace." After all, this is so logical and so obvious, who could disagree?

We could.

There's a paradox in marketing. While everyone believes that the better product will win in the marketplace, the worst possible strategy for any company is to try to produce a "better product." Why? Because the leader in your field already has the perception of producing the better product. If you try to claim that your product is better, the prospect thinks, "No, it can't be better, otherwise *they* would be the leader." Yet what do most companies try to do? They try to: (a) produce a better product, and (b) communicate that difference to customers and prospects. It's easy to do (a) but it's almost impossible to do (b). Is Royal Crown Cola better tasting than Coca-Cola? Royal Crown thinks so, and their research shows that prospects prefer the taste of Royal Crown to Coca-Cola Classic by 57% to 43%. That's a pretty big difference. Yet Royal Crown Cola has only 2% of the market. What they need to do, you might be thinking, is to communicate that difference. Well, they've tried, and it doesn't work; prospects too easily conclude: "If Royal Crown was the better tasting cola, *they* would be the leader, not Coke. There must be something wrong with the research."

WHAT'S IMPORTANT: WHO'S FIRST?

It's our experience that 90+% of all marketing programs are based on communicating the essence of the better product or service. Unless you are already the leader, these programs are bound to fail because the prospect assumes that the leader must have the better product or service. But how did the leader achieve its leadership? Not by introducing a better product or service; invariably the leader in the category got to be the leader by being the first brand in the category. Companies such as Coca-Cola, CNN, Dell, Hoover, Pizza Hut, Rolex, and Xerox are all globally recognized as leaders in their respective fields. Some consultants have called this leadership phenomenon, "the first mover advantage," but that is not so. It's an advantage, but it's not the reason that most leader brands are first in their categories. It's the "first minder" advantage. That is, the brand that gets into the mind first is the winner, not the brand that is the first in the category. For examples: Duryea was the first automobile on the road, but never got into the mind. Ford was the first automobile in the mind. MITS Altair 8800 was the first personal computer, but never got into the mind. Apple was the first personal computer to get into the mind. Du Mont made the first television set. Hurley, the first washing machine. But these and many other brands failed to get into the minds of their prospects. You don't win in the marketplace. You win in the mind.

EXAMPLES ABOUND

If you weren't first in your category and you can't win by being better, what can you do?

The answer is obvious: start a new category you can be first in. Marketing is more a battle of categories than it is a battle of products. Winning companies think category first and product second. They try to categorize what they do, not in terms of being better, but in terms of being different.

When Procter & Gamble introduced Tide many years ago, they could have called the product a "new, improved soap." Tide was a soap then, and Tide is a soap today, in the sense that soap is a "cleansing agent." But Tide was made from synthetic materials rather than the fats and lye found in traditional cleaning products like Ivory, Oxydol, and Rinso. Tide could have been called a synthetic soap, but that would have nailed the brand to the soap category. So Procter & Gamble called Tide the "first detergent," a totally new category and even today Tide is the leading brand of detergent.

When Charles Schwab set up Charles Schwab & Co., he could have focused on providing better service to stock buyers. But he didn't. Instead he decided to launch the first discount stock brokerage company, and today Charles Schwab & Co. is one of the leading stock brokerage firms in the country.

When Michael Dell set up Dell Computer Corporation, he could have sold his "better" products through conventional computer stores, but he didn't. Instead he launched the first brand of personal computer sold direct by phone. Today Dell Computer Corporation is the world's largest seller of personal computers and still doesn't sell any computers through conventional computer stores.

HOW TO START?

Before you launch (or relaunch) a new product or service, ask yourself the following questions:

1. What is the name of the category? Not a name that you might like, but a name the industry gives the category.
2. What is the brand name of the leader in the category? Not necessarily the sales leader, but the brand that customers perceive to be the leader.
3. If there is no dominant brand, or at least not a dominant brand in the mind of most prospects, jump right in with your product or service and try to quickly establish your leadership. Cut prices, cut deals, hire sales people, launch massive publicity campaigns, do everything you can to seize the leadership position before someone else does.
4. Promote your brand as the leading brand. "It's so easy to use," says AOL, "no wonder it's number one." Leave no piece of paper or Web site or TV advertisement or radio commercial without mentioning your leadership. Leadership is the most important aspect of any marketing program. Why? Prospects assume the better product or service will win in the marketplace. Therefore, if you are the leader, you must have the better product.
5. If there is a dominant brand, then move on and set up a new category you can be first in. But make sure you have a new name to match the new category. You can get into serious trouble if you try to use an existing name.

6 You can't dictate the category name. Only the industry and the media can do that. Therefore you have to launch your new brand with publicity and get the media to establish the category name for you.

MAKING IT HAPPEN

There's almost always a way to set up a new category. Unfortunately, most companies refuse to even consider the possibility of a new category because "there's no market." Of course, there's no market. If there were, it wouldn't be a new category. This presumed "logic" is the most difficult thing to overcome. You have to have faith that you can succeed in getting acceptance for a new category. What was the market for personal computers sold by phone before Michael Dell launched Dell Computer Corporation? Zero. What was the market for sports drinks before Gatorade was launched? Zero. What was the market for discount brokerage firms before Charles Schwab was launched? Zero.

Furthermore, a new category doesn't necessarily represent a big, technological advance. Soapsoft, the first liquid soap, was a big commercial success. How difficult is it to take a tub of soap and liquefy it? How difficult is it to take regular beer and add water? Miller Lite, the first light beer, was a big success, but ultimately paid a big penalty for its success. Instead of creating a new brand to match the new category, they used a line extension name which just about killed their regular beer brand (Miller High Life) and caused them to lose their light beer leadership to the competition. A new category needs a new name.

The IBM PC was the first 16-bit, serious, office personal computer, but the line extension name caused IBM to ultimately lose their personal computer leadership to first Compaq and then Dell Computer Corporation. VisiCalc was the first spreadsheet for personal computers when all personal computers used 8-bit operating systems. Lotus 1–2–3 was the first spreadsheet for 16-bit, IBM-type personal computers, but lost its leadership to Excel, which was the first spreadsheet to use Microsoft Windows.

Listerine was the first mouthwash, but it was a bad-tasting mouthwash, hence the slogan, "the taste you hate, twice a day." Except for Procter & Gamble, all competitors in the category thought that mouthwash had to taste bad. P&G introduced Scope, the first good-tasting mouthwash, which is neck and neck (or mouth and mouth) with Listerine for leadership in the category.

Marketing is not a battle of products. Marketing is a battle of perceptions. And to win the battle of perceptions you have to become the leader in a category. Prospects assume the leader must be better because "everybody knows the better product or service will win in the marketplace." How do you become the leader? You launch a new category you can be first in. It doesn't have to be a big technological advance. Sometimes the simple ideas are the easiest to get into the mind. And where do you win the battle? You win the battle inside the mind of the prospect.

Al Ries and Laura Ries are a father and daughter team. Al Ries is chairman and Laura Ries is president of Ries & Ries, a marketing strategy firm located in Roswell, Georgia, which they founded in 1994. The company now has affiliates around the world (www.ries.com). Their books include *The 22 Immutable Laws of Branding* (Harper-Collins, 1998) and *The 11 Immutable Laws of Internet Branding* (HarperCollins, 2000).

Creating Powerful Brands

Paul Stobart

Put simply, a brand is the difference between a bottle of sugared, flavored, carbonated water and a bottle of Coca-Cola. It is the sum of the functional and emotional characteristics, both tangible and intangible, that a consumer attributes to a product or service. These characteristics are embodied in a name, trademark, symbol, or design, or any combination of these.

However, this definition is being increasingly stretched. As the Internet grows ever more pervasive, many online brands have virtually no tangible attributes. It could be argued that brands such as Amazon and Yahoo! exist purely in virtual reality. Moreover, the concept of branding can no longer be restricted to products and services. Movie stars, politicians, and company executives are all realizing that success is dependent on their ability to market themselves as brands.

WHY ARE BRANDS IMPORTANT?

For most companies brands are their primary source of competitive advantage and their most valuable strategic asset. Without brands we'd live in a world of commodities—undifferentiated products that are traded solely on price, according to the laws of supply and demand. Branding enables companies to actively influence the demand side of the equation by encouraging consumers to base their purchase decisions on factors other than price.

Brands are also important for consumers. They enable consumers to make informed purchase decisions and help them to navigate their way through the bewildering number of alternatives that exist in any product category. It can also be argued that brands enrich our lives. In a world in which our basic needs have been satisfied, brands give us something to which we can aspire and help in defining our own identities. This, however, is a question of ideology, and many would disagree.

SOURCES OF DIFFERENTIATION

Differentiation is the most important concept in the creation of powerful brands. Essentially brands can be differentiated in terms of product and/or service, leading to four generic brand types.

1 Where an offering is differentiated neither in terms of product nor service, it is a *commodity*. Precious metals and staple food products are still largely traded as commodities (though the increasing demand for organic produce is changing this).

2 Where an offering is differentiated in product, but not in service terms, it is a *product brand*. Product brands can be further differentiated in terms of intrinsic (or functional) benefits and extrinsic (or emotional) benefits. In practice most consumer goods are product brands, and most contain elements of both intrinsic and extrinsic differentiation. Hi-fi manufacturers focus primarily on the

functionality of their products, while most mainstream soft-drink brands are differentiated largely in terms of image. The marketing of automobiles, one of the most potent symbols of status and way of life, plays on both function and emotion.

3 An offering based on providing an intangible service is a *service brand*. Financial services are classic examples. Creating service brands can prove difficult because, unlike packaged goods, delivering a service to the consumer relies heavily on humans, and humans are notoriously less reliable than machines.

4 An offering differentiated in both product and service terms is a *system brand*. The McDonald's experience is based on a combination of the quality of the food, the speed of the service, and the cleanliness of the restaurant.

THE BUILDING BLOCKS OF BRAND CREATION

The *brand proposition* is the statement of the functional and emotional benefits that a company believes its product or service offers to the consumer. Coca-Cola's brand proposition is a mixture of functional benefits (taste, refreshment) and emotional benefits (good wholesome fun).

Brand positioning is a description of those at whom the brand is aimed (the target audience) and where it stands relative to the competition.

Brand identity (or *brand image*) is the aggregation of the words, images, and ideas that the consumer associates with a brand. There is an increasing tendency to person-ify brands, and companies talk about brand personality and brand attitude. This is particularly important in youth markets, in which consumers regard brands as state-ments of their beliefs and preferences.

THE BRAND-BUILDER'S TOOLBOX

Successful brand creation starts with product design. But it's not just about how the product performs, it's also about how it looks. When Dyson turned the vacuum cleaner market upside down, it was due not only to the revolutionary technology, but also to the fact that its products looked like nothing else on earth!

In the fast-moving consumer-goods sector, packaging is also a key source of dif-ferentiation, both as a powerful tool for creating brand identity and as a means whereby brands can stand out from the crowd on increasingly cluttered supermarket shelves.

Advertising is perhaps the brand manager's most potent tool. Print and broadcast media not only represent a cost-effective mechanism for reaching mass audiences, they also have the power to influence consumer behavior. The press is a particularly effective medium for communicating complex messages, while TV advertising, with its beguiling interplay of sounds and pictures, is ideal for building brand image.

In recent years, however, the brand manager's task has become increasingly complex. Brands have proliferated, media have fragmented, and consumers have become more cynical. Brand owners have had to become more innovative, constantly reinvent-ing their brands to keep one step ahead of their competitors and their consumers.

Technology has facilitated increasingly sophisticated consumer segmentation techniques, and many brand owners are moving from a *one-to-many* to a *one-to-one* marketing model.

MEASURING BRAND EQUITY

If brands are a company's most valuable strategic asset, it makes sense to take good care of them. While it is difficult to prove a statistical relationship between advertising and sales because of the sheer number of variables involved, it is possible to prove a relationship between advertising and awareness and between awareness and sales. For this reason most companies track brand awareness levels, together with other measures such as brand loyalty and purchase intention.

It is also important to track brand image, to make sure that the differentiating elements of brand identity a company is attempting to communicate are being received accurately by the consumer. One reason for doing this is to gauge to what extent brand equity can be leveraged into line extensions or new products. Virgin is the classic example of this, with the brand now spanning airlines, trains, soft drinks, and financial services.

In recent years many brand owners have attempted to assign an economic value to their brands on the balance sheet. The brand consultancy Interbrand has been at the forefront of this process, though the accounting profession has yet to fully embrace the concept.

BRANDS IN THE NEW ECONOMY

It took radio 38 years to reach an audience of 50 million, while TV took 13 years. At current growth rates the Internet will reach the same audience in less than five years. The Internet is the brand manager's dream: it's instantaneous; it enables one-to-one communication; it's interactive, and it's multimedia, integrating text, sound, and images.

Yet many companies are realizing that creating brands at Internet speed is not as easy as it sounds. Many dot-com startups have been able to create new businesses virtually overnight, unencumbered by the baggage of the old economy, but consumers have been less willing to buy into these new brands. The most successful online brands are arguably those that are rooted in the old economy but have harnessed the Internet to extend their brand franchise.

MAKING IT HAPPEN

Brand building in the Internet age still depends on fundamental principles:
- Seek above all to differentiate the product and/or service elements of your offerings from those of your competitors.
- Build the brand proposition from the functional and emotional benefits you believe your product or service offers to customers.
- Use sophisticated consumer segmentation techniques to move from a one-to-many to a one-to-one marketing model.
- Track brand image to make sure that the differentiating elements of brand identity are being received accurately by the consumer.

- Harness the Internet to extend the customer franchise of your most successful offline brands.
- Work on every aspect of the organization, from employee behavior to premises, so as to reflect and reinforce brand values.

While brands are undoubtedly here to stay, there is growing evidence of a consumer backlash. Ironically it's the Internet that's encouraging consumers, sick of being marketed to by faceless corporations, to demand a dialog with brand owners.

Moreover, disgruntled consumers are using the Internet to undermine the brand equity that has been expensively created by these same faceless corporations. These voices of dissent range from the humorous (www.ihatemanunited.com) to the more sinister (www.aolwatch.org).

Paul Stobart, a qualified chartered accountant, spent seven years with a London-based merchant bank before moving to Interbrand, an international branding and marketing services consulting firm. During eight years at Interbrand he held a number of positions, most recently as chairman of European operations. He is now chief operating officer of Sage, overseeing the continuing development of the Sage brand as a powerful marketing tool. He is the editor of *Brand Power* (New York University Press, 1994), a book examining the branding strategies of leading international brand owners.

Transforming Business by Making It an Experience

B. Joseph Pine II

Joe Pine has the unique distinction of having written two books that will be seen as seminal in the 21st century. In *Mass Customization*, he outlined how companies can efficiently provide individually customized goods and services. And, with coauthor James Gilmore, Joe advanced the idea in *The Experience Economy* that goods and services are no longer enough—they're becoming basic commodities. Here, Joe tells not only what these books mean to management, but how they essentially interconnect and project what it will mean to lead in the businesses of tomorrow.

As big a shift as is happening in business today, in 50 years the business world will undergo an even more dramatic shift.

If you think about it, it was almost exactly 50 years ago that the economy shifted from an industrial base to a service base. It was the mass production of goods that made America the number one economic power in the world, but beginning around 1950, more people began to earn their incomes from delivering intangible services than from making physical goods or extracting natural commodities. It took, however, almost 30 years for the trend to be fully recognized, at which time many pundits and professors decried the very notion that an economy could be built on anything other than the hard and tangible. Remember all the complaints about manufacturing jobs going away, about production moving offshore, about the very hollowing of America? We don't hear those particular protests any longer, even though the goods and commodities sectors combined have shrunk to less than 20% of employment and GDP. Indeed, it was the very loss of manufacturing jobs that opened the door to all the entrepreneurial talent which has made today's business world such a dynamic place through service innovations.

One of the effects of the burgeoning service economy was that goods became commoditized. Customers—whether consumers or businesses—simply valued the service more than the good. Today, we see the same thing happening to services; they're also being commoditized, where customers care more about price than any other factor.

So now we are in the midst of another economic shift, to an experience economy. The predominant economic activity is rapidly becoming staging experiences— memorable events that engage each customer in an inherently personal way. The prototypical experience is, of course, going to Walt Disney World. Sure, one buys food and parking services and goods as memorabilia; but the reason one goes is for that shared family experience that lasts for months and even years afterward. Hard Rock Cafés serve food against the backdrop of staging memorable musical moments. And Recreation Equipment Incorporated (REI) places 65-foot climbing mountains and other experiences in its stores to get consumers to experience the goods before they buy them. Those businesses—whatever their product or service line—that miss the shift to experiences will be marginalized.

But now let's look 50 years into the future. Then, experiences will also become commoditized, and businesses will need to shift again to sell a fifth and final economic offering: transformations. The transformation economy will be one in which companies help customers change via life-transforming experiences—where the customer is the product. It may sound like something out of H. G. Wells, but think more of Michael Douglas's film, *The Game*, in which the main character willingly plays a game that takes him way out of his comfort zone, challenges him as a human being, and transforms him at the end. Many companies are already naturally in the transformation business, including fitness centers, hospitals, schools, and consultants. But today each of these charge for the mere service or experience, not for the transformation. In the future, they'll be paid based on the demonstrated outcome their customers achieve—and there is no more economic value to be gained than by helping someone achieve their aspirations.

So what's happening in the business world means that managers need a completely new skill set in order to prosper in the emerging experience economy and forthcoming transformation economy. They'll need a new skill set even to participate.

First, in terms of the experience economy, managers must realize that work is theater. I'm not using a metaphor here. Whenever workers are in front of guests, they are acting, and need to act in a way that turns the interaction into a memorable event. Managers, therefore, must help their workers take on a role, characterize that role, rehearse it, and then perform it on the bare stage of business.

Then, in terms of the transformation economy, the key skills are caring and empathy. We used to talk about understanding a customer's problems and then providing solutions. This is much more. Managers must care for individuals enough truly to understand their aspirations, and to help them achieve those aspirations. It was, I believe, a Woody Allen character who said "Sincerity—if you can fake that, you've got it made." Well, what I'm suggesting is no joke—you won't be able to fake empathy. The new economic landscape demands authenticity. Why? Educated, demanding customers simply will not deal with businesses that are little more than smoke and mirrors.

In this regard, my close friend and business partner, Jim Gilmore coined the term "world-view segmentation" to describe what's starting to happen in the business world. Jim's point is a good one: customers increasingly will not buy from, nor support, a business that does not share their own world view. In the same way, people will not work for companies that are at odds with their world views. They'll do business with or work for only those enterprises that have the same set of values and make the same moral choices as they do. So everything that Jim and I talk about has both external and internal implications. Just as companies must stage experiences and guide transformations to forestall commoditization in their industries, they must stage authentic, life-transforming internal experiences to enable employees to achieve their work aspirations, and become better workers, in all the senses that word implies.

And just as companies must mass-customize their economic offerings to attract and keep customers, so must they mass-customize their compensation systems and development plans to attract and keep their workers.

Mass-customization is not at all ancillary to this discussion. My work there led to the discovery of experiences and transformations as distinct economic offerings. I recognized that mass-customizing a product automatically turned it into a service, and applying the same learning process, discovered that mass-customizing services turned them into experiences, and mass-customizing experiences turned them into transformations.

Therefore, I owe a great debt to Stan Davis, who first coined the term "mass-customizing" in his compelling and terrific 1987 book, *Future Perfect*. I first read it when I was a strategic planner at IBM in the late 1980s, and it changed my life. During the development of the AS/400 computer system, I managed a cross-functional team that brought customers and business partners into the development process. And I learned that every customer was unique. They wanted different characteristics for their systems, they wanted different software, they wanted to integrate the systems in different ways. We had designed the system for a large, homogenous marketplace that simply did not exist! So when I read Stan Davis's book, it suddenly all made sense. I worked to get his ideas into IBM's plans and strategies, and when the company sent me to the Massachusetts Institute of Technology (MIT) to get my master's degree, I spent that entire time investigating the subject further. I eventually turned my thesis into my first book, *Mass Customization*, for which I was proud that Stan consented to write the introduction.

As I think back to that time, what's amazing is how it all really connects. Building a physical good that's unique for each and every customer—as IBM learned to do with computers—is part and parcel of providing a special experience that connects in a unique way to each and every guest. As we move to the experience economy and, eventually, through it to the transformational economy, it's crucial to understand that experiences happen inside each person individually—and aspirations belong to each person in unique ways. Goods and services are becoming commodities today; there's nothing special about them. Leaders who want to make their businesses stand out will have to do more. They'll have to stage memorable experiences for their customers, and they'll have to help their customers become the people (and businesses) they've always wanted to be.

Delivering and Delighting—
A New Spirit at Work

Richard C. Whiteley

In speeches and company visits over many years, I have often been asked the same questions. Lower level managers, usually in a service function, ask; "How can I get senior management to believe in delighting customers as much as I believe in it?" With executives, the question flips: "How can I get our people to pay attention to our customers?"

These questions mirror the frustration of many organizations which are trying to reorient themselves around customers. Too often, neither leaders nor employees seem to be committed; worse, each side seems to be blaming the other. Managers must create four conditions to help employees feel a genuine passion for serving the customer; happily, there are three best practices that leaders can employ to create this most desired attitude.

CREATE CONDITIONS FOR CHANGE

The complexity, challenge, and time required for an organization to become truly customer-centric are usually underestimated. It is not just about introducing a new program, training customer contact people to smile over the phone, or conducting a few customer focus groups. Rather, it is about changing the culture of the organization, a challenge that may seem as difficult as, say, rewiring your own DNA. The most successful and dramatic transformation of an organization's culture I have witnessed took place in the 1980s and was led by Sir Colin Marshall at British Airways. When he arrived at the government-owned airline BOAC, it was losing money, abusing customers, and not doing well by its employees. Several years after Sir Colin privatized the company, it was commended for having the most improved service in the industry and for being the most profitable airline in the world. By any standard this remains one of the classic cultural turnarounds.

Study the BA success and others like it and patterns emerge of management actions that help create conditions that assist each and every employee to commit to the new direction and engage in the personal change that is required to bring the customer into the equation at all levels of the organization. These actions are to:

1 articulate and promote the new direction;
2 make sure that each employee knows what is expected;
3 see that each employee has the skills to do what is expected;
4 motivate each employee to do what is expected.

Looking at these four conditions, it is clear that they are deeply based in common sense. But you would be amazed at how difficult it is to implement them. Common sense, it has been said many times, is unfortunately not common at all.

Articulate and Promote the New Direction. A study by Bain & Company asked C.E.O.s to rate their level of confidence in their ability to perform various aspects of their job. Of those asked, 85% felt they handled strategy development well; strategy execution, conversely, dropped off dramatically to 40%. When asked about aligning their people with their company's strategy, the response was an anemic 10%. Articulating and promoting the new direction speaks directly to this deficit.

- **Create a clear vision and value statement to direct the organization.** This is not a new idea (and for many managers it may fall into the category of been there, done that); many organizations have vision and value statements that seem to have little influence on day-to-day operations and decisions. It helps to have a vision and values audit to test the extent to which adopted vision and values are truly guiding the company and having a positive impact.
- **Share the strategy of the organization with all employees.** Ironically, a company's strategy is often deemed so confidential that it is not shared with employees, the people who have to make it happen. Sam Walton knew better; his policy was to share each Wal-Mart store's vital performance information with all employees, even part-timers. He reasoned that they were directly responsible for Wal-Mart's success.
- **Actively promote the new direction.** When Sydney Electricity first won Australia's national quality award, I asked C.E.O. John Gillespie what his most difficult challenge was in achieving this honor. He responded that continually selling the vision, repeating it with enthusiasm over and over again at every meeting with one or more of his employees, was the hardest. It simply is not good enough to send an e-mail to all employees stating the new direction.

Make Sure Each Employee Knows What Is Expected. In a multiyear research program that studied 400 organizations, 80,000 managers, and over one million employees, the Gallup Organization found that one of the factors that correlated highly with an organization's success was employees knowing what is expected of them. Sounds obvious, but this is never truer than when a company is changing its strategy. Some key steps are required:

- **Use the chain of command to discuss and explain what is expected.** When Michael Abrashoff, the commanding officer of the U.S.S. Benfold, took command of the beleaguered, poorly performing destroyer, he first had to establish new standards of behavior. He met in small groups with his 300 officers and enlisted men and women to make sure that they understood the rationale for the changes he was implementing and what their personal impact would be. Under his command the ship went on to establish training, readiness, and retention records and won the coveted Spokane Trophy for operational readiness.
- **Use your hierarchy to communicate new expectations.** Have all managers meet with their people and explain the rationale for the change and what this means for them. The more a picture can be created of appropriate new behavior, the more it is likely to become part of each employee's daily routine.

- **Have employees create a line-of-sight map between them and your customers.** A simple yet powerful exercise: ask employees to start with their location in the organization and create a visual trail direct to customers. While most are not in direct contact with external customers, they all have internal customers within the organization. Employees soon realize that a glitch in the internal customer relationship inevitably leads to a problem for external customers.
- **Put the spotlight on early adopters.** In any organizational change there are fence sitters and early adopters. Fence sitters do little but sit around, complain about another *program du jour*, and adopt an attitude of "Change is good . . . you go first." In contrast the early adopters make a sincere (though sometimes awkward) effort at trying on the new behaviors to make the strategy work. Since peer success is a powerful influencer, purposely seek out these early adopters and publicly praise their efforts to change. Don't wait until all results are in; it's the effort to try things differently that you are actually rewarding. Results will follow.

See that Each Employee Has the Skills to Do What Is Expected.   Once people have an idea of what is expected, it is a mistake to assume that they actually have the necessary skills to accomplish the stated goals. Van Kampen Investments, a mutual fund company that consistently wins its industry's top award for customer service, believes that the key to this success is employee training. How to start?

- **Conduct internal best practices research.** Identify best performers in each job category and compare them with their marginally-performing counterparts. Identify what superior performers do distinctly. Once critical competences are identified, training exercises can be created to develop these skills in every employee.
- **Conduct a strategic training audit.** This simple process will pay great dividends. Create a matrix that lists the critical competencies required for each job in your company on the left vertical axis, and each of your training programs along the top horizontal axis. Then, on a scale of 1 to 5, simply rate each program's contribution to the development of each competency. This will help purge redundant programs and fill gaps in competency development.
- **Make your employees your best trainers.** Rather than assigning all development to your company trainers, make it part of employees' jobs to help. Pret A Manger is a highly successful chain of sandwich shops in the United Kingdom (and now the United States) with legendary service. Many frontline staff (half!) have been promoted to Team Manager Trainer, responsible for training new hires.

Motivate Each Employee to Do What Is Expected.   Now comes the hard part: getting people to actually use newly-developed skills. Assuming that the compensation and reward system is running smoothly, what are some of the other practices that can create an organization-wide passion for serving the customer?

- **Get everyone in the game.** In recent years much has been written about participative management. Why? Because it works. This means engaging in practices like asking employees to help create the vision and values, seeking their opinions on strategic issues, inviting them to innovate and create new processes, and authorizing them to solve problems now—without having to go through layers of approval. A survey of 551 large employers by Watson Wyatt found that people are more motivated when they believe they have an important place in the organization.
- **Introduce the face of the customer.** Of course, appropriate metrics based on customer behavior and feedback are also essential. While the *voice of the customer* continues to be a critical driver here, consider introducing *the face of the customer*. This means finding ways to personalize the metrics. For example, videotape focus groups and share the results with every employee. Medical products manufacturer Medtronics keeps employees focused on its real purpose by bringing doctors' patients and their families into the company to share their stories of survival. Such sessions are both inspiring and moving.
- **Make it fun.** With the seriousness and sometimes outright fear caused by downsizings, mergers, stock price collapses, increased working hours, and a near-maniacal focus on quarterly earnings, all too often the fun has been squeezed out of work. In 2000 the United States lost $1.5 billion in productivity to stress-related absenteeism. This is more than the total profitability of the *Fortune* 500. It is the unquestioned responsibility of leaders to help put the fun back in to work. In a survey of 1,000 peak performers, Louis Harris and Associates asked what kind of workplace they would be reluctant to leave. Their answer? One that promotes fun.

Changing an organization's culture is always a complex, even daunting, task. In order to become customer-centered the leaders of a corporation must first be willing to change themselves. It is their responsibility to create the four conditions cited above that will support each and every employee in understanding the new direction, knowing what is expected, and having the skills and motivation to do what is expected.

Richard C. Whiteley is a successful entrepreneur, writer, and professional speaker. He is the principal of The Whiteley Group and formerly cofounder of The Forum Corporation. He has written three best-selling, award-winning books: *The Customer Driven Company* (Perseus, 1991), *Customer-Centered Growth* (Perseus, 1996) and *Love the Work You're With* (Henry Holt, 2001). A new book, *The Corporate Shaman*, was published in 2002 by HarperCollins.

Marketing to the "Real-time" Consumer

Geoff Mott and Regis McKenna

Two important questions arise in relation to marketing and the Internet:

1   How does the Internet affect or change the marketing process?
2   How is marketing practiced on the Internet and what room is there for improvement?

According to Peter Drucker in *The Practice of Management*, only two things matter in the corporation: marketing and innovation. This challenging statement suggests that marketing has a key role to play in the enterprise. We would submit that because of the "real-time" connection to the customer and the enterprise value chain, the Internet increases the urgency and criticality of that role. Marketing should embrace activities ranging from managing the product specification process, often with internal and external groups, to operations and logistics, relationships management, and other key business processes that get little mention in the Internet marketing debate.

ENTER THE INTERNET

The Internet affects every facet of a firm's value-delivery system, providing critical feedback and insight about the company and its partners/channels: the efficiency and effectiveness of its product/service design and delivery; who the customers are, what they think, and what they value; and how the competition is performing. Companies become great because they build sustainable business infrastructures that are superior to their competitors, and leverage those infrastructures to deliver more value to each customer. The infrastructures that matter most are R&D, operations, logistics, distribution, and positioning. Marketing should be critically linked to, if not driving, this infrastructure, because it is visible to the customer and shapes the customer's perspective of the firm.

The Internet is, above all else, a unique vehicle for facilitating and enhancing the performance of this business infrastructure. It helps companies with strong and targeted value propositions develop much richer dialog with their customers and, as a result, improve innovations in products and services to make the consumer experience even richer and more relevant. An excellent example of this is Lego, which leveraged the Internet to develop and launch blockbuster products like Mindstorms.

CURRENT INTERNET MARKETING PRACTICES: A FOR EFFORT, F FOR RESULTS

The overall track record of marketing in leveraging the Internet has been dismal. Because it is a new landscape, a series of myths have grown up around the Internet as a marketing medium, myths that have proven expensive and frequently disastrous to many of the businesses that bought into them.

Myth 1: The Internet Is a Great Customer Acquisition Vehicle. On average the Internet costs three to ten times as much as acquiring customers through other retail channels, such as stores or catalogs. The problem is partly hit rate (very low indeed) and partly the initial cost of getting people to a new site. While the cost of acquiring real estate on a Web portal has declined substantially in the recent past, and while there is no doubt that the Internet can serve as a very effective marketing tool, customer acquisition is a very tough process this way.

Myth 2: The Internet Is a Great Messaging and Advertising Medium. A lot of advertising money is spent either to reinforce the presence of brands that have massive distribution advantages or to encourage greater recognition among existing customers. Some money is spent on building awareness for new products, but most of these are line extensions of existing products. Even so, most line extensions fail (upward of 75%), while more than 90% of truly new products fail.

Internet advertising is supposed to be more targeted since there are many more "channels" than in traditional media. Increasingly, online advertising is concentrated among the few big properties, especially Yahoo and AOL, that offer economies of scale and are likely to survive the current online advertising shake-out. As a result, online advertising is every bit as mass-market and "broadcast" as traditional e-media advertising, notwithstanding personalized home pages and so-called "viral marketing." In an era of superabundance of customer choice in most product categories, the Internet needs to be viewed more as a *listening* than as a *broadcast* medium, a platform more for understanding than for declaiming.

Myth 3: The Internet Makes 1:1 Marketing a Reality. Technologies like collaborative filtering and some new preference-matching programs are supposed to tailor online offerings to the needs of individual consumers. They fall short because they lack context for the suggestions they put forward, the kind of context that only a knowledgeable individual in a store or on the phone could bring to customer interactions. Listening technologies are pervasive, from the ATM to the check-out counter, to the remote network management console. Marketing has yet to recognize these listening systems for what they are, contextual windows on the 1:1 customer relationship.

MARKETING IN THE INTERNET AGE

The myths described above make most current marketing practices on the Internet only marginally valuable and successful. We need to think not about Internet marketing but about marketing in the Internet age—the totality of the marketing challenge in an age where business processes are increasingly mediated by the Internet.

Many organizations have underestimated the extent to which the Internet really does represent a new kind of technology-mediated value proposition. Technology tends to drive rapid commoditization. The Internet supports that trend by virtue of the access it affords to comparison information. As a result, many online companies have rapidly descended to commodity status, resulting in unsustainable business models. A classic example is Priceline, which is now facing competition not only from travel sites such as Orbitz, but also airline-specific sites such as Southwest.com.

On the other hand, the "new economy" argument has generally failed because it decouples the Internet from the rest of the business system. Three hundred beauty sites opened for business in the 1997–2000 period, almost none of which understood that without the availability of top brands such as Lauder and Lancôme they would not be interesting to consumers, despite virtual makeover software, digital fragrance generators, and other technology gimmickry. In contrast, one of the very few successful Internet companies (measured in terms of growth and profitability) is eBay, which brilliantly defined its role in the marketplace as the key intermediary, and enlisted other players to manage key business processes such as payments and logistics.

The challenge for marketers in the Internet age is *marketing at the core*. It requires an understanding of customer pain points (an ability to listen rather than talk), a familiarity with the economics of cost-to-serve and, above all, an approach to customers that is based upon a life-cycle relationship management process.

As an example of the importance of marketing as a repository of customer business process expertise, Citibank has one of the more highly developed Internet-based innovation and marketing strategies in the financial services sector. The company has applied superior marketing insight into the way technology can completely change the value proposition to a key target market—corporate C.F.O.s. These customers have traditionally been served by "stovepiped" product lines, but innovative marketers like Citibank understand that C.F.O.s are really interested in managing their day-to-day activities in a much more integrated fashion. The result has been measurable share gain in corporate financial services. Instead of driving temporary, transient product *differentiation*, they have used Internet platforms to deliver sustainable business value to customers via effective process *integration*.

MAKING IT HAPPEN

Answering these questions is an excellent prescription for any executive who wishes to understand what marketing should know about customers and the role of the Internet:

- How does the Web deliver value to customers, business partners, and my own company?
- Who am I serving with my Web presence, and do the economics deliver enough return to the value network to justify the use of the Web?
- What is the whole product that I need to bring to my Web business, including, where necessary, non-Web components and partnership components?
- How do I guarantee extraordinary value delivery on the Web, manage that value delivery over time for my customers, and build brand value from that total customer experience?
- How does the Web fit into that total relationship with the customer and why? What roles should it play at different stages of the relationship?
- Where should the Web fit organizationally, such that it leverages and enhances my total marketing strategy and implementation plan?
- How do I measure success in terms of new customers, repeat customers, loyal customers, total revenue and margin growth, new product success rates, partner business and profitability growth, and so on?

The Web is one of the greatest resources marketers have ever had at their disposal. Successful sites all tend to have the property of expanding consumer choice and control in terms of *how the relationship is managed* without compromising the traditional basis for consumer preference, the choice and control over *what is delivered*. The vast majority of these firms successfully align the rich contextual options of the Internet with a coherent set of content and commerce options that integrate across all relevant touchpoints and distribution channels, electronic or otherwise.

In the short term, all companies can use the Web as a particular part of their marketing approach, reinforcing their ability to understand and deliver value to customers, underscoring their ability to deliver tailored value propositions, facilitating better channel relationships via information sharing, and generally extending their presence to become more pervasive and more relevant to customers and business partners.

In the longer run, the Web can help marketing reassert some of the functions that it used to have a large say in but has lost control over in the last decade, such as product definition, control of the value proposition and how it is positioned, a measure of brand control (especially concerning the customer's total brand experience), and even what price is charged and the role of price in the decision process.

Regis McKenna has been a pioneer of high-tech marketing since launching his Silicon Valley-based marketing strategy firm in 1970. He has worked with a wide variety of entrepreneurial start-ups and established multinationals worldwide, and serves on the boards of many organizations, including the Santa Clara University Center for Science, Technology, and Society and the Silicon Valley Children's Fund. He is the author of *Relationship Marketing* (Perseus, reissue 2003), *Real Time* (Harvard Business School Press, 1999) and *Total Access* (Harvard Business School Press, 2002), and many articles on technology, marketing, and customer relationship management. Geoff Mott has served as C.E.O. of The McKenna Group, an international consulting firm specializing in the application of information and telecommunications technologies and markets. He speaks regularly at conferences on various topics, including data networking and business strategies on the Internet.

The Second Coming of Service

Karl Albrecht

Many firms, particularly in the United States, ran off their rails, strategically speaking, during the Internet craze of the late 1990s. Hypnotized by the e-commerce story, many dot-com businesses made strategic blunders that would be unforgivable on the part of first-year MBA students. Executive teams of many established firms, gripped by the fear of being left behind, threw money at anything that looked as if it might qualify as an Internet strategy.

Apart from the loss of billions of dollars by investors and ill-advised expenditures by established firms, the biggest victim was the customer. Internet operators set back the cause of service quality by a good ten years in some sectors, and the implosion of dot-mania left an ideological vacuum in the minds of many executives.

A more realistic appraisal of the role of IT in business has forced a return to basic principles: focus on the customer and value creation, culture building, skillful execution of quality practices, and inspired leadership. This return to basic truths may unfold as a second coming of customer focus.

WHAT HAPPENED TO SERVICE?

In 1985 the business world embraced the concept of service management with remarkable enthusiasm. There were books, articles, conferences, seminars, training programs, videos, newsletters, consulting firms, and even professional societies and academic research programs aimed at making customer focus a critical and permanent part of Western management thinking. Even the management gurus, established names on other topics, were moved to declare the primacy of customer value.

The wave didn't last. The service revolution was hijacked somewhere along the road to victory. Like most other management movements before it—management by objectives, participative management, productivity, and quality management—customer focus became the object of intense flirtation by many firms, but ultimately the infatuation faded. The same fate befell several other revolutions: TQM, reengineering, and ISO 9000.

The real value and potential impact of the service management model are yet to be realized. We're coming to a stage in business worldwide, in which we will need its principles more than ever. Western management thinking has lost its way in recent years, particularly with the mindless infatuation with all things digital. There is a deep underlying need, only partly articulated, to return to the most basic and timeless precepts of leadership, management, and enterprise thinking.

THE TECTONIC SHIFT AWAY FROM SERVICE

Around 1995, when TQM, ISO 9000, and service quality movements were fading, U.S. business began to feel the pressure of a more primitive shift in emphasis. U.S. enterprises, and to a lesser extent firms in other countries, moved into a reconstruction phase. An unprecedented period of mergers, acquisitions, and the dramatic growth of retail giants got mixed in with business breakups, spinoffs, delayering, outsourcing, and partnering. A growing economy coupled with low unemployment rates and a remarkably flexible workforce enabled U.S. firms to rearrange themselves to maximize their strengths.

Key phrases such as "core competencies," "strategic partnering," and "supply-chain management" replaced the language of service, quality, and customer value. Thus began an ideological drift in U.S. management thinking toward *resource-based* rather than *value-based* competition. A large banking corporation finds it difficult to win more customers by adding value or reinventing its service package, but it's easy to find profit growth by buying up its smaller competitors. Why have competing banks on opposite sides of the street? Let's just buy out the other bank, close its branches, and add its customers to our inventory.

Why should a large airline try to offer better service when all airlines have conditioned their customers to make their choices solely on the basis of price? Why not buy up or force out the smaller airlines and relieve the pricing pressure? Why waste time changing customer-service programs that just fizzle out anyway?

This is not to suggest that no companies are interested in service quality as a competitive factor: surely firms like Disney and Federal Express are still in a class by themselves. However, the example set by the giant firms, namely buying their competitors and kidnapping their customers, has drawn more attention in recent years.

THE PENDULUM RETURNS?

Has the so-called new economy lived up to its image? Or is it an intellectual chimera?

Actually, there's no such thing as a new economy (or an old economy) as preached by the Internet hucksters, who managed to separate several billion dollars from investors, venture capitalists, and corporate executives. This warped notion of two economies will eventually be seen as one of the most serious conceptual blunders in business thinking of the last 50 years.

There is only one economy: the ever-new, ever-evolving economy of continuous creative destruction, described by theorist Joseph Schumpeter. Information is, and will continue to be, an important resource for economic development, but it is not in itself a—and certainly not *the*—new economy. Nor is the high-tech industry the primary driver of economic growth, as so many business writers have declared. Even Peter Drucker, the *eminence grise* of management theology, has wrongly characterized the U.S. economy as information-based. When the fantasy begins to fade, economists, business leaders, journalists, and management theorists will see the information phenomenon in a more realistic perspective: as an inseparable part of the economic structure, but not the magical engine of it.

Information is one of the five key factors of economic growth and development: land, capital infrastructure, energy, labor, and information. Why arbitrarily declare one factor profoundly more important than the others? It is impossible to do anything with information—create it, manipulate it, store it, duplicate it, transmit it, or present it for consumption—without also consuming energy, usually in the form of electricity. Information is not free, and on a macro scale it isn't even cheap.

As business leaders return to the idea of customer value as the ultimate driving force of business success, they will turn a new page in their understanding of the potential of IT, online technology, and abundant information. Instead of trying to turn their businesses into vending machines and building an impersonal digital moat around their companies by replacing people with software, they will begin to see a wholly different set of strategies for using information as a strategic weapon. This understanding will change the meaning of the customer-value focus and reshape our thought processes as they relate to the use of information in business.

Some examples include:

USAA is the premier provider of insurance services to U.S. military personnel. Founded in 1922 by a group of army officers, the firm has never lost its focus on delivering value to its special population of customers with their special needs. It has stayed at the forefront of applying information technology—with a human face—to the insurance business. With 90% of all military personnel buying their products and a 97% customer retention rate, the firm has proven that customer value counts.

REI (Recreational Equipment, Inc.) is the outfitter of choice for over a million outdoor sports fans and adventure enthusiasts. Successful since 1938, the firm has recently achieved a brilliant convergence of bricks and clicks by marrying online technology and its existing experience of interactive retail stores. Customers can interact seamlessly with its 55 retail outlets in 23 states and its in-depth resources for ordering, advice, and information on its Web site.

Walt Disney's commercial kingdom retains its unchallenged position as a provider of outstanding services in its chosen domain of entertainment. Based in Burbank, California, the Walt Disney Company is the third-largest media and entertainment conglomerate in the world, with operations encompassing movies, broadcasting, the Internet, and theme parks. Its Tokyo Disney Resort draws 16.5 million people a year. Disneyland Paris has emerged as one of the preeminent entertainment destinations in Europe. In all cases the customer experience is the focus of Disney's business operation.

MAKING IT HAPPEN
Implementing a strategy that maximizes customer value involves the following steps:

- **Refocus on the customer.** Are you conducting customer research on a regular basis? Do people understand what customer value is in your line of business, and do they know how to deliver it? Do you have a workable system for measuring customer perceptions of value? Do you share findings throughout the organization?
- **Reinvent the service strategy.** What is your core benefit premise, that is, the *customer-value proposition* on which you base your business model, the design of your service systems, and the operation of the enterprise? Does it make sense? Does everyone in the organization understand it and take it seriously? Is it time to rethink the business model or realign the priorities?

- **Build organizational intelligence.** Conduct a comprehensive review of your operating systems and an audit of their capacity to deliver on the business strategy. Look for evidence of system craziness, or lack of intelligence. Align the systems, the processes, and the people to the critical success factors of the business.
- **Reenlist the people.** Too many crises, priorities, and brushfires can distract the leaders of the enterprise and put them out of touch with the culture. How well do you understand employees today? What do they want? What do they seek in their jobs and careers? What frustrates them, inhibits them, or demotivates them? Are they switched on, switched off, or just glowing at half-wattage? Get the energy up and get the heads all pointing in the same direction.

In the present confusing and rapidly changing business environment, enterprise leaders at all levels must learn to see beyond fads and folklore and concentrate ever more tenaciously on the timeless truths of business:

- Make sure you are selling what the customer wants to buy.
- Concentrate your resources on the strategic advantage.
- Align the systems to meet the mission.
- Mobilize the culture.
- Make technology your servant, not your master.
- Stay on message.

The winning enterprises of the next decade won't be those whose leaders chase fads and fantasies, but those who can integrate new knowledge and new possibilities with their own trusted understanding of the basic truths of business success.

Dr. Karl Albrecht is a management consultant, futurist, speaker, and author. He has written more than 25 books on business performance, including the best-selling *Service America!: Doing Business in the New Economy* (with Ron Zemke; McGraw-Hill, 2001). As chairman of Karl Albrecht International, he oversees the practical application of his ideas through a consulting group, a seminar firm, and publishing company. For more information, please see the Web site, www.KarlAlbrecht.com.

The Power of Identity

Wally Olins

Organizations have a unique identity that can be employed as a valuable asset. Corporations currently face challenges to their identity from all sides. These challenges are increasingly prompting company boards to regard identity as an important topic. These are the most common problems regarding identity management:

- Products and services are increasingly becoming more similar, making customers purchase products on an emotional basis—a projected sense of corporate personality and rapport with customers boosts business. How can Shell, Texaco, and BP differentiate their products from each other so as to provide competitive advantage?
- Corporate mergers are on the rise, disregarding local boundaries and charging leaders with the problem of how to create a new identity from two old ones. Daimler Chrysler is a good example.
- Organizations are forced through changing technologies, deregulation, and globalization to alter the nature of their business and to manage corporate identity through change and uncertainty.

Corporate identity provides a bedrock of valuable resources, such as goodwill, loyalty, and respect among customers, while internally providing a strategic direction for every member of an organization.

WHAT IS IDENTITY?

Every organization carries out thousands of transactions every day. In each transaction the organization is in some way presenting itself—or part of itself—to the various groups of people it deals with. The totality of the way the organization presents itself can be called its identity. What different audiences perceive is often called its image.

Because the range of its activities is so vast, and the manifestations of identity are so diverse, the corporation needs actively and explicitly to manage its identity. Identity management should be seen as a corporate resource embracing each and every part of the organization.

Identity can project four ideas: who you are; what you do; how you do it; where you want to go.

The Four Vectors. Identity manifests itself primarily through:

- products and services—what you make or sell (think of BMW);
- environments—where you make or sell it (Hilton Hotels);
- communications—how you talk about your product, both internally and externally (Coca-Cola);
- behavior—how you behave to your employees and the world outside (Southwest Airlines).

The balance among these four is rarely equal, and an early priority in creating any identity program is to determine which predominates.

The Central Idea/Vision. The idea behind an identity program is that in everything the organization does or produces, it should project a clear idea of what it is and what its aims are.

Name/Logo. At the heart of the visual identity is the hierarchy and identification system and the way it is reflected in symbols, logotypes, and marks. The symbol is highly visible. Its prime purpose is to present the idea of the corporation with impact, brevity, and immediacy.

It is sometimes necessary to change the symbol in order to signify a change in direction, as, for example, BP Amoco did. In other cases (for example, Renault or Shell) modification may be more appropriate.

Sometimes it's appropriate to change the name of a corporation for legal reasons or for clarity. Name changes are, however, frequently misunderstood and always excite high levels of emotion, particularly in the media.

Audiences. The audiences of an organization are those people who come into contact with it in any way. It is often assumed that the most important audience for any corporation is its customers. In a service business, however, employees are by far the most significant audience. They transmit the identity of the organization to customers, so they have to live it.

There are both internal and external audiences. The internal audience comprises staff members and their families. External audiences include shareholders, competitors, suppliers, and partners, the financial world, and opinion-formers of all kinds. These audiences are not always separate and independent; to some extent they do overlap.

Types of Corporate Identity. The identity of most corporations can be assigned to one of three general categories: monolithic, endorsed, or branded.

Monolithic identity. Here the organization uses one name and one visual system throughout all of its interactions. Because everything that the organization does has the same name, style, and character, each part supports the other. Virgin is the most high-profile example of this type of identity. The name and identity of Virgin is not associated so much with what it does, but with what it is, how it behaves, and what it seems to stand for.

Endorsed identity. Most corporations grow at least partly by acquisition. The acquiring corporation is often eager to preserve the goodwill (equity) associated with its acquisitions. Under an endorsed identity strategy, the parent endorses its subsidiaries with the corporate name and sometimes its visual style. Nestlé and P&O are examples.

Branded identity. Some companies, especially those in the consumer products field, separate their corporate identity from the identities of the brands they own, for example, Unilever, Diageo, and LVMH. The final customer identifies with the brand, other audiences with the corporation. Brands have names, reputations, life cycles, and personalities of their own, and they may even compete with other brands from the same corporation.

STARTING AND MANAGING A PROGRAM

The following points should be considered when implementing a corporate identity program:

- Is it part of a corporate turnaround?
- Does it inspire, invigorate, and create more cohesion internally?
- Is it intended to increase the share price?
- Is it focused on helping to integrate newly acquired companies?
- Is it a response to competitive pressures?

When a corporate identity program is initiated, a senior individual in the organization must be appointed to manage it, and change should be implemented in a clear and goal-focused manner. Most organizations will need outside assistance from branding, identity, or design consultants. As with every corporate activity, the identity program needs a power base, financial controls, and clear lines of authority. A working party should be formed, which should report to a steering group.

THE STAGES OF WORK

Stage One: investigation, analysis, and strategic recommendations. The organization has to take an objective look at how it is perceived by its various audiences and how these perceptions compare with its aspirations. If the existing identity is seen as fragmented, unclear, old-fashioned, or ineffective, senior managers need to agree on the action required to change perceptions. Stage One ends with recommendations for action.

Stage Two: development of the identity. Depending on the results of Stage One, it may be necessary to change the identity of the corporation completely, including name and visual style (Accenture); to keep the same name but change the identity visually (BP Amoco), or simply to make some changes.

Changes of name and visual style are expensive and time-consuming, and they clearly signal to the marketplace that the organization is making a new promise or moving in a new direction. This kind of change makes a promise of changed performance that has to be fulfilled. Never promise more than you can deliver.

On the basis of the recommendations made in Stage One, consultants develop an identity system based on the endorsed or branded model. The identity system usually consists of a name (or names), mark or logo, main and subsidiary typefaces, and colors. These will be applied to materials such as letterheads, Web sites, and products.

Stage Three: implementation. The new identity has to be codified so that it can be used in the organization and by relevant outside suppliers. Manuals are prepared containing all the identity elements and their precise specifications for a variety of applications. The manual should also demonstrate the spirit that lies behind the organization.

Stage Four: launch and introduction. If the new corporate identity program is to work, it has to be launched with enthusiasm and commitment. The launch is the first major opportunity for the company's leaders to present the identity as a significant corporate resource and to integrate it into the organizational structure.

Never trivialize your corporate identity. Explain that the new identity is the outward sign of change and explain what that change means. Internal audiences want to know what, why, and particularly how it will affect them as individuals. External audiences only want to know why and how much.

The Spanish oil company Repsol was formed in the 1980s from Instituto Nacional de Hidrocarburos (INH). INH was a state monopoly with low standards of service, old and badly-maintained service stations, and a plethora of names and identities. The central idea/vision emerged naturally from the corporation's new positioning. Spain had just entered the European Union and the corporation had to defend its position. INH had to be revitalized and eventually privatized. Repsol had the opportunity to become the model for a revitalized Spain. It could become and be seen as new Spain's industrial and commercial flagship. This was the vision that was presented to and agreed on by the board.

The naming structure and visual identity followed from this brief. The name INH was abandoned in favor of one of the company's brands, Repsol, and a mono-lithic identity structure was adopted in order to give the organization strength and coherence. A new design was part of the program of change.

MAKING IT HAPPEN
The following steps will help you create and build your corporate identity:
- Develop your corporate identity to project the company's approach, values, distinctiveness, and direction.
- Concentrate primarily on three "tangibles": your products and services, the environments where you make or sell them, and communications.
- Treat the intangibles of behavior—how you behave to your employees and the world outside—as vital.
- As a priority, determine early which of the above four tangible and intangible factors predominates.
- Before starting a corporate identity program, decide what you want it to achieve in the longer term.
- Construct the program in the four stages recommended above.

All corporations have an identity, irrespective of whether they control it or effectively manage it. By concentrating on developing a desirable corporate identity and project-ing it to customers, as well as employing it as a tool to provide internal direction and orientate strategic development, organizational efficiency can be raised. Remember that a corporate identity program harnesses and manages a valuable corporate asset.

Wally Olins is one of the world's most experienced experts on corporate identity and branding. His main interests are the big ideas behind organizations, mergers, and acqui-sitions, and he has a particular fascination with the branding of regions and nations. His publications include *The New Guide to Identity* (Gower, 1995) and *Trading Identities* (Foreign Policy Centre, 1999).

The Dance of Authenticity

Watts Wacker and Ryan Mathews

Watts Wacker, founder and director of FirstMatter, LLC, has written essays for publications as diverse as *Architectural Record* and *Scientific American*. He also writes a column for *Entrepreneur Magazine*. With Jim Taylor he is the coauthor of *The 500-Year Delta* (Harper-Business, 1997), which has been translated into 10 languages, and *The Visionary's Handbook* (HarperBusiness, 2000). Ryan Mathews has leveraged his 18 years of experience in retailing to become a top authority on emerging retail channels, electronic commerce, and the future of wholesaling, retailing, and food service. He has pioneered studies in consumerism, including ethnic marketing and non-linear virtual supply chain modeling. He is the coauthor, with Fred Crawford, of *The Myth of Excellence* (Crown, 2001). Together, Wacker and Mathews are coauthors of *The Deviant's Advantage* (Crown, 2002).

Martin Heidegger, despite his politics perhaps still the greatest metaphysician of the 20th century, argued that the fact that our existence is embodied in cultural context explains our apparently collective predisposition to inauthenticity. Confronted by our fears, he argued, we almost instinctively choose the comfort of anonymity over the burdens of authenticity. As Heidegger saw it, we flee from the core issue of our existence (death) and insulate ourselves in mantles of social convention and conformity, voluntarily abdicating the right and ability to seize control of and define our own lives. In Heidegger's lexicon, authenticity is achieved only when we face what he calls "being-toward-death." Heidegger wasn't alone. In *Hero with a Thousand Faces*, Joseph Campbell echoed the German philosopher when he wrote ". . . the hero would be no hero if death held for him any terror; the first condition is reconciliation with the grave."

To be authentic, Heidegger argued, is to be transformed: to face up clearly and honestly to the responsibility for what one's own life adds up to in its entirety, and to seize onto the possibilities present in our community or shared "heritage" in order to realize a communal "destiny." We agree with Heidegger and Campbell. Authenticity isn't defined by a single act or an isolated moment in time, for either an individual or a corporation. Rather it's a sum total of all the aspects of an individual's or business's being-in-the-world, both their inner being and their public face and presence. Authenticity, then, is about a life, and, by extension, a life's work. In the case of a business, it's about a brand's or company's life and its lifetime relationships with customers or consumers. Authenticity is both life's greatest achievement and, historically, its most daunting challenge. We believe that from this day forward, life, both individual and collective, will be characterized by what we call "the abolition of context" or the most complete absence of a unifying and defining social canon. If achieving authenticity has been difficult in the past, it will exponentially be more difficult in the future.

As a society and as individuals we're at best ambivalent about authenticity. On the one hand we ostensibly demand the authentic and on the other we live lives slavishly devoted to the heedless and mindless pursuit of the shallow and the banal. We speak of pursuing the eternal truths—love, peace, and freedom—while all the while we're enslaved by style and convention. This ambivalence infects everything we do, from the trivial to the transcendent. We claim to be devoted to the authentic, but we are addicted to the new, no matter how superficial it is. Even our rebellions and statements of personal eccentricity are calculated. We coast through existence as self-styled bohemians in BMWs and as intellectuals pondering the cosmic meaning of MTV. We are publicly virtuous and privately venial.

Our collective obsession with the new—which, we reassure ourselves, is the quest for the authentic, the real thing—deploys cool-hunters, trend pimps, hip social chroniclers, and mass media vampires who are all desperately competing for their next fix of virgin audio and/or visual context that will lead them deeper and deeper toward what they perceive to be the edge in search of the next *real* big thing. The irony, of course, is that authenticity is far more often a casualty rather than a characteristic of social acceptance. The faster we drag products, ideas, or individuals from their origins on the fringe toward the center of convention, the faster we kill their authenticity. And, more often than not, once something has survived the gauntlet of inauthenticity and reached the center of convention, it is routinely rejected as passé and passed over to make room for something "more real," which is destined to meet the same fate. This should come as no surprise, given that we've handed our search for authenticity proxies over to "cool hunters," rarely more than trend pimps, and market analysts who rarely leave the comfort of their offices to deal with real customers *in situ*.

Is it possible to balance our insatiable craving for the authentic with our ravenous appetite for the superficial and phoney? Clearly, one of the reasons our search for authenticity yields such barren fruit is that we generally begin it in the wrong places. Really authentic things exist at either end of a continuum that begins beyond the edge we're always told to live on at a place we call "the Fringe," which extends outside the sterile and artificial confines of mainstream social convention. The Fringe is the place where the primordial soup of innovation and creativity resides. Most ideas, people, and products moving out of that part of the continuum lose part or all their authenticity on the journey.

Businesses are as inept in their pursuits of authenticity as people are. Each year global businesses spend billions of dollars prattling on about how their product is genuine; their service personalized, intimate, and engaged; their prices the lowest possible, and about how their companies are devoted to the selfless altruistic principle of the betterment of consumer lives. No wonder we don't trust them! Businesses can't declare themselves to be authentic; that's the customer's job. Brands can't assert they are authentic; they can only be seen as such. And when marketing and advertising tread too close to reality—as in the case of Benetton—they often fall foul of it. Of course, that isn't to say that businesses can't act authentically. Reebok is heavily engaged in the struggle for human rights, values reflected in both its corporate philanthropy and its supply-chain labor policies, but it publicly underplays most of these efforts. Contrast this with the spate of cause-related marketing schemes selling everything from over-priced consumer goods to financial services.

As Heidegger noted, we generally fail in our attempts to be authentic and that failure is generally tied back to fear. Most companies are afraid to tell their story, because they understand they have no real story to tell. As the 21st century unfolds, we believe authenticity may be the primary criterion to differentiate products. Technology has simply moved too fast for it to be credible that one can sustain a product innovation on a proprietary basis for any length of time. The best most businesses can hope to enjoy is a six-month innovation advantage before their competitors introduce a similar, and often improved and lower-cost, version of their product. After all, they don't have to recoup all those burdensome research and development costs. Authenticity by its very nature can't be copied, and any attempt to do so makes the clone appear all the more phoney.

Another way to look at this is to say that whatever a company or organization does inherently exists outside the domain of authenticity. Authenticity only comes into play when you stop listening to what a company says and begin examining how it lives and what it believes. The search for authenticity—personal or commercial—isn't easy. If it were, we'd live in a much different world. But no matter how difficult the goal, it's more than worth the effort.

We began this discussion with Martin Heidegger and we'd like to conclude it with the French philosopher, journalist, novelist, and playwright Albert Camus. Camus's work often dealt with antiheroes who acted out of authenticity, which he defined as freedom from any conventional expectations about what "human nature" required in a situation. His characters embrace total personal responsibility and, in their best moments, share an almost painful lucidity that disallows them from living in what Camus called bad faith, or lying to themselves. Obviously, from the point of view of the mainstream, Camus's "heroes" are deviants, oddities, and, in fact, often criminals. Given the inauthenticity of the world, any genuine act is almost invariably suspect.

Indeed, whenever a business comes dangerously close to acting authentically it is attacked—by prying mediavistas looking for a corporate Achilles heel; by analysts ready to downgrade companies who are honest, and by individuals who have been schooled in the arts of skepticism and negativity. No wonder so many businesses opt for the inauthentic! It generally pays better.

Earlier we said that authenticity might be the only area of sustainable competitive differentiation. In the same way an individual must choose whether to live his or her life authentically or to conform to the inauthentic demands of society or business, commercial entities must choose whether or not they will walk the path of authenticity. Remember, customer rhetoric aside, being authentic isn't always a commercially successful formula. For one thing, authenticity is often expensive. Great artistic masterpieces are more commanding than cheap prints, but if you had a dime for every image of the Mona Lisa ever produced you could buy the original and the Louvre it sits in. For another, it's rarely socially acceptable. Big Mama Thornton's version of "Hound Dog" is authentic; Elvis Presley's was a commercial success. Somehow white America just wasn't ready for a black woman who dressed in men's clothes growling about illicit sex. Elvis didn't change the words much, but he ratcheted down the menacing attitude enough to not scare the Caucasians. But perhaps authenticity's single largest failing as a market offering is its tendency to remind us of our own inauthenticity. Most of us don't do well by comparison when we find ourselves in the presence of the truly real, the nakedly honest, or something that is undeniably itself. So we choose the comfort of the inauthentic, that which lets us live our lies without challenge or protest.

Things may be a bit different in the 21st century, however. The empty promises of inauthenticity have delivered us into a world of dangerous social inequality, political instability, and a growing consolidation across a broad band of commercial markets. Inauthenticity, it seems, is a scalable offering. The battle, so close to the hearts of 20th century existentialists like Heidegger and Camus, is intensifying in the 21st century. We live in a world in which the inauthentic sells at the same time as the antihero—from the terrorist to the entrepreneurial maverick—routinely triumphs, at least in the short run. We believe both trends. If Camus was correct, are these signs that an authentic world isn't far away?

Beyond Strategy: Market-based Capabilities

Jean-Claude Larréché

Beyond strategy, great business leadership requires building intangible assets for sustainable long-term success. Market-based capabilities are intangible assets that influence the competitive success of a firm in its markets. In this piece, Jean-Claude Larréché, the Alfred H. Heineken Chaired Professor of Marketing at INSEAD in Fontainebleau, France, sets out his views on four selected key issues concerning market-based capabilities: the concept, measurement, emergence of capability gaps in specific business sectors, and development of distinctive superior capability profiles.

Ever since the advent of modern management, the business community—corporations, consulting companies, and business schools alike—has been striving to understand what makes some companies more successful than others. From Peter Drucker's first book in the late 1940s through *In Search of Excellence* and several generations of other bestsellers, ample guidance has become available on this most important subject. And "strategy" has now become more of a buzzword in business than in the military.

Jack Welch, as the new chairman of General Electric, came to his first meeting with financial analysts with a "big" message, organized in two parts: "hard" issues—the strategic requirement of being no. 1 or no. 2 in each business unit—and "soft" issues such as the human element. While the soft issues were essential to General Electric's success for the next decades, the analysts' reaction was cold. In Jack Welch's words: "About halfway through, I had the impression that I would have gotten as much interest if I'd talked about my Ph.D. thesis on drop-wise condensation."

Since that time, the more progressive business leaders and observers have, fortunately, become more enlightened and followed Jack Welch's example. In the search for key success factors, there has been a growing recognition of the importance of intangible assets, or capabilities, such as human resources, customer orientation, corporate culture, or brands. Simultaneously, there has been an increased focus on evaluating these capabilities in terms of their impact on the competitive success of the firm in its markets, not in terms of technically-defined criteria. This is emphasized in the expression "market-based capabilities".

Some companies have capabilities that are "technically correct" but ineffective when it comes to winning in the marketplace. For example, they may have an impressive, well-written mission statement with all the "right" ingredients, which nonetheless causes confusion or cynicism resulting in reduced effectiveness. They may have sophisticated systems based on the latest technologies with wonderful real-time features, but to no avail if these are seen by front-line staff to be more of a competitive handicap than a competitive advantage. On the other hand, companies like Virgin Atlantic, First Direct, or Amazon.com have great competitive fitness capabilities from relatively small investments. There is no need to be a large firm to have great fundamental capabilities. In fact, sometimes the opposite is true; in large firms the muscles can turn to fat so the firm becomes heavier, ineffective, and handicapped in the market-place.

The opportunities for improving market-based capabilities for most companies are huge. Opportunities are uncovered by asking a few fundamental questions, not typically asked in the "normal" process of running a business. How fit, in the absolute and relative to my competitors, are these capabilities that are the life blood of the unit I am leading? What progress has been made in the last five years? What is the current trend? What am I going to do about it? At times, responding to these opportunities requires investment, but in other cases it is more a matter of doing less and focusing more. The executive or manager cannot escape responsibility for the competitive fitness of the unit he or she is in charge of. This responsibility is at the core of leadership.

An important leadership gap is the inability to measure intangible capabilities. In the Competitive Fitness of Global Firms initiative at INSEAD, a framework and an assessment methodology have been developed to evaluate the fundamental capabilities driving the success of the modern firm. This work has been based on available published research, long-term analyses of about 40 corporations, in-depth case studies, and the cooperation of selected firms.

The Competitive Fitness of Global Firms framework includes 12 fundamental capabilities: Mission and Vision, Customer Orientation, Corporate Culture, Organization and Systems, Planning and Intelligence, Human Resources, Technical Resources, Innovation, Market Strategy, Marketing Operations, International, and Performance. The measurement methodology is based on a diagnostic tool containing 182 indicators to estimate scores on the 12 capabilities. The methodology is available for use by executives at any level in a firm.

Since 1998 a survey has been conducted annually to provide international capability benchmarks on which executives can compare their scores with competitors. This survey covers eight sectors comprising more than 300 of the largest firms from Europe and North America. The *Report on the Competitive Fitness of Global Firms*, based on this survey, is published each year in February.

A competitive advantage in terms of capabilities is the ultimate form of competitive advantage. Products and technologies are visible and well defined and can be imitated by those ready to make the investment. By contrast, capabilities are often intangible and made up of elemental parts-innovation, human resources, corporate culture. Capabilities also tend to endure and provide a competitive edge for a firm in various markets, not just a specific area or segment. A capability advantage is pervasive and sustainable and can therefore be an important engine of value creation for the short and long term.

In the past, "industry practices" prevailed in separate sectors. There was an acceptable way to run a bank, a chemical group, or a consumer goods company. Industry associations, management transfers, and the leadership of large companies contributed to the establishment of these norms. We can now observe a wider gap being created between the capabilities of different firms in the same sector, and recognize that the trend leaders are not always the largest firms.

The *Report on the Competitive Fitness of Global Firms* provides some illustrations of this phenomenon in many sectors. Many financial services firms still believe in an old industry "truth" that innovation advantages are not possible because products are imitated easily. In reality, some firms find ways to go from strength to strength while others lag behind in innovation and other key capabilities. These latter firms are unaware of their sliding competitiveness as they do not have access to a quantified benchmark. They run the risk of realizing it only when their performance suffers, by which time it will be even more difficult to correct the situation.

Does this mean that all the fittest firms need to be equally strong on all capabilities? Certainly not. The *Report on Corporate Competitive Fitness* shows that the fittest firms very often have a personality, a distinctive competitive fitness profile. There is a unique "capability look" about the fittest companies in a given sector, reminiscent of a specific face, silhouette, or fingerprint.

In addition to a vast array of observations on market-based capabilities, the *Report on the Competitive Fitness of Global Firms* contains the capability profiles of more than 60 firms in eight sectors. These are the fittest firms among those included in the survey; firms such as Diageo, Exxon Mobil, and Eli Lilly. All these firms score highly on overall corporate competitive fitness. They are above their sector's averages on most of the capabilities. In addition, they have a strong atypical profile, the expression of a unique personality that is the result of strong crafting. It may have been achieved over generations or through recent transformations and actions, but such competitive fitness profiles are not developed just through the "normal" way of running a business. It requires strong leadership to invest in what Jack Welch called "soft values." Beyond strategy, the selection of priorities for further capability development is a crucial task of leadership.

Beyond short-term results is strategy; beyond strategy are market-based capabilities. By focusing on short-term results, or on a narrow strategy, some businesses are cutting into both fat and muscle. In the process, they are digging the hole into which they will eventually collapse. The challenge of great leadership is to deliver at all three levels: results, strategy, and market-based capabilities. The latter are the most important for sustainable long-term success. Unfortunately, market-based capabilities are also the most difficult element to comprehend and the easiest to neglect. Effective management of a business's intangible assets requires the three steps described in this article: measuring market-based capabilities, monitoring the emergence of capability gaps in relevant business sectors, and investing in the development of a distinctive superior capability profile.

Strategic Agility

John Wells

With the crash of technology stocks turning into a general economic slump, top management focus is shifting from investing in new technology and business ideas to cutting costs. But badly directed cost-cutting delivers no better return on investment than the speculation in e-commerce that was so characteristic of the 2000 boom. When the pressure is on to cut costs, a C.E.O. has a tough choice to make: simply make bold cuts without consideration of future needs, or invest in taking the first steps to building a much more agile business platform that will allow the firm to exploit future opportunities and respond more quickly to change.

How quickly times change. How short investors' memories are. One minute the stock market is booming and companies are being driven to invest in e-commerce at almost any cost to protect their stock rating. The next minute the e-bubble has burst and no C.E.O. who wants to stay on the job is talking about new e-commerce initiatives. It's time for consolidation, focus, cutting costs.

This is unfortunate because e-commerce, wisely deployed, provides a powerful competitive weapon in a downturn as well as in boom times. But this is not what investors want to hear. They insist that now is the time for bold announcements to cut costs and reduce head count, and there are several approaches to choose from.

THE SIX LEVELS OF COST MANAGEMENT

Level Zero cost management: talking about it. The simplest and least-disruptive approach to cost-cutting is to talk about it but not actually do much. This is common practice in companies that acquire other businesses with the promise of major cost-reduction synergies that then fail to materialize. For instance, Bank of America, which grew from Nations Bank into the number one U.S. consumer bank in a 30-year binge of more than 100 acquisitions, never realized major cost synergies until a new management came in.

Level One cost management: arbitrary cuts. A more dramatic approach to cost management is to cut all discretionary expenses (consultants, bowls of fresh fruit) and demand head count reductions across the board. But cutting costs without tackling the underlying causes is often a short-lived solution. Costs have a nasty habit of growing back. Savings promised by the majority of cost-reduction programs disappear within two years, never delivering the returns required to justify the high price paid for them.

Level One cost management is fast, decisive, and sometimes very necessary in a crisis, but it's seldom optimal. While it may be a short-term palliative for investors, it is seldom in the best long-term interests of the corporation.

Level Two cost management: redesign business processes to meet today's needs. Rather than simply cutting costs, the challenge is to deal with the underlying causes of cost. This takes reengineering business processes to design costs out. Rather than simply reducing the amount of resource allocated to an old process in the hope that it will work harder, the objective is to redesign the process so that it requires less resource in the first place. This is more thoughtful—and more effective—cost-cutting.

Level Three cost management: redesign business processes to meet tomorrow's needs. There is a danger of changing processes to meet today's immediate needs without paying attention to the future, so that when business improves another expensive process redesign is required. Every C.E.O. knows there are a host of actions that must be taken if the firm is to prosper, but some must be deferred until financial conditions improve and shareholders have more of an appetite for investment. The process redesign should take these into account, ensuring that the firm is ready to expand its activities when the time is ripe.

Level Four cost management: meeting unforeseen needs. But how can an organization *really* be future-proof? What about those unforeseen events that demand sudden changes? It's not possible to design a set of business processes to meet every eventuality. And yet an organization can't afford to redesign all of its processes every time it encounters change. The challenge is to shape a process architecture that can be more easily adapted to change.

The way to achieve this is to shape processes in a way that decouples them from each other as much as possible, allowing local changes to be made in a single process without major redesign of the total system. This is component-based process architecture.

Level Five cost management: self-adaptive systems. Decoupling processes also allows the team of people responsible for operating each process to look for improvements continuously. If they are incentivized to behave in this way, then when changes occur the process is quickly modified to meet the new needs. The process and the people who operate it form a component of the organization.

To be really adaptive, the component team must have the ability to modify and improve the process themselves. This makes for really rapid response. The component, and the organization as a whole, then become much more agile and adaptive.

STRATEGIC AGILITY IN ACTION

Wells Fargo saw the opportunity to offer loans to small businesses on the Web, collecting credit-check information on each applicant in real time to decide on whether to approve a loan. The company envisaged an automated loan manager and backroom support service that were much more cost-effective than the human variety.

The initial service was very well received. Not only did it cut costs, but it provided much quicker response to the customer, and it began driving up market share.

The next challenge came when Wells Fargo wanted to change its criteria for making loans. This process had traditionally taken up to six months, limiting flexibility and responsiveness to changing market demands. One solution would have been simply to wire in the new loan criteria. However, sufficiently dissatisfied by its past experience, in this phase Wells Fargo sought to componentize the system, isolating the criteria from the rest of the system so that they could be changed more easily. Moreover, rather than simply inserting a new set of criteria into the criteria module, the company built a criteria generator. Instead of requiring expensive IT resource to change the criteria, the department managers could do it themselves, taking days instead of months.

Far from limiting the number of criteria, Wells Fargo made its solution even smarter by making sure that the criteria component allowed the addition of more, as yet unidentified, criteria, providing the system with the agility to react to the unknown. The bank avoided the temptation to implement a Level Two solution and moved directly to a Level Five solution, dealing with known changes and changes as yet unknown, while empowering the management team to look continuously for improvements.

The Implications for Information Systems: Componentized Systems Architecture. Redesigning processes almost always means changing the information systems that support the processes. And the trouble is that old legacy systems get in the way. Hence the frustration with IT departments. Rather than being seen as the driver of change, IT is often seen as the greatest impediment to change in large organizations.

Old legacy platforms are typically hugely complex systems tied together to help run the company. A minor change in one part of the system can have major and unpredictable impact on other parts, rather like the proverbial butterfly that starts a hurricane in the Caribbean by fluttering in South America.

The challenge for legacy IT systems is the same as for organizational processes: to be able to break them down into loosely-coupled components, so that each component can be changed without affecting the organization as a whole.

The IT components must map 100% onto organizational process components, so that when a department component sees opportunities for improvement it can change without disrupting the whole organization. The IT system can be adapted in parallel to support the change without changing the whole IT system. The capacity for change when this alignment is achieved is obviously very large.

Deal With Today's Challenge with Tomorrow in Mind. But when a company is facing major economic challenges, how can it find time to worry about componentizing its IT platform? The reality is that a company must be guided by its component architecture whenever it makes change. Take the current plethora of legacy systems and identify the role each will play in a more flexible componentized architecture. In the context of a clear long-term view, legacy systems can be changed in ways that contribute to the long-term agenda.

John Wells is currently senior partner with Netdecisions, a global strategy and technology company, responsible for strategy, knowledge management, innovation, and learning. Netdecisions works with global companies to help them adjust to the strategic impact of technology and become more agile in response. His career started at Unilever in London, where he trained as a cost and management accountant. He has worked in numerous companies, including the Boston Consulting Group, PepsiCo,

Corporate-level Strategy

David R. Sadtler

Implementing a successful corporate-level strategy has become an urgent priority for all conglomerates. Parent companies must demonstrate that they are creating shareholder value by their own actions and initiatives, and not just reaping the profits of the businesses in their charge. The sanctions for being seen to fail in this challenge can be severe. At the very least, share prices will suffer; at the other extreme, predators will force a breakup.

A FRAMEWORK

The challenge of corporate-level strategy is to ensure that value is being added to every business in the company's portfolio. That value must, of course, be in excess of its cost. Conglomerates with good corporate strategies do even better: they add more value than other companies in the same businesses.

Insuring that this value-added process is productive requires several actions by top management:

First, it must identify ways in which each business can be helped. This help must make possible a major improvement in business performance. Without an understanding of where improvement potential exists, the search for value added cannot be real and substantial. These improvement opportunities should be identified and agreed on through managerial dialogue and business-planning systems.

Second, central management must make sure that it possesses the skills to provide the help needed. Different kinds of improvement opportunities require different forms of help. Management must see that it has those capabilities.

Third, it must construct a portfolio of businesses in which this constructive fit—useful skills attuned to the needs of the businesses—exists. How businesses can be helped is bound to change over time. The strength of the fit must be continually reappraised.

Fourth, management must ensure that it is sufficiently familiar with the requirements for the success of each business and that it will not damage that business, whether by approving the wrong investment proposals, appointing the wrong general managers, or giving poor strategic guidance.

QUESTIONS FOR MANAGEMENT

The pursuit of added value often presents managers with challenging issues to resolve.

How can we grow if our core business is limited in terms of further expansion? This question arises when management has divested businesses that didn't fit and is left with one core business. If it has a commanding market share, competes in a nongrowing market, and has little opportunity for overseas expansion, the dilemma can be a real one. This is especially true in an era in which capital markets reject diversification and demand that companies stick to their knitting.

Capital markets are wary of any form of corporate diversification. They are simply being pragmatic: experience has shown them that diversification doesn't work well. What is the single-business company to do to find growth opportunities? There are four possible answers:

First, seek a way to reinvent the business by looking for new customers, new markets, new ways to present the product, and a better package of customer value to offer. Even commodity products can be differentiated by offering them in a different service context. Do make certain that growth limits really have been reached.

Second, consider moves into related businesses that share existing resources and skills. Such initiatives should possess the same requirements for success. If not, the management skills both at the business-unit level and in the parent company may be inadequate to the challenge.

Third, operate a nursery of new ideas. Business unit managers are always on the lookout for new products and markets. The more promising should be regarded as new-product research and development initiatives. Those that offer promise can then receive modest investment until there is a persuasive reason to make a serious commitment.

Finally, although unconventional in today's environment, it may be smart simply to operate the existing low-growth business for cash flow, eschewing major growth aspirations. Mature industries can often be sustained for a long time without heavy investment and achieve above-average returns.

What's wrong with vertical integration as a way of extending the opportunities for a stagnant business? In other words, why shouldn't we acquire our customer to guarantee an outlet for our products?

Vertical integration has increasingly lost favor among thoughtful managers. While it may seem like a sensible proposition to guarantee a supply of raw materials or markets for your products, vertical integration frequently exhibits three major shortcomings:

First, when one division sells products to another division, disagreement often arises about transfer pricing and product and service quality. The selling division realizes it has a captive customer and often works less hard to retain the business. Much time is wasted resolving such intramural issues.

Second, entry into new upstream or downstream businesses often involves competing with your existing customers. Several corporate breakups have been the result of the realization that this problem was insoluble under the existing ownership arrangements.

Third, entry into new businesses often involves dealing with differing requirements for success; it thus requires a new range of managerial skills and capabilities, both at the business-unit level and in the parent company. Mistakes are made, and the business suffers competitively.

Is it wise to limit the number of eggs in our basket? Management teams often seek positions in different industrial sectors simply to spread risk. They reason that when one sector is unattractive owing to a cyclical market turndown, other sectors can take up the slack. While this can give comfort to management teams, it's an unwise strategy in today's markets. Capital markets will say: "We can spread our own risk; you do what you know how to do." The management team that focuses its effort and investment on areas in which it has demonstrable skills will be rewarded appropriately in capital pricing.

DEMERGER AND BREAKUP

When it becomes clear that a failed corporate strategy is in place—when you recognize that substantial and discernible value is not being added—the question of portfolio changes arises. In some cases this may involve simply a trade, sale, or demerger of the business for which there is no fit. Sometimes, when the value-added formula has substantially dissipated, total breakup is indicated: the company ceases to exist in its entirety and breaks into several pieces.

Successful corporate strategists believe in the primacy of value added. They constantly seek out ways to provide the kind of help the businesses in the corporate portfolio need. They continually search for major improvement opportunities among the businesses. They adjust both their portfolio of businesses and the capabilities of the parent company to provide a continuing match between the needs of the business units and what the parent can provide. And when the businesses need no further help of the sort they can offer—and this often happens—they wish them Godspeed and release them into the outside world.

A CASE IN POINT

The U.K. conglomerate Hanson Trust offers a superb example of how to do it right. During the 1970s and 1980s it built a portfolio of low-tech, mature businesses by means of acquisition and disposal. It sought out undermanaged companies with major positions in mature businesses who were looking for opportunities to strengthen their competitive position by tight, disciplined management. When its acquisitions brought in businesses that didn't fit Hanson's profile, they were disposed of. Hanson was clear about its value-added formula: it found businesses whose fortunes could be dramatically improved through tight financial discipline and strong general management motivation. It worked well and shareholders benefited greatly.

In the 1990s it became apparent that the formula no longer had much to offer shareholders. Major opportunities for the Hanson treatment were waning, especially in the United Kingdom and the United States. All the fat targets had been exploited. At the same time computer-facilitated financial control systems made Hanson's approach an ordinary corporate capability. Finally the businesses in the Hanson stable became so well run that there was little improvement potential left. Realizing that the value-added formula had become obsolete, the company broke itself up into five pieces, each one of which has thrived competitively on its own.

The same caution should be applied to overseas diversification. Some management teams intentionally direct investment to different parts of the world in order to limit exposure in any one area. Unless such geographic expansion is initiated to strengthen one's competitive positioning in a particular global marketplace, the investment community is likely to scorn this form of expansion. There are simply too many downsides to investment abroad to undertake it without a solid competitive business rationale. Currency exposure, entry into alien market environments, and bone-wearying travel all represent significant costs of expanding internationally.

MANAGING YOUR PORTFOLIO

The following principles should help guide the process of planning your strategic portfolio.

Make sure that value is being added to every business in the portfolio by identifying ways in which each can be helped to achieve major improvement in performance.

Restrict the portfolio to activities in which a constructive fit—useful skills attuned to the needs of the businesses—exists at the center.

If growth prospects appear limited, try reinvention, moves into related businesses, new ideas, or a cash-cow strategy.

Consider vertical integration as a way of extending strategic opportunities.

Focus effort and investment on areas in which you have demonstrable skills: don't diversify into unknown areas.

When substantial and discernible value is not being added, change the portfolio.

David R. Sadtler is a Fellow of the Ashridge Strategic Management Centre in London, and a teacher and consultant on questions of strategy at both the corporate and business unit levels. He is the author of a number of articles on the issues and challenges of corporate-level strategy. He was the cofounder and executive vice president of Medi-Computer Corporation, and served as the first president of Vickers America Inc. He is a coauthor of *Breakup! When Large Companies Are Worth More Dead Than Alive* (Free Press, 1997) and *Successful Business Acquisition* (Delta Sierra, 2000). For more information, see www.sadtler.demon.co.uk.

Why Mergers Fail and How to Prevent It

Susan Cartwright

The incidence of M & A has continued to increase significantly during the last decade, both domestically and internationally. The sectors most affected by M & A activity have been service- and knowledge-based industries such as banking, insurance, pharmaceuticals, and leisure. Although M & A is a popular means of increasing or protecting market share, the strategy does not always deliver what is expected in terms of increased profitability or economies of scale. While the motives for merger can variously be described as practical, psychological, or opportunist, the objective of all related M & A is to achieve synergy, or what is commonly referred to as the 2 + 2 = 5 effect. However, as many organizations learn to their cost, the mere recognition of potential synergy is no guarantee that the combination will actually realize that potential.

MERGER FAILURE RATES

The burning question remains—why do so many mergers fail to live up to shareholder expectations? In the short term, many seemingly successful acquisitions look good, but disappointing productivity levels are often masked by onetime cost savings, asset disposals, or astute tax maneuvers that inflate balance-sheet figures during the first few years.

Merger gains are notoriously difficult to assess. There are problems in selecting appropriate indices to make any assessment, as well as difficulties in deciding on a suitable measurement period. Typically the criteria selected by analysts are:

- profit-to-earning ratios
- stock-price fluctuations
- managerial assessments

Irrespective of the evaluation method selected, the evidence on M & A performance is consistent in suggesting that a high proportion of M & As are financially unsuccessful. U.S. sources place merger failure rates as high as 80%, with evidence indicating that around half of mergers fail to meet financial expectations. A much-cited McKinsey study presents evidence arguing that most organizations would have received a better return on their investment if they had merely banked their money instead of buying another company. Consequently, many commentators have concluded that the true beneficiaries from M & A activity are those who sell their shares when deals are announced and the marriage brokers—the bankers, lawyers, and accountants—who arrange, advise, and execute the deals.

TRADITIONAL REASONS FOR MERGER FAILURE

M & A is still regarded by many decision makers as an exclusively rational, financial, and strategic activity, and not as a human collaboration. Financial and strategic considerations, along with price and availability, therefore dominate target selection, overriding the soft issues such as people and cultural fit. Explanations of merger failure or underperformance tend to focus on reexamining the factors that prompted the initial selection decision, for example: payment of an overinflated price for the acquired company; poor strategic fit; failure to achieve potential economies of scale because of financial mismanagement or incompetence; or sudden and unpredicted changes in market conditions.

This ground has been well trodden, yet the rate of merger, acquisition, and joint-venture success has improved little. Clearly these factors may contribute to disappointing M & A outcomes, but this conventional wisdom only part explains what goes wrong in M & A management.

THE FORGOTTEN FACTOR IN M & A
The false distinction that has developed between hard and soft merger issues has been extremely unhelpful in extending our understanding of merger failure, as it separates the impact of the merger on the individual from its financial impact on the organization. Successful M & A outcomes are linked closely to the extent to which management is able to integrate organizational members and their cultures and sensitively address and minimize individuals' concerns.

By representing sudden and major change, mergers generate considerable uncertainty and feelings of powerlessness. This can lead to reduced morale, job and career dissatisfaction, employee stress, and uncertainty. Rather than increased profitability, mergers have become associated with a variety of negative behavioral outcomes such as acts of sabotage and petty theft; increased staff turnover, with rates reported as high as 60%; increased sickness, and absenteeism.

Ironically, this occurs at the very time when organizations need and expect greater employee loyalty, flexibility, cooperation, and productivity.

PEOPLE FACTORS ASSOCIATED WITH M & A FAILURE
Studies like the one conducted by the British Institute of Management have identified a range of people factors associated with unsuccessful M & A. These include: underestimating the difficulties of merging two cultures; underestimating the problem of skills transfer; demotivation of employees; departure of key people; expenditure of too much energy on doing the deal at the expense of postmerger planning; lack of clear responsibilities, leading to postmerger conflicts; too narrow a focus on internal issues to the neglect of the customers and the external environment, and insufficient research about the merger partner or acquired organization.

DIFFERENCES BETWEEN MERGERS AND ACQUISITIONS
In terms of employee response, whether the transaction is described as a merger or an acquisition, the event will trigger uncertainty and fears of job losses. However, there are important differences. In an acquisition, power is substantially assumed by the new parent. Change is usually swift and often brutal as the acquirer imposes its own control systems and financial restraints. Parties to a merger are likely to be more

evenly matched in terms of size, and the power and cultural dynamics of the combination are more ambiguous. Integration is a more drawn-out process.

This has implications for the individual. During an acquisition there is often more overt conflict and resistance, and a sense of powerlessness. In mergers, however, because of the prolonged period between the initial announcement and actual integration, uncertainty and anxiety continue for a much longer time as the organization remains in a state of limbo.

CULTURAL COMPATIBILITY

The process of the merger is often likened to marriage. In the same way that clashes of personality and misunderstanding lead to difficulties in personal relationships, differences in organizational cultures, communication problems, and mistaken assumptions lead to conflicts in organizational partnerships.

Mergers are rarely a marriage of equals, and it's still the case that most acquirers or dominant merger partners pursue a strategy of cultural absorption; the acquired company or smaller merger partner is expected to assimilate and adopt the culture of the other. Whether the outcome is successful depends upon the willingness of organizational members to surrender their own culture and at the same time perceive that the other culture is attractive and therefore worth adopting.

Cultural similarity may make absorption easier than when the two cultures are very different, yet the process of due diligence rarely extends to evaluating the degree of cultural fit. Furthermore, few organizations bother to try to understand the cultural values and strengths of the acquiring workforce or their merger partners in order to inform and guide the way in which they should go about introducing change.

MAKING IT HAPPEN

Making a good organizational marriage currently seems to be a matter of chance and luck. This needs to change so that there is a greater awareness of the people issues involved and consequently a more informed integration strategy. Some basic guidelines for more effective management include:

- extension of the due diligence process to incorporate issues of cultural fit;
- greater involvement of human resource professionals;
- the conducting of culture audits before the introduction of change management initiatives;
- increased communication and involvement of employees at all levels in the integration process;
- the introduction of mechanisms to monitor employee stress levels;
- fair and objective reselection processes;
- providing management with the skills and training to sensitively handle M & A issues such as insecurity and redundancy.

Paul Hodder was involved as director of human resource management in the formation of Aeon Risk Services, a merger of four rather different retail-insurance-broking and risk-management companies. A major theme of their integration process was the formation of a series of task groups to review and identify best practice. Another part involved an organization-wide training program to provide individuals with life skills to help them initiate and cope with change, to improve teamwork, and to develop support networks. Enthusiasm for the program has provided several hundred change champions to lead change projects and assume support and mentoring roles. Good communication of early wins and successes has reassured organizational members that the changes are working and are beneficial.

Despite thorough pre-merger procedures, mergers continue to fall far short of financial expectations. The single biggest cause of this failure rate is poor integration following the acquisition. The identification of the target company, the subsequent and often drawn-out negotiations, and attending to the myriad of financial, technical, and legal details are all exhausting activities. Once the target company has been acquired, little energy or motivation is left to plan and implement the integration of the people and cultures following the merger. It seems nonsensical to waste all the resources and energy that has gone into the merger, through inadequate planning of the integration stage of the process, yet all too often organizations do just that. Without a properly planned integration process or its effective implementation, mergers will not be able to achieve the full potential of the acquisition.

Dr. Susan Cartwright is senior lecturer in organizational psychology at the Manchester School of Management, UMIST. Her research interests and publications are in the area of occupational stress and organizational culture and change, particularly in the context of mergers, acquisitions, and joint ventures. She has worked extensively with public and private organizations on a variety of projects related to stress management and human merger integration. She is currently coeditor of the *Leadership and Organization Development Journal* and book review editor for *Stress Medicine*. She is coauthor with Cary L. Cooper, of *Managing Workplace Stress* (Sage, 1997).

Power Struggling and Power Sharing

Jonas Ridderstråle

Information technology (IT) opens many opportunities for wealth creation but, from a more general economic point of view, IT in general—and the Net in particular—is best thought of as profit enemy no. 1. The current trends of digitization, deregulation, and globalization are altering the balance of power between those who sell and those who buy, on the one hand, and between capital and competence investors on the other. Combined, these changes make it increasingly difficult for firms to show a profit. Companies must respond by coming up with imaginative strategies to enhance the value of their intellectual capital.

MARKETS MEET MARX

Welcome to the information jungle, where markets flourish because they feed and breed on information. Some 30 years ago only 40% of all individuals lived within a market system. Now around 90% do so. The advent of what we might call global marketification has caused three identifiable trends:

1 *Overcapacity* is often the norm: 40% in automobiles, 100% in bulk chemicals, and 140% in computers.

2 While more products and services are available, they're often incredibly similar: *commoditization* rules.

3 The costs to find the best deal are falling dramatically; thanks to search power, comparison shopping has become a picnic.

In effect we're moving closer to a state of perfect competition. Power is transferred from those who sell to those who buy. The new consumer is a demanding dictator. The stupid, humble, and loyal customer is about to die.

Knowledge is our most critical resource. And just who owns that? We, as individuals, are the owners of our brains. Karl Marx was right: people now control the most critical resources—though individually, not collectively. Modern firms depend heavily on their *core competents*, that is, individuals who make competencies happen. Bill Gates once claimed that if 20 people left Microsoft, the company would risk bankruptcy. Competents are walking monopolies. They stay only as long as the organization can offer something they want. Power is now in the process of being transferred from capital owners to competence owners.

Companies will accordingly do business with demanding dictators, and negotiate salaries and stock-option plans with the business world's equivalents of Madonna and Tiger Woods. Indeed, one plausible hypothesis is that the more Web-based and knowledge-intensive the business, the less chance that any of the eventual profits will end up in the pockets of the purely financial investors of the company.

Any organization relies on a mix of financial and intellectual capital. Now exchange rates are changing. Financial capital is in the process of being devalued. To prosper, organizations must counter the forces of consumer and competent control by boosting their intellectual capital in three primary ways:

1 attracting human capital;
2 transforming it into structural capital, while simultaneously;
3 building customer capital.

HARNESSING HUMAN CAPITAL

Talented individuals have alternatives every minute, every day. Where competition in the labor market is increasingly generic, we're all players in a great global attraction game. Success is contingent on exploiting the fact that human beings simultaneously want to express their individuality and their need for belonging.

Individual Personalization. Attracting talent calls for a more personalized company. Today smart people hire organizations rather than vice versa. Competents have a choice: the organization is disposable, a temporary home. And human beings are not bulk goods. We differ. Firms either manage this differentiation or watch their most precious resources walk away. The consequence is that each and every little system needs to be personalized.

Organizational Tribalization. Peter Hagström has helped shaped my thinking on this immeasurably. Not only are people individualistic creatures, we also want to belong. Firms with a future will build organizational tribes in which employees share common traits or interests—rewards, ownership, culture, whatever. Today we see successful companies recruiting people with the right attitude, then training them in skills. Look at Hell's Angels or Greenpeace. Just imagine Hell's Angels hiring for skills! These organizations hire for attitude, because the half-life of knowledge is coming down fast, and it's easier for most of us to change our skills than our values.

SECURING STRUCTURAL CAPITAL

From the outlook of the firm, human capital is best thought of as a liability, while structural capital is definitely an asset on the balance sheet. Companies must therefore transform both the know-how and know-who components of their knowledge bases.

Knowledge Codification. The typical company may suffer not from knowing too little, but rather from not knowing what it knows. A critical task is thus to turn core competents into core competencies that are shared throughout the entire organization. Codification means collecting the knowledge of competents or *competeams* and transferring it to the organizational level. This way the firm not only provides others in the organization with an opportunity to learn, but becomes less dependent on a few competents.

Corporate Socialization. By working in teams and spending time together after work, people in groups soon develop tacit knowledge. Tacit knowledge makes it more difficult for competitors to imitate, and for competents to quit with their skill-sets intact. When knowledge is a combination of know-how and know-who, part of it will be nested in a network of relationships with existing colleagues. Anyone threatening to leave can thus only bring the intrapersonal skills along. Socialization = tacit knowledge = knowledge handcuffs.

CREATING CUSTOMER CAPITAL

In a world of customer control, companies will have to come up with new ways to deal with these demanding dictators. Once again the dual nature of humans, comprising elements of both individualism and collectivism, must be exploited.

Customer Tribalization. We all grew up in a world in which physical proximity ruled. Yesterday's tribes were geographically structured: Russians and Americans. The new tribes are biographically structured: they are global tribes of people who actually believe they have something in common, no matter where they were born. In a geographically structured world, companies competed for the local average. Smart firms today go for the global extremes. Consider the case of G & L Internet Bank, the first U.S. bank for homosexuals (G stands for gay and L for lesbian). The basic idea is to target the 21 million or so homosexuals (a group with a combined annual budget of some $800 billion), then to go global.

A second kind of global tribe is more transactional—*buyographical* rather than biographical. While demanding dictators may constitute powerful forces individually, just imagine what happens when they link up. And in a networked world they will. Tribes of customers will interact and create customer unions. So entrepreneurial firms provide platforms on which customers can indeed aggregate their demand. Just look at LetsBuyIt.com, an Internet auction house/coshopper. The company allows you to link with other consumers (anywhere!) who are interested in buying the same product. Whether LetsBuyIt or someone else will eventually dominate the market is beside the point. Coshopping sites will become to global buyographical tribes what traditional co-ops once were to blue-collar workers in the industrial society.

Total Customization. Within a consumer tribe there must be room for personalization and individual differences. Niches are becoming ever smaller in our fragmenting world. Recent technological developments open up many new opportunities for mass customization. But total customization involves more than the customer offering—it must encompass the entire experience. Innovative organizations help people avoid information overload and aid them in making smart choices. Either companies focus on internally producing this service by employing experts, aggregating information, and comparing prices (the way Pricerunner.com does), or they choose to more actively involve the consumers in the process (as does Amazon.com).

ALL YOU NEED IS LOVE

Given today's almost endless choices for customers and competents, only those companies that realize success rests with capturing the emotional human being will stand a chance. Moving from abundance to affection is a question not of applying more reason, but of fusing functionality with ethics and aesthetics. Logic leads to conclusions. Emotions trigger action. Sensibility rather than sense is the inevitable way forward.

Sounds too touchy-feely? There is hard evidence to prove it. Research in neuroscience shows that the brain's limbic system, which governs our feelings, is more powerful than the neocortex that controls intellect. The traffic instructions in our brains are clear: emotions have precedence.

MAKING IT HAPPEN
Define your organizational tribe by asking: who are we and where do we want to go? Then:

- Hire people for attitude and then train them for skill.
- Replace job descriptions with motivation descriptions.
- Personalize all aspects of all systems and contracts for all competents.
- Get competents to share their competencies—collect, codify, and communicate.
- Promote socialization at and away from work to develop knowledge handcuffs.
- Invite customers to join your tribe—and then constantly reinforce the bond.
- Customize the entire experience for the consumer, not only the customer offering.
- Remember that people differ. Figure out what makes customers and competents mad, sad, and glad. Then ask yourself that question—over and over again.

As digitization, combined with deregulation and globalization, perfects the global market economy, IT is enabling many of the strategies outlined above. Yet for a company to exist just on the Web is a bit like having a toilet back at the office—necessary, but not sufficient for the creation of a sustainable competitive advantage. IT merely provides the means to an end. The road to the future may end up in Silicon Valley, but it must start in Soul and pass through Values on the way to e-(motional) business.

———•———

Jonas Ridderstråle is Assistant Professor at the Center for Advanced Studies in Leadership at the Stockholm School of Economics, Sweden. He is the author of *Global Innovation: Managing International Innovation Projects at ABB and Electrolux* (IIB, Stockholm, 1996) and *Funky Business: Talent Makes Capital Dance* (Financial Times Prentice Hall, 1999). The latter, cowritten with Kjell Nordström, is an international bestseller that has been translated into more than 25 languages and has its own Web site at www.funkybusiness.com.

Toward a Total Global Strategy

George Yip

In the 1980s and the 1990s, many companies were still debating whether they should globalize. For most, this debate has now ended. Companies assume that they should globalize unless they can find very good reasons not to.

The spread of the Internet and the Web provides one compelling reason. Any company that creates a Web site has instant global reach, with corresponding demands for delivery and service. In addition, evidence shows that companies that globalize achieve better competitive and financial performance.

But globalizing, in the sense of spreading activities around the world, is not enough. Companies also need to be globally integrated. They need globally coherent strategies, global networks, and the ability to maximize profits on a global basis. However, turning a collection of country businesses into one worldwide business that has an integrated, global strategy is not easy. It presents one of the stiffest challenges for managers today, and is the acid test of a well-managed company.

THE CASE FOR GLOBALIZATION

Whatever the anti-globalization protestors may say to the contrary, a range of forces is driving companies around the world to globalize. Many managers view this as expanding their participation in foreign markets. But companies also need to globalize in another sense. They need to integrate their worldwide strategy. This contrasts with the traditional multinational approach.

In the past, multinationals have tended to set up country subsidiaries that design, produce, and market products or services that were tailored to local needs. But this model is now in question. Increasingly, the multinational approach is seen as a "multi-local strategy" rather than a truly global strategy.

Today, a growing number of managers are asking, if they are in a global industry, whether their business should have a global strategy. Better questions are: how global is our industry, and how global should our business strategy be? This is because virtually every industry has aspects that are global or potentially global. But some industries have more aspects that are global, and more intensely so.

Similarly, a strategy can be more or less global in its different elements. An industry is global to the extent that there are inter-country connections. A strategy is global to the extent that it is integrated across countries. Global strategy should not be equated with any one element—standardized products, or worldwide market coverage, or a global manufacturing network. Instead, global strategy should be a flexible combination of many elements.

BEYOND THE MULTINATIONAL MODEL

Recent and coming changes make it likely that in many industries a global strategy will be more successful than a multilocal one. Indeed, having a sound global strategy may well be the requirement for survival as the changes accelerate. These changes include: the increasing convergence of consumer tastes across countries; the reduction of tariff and non-tariff barriers; technology investments that are becoming too expensive to amortize in one market only, and competitors who are moving from country-by-country competition to global competition.

In the 1990s, the world saw greater convergence in customer needs and tastes; the drastic reduction of many government barriers to free trade and investment; an acceleration of enablers in communications, and a surge in globally-applicable new technological products and services. All this does not mean that every industry has become entirely global. But today, nearly every industry has a significant global segment in which customers prefer products or services that are much more global in nature.

Around the global segments, however, regional, national, or sub-national niches still exist. The size of the global segment varies, from very large in the personal computer industry, to relatively small in many parts of the food industry. But the global segment is increasing in size in nearly all cases.

TUMBLING BARRIERS TO TRADE

Around the world, trade barriers continue to fall. The most important examples include: the North American Free Trade Agreement among the United States, Canada, and Mexico; the continuing integration of the European Union; the formation of the new World Trade Organization in 1995, and China joining that body in 2001. The Asian Crisis of 1997 to 1999 has also helped to open up economies such as Japan and South Korea.

At the same time, the rise of the newly industrializing countries (NICs) such as Hong Kong, Taiwan, South Korea, Singapore, Thailand, Malaysia, Mexico, and Brazil has increased the number of viable sites for sophisticated manufacturing operations with low labor costs. Even China and India are beginning to join the industrialized world and the global market economy.

Almost every product or service market in the major world economies now has foreign competitors. They compete to sell everything from computers, to fast food, or medical diagnostic equipment. Increasing foreign competition is itself a reason for a business to globalize in order to gain the size and skills to compete more effectively. But an even greater spur to globalization is the advent of new global competitors who manage and compete on an integrated global basis.

THE GLOBAL REVOLUTION

In the 1980s these global competitors were primarily Japanese. Their central approach to global competition was one of the factors that allowed Japanese companies to conquer so many Western markets. In the 1990s, American and European companies responded to the Japanese challenge by focusing much more on quality. This was exemplified by the adoption of "six-sigma" quality by General Electric and Motorola. In addition, a growing number of American and, especially, European companies began to develop new models of globalization that were more flexible than the centralized Japanese approach. Companies such as Asea Brown Boveri, for example, developed networked models that combined the benefits of both global integration and national responsiveness.

In recent years, the communications and information revolution has also made it much easier to apply a globally-integrated approach to management. Improvements in air travel, computers, satellites and telecommunications make it much easier to communicate with, and control, far-flung operations. Today, in a world where e-mail has become pervasive, it is easy to forget the dramatic impact of the humble facsimile machine. Its immediacy plugged every executive's desk into the global market. The Internet and the Web completed this revolution.

CASES IN POINT

Gillette, the U.S. shaving products company, provides one of the most aggressive examples of globally standardized strategy. While many corporate strategies still regard local adaptations as essential to their success in foreign markets, Gillette minimizes adaptation for cultural differences. The company sells the same products, uses the same production methods, enforces the same corporate policies, and uses the same advertising in every country where it conducts business.

The results are impressive. The company now dominates the shaver market with a 70% market share worldwide. The main advantages of this business model are scale and flexibility, most notable in research and development costs and leveraging intellectual capital across the globe. In addition, the company is more nimble. This was demonstrated during the Asian crisis in the late 1990s. Rather than maintain advertising expenditures in an area with flat to negative growth, Gillette chose to shift its marketing funds to Eastern Europe, where better sales growth was forecast. It is because the company treats the world as one region that it has such flexibility in its operations.

Toyota is another company that has benefited from an integrated global approach. It recognized early that in the automobile industry, where some local customization is essential, a global strategy requires multi-regional production. In the late 1990s, Toyota spent over $10 billion on global expansion in an aggressive effort to become the first truly globally organized car manufacturer. The company developed manufacturing hubs in the three major markets—North America, Europe, and Asia—with the ability to customize vehicles for regional markets.

Such extensive coverage now allows Toyota to react quickly to local tastes, bypass regional trade barriers, and utilize locally based suppliers to increase cost efficiencies. The company set up an assembly plant in the United States as early as 1987 and continued expansion at a number of sites there and in Canada throughout the 1990s.

In Europe, by 2001, Toyota had a regional parts center in Belgium, and manufacturing plants in the United Kingdom, France, and Turkey (another was scheduled to open in Poland in 2002). This local production allows Toyota to bypass tariffs and locally produce Toyota's "Europe Car." In Asia, a local network of suppliers and assembly hubs allows Toyota to build sturdy, simply-designed, low-priced cars that appeal to the Asian consumer.

MAKING IT HAPPEN

So how can companies create truly global strategies? For most, there are three separate stages involved.

1 **Developing the core strategy**: this is the basis of sustainable strategic advantage. It is usually, but not necessarily, developed for the home country first. Without a sound core strategy to build upon, a global strategy cannot be successful.

2 **Internationalizing the core strategy**: this stage involves the international expansion of activities, and adaptation of the core strategy. Companies need to have mastered the basics of international business before they can attempt a global strategy (because the latter often involves breaking the rules of international business).

3 **Globalizing the international strategy**: this involves integrating the strategy across countries to leverage the company's total global potential.

Multinational companies are usually adept at the first two steps. What they are less familiar with is the third stage. For one thing, total globalization runs counter to the accepted wisdom of tailoring for national markets. Yet, it is this third step that is vital to creating a successful total global strategy.

The first step towards a global strategy, then, is the creation of a viable core strategy. This involves several key elements:

- selection of the type of products or services that the business offers;
- the types of customers that the business serves;
- the geographic markets served;
- major sources of sustainable competitive advantage;
- functional strategy for each of the most important value-adding activities;
- competitive posture, including the selection of competitors to target;
- investment strategy.

At the second stage, a business expands outside its home market and needs to internationalize its core business strategy. The key to internationalizing is to select the geographic markets in which to compete. This choice has much more importance for an international business than for a national business.

For most businesses, international market selection presents issues that are much more challenging. These include the role of barriers to trade—such as import tariffs and quotas, and foreign ownership rules—as well as differences from the home country in laws, language, tastes, and behavior. Other aspects of internationalization strategy involve how to adapt products and programs to take account of foreign needs, preferences, culture, language, climate, and so on.

Typically, the end result is that the company ends up with strategies and approaches that involve large differences among countries. These differences can then weaken the company's worldwide cost position, quality, customer preference, and competitive leverage.

This is where a global strategy comes in. It involves strategic integration across all markets to leverage competitive advantage.

A key issue here is: what aspects of strategy should be globalized? Managers can answer this question by analyzing industry conditions or "industry globalization drivers." This provides the basis for evaluating the benefits and costs of globalization, and creates a clearer understanding of the different ways in which a globalization strategy can be used through the use of "global strategy levers."

Industry globalization drivers are externally determined by industry conditions or by the economics of the business. They fall into four groups—market, cost, government, and competitive drivers.

Taken together, these represent the industry conditions that determine the potential and need for competing with a global strategy. Each group of drivers is different for each industry and can also change over time.

Global strategy levers, on the other hand, are the choices available to the business. They operate along five dimensions. Market participation—involves the choice of country-markets, and the level of activity. Products/services—involves the extent to which business offers the same or different products in different countries. Location of value-adding activities—involves the choice of where to locate each of the activities that comprise the entire value-added chain, from research to production to after sales service. Marketing—involves the extent to which a business uses the same brand names, advertising and other marketing elements in different countries. Competitive moves—involves the extent to which a worldwide business makes competitive moves in individual countries as part of a global competitive strategy.

A global strategy should aim to ensure that all global strategy levers are optimally positioned relative to the industry drivers, and relative to the position and resources of the business and its parent company. In this way, a company ensures that the global whole is greater than the sum of its local parts.

———

George Yip, Professor of Strategic and International Management at London Business School, is one of the world's leading authorities on global strategy and marketing, internationalization and multinational strategies for the Asia-Pacific region. His widely-acclaimed books include *Total Global Strategy* (Prentice Hall, 2nd. ed., 2002), *Asian Advantage* (Perseus, 1998), and *Strategies for Central and Eastern Europe* (Palgrave, 2000).

Strategy in Turbulent Times

Costas Markides

In our turbulent and uncertain times it is tempting for companies to wonder whether they do actually require a strategy. They do.

By way of proof, imagine that you find yourself in the middle of a dark and hostile jungle. If you want to get out of the jungle, do you need a strategy?

Think about it. In the dense foliage you cannot see farther than a few feet. You want to get out of this jungle, but you don't know how and you don't know which way to turn. There is total uncertainty. How then can you get out alive? Well, the last thing you want to do is to stay still, paralyzed by uncertainty. You need to analyze your position based on the available information and then decide on a direction. That's the first principle of strategy—the need to make difficult choices based on what information you have at the time. You take stock, gather information based on that, and then start walking. The worst thing is to stay still. That's the second principle of strategy— the need to stop analyzing and start doing, even if you are not entirely sure that what you are doing is going to turn out to be the right thing.

After you start walking, new information comes your way. The new information may allow you to revise your original direction. That's the third principle of strategy—the need to learn as you go along and modify your strategy through trial and error. If you meet a wild animal or run into a canyon, your strategy (or direction) has to change. Therefore, strategy is all about making difficult choices in the face of uncertainty, and then learning as you go along and adjusting your original choices. When you think of it like this, it's obvious that you need a strategy—even (or especially) in times of uncertainty.

THE SEARCH FOR DIFFERENCE

If strategy is necessary, the next question is how to come up with a *differentiated* strategy.

In many industries competing companies have the same suppliers, are structured in much the same way, receive their information from the same sources, use the same consultants, and so on. They receive much the same information. And yet some pursue genuinely different strategies.

The difference lies in mental processing. How companies process the information around them will determine what they do.

Indeed, this is what differentiates innovators from other companies. Most companies try to become better than their competitors. But for almost all companies other than the established leader, being better is not the right way. They need to play a different game. Look at EasyJet, e*trade, or Schwab. These are companies intent, not on being better, but on playing a different game. They thought of new ways of playing the game. The managers of these companies face the same information as everyone else in their industries, yet they process this information differently and come up with differentiated strategies. Companies get the same inputs, but it's what they do with the inputs to change the rules of the game that matters.

ESTABLISHED BUT DIFFERENT

Many established companies develop a winning strategy and then spend all their time trying to improve it and make it better. They rarely consider "cannibalizing" their current strategy in favor of a different one. They judge the risks of doing so too high. Yet all around us established companies are being toppled by newcomers that adopt different strategies.

The solution? Companies must continue to improve their existing strategies, but they must also continuously strive to discover new or different strategies. They should try to be better and different at the same time.

PLAYING TWO GAMES

The question is, how can a company play two games simultaneously? Harvard Business School's Michael Porter suggests that doing this is so difficult that most companies that attempt it will fail. His advice is for companies to focus on only one game. His Harvard colleague Clay Christensen suggests that a company can play two games at the same time, but that the new game needs to be separate from the main business.

My own research suggests that although it's difficult, companies can still play two games without necessarily separating them. More importantly, it implies that when established companies are attacked by a new way of playing the game, they do not necessarily have to respond by adopting the new game.

What established companies need to appreciate is that the new, disruptive ways of playing the game are not God-sent. The new ways are not preordained to win out. Established companies could respond by killing off the new ways. For example, why is Internet banking the game of the future? Is it more convenient or more efficient than traditional banking? Why don't banks respond to Internet banking, *not* by adopting it, but by making their traditional operations so good that consumers simply wouldn't find banking over the Internet an attractive proposition?

CASES IN POINT

Look at what happened with Gillette back in the 1970s when it came under attack by Bic. The strategy adopted by Bic was certainly different from Gillette's. But Gillette didn't respond by adopting the Bic strategy. Instead, it invested $1 billion in its existing strategy to develop a superior product—the Mach 3—which was then used to destroy Bic and the disposable razor threat. Who buys disposable razors now?

Consider also the case of Swatch. In the 1970s the Swiss watchmakers competed on the basis of their craftsmanship. Then Japanese companies (like Seiko) attacked by offering better prices, the latest technology, more features. Everybody thought that this would be the end of the Swiss watch industry. Instead, Swatch hit back at the Japanese. But rather than trying to compete with them on their terms (that is, price and features), Swatch introduced a new competitive dimension—style and design—as the basis for competition.

Consider Merrill Lynch today. It competes on the basis of research and advice. Schwab and e*trade have now attacked it on the basis of cheaper transaction costs and faster execution of trades. Merrill Lynch will not succeed against them if it, too, chooses to play the price and speed game. What it has to do is innovate and discover new competitive dimensions—different reasons why a customer should buy from Merrill Lynch.

CONFUSING CREATIVITY AND INNOVATION

One of the problems is that the difference between innovation and creativity (or invention) is often misunderstood. Coming up with new ideas is not innovation—it's creativity. Innovation is deciding which ideas to select and implement to create value. A lot of research tends to emphasize creativity rather than innovation.

Innovation is about coming up with ideas and then finding ways to scale them up to create mass markets out of them.

For example, consider the market for PCs. Who is the innovator in this market? Most people think the answer is Apple, or perhaps Osborne. But who really created the mass market for PCs? Who should be credited with the fact that the personal computer is not some high-tech gimmick that only nerds use, but is instead a fixture in every home? The answer is simple—IBM. IBM scaled it up. IBM created the mass market. Yet nobody considers IBM as an innovator.

Therefore, innovation is not just coming up with ideas but also scaling them up to create big markets. Most of the dot-coms failed because they didn't know how to sell to customers, to bring ideas to a mass market.

The trouble is that while coming up with ideas is celebrated as innovative, the act of scaling them up into big markets is not. Even worse, scaling up—rather than coming up with new ideas—is what big companies are good at, but they often forget this and try instead to become brilliantly creative like the small startups. Instead of taking the ideas of others and converting them into big markets, they focus on coming up with ideas themselves and waste time and resources trying to do so. Unfortunately, this is what small firms excel at.

CONVERTING BIG FIRMS INTO SMALL FIRMS

Over the last ten years we have tried to convert big firms into small firms. There's a lot of talk about injecting big corporations with the entrepreneurial culture of the small firm, or breaking up the big ones to make them as agile and flexible as the small ones. This won't happen. The big firm will never become as creative as the small firm. What the big corporation is good at is scaling up, not creativity. Our attention should shift toward making the big corporation better at what it is good at—not making it like the small ones.

We have a cultural bias in favor of coming up with ideas, and a real lack of appreciation for the challenging task of taking the idea and converting it into a mass market. Similarly, there is a bias in defining innovation as something new. But the real trick is how to convert something new from being a plaything of the few into the mass market.

MAKING IT HAPPEN

If you ask a group of C.E.O.s how to make their organizations more innovative, you'll get a long laundry list of ideas on how to do it—allow experiments, reward new ideas, don't punish mistakes, and so on. The problem is not that they don't know how to do it, but that it doesn't happen.

So why don't they do it? Senior executives know what they can do to promote innovation, but the personal risks are simply too high. Innovation carries a huge personal risk; how many people will actually put themselves on the line? After all, what they get evaluated on at the end of the year isn't generating innovative ideas, it's delivering the numbers.

Over and above this, we tend to forget that innovation is an art. Even if you have all the ingredients, it doesn't guarantee that you'll get innovation. The key is how you put it all together. The baking of the cake is more important than its raw materials.

To make it happen we need to train people *how* to think, not what to think. We also need to give people a sense that organizations are not there simply to make money for individuals and the company, but that they have a social purpose in the community. The important thing is for young people to get into business not only because it's a good way to make money, but also because through their companies they can help create something that improves the state of the world.

Take the young people who worked as a team to develop the Apple Mac as an example. They weren't just making a computer, they were on a mission to change the way people thought about computers. In the end, galvanizing people isn't about money, but about having a purpose beyond money. Making money is implicit.

The modern corporation is very delicate. It must be able to make an accurate assessment of the external environment so it takes the right strategic position. In addition, the organization must also remain true to its unwritten moral contract with employees. This contract promises to provide employees with an environment that sustains them and allows them to grow as individuals.

This delicate balancing act requires a new kind of corporation, one with different structures, processes, mindsets, and behaviors than has been the norm for the last 50 years. We need to totally rethink how we manage corporations.

If they are to be flexible and fluid, companies need to become ameba-like—able to move one way while always responding to local stimuli and changing direction in response to new information from the environment.

This can only be achieved by giving people autonomy and the freedom to monitor what's going on around them and respond as they see fit.

Costas Markides is Robert P. Bauman Professor of Strategic Leadership at London Business School. His books include *Strategic Thinking for the Next Economy* (co-edited with Michael Cusumano, 2001) and *All the Right Moves: A Guide to Crafting Breakthrough Strategy* (Harvard Business School Press, 1999).

Competitor Analysis: From Data to Insight

Liam Fahey

Executives, among others, often misconstrue why competitor analysis (CA) is conducted. Its purpose and benefits are not just to learn about one's competitors. Competitors are analyzed as one means of learning about the broader competitive environment—that is, in order to generate insights into customers, distribution channels, suppliers, technology, and competitive dynamics. In the same vein, CA is also used to reflect on and learn about one's own organization—its vulnerabilities, limitations, and capabilities relative to current and potential rivals.

WHICH COMPETITORS MERIT ATTENTION?

Potential insight is sometimes unnecessarily constrained in many firms because too much attention is devoted to *current* large-market-share competitors and far too little to other types of current and potential competitors. Critical insight into change in customers' buying behaviors often emanates from analysis of small(er) rivals or of functional substitute rivals. And, sometimes, it is especially useful to "invent" a competitor that is not yet in the marketplace—for example, one created by the alliance and integration of two smaller rivals, which would then develop and introduce a range of products new to the market—and use it as a reference point to challenge the firm's existing strategy or potential strategy alternatives.

THE PROCESS OF ANALYSIS

The core of the analysis process in CA can be simply stated: identify relevant indicators from competitors' behaviors, actions, and words, then draw inferences as to what change along those indicators would imply for what the competitor might do in the future (for example, how it might change its strategy), or what it might suggest about developments in the broader marketplace (such as how fast specific products might come to the market or how quickly other products might penetrate particular customer segments). It is especially important to emphasize that CA is always about detecting change in and around competitors and assessing what that change implies for the competitor itself, for the marketplace in general, or for your own organization.

THE FOCUS OF COMPETITOR ANALYSIS

A central competitor-analysis question confronts every organization: *what is it about our rivals that we should analyze?* Or, stated differently, what do we need to know about our current and potential rivals? When competitor analysis is driven by a perspective that views it as a source of learning about both the competitive environment and our own organization, however, and not just as a source of learning about our rivals, then a number of other core focal points of analysis quickly surface.

We need to learn about:

- The competitor's *marketplace strategy*: how it tries to outmaneuver rivals in the marketplace.
- The competitor's *activity/value chain*: how it organizes itself to develop and execute its marketplace strategy.
- The competitor's *alliances and networks*: what other organizations it aligns with and how it manages its network of alliances.
- The competitor's *assumptions*: what the competitor assumes about the marketplace and itself.
- The competitor's *assets and capabilities*: what enables the competitor to compete.
- The competitor's *organizational infrastructure and culture*: the nature of the competitor's organization.

CAPTURING COMPETITORS' MARKETPLACE STRATEGIES

Let us take marketplace strategy to quickly illustrate some key points in how to conduct CA.

Understanding a competitor's marketplace strategy requires you to answer three fundamental, highly interrelated questions related to the rival's marketplace scope, posture, and goals—the three central elements in any firm's marketplace strategy:

1 What product-markets does the competitor compete in (or want to compete in)?
2 How does it compete in those product-markets to attract, win, and retain customers?
3 What does it seek to achieve in those product-markets?

You can now think about the critical indicators associated with each question. Question (1) involves indicators associated with products and customers: the range of products offered; the variety within each product line; the segments of customers reached; differences across the segments, etc.

Indicators that allow posture to be identified depend upon the relevant dimensions associated with its key modes of competing or providing value to customers—product line width, product features, functionality, service, availability, image and reputation, selling and relationships, and price. For example, for a car manufacturer, functionality might involve a number of dimensions, each giving rise to specific indicators: takeoff speed (how fast can the car go from zero to 60 mph); braking speed (how fast can you stop the car going at 40 mph); gasoline consumption (how many miles will the car go on a gallon of gasoline); reliability (on average, how often does this type of car have to be repaired).

Indicators that allow marketplace goals to be inferred are also specific to the particular type of goal: product, customer, market share, share of customer, etc.

One great merit of attention to indicators is that they guide you to relevant data sources. The overarching question is always: *What sources might provide data on this particular indicator?* You should always begin by asking which individuals or units within your own organization might possess the required data and what the external sources might be.

For example, a team of competitor analysts in one automobile manufacturer wished to know the terms and conditions associated with purchases of key components from particular suppliers, such as specific types of glass from a well-known international glass manufacturer and specific types of plastic from a local supplier. They discovered that their own internal purchasing department already possessed most of the required data.

The essence of the analysis task then becomes the derivation of inferences from the change detected along relevant indicators. For example, change along a number of indicators specific to the posture's modes of competition, as discussed above, could reveal that a competitor is moving its posture to increasingly add value for customers in terms of a broader range of service dimensions or through introducing new forms of functionality or by developing more intensive relationships with high-end customers.

ASSESSING COMPETITORS' MARKETPLACE STRATEGIES

Analysis only generates real insight when it turns to assessing what change in the competitor's strategy indicates the current, emerging, and potential change in the broader competitive context, and what such change in turn implies for the firm's current and potential strategy, decisions, and actions.

Assessment begins by evaluating the performance of the rival's strategy. Is it resulting in market-share gain? Is it leading to a greater share of individual customers? Is it building greater brand name and reputation (that in turn could be the basis of further market-share gain)?

Assessment then addresses how well the rival's strategy is performing compared to other rivals or to our own firm's strategy. For example, with regard to specific customer segments, or even individual customers, is the competitor or our own firm providing greater value along the modes of competition? Based upon customers' judgments, who is providing superior functionality? Who is providing more useful services? Whose image and reputation is more appealing to customers? It is important to note that these assessments must be based in large measure on the judgments of the customers themselves.

Assessment then aims to determine what change in the rival's marketplace strategy might portend for change in the emerging and potential marketplace. For example, customers' positive responses to a rival's recently introduced product might suggest significant shifts in the value customers will increasingly demand from their suppliers. If the firm misses this signal, it could commit extensive investment to products that will be less appealing to the market.

To cite one more illustration, if a competitor appears to be committing extensive resources to introducing new product lines, to going after new customer segments, and to seeking a greater share of existing customers, then it may well significantly shift the dynamics of rivalry over time. Its rivals may find that their old ways of competing may no longer be sufficient to retain existing customers, much less attract new ones.

Assessment of change in competitors' marketplace strategy can also lead to strong judgments about what type of marketplace strategy might be required to win in particular product domains or specific geographic regions. For example, in one product area, one computer firm concluded from the analysis of a dominant rival's marketplace strategy change, and from the product initiatives of a recent entrant, that the only way any firm could succeed in this product/technology was to develop multiple alliances with a range of vendors (so that it could continue to develop state-of-the-art products) and with a range of value-added resellers and other type of retailers (so that it could guarantee rapid access to large segments of customer).

Assessment concludes by identifying specific implications for one's own firm. For example, do the marketplace implications of change in the rival's strategy suggest that one is missing an emerging marketplace opportunity or that one should be moving faster to penetrate a specific customer segment? Often, assessment reveals key vulnerabilities not just in one's own marketplace strategy but also in one's assets and capabilities.

MAKING IT HAPPEN

In summary, competitor analysis can lead to significant new insights into the world around us, as well as into our own organization.

- Focus on analyzing the information gained on competitors in order to reflect on and learn one's own organization's vulnerabilities, capabilities, and future direction.
- Examine six areas of competitor activity: marketplace strategy; activity/value chain; alliances and networks; assumptions; assets and capabilities; and organizational infrastructure and culture.
- Ask what sources can provide the data you need. Look internally for sources of information first.
- Always consider what a change in competitor's activity indicates about the potential change in a broader competitive context.

While many managers feel that it's all they can do to collect and analyze information about their own business, one cannot really compete in today's business environment without some understanding of what the competition is up to. Competitor analysis is a new aspect of a manager's job, and it has rapidly become a respected discipline. However, analyzing the ways of one's competitors is valuable only when a company subsequently makes decisions about how it can perform better, based on a wider view of what's happening in the marketplace.

Liam Fahey is adjunct professor of strategic management at Babson College, Massachusetts, and visiting professor of strategic management at the Cranfield School of Management in the United Kingdom. His research, teaching, and consulting centers on competitive strategy, macroenvironmental and competitor analysis, with special emphasis on linking strategy, scenarios, and knowledge. Fahey is the author or editor of eight books and over 40 articles or book chapters. His most recent books, published by John Wiley, include *Learning from the Future* (1998), *Competitors: Outwitting, Outmaneuvering and Outperforming* (1999), and *The Portable MBA in Strategy* (2nd ed., 2001).

Setting Objectives for a Business

Allan A. Kennedy

Managing is the task of moving an enterprise toward a defined objective. Most of the disciplines of management—budgeting, strategic planning, performance monitoring—take as a given that an appropriate objective has been set. Given the central role that objectives or targets play in most management actions, it is critical that they be set correctly. It may seem trite to point out, but it is none the less valid: if inappropriate objectives are set for a business, inappropriate outcomes will occur.

What constitutes appropriate objectives for a business? As business and management have evolved, thinking about what constitutes an appropriate objective has evolved as well. Throughout this evolution, there has been an ongoing tension between financial goals and objectives and nonfinancial objectives. If business exists primarily or solely to make a profit (a highly quantifiable outcome), then relatively simple financial objectives suffice, argue some. Others say that business exists to serve simultaneously the needs of various constituencies—shareholders, customers, suppliers, employees, communities. The interests of these various legitimate constituencies are not always quantifiable, leading to a school of thought that puts greater emphasis on nonfinancial objectives. The history of business would suggest that both types of objectives are important.

A BRIEF HISTORY OF BUSINESS OBJECTIVES

Most businesses that were launched in the 19th century began their life as some form of family enterprise. As family businesses, their objectives were quite clear: to provide an ongoing source of income and, where necessary, employment for current and future members of the family.

As the technology of management has evolved, ideas about what constitutes the right objective for a business have changed. In his book *Concept of the Corporation*, first published in 1946, Peter Drucker described the purpose of a corporation as generating the maximum profit achievable from its operations. He went on to comment on the potential conflict between this purpose and society's expectation that the job of business was to maximize the production of cheap goods and services for consumption. To a modern observer, Drucker's thinking seems simplistic.

Drucker based his comments on work he had done with General Motors (GM), then the largest industrial enterprise in the world. The people he worked with in GM were convinced he got it wrong. To set the record straight, the legendary leader of General Motors from 1923 until 1946, Alfred P. Sloan, Jr., wrote his own account of the GM system of management, which he called *My Years with General Motors*. In that book, Sloan described a high-level task force effort he led in 1920 to define the concept of GM's business. He articulated a purpose for GM's business quite different from Drucker's version. "We made the assumption . . . that the first purpose in . . .

establishment of a business [is that it] will pay *satisfactory* dividends and *preserve* and *increase* its capital value" [emphasis added].

As a reflection of Sloan's influence in the business world, in the 1950s and 1960s most businesses sought to operate with a conservative balance sheet while showing steady signs of growth in sales, assets, profits, dividends, and shareholder equity.

During the 1950s and 1960s, new types of companies emerged on the familiar business landscape. These companies were young, entrepreneurial, and managed by hands-on practitioners, each in his own fashion on a mission. This new breed included the likes of Hewlett-Packard, a company set up to make useful technical contributions in a variety of engineering markets. It also included companies like Wal-Mart, whose driving rationale was providing superior value to its customers.

All of these new companies were in business to make a profit, both as a return to their investors and as a measure of the value of what they were doing as a company. These financial objectives were, however, secondary to their broader institutional objectives. Because many of these new companies grew very rapidly and became, relatively speaking, darlings of the stock market, many established companies modified their traditional objectives to focus on achieving specified levels of growth in revenues and profits in an attempt to keep pace.

In the late 1970s, a new theory about appropriate objectives for business was developed by academics specializing in the complex area of accounting. Their theory held that since shareholders owned companies, the real objective of business should be maximizing shareholder value. They went on to point out that conventional accounting measures of profitability, such as earnings per share of public companies, were very poor proxies indeed for the true value of a company. Instead they urged business people to focus on the present value of future cashflow streams as a truer measure of value. Most managers ignored this advice for all practical purposes, but some specialized investment bankers, who came to be known as "corporate raiders" or "leveraged buyout bankers," took the insights of the academics very seriously.

The immediate result was an unprecedented wave of corporate takeovers during the 1980s. The longer-term result was a fundamental rethinking of what business was all about by most managers, as they adopted shareholder-value thinking as a means of defending themselves from the corporate raiders.

Throughout the 1990s, maximizing shareholder value was the driving purpose of most businesses, and managers did virtually anything they could to ensure that their stock price—the most direct proxy for shareholder value—rose steadily.

LIMITATIONS OF RELYING SOLELY ON FINANCIAL OBJECTIVES

The stock market boom of the 1990s seemed to prove that focusing on shareholder value was the right way to run a business. But the boom of the 1990s gave way to the economic slowdown and stock market correction of 2000 and 2001. With the change in the business climate, the problems associated with over-reliance on maximizing shareholder value became apparent. With an exclusive focus on rewarding shareholders, many companies simply failed to take care of the legitimate needs of the other constituencies they depended on to provide them with a profitable future. As a result, these other constituencies rebelled.

Employees, having been treated as commodities by the companies they worked for, stopped being loyal to their employers and sold their services to the highest bidder. Especially for high-tech companies in places like Silicon Valley, this change in the labor marketplace forced employers to pay top dollar to get the talent they needed, and left them saddled with the costs inherent in a high-turnover workforce.

Suppliers, who had been forced to accept lower and lower prices for providing ever-increasing amounts of service to their customers, banded together in a last-ditch effort to survive. In some very important sectors like the automobile industry, this led to more concentrated groups of suppliers who had more market power than the customers they served.

Customers, whose choices had been limited by companies intent on pruning product lines and closing outlets to produce higher immediate profits, responded by steadily reducing their loyalty to brands and increasingly shopping for the lowest price available, regardless of the consequences for the companies that supplied them.

Governments, which had once bent over backwards to entice companies to invest, increasingly eliminated investment subsidies and began negotiating tighter and tighter agreements and strictly enforcing the terms of these agreements.

The net effect of these changes in the business environment is that the path to future growth and profitability is compromised for many of the companies that so excelled in their pursuit of shareholder value.

THE STAYING POWER OF NONFINANCIAL OBJECTIVES

Why do some companies seem to thrive over a very long period of time, while others have a brief moment in the sun and then recede into obscurity? There are a number of factors that account for this long-term pattern of success, including leadership, the quality of management, and the dynamics of the markets they serve. James Collins and Jerry Porras in their landmark book, *Built to Last*, suggest there is one common element. Companies that thrive for a long time all have a nonfinancial vision of what they are in business to accomplish. The 3M company exists to create useful products through innovation. Boeing exists to be at the leading edge of the aeronautics field. Marriott has a mission to make its customers feel like they have a home away from home. Johnson & Johnson exists to help alleviate pain and suffering. All of these companies, and the others cited by Collins and Porras, also work hard to make a profit and return value to their shareholders. However, producing profits and generating value for their shareholders was a byproduct of the broader objectives each of these companies sought to pursue.

Why this should be so is actually quite simple. Most people who work for companies need a broader goal than purely a financial one to motivate them to perform at their best. The companies profiled by Collins and Porras provided their people with just such a broader mission, treated them as full partners in the pursuit of this broader goal, and as a result realized higher levels of commitment and motivation from them. The companies reward this higher level of commitment and loyalty with policies appropriate to maintaining an ongoing partnership. To be viable and successful, every business must set and work hard to achieve a series of financial goals and objectives. But having financial objectives alone will not produce superior performance over the long term.

MAKING IT HAPPEN

How can a manager at any level of business decide whether or not the objectives set for the business are sound? There are no firm rules to rely on, but there are some common-sense tests any manager can apply to determine whether the objectives set are:

- compelling—capable of getting someone's attention;
- motivating—likely to inspire someone to put in extra effort;
- consistent—able to be met without compromise;
- achievable—reachable with reasonable levels of effort and commitment;
- distinguishing—something that when achieved will set the company or business apart from others;
- competitively superior—difficult enough to attain so that the achievement will produce superior rewards from the markets served and the investing public;
- satisfying—of such a nature that the achievement of the objective will produce a personal sense of satisfaction among those who contributed;
- lasting—likely to pass the test of time.

Tests like these are applicable to financial as well as nonfinancial objectives.

Making a profit and delivering value to shareholders is motivating indeed for anyone engaged in business. However, it is simply not a sufficient motivator to produce the kind of extra effort over a long period of time that produces superior long-term performance.

Allan A. Kennedy is a Boston-based management consultant and writer. He is co-author with Terrence Deal of *Corporate Cultures* (Perseus, reissue 2000) and *The New Corporate Cultures* (Perseus, 1999). He has also written *The End of Shareholder Value* (Perseus, 2000) and numerous articles.

The Balanced Scorecard

Robert S. Kaplan and David P. Norton

The Balanced Scorecard is a performance measurement and management system using objectives and measures in four interrelated perspectives—financial, customer, internal process, and learning and growth. We introduced the Balanced Scorecard in the early 1990s because we believed that an exclusive reliance on financial measures in a management system would be insufficient for the 21st century. Strategies for creating value had shifted from managing tangible assets to knowledge-based strategies that created and deployed an organization's intangible assets, including customer relationships, innovative products and services, high-quality operating processes, and the skills, knowledge, and motivation of its workforce.

Organizations such as Mobil North American Marketing and Refining, Cigna Property and Casualty Insurance, Brown and Root Engineering Services, and Chemical (Chase) Bank implemented the Balanced Scorecard, embedded it into their management systems, and achieved breakthrough performance within two years. Our research has revealed a set of five principles, built around the Balanced Scorecard system, that enabled these and other organizations to execute their strategies rapidly.

Principle 1: Mobilize Change through Executive Leadership. The single most important condition for success is the ownership and active involvement of the executive team. A Balanced Scorecard program starts with the recognition that it is not a "metrics" project; it's a change project. Initially, executive leaders must *mobilize* the organization, creating momentum to get the process launched. Once mobilized, leadership focus shifts to *governance* to install the new performance model. Gradually a new management system evolves—a *strategic management system* that institutionalizes the new cultural values and processes into a new system for managing. Convergence to the system can take two to three years.

Principle 2: Translate the Strategy into Operational Terms. The objectives and measures on a Balanced Scorecard help executive teams better understand and articulate their strategies. The scorecard provides a framework for organizing strategic objectives into four perspectives:

1 *Financial*—the strategy for growth, profitability, and risk, viewed from the perspective of the shareholder.
2 *Customer*—the strategy for creating value and differentiation from the perspective of the customer.
3 *Internal Business Processes*—the strategic priorities for various business processes that create customer and shareholder satisfaction.
4 *Learning and Growth*—the priorities to create a climate that supports organizational change, innovation, and growth.

From work done with an initial set of implementers, we developed a strategy map to provide a graphical representation of a well-constructed Balanced Scorecard. A strategy map, a logical and comprehensive architecture for describing strategy, specifies the critical elements and their linkages for an organization's strategy. It creates a common point of reference for all organization units and their employees.

Organizations build strategy maps from the top down, starting with the destination and then charting the routes that lead there. Corporate executives first review their mission statement (why their company exists) and core values (what their company believes in). From that information, they develop their strategic vision (what their company wants to become). This vision creates a clear picture of the company's overall goal.

Once the strategy map has been defined and agreed to by the executive team, the design of a scorecard with measures and targets is a straightforward process. The strategy map approach illustrates the idea that Balanced Scorecards should not just be collections of financial and nonfinancial measures organized into four perspectives. Balanced Scorecards should reflect the strategy of the organization. A good test is whether you can understand the strategy by looking only at the scorecard and its strategy map.

Principle 3: Align the Organization to the Strategy. The Balanced Scorecard is a powerful tool to describe a business unit's strategy. But organizations consist of numerous sectors, business units, and specialized departments, each with its own operations and often its own strategy. For synergy to occur across these diverse units, the strategies across these units need to be coordinated. The Balanced Scorecard helps to define the strategic linkages that integrate the performance of multiple organizations. Each unit formulates a strategy appropriate for its target market in light of the specific circumstances it faces—competitors, market opportunities, and critical processes—but that is consistent with the themes and priorities of the corporation or division. The measures at the individual business unit levels do not have to add to a corporate or divisional measure, unlike financial measures that aggregate easily from sub-units to departments to higher organizational levels. The business unit managers choose local measures that *influence,* but are not necessarily identical to, the corporate scorecard measures.

Beyond aligning the business units, strategy-focused organizations must also align their staff functions and shared-service units, such as human resources, information technology, purchasing, environmental, and finance. Often this alignment is accomplished with a service agreement between each functional department and the business units. The service agreement defines the menu of services to be provided, including their functionality, quality level and cost.

When this process is complete, all the organizational units—line business units and staff functions—have well-defined strategies that are articulated and measured by Balanced Scorecards and strategy maps. This alignment allows corporate-level synergies to emerge, in which the whole exceeds the sum of the individual parts.

Linkages can also be established across corporate boundaries to define relationships with key suppliers, customers, outsourcing vendors and joint ventures. Companies use such scorecards with external parties to be explicit about (1) the objectives of the relationship and (2) how to measure the contribution of each party to the relationship in ways other than just price or cost.

Principle 4: Make Strategy Everyone's Everyday Job. The C.E.O.s and senior leadership teams of organizations that adopted the Balanced Scorecard understood that they could not implement the new strategy by themselves. They wanted contributions from everyone in the organization. This is not top-down *direction.* This is top-down *communication* and bottom-up *implementation.* Three processes are required:

- **Use communication and education to create awareness.** A prerequisite for implementing strategy is that all employees understand the strategy. A consistent and continuing communication program is the foundation for organizational alignment.
- **Align personal objectives with the strategy.** Companies challenge individuals and departments at lower levels to develop their own objectives in light of the broader priorities; in some cases, personal scorecards are used to set *personal objectives.*
- **Link compensation to the scorecard.** To modify behavior as required by the strategy and as defined in the scorecard, change *must* be reinforced through incentive compensation. When the incentive compensation program becomes linked to the Balanced Scorecard, interest in the details of the strategy increases.

Principle 5: Make Strategy a Continual Process. Companies adopt a new "double-loop process" to manage strategy. The first step *links strategy to the budgeting process.* Managers use the Balanced Scorecard as a screen to evaluate potential investments and initiatives that will develop entirely new capabilities, reach new customers and markets, and make radical improvements in existing processes and capabilities. This distinction is essential. Just as the Balanced Scorecard attempts to protect long-term objectives from short-term sub-optimization, the budgeting process must protect the long-term initiatives from the pressures to deliver short-term financial performance.

The second step introduces a *simple management meeting* to review strategy. As obvious as this step sounds, such meetings didn't exist in the past. Now management meetings are scheduled on a monthly or quarterly basis to discuss the Balanced Scorecard, so that a broad spectrum of managers comes together to monitor organizational performance against the short-term targets for the scorecard's financial and non-financial measures. This process creates a focus on the strategy that did not exist before.

Information feedback systems change to support the new management meetings. Many organizations create an *open reporting* environment, in which performance results are made available to everyone in the organization. Building upon the principle that "strategy is everyone's job," they empower "everyone" by giving them the knowledge needed to do their jobs.

Finally, a *process for learning and adapting the strategy* evolves. As the scorecard is put into action and feedback systems begin their reporting on actual results, the organization tests the hypotheses underlying its strategy, to see whether the strategy is delivering the expected results.

A new kind of energy is created. People use terms like "fun" and "exciting" to describe the management meetings. One senior executive reported that the meetings became so popular, there was standing room only . . . he could have sold tickets to them.

Companies also use the meetings to search for new strategic opportunities that aren't currently on their scorecard. New challenges arise externally, and ideas and learning emerge internally from within the organization. Rather than waiting for next year's budget cycle, the priorities and the scorecards are updated immediately. Much like a navigator guiding a vessel on a long-term journey, constantly sensing the shifting winds and currents and constantly adapting the course, the executives of successful companies use the ideas and learning generated by their organization to fine-tune their strategies. Instead of being an annual event, strategy formulation, testing, and revision became a continual process.

The Balanced Scorecard enables organizations to introduce a new governance and review process—one focused on strategy, not tactics. The new governance process emphasizes learning, team problem solving, and coaching. Review meetings look into the future—exploring how to implement strategy more effectively, and identifying the changes to be made to the strategy—based on what has been learned.

This is a management process attuned to the needs of contemporary businesses. The essential ingredient is a simple framework—the Balanced Scorecard and its representation on a strategy map—that allows strategy to be clearly articulated. The Balanced Scorecard becomes the heart of the management system that strategy-focused organizations will use to build their future.

Robert S. Kaplan is the Marvin Bower Professor of Leadership Development at Harvard Business School. His research, teaching, and consulting focus on linking cost and performance measurement systems to strategy implementation and operational excellence. With David Norton, Kaplan developed the Balanced Scorecard, an aid to achieving strategy by showing how key measures interrelate to track progress toward strategy, and both Kaplan and Norton serve as directors with the Balanced Scorecard Collaborative—a global network to support organizations implementing the method. Their most recent books include *The Strategy-focused Organization* (Harvard Business School Press, 2001) and *The Balanced Scorecard* (Harvard Business School Press, 1996). David P. Norton is President, C.E.O., and cofounder of Renaissance Solutions Inc., a management consulting and systems integration firm. Prior to Renaissance, Norton cofounded and spent 17 years as President of Nolan, Norton & Company, which was acquired by Peat Marwick.

Competing on Costs

Dinna Louise C. Dayao

Nissan slashed 10% from its 2000 bill for auto parts by dropping its most inefficient suppliers and consolidating orders with the most cost-conscious ones. The resulting savings of at least $2.5 billion went straight to the automaker's bottom line. Minor Food Group, which owns franchises for pizza restaurants, ice-cream outlets, and steakhouses scattered all over Thailand, survived the Asian financial crisis through a strategy of price-cutting and streamlining. As a result, the fast-food company's net profits rose to a record 178 million baht in 1998, from 82 million baht in 1997. Electrolux has shed a third of its work force—40,000 jobs—since 1997. The tactic helped the Stockholm-based appliance giant boost its operating income by 8% in 2000, to $760 million, on sales of $12.4 billion.

Faced with a difficult economic environment, competitive pressures, or internal crisis, many companies switch to a cost-cutting mode as a short-term defensive tactic. However, low-cost leaders like Taiwan-based Quanta Computer, the Philippine fast-food company Jollibee Foods, the Indonesian retailer Ramayana Lestari Santosa (RLS), and Japan's Fast Retailing don't wait for a crisis to contain costs. They focus on cost control as a strategic imperative. This facilitates improvement in market position and drives bottom-line growth.

Instead of merely focusing on cost reduction, low-cost leaders rethink the very core of their companies' internal value chain—the distinct activities needed to create their products or services. They typically:

- optimize the operating efficiency of facilities and resources;
- pursue cost reductions through tight procedural controls, and avoidance or elimination of marginal customer accounts;
- minimize (but do not remove entirely) costs, and increase efficiency in areas like research and development.

As a result they reap real and lasting breakthroughs, for example, increased productivity, reduced cycle time, and lower input costs, and they can produce goods or deliver services for less money than their competitors. This translates into better profitability and potentially more cash flow. Indirectly, it also provides other significant benefits, such as better customer service and enhanced customer retention and loyalty.

The position of low-cost leader assumes greater importance as more products and services, from cellular phones and computers to financial services and utilities, become perceived as commodities. In markets in which price is the sole factor in the customer's purchase decision, why not be the leader?

COMMON TRAITS OF LOW-COST LEADERS
How do low-cost leaders deliver products and services at the lowest prices? These companies share the following traits.

They Are Fantastic at Containing Costs.   Fast Retailing, Japan's third-largest seller of clothing, cut costs drastically by focusing on a few core products and buying in bulk from low-cost manufacturers, mostly in China. The retailer's competitive prices help to build consumer loyalty. Its chain of 500 no-frills outlets was expected to rack up total sales of $3.3 billion in 2001.

RLS, which operates a chain of department stores across Indonesia, not only contains its recurrent operating expenses, it also uses capital in a very efficient manner. The company rents store space rather than owning it and uses supplier credit to fund working capital.

Askul, which supplies 1.5 million Japanese small businesses with office supplies, keeps costs low by buying direct from manufacturers. The company passes on savings of up to 40% to its customers. Combine that with a catalog of more than 12,000 items and guaranteed delivery within 24 hours, and you get a fast-growing company with sales of $615 million for the year ending May 2001.

They Are Operationally Excellent and Efficient.   How does the largest single provider of eye surgery in the world keep the cost of performing a cataract operation down to about $10, when it costs hospitals in the United States about $1,650 to perform the same operation? Aravind Eye Hospitals in India slashes costs by putting two or more patients in an operating room at the same time. Hospitals in the United States don't allow more than one patient at a time in surgery, but Aravind hasn't experienced any problems with infections.

Aravind's doctors have created equipment that allows a surgeon to perform one 10- to 20-minute operation, then swivel around to work on the next patient. They're so productive that the hospital has a gross margin of 40% despite the fact that 70% of its patients pay nothing, or close to nothing, and the hospital doesn't depend on donations. Crucially, this example highlights the fact that operational efficiency does not mean reducing quality standards.

Efficiency helped Quanta earn an estimated $3.8 billion in revenues in 2001. The Taiwanese electronics designer-manufacturer, which specializes in laptops, cellphones, and servers, boasts of flexible, round-the-clock manufacturing lines that mass-produce notebook computers with different product specifications and configurations for customers such as Dell, Compaq, and Apple. A computerized and automated warehouse feeds parts to the conveyor belts. Quanta fulfills orders received electronically from U.S. brands, sellers, or even end users within five working days—two to manufacture the machines, configured to specs, and three for FedEx shipment. It's no wonder that Quanta shipped 4 million notebook units in 2001, 50% more than in 2000—and one-seventh of all the notebooks sold anywhere in the world.

They Know That Cheap Is not Necessarily a Synonym for Low Quality.   Toyota is well on its way to becoming the world's lowest-cost producer of highest-quality automobiles. The Japanese automaker had just 115 problems per 100 vehicles, compared with 162 for Ford. Its average warranty cost per vehicle is a low $400, versus $650 at Ford and $550 at General Motors. As a result, Toyota enjoys a cost advantage of $1,800 per vehicle over Ford because of its greater efficiency and consequent ability to command high prices.

Nearly 90% of all items sold by Fast Retailing are made in China under exclusive contracts. The company keeps strict tabs on quality and offers an unconditional money-back guarantee—still a rarity among Japanese retailers.

They Keep Loyal Customers and Attract New Ones. When McDonald's Japan halved weekday hamburger prices in 2000, the move attracted a whole new clientele, instead of eating into earnings. What used to be a teen hangout is now frequented by businesspeople.

In the Philippines, fast-food market leader Jollibee achieved the same result. The company offered value meals at different price points during the financial crisis and pulled in new customers, as high-income families switched from gourmet restaurants to fast food in order to cut spending.

They Nurture a Culture That Abhors Waste and Is Constantly Aware of the Need to Control Costs. HSBC Holdings, one of the largest and most efficient banking and financial services organizations in the world, prides itself on being fanatical about expense discipline. Chairman John Bond sets the example for frugality. He's known to turn off the lights when he leaves his office, to fly economy, and to take the subway to work. Other HSBC executives follow his lead—when they travel they rarely fly first class, and they stay at middle-range instead of five-star hotels. The bottom-line benefits are considerable: a smaller and predominantly domestic U.K. competitor spends twice as much on travel and entertainment as does HSBC, which operates on every continent.

Cost consciousness is also a hallmark of the management of Singapore Airlines (SIA). SIA's unassuming C.E.O., Cheong Choong Kong, works in a small office at headquarters and sometimes travels economy class on his own airline. SIA executives get no stock options and no special dining room, not even a free parking space. Rigorous cost control has resulted in a strong balance sheet with very little debt and more than $1 billion in liquid assets. SIA's deep pockets enabled the company to expand its holdings, invest $300 million in an ambitious transformation of air-passenger service, and post significant earnings when other airlines were swooning at the height of the Asian financial crisis.

MAKING IT HAPPEN

These success stories demonstrate that low-cost leadership is a proven approach to successful competition in the marketplace. They follow these fundamental principles:

- Understand the bare bones of your company. Ask the most fundamental questions about each activity needed to create your product or service.
- Distinguish between low-cost and high-cost activities. Determine what controls the cost of each activity.
- Keep the activities that add value. Compress, eliminate, or outsource those that don't.
- Identify cost-reduction opportunities and implement those ideas. Aggressively pursue cost savings throughout the value chain.
- Consider how to build a culture of cost control within the organization. Making cost control a strategic imperative, and leading by example, may help increase its prominence.

By asking fundamental questions about the processes that create your product or service, by grasping which activities are low-cost and which are high-cost, by eliminating process steps that truly do not add value, and by leveraging all cost-reduction opportunities, any company can compete with a low-cost advantage.

Dinna Louise C. Dayao is the author of *Asian Business Wisdom: Lessons from the Region's Best and Brightest Business Leaders* and its revised edition, *Asian Business Wisdom: From Deals to Dot.Coms*, published by John Wiley in 2000 and 2001, respectively. Both books feature insightful and informative articles from visionary Asian C.E.O.s. As a freelance writer and editor, Dayao has contributed articles on management, executive lifestyle, and telecommunications to publications such as *Chief Executive China* and *Worldroom.com*. She is based in Makati City in the Philippines.

Allocating Corporate Capital Fairly

John L. Mariotti

The appetite of organizations for capital is insatiable. Understanding the nature of capital and its effective allocation is essential to organizational success. Classical economics defines land, labor, and capital as the determinants of wealth, each being exclusive to its owner. Now there is a fourth determinant of wealth—information—and it is nonexclusive. The more information is shared, the more valuable it becomes. Business is a game in which the score is kept in money, and thus allocation of capital is a critical decision.

The challenge is to decide which division, project, or acquisition gets the scarce capital. The challenge varies with the source of capital. Venture capitalists' tolerance for risk is offset by their high return expectations. The low risk of municipal bonds and banks is matched by low returns. Corporations, striving to enhance shareholder value, must match investment choices to their investors' expectations. Such is the world of being *your brother's banker*.

ALLOCATING CAPITAL

Investment models of prior eras are tested, changed, and then validated or proved flawed. The venture-capital-driven dot-coms appeared to exist in a new reality where the old rules of finance were suspended. The reality of the situation reemerged, and these returnless enterprises disappeared. Their mounting million-dollar losses with no profit in sight led to their inevitable and rapid demise.

The principles of sound fiscal management and capital allocation still applied. If capital is allocated foolishly to poorly-defined projects, it is wasted. The game is a simple one: invest in projects with the greatest return and the lowest risk. Deciding which ventures to invest in has always occupied management. Corporations have developed many quantitative methods for allocating capital. Most of these remain valid, but they share one problem: they all depend on someone's forecast of the future, and this is risky. The challenge is to allocate capital to well-thought-out opportunities that have a reasonable chance of earning good capital returns.

The Plan: Allocation for Strategic Purposes. Capital allocation must be aligned with the strategic purposes and objectives of the corporation. The implication is that these are well defined and clearly understood. However, this is frequently not the case; too often their meaning is unclear or hidden from decision makers.

The Typical Practice: A Capital Budget. Organizations develop capital expenditure budget needs for annual review by boards and banks. A common breakdown of capital budgets is by category or type of expenditure—for example, new products, new facilities, maintenance of existing products or facilities, infrastructure needs. This is a theoretically sound method, since each category has a different strategic purpose: for example, sustaining current activities or revenue streams, creating new revenue streams, or providing infrastructure to support current or new business needs. These category splits are intended to allow senior management and boards to allocate capital fairly according to the company's strategic needs.

The problem with this approach is that there is an enormous gap between the theory of developing capital expenditure budgets and the actual practice of the process. This traditional route is a sure path to sustaining mediocrity.

THE CAPITAL APPROPRIATION PROCESS

When management has determined what it believes is an effective use of capital, it must find a means to communicate that need and its worthiness relative to other needs. Larger organizations use a formal capital appropriation process. This process involves documentation of the intended use, description of the assets to be acquired, time frames for the investments, and benefits to be gained. A financial analysis is a required part of the capital appropriation request.

The methods used to compare and evaluate capital investments use projections of future revenue streams and a calculation of some combination of:

- internal rate of return (IRR)
- net present value (NPV)
- breakeven
- economic value added (EVA)
- economic profit created (EP)
- risk-adjusted return on capital (RAROC)

This approach will reward the best analysts, politicians, and sycophants, but not the best projects. The most innovative high-potential projects are seldom easy to quantify, analyze, and define. Yet these are the very ideas that turn out to be outstanding—but only in retrospect and only if they ever get funded.

For reasons of personal or organizational pride, differing goals, or political power, appropriation requests often do not match corporate goals. Competing executives or organizations will scuffle for scarce capital, and even if their intentions are good the resulting conflicts can be ugly. Who is to resolve these conflicts?

APPROVALS AND THE CAPITAL APPROPRIATION COMMITTEE

In some companies the authority level for heads of business units is high—assuming funds have been budgeted—in the category needed. This means there is a chance that good, innovative ideas might receive financing. In central-control-oriented companies spending approval levels are kept low, forcing corporate reviews of most investments.

Appropriation requests go up the ladder to be approved by successively higher levels of management. The originator's chain of command is a normal path in addition to gatekeepers from finance and accounting. Other functions affected often have sign-off rights, too. This makes the process time-consuming, bureaucratic, and often contentious. Such processes will wring the creativity out of any proposal, replacing it with conservatism, caution, and capital constipation.

After running the divisional bureaucratic gauntlet, the appropriation goes to the corporate capital appropriation committee, where it is subjected to more scrutiny.

This review is supposedly based on alignment with corporate strategies, the return versus competing capital needs from other units, and the requesting unit's budget. The larger the organization the more levels there may be, but the process varies surprisingly little from company to company.

When the Cleveland, Ohio, manufacturing company Manco, Inc. was growing through the $100 million sales level, it implemented a formal but streamlined capital approval process. Since its acquisition by the Henkel Group this process now includes approval at corporate level in Dusseldorf, Germany. Some may consider this necessary; it is, however, slower. The successive layers of capital appropriation processes and committees can slow down or even kill good ideas.

Historically, depreciation was designed to replace assets by taking noncash charges to expenses, thereby reserving the money for new expenditures. Thus, it became normal for capital allocation to equal depreciation. To spend more is equivalent to putting in new money, and to spend less is in effect using up the business. Many lending agreements contain restrictive covenants that limit capital spending to formulas—the right spending level is a function of what happened in the past divided by some accountant's factors. The obvious corollary is that, if the company is struggling, it will be starved of the necessary capital to rebuild.

OTHER CHALLENGES IN CAPITAL ALLOCATION

There are many other issues. Cash-rich companies also have a problem. A low return on conservatively-invested cash reduces the return on assets. Corporations are expected to earn higher returns than banks (or bonds). A common alternative is to repurchase stock.

In other cases, company treasurers are tempted to use high-risk investments like derivatives. Multinational companies have another issue: currency fluctuations. Shifting exchange rates can negate the best analyses, making investments much better—or worse. Hedging currency by buying futures can protect the downside, but, like all insurance, this comes at a cost. This can often seem little better than gambling.

Then there are fiascoes in which capital allocation is based on equity markets and stock prices. The dot-com deals involving stock swaps quickly revealed the flaws here: huge profits disappeared overnight, replaced by unexpected write-offs. The pricing of deals is destroyed in a blink when stock prices fluctuate wildly. Carefully-negotiated deals combining cash and stock might as well have been decided on a roulette wheel—long odds and large potential losses.

Furthermore, what happens to budgeted but unused money? The government model—use it or lose it—is often used. The rush to spend unused budgeted capital results in waste, misallocation, or both.

NONMONEY "CAPITAL"

Finally, there are noncapital resources, such as people, knowledge, or time. If these were not available, all the capital in the world would not help. Capital must be spent wisely or else allocating it wisely is useless. People spend the capital. So if you are to be your brother's banker in allocating capital, the most important question you can ask is not what it will be spent on. Rather, it is who will be spending it and what their track record is. Choosing the right people to bet on is the critical decision. Then and only then are all the other processes useful and important.

An Alternative to Allocation?   In the new economy capital flowed freely to those perceived to deserve it (and the perceived undeserving were starved). Forget that many of the decisions were bad ones, and consider the concept. Instead of allocating capital, think in terms of earning it and deserving it. Unconventional ideas seldom survive the bureaucratic battles, particularly if they threaten to cannibalize existing businesses. Silicon Valley taught us that in a venture-capital-rich climate, an idea either attracts capital or it doesn't—no corporate committee says yea or nay—then it must prove that the capital it attracted was deserved by succeeding with it.

Companies usually allocate capital on the basis of one of three mindsets.

- The first is *protecting the past*, in which case they will always be following the competition and reacting to a leader's moves, simply trying to hang on to past glories.

- The second mindset is the attractive trap of *perfecting the present*. Such moves are always easier to analyze, and make short-term strategic goals. The problems arise when a new, disruptive technology or a revolutionary competitor enters the fray, upsetting the applecart.

- The third mindset is the critical one, to allocate capital by investing in *finding the future*. This is harder and riskier, but it is the only true path to success.

Few traditional appropriation processes accommodate this approach, which is why so few companies succeed over the long term. Companies trying to find the future are often led by escapees from the other kinds of companies—people seeking outlets for creative brilliance and people thwarted by capital appropriations processes, restrictive policies, and countless committees.

The best rule for capital allocation is to allocate very little to protecting the past and just enough to perfecting the present, leaving plenty to spend on finding the future. That is where real wealth and excitement lies.

———————

John L. Mariotti is a consultant, writer and speaker, and is President and C.E.O. of The Enterprise Group. He is a former corporate president and serves on the boards of four companies. His three latest books are in the Capstone *Smart Things to Know About* series: *Brands & Branding* (1999), *Marketing* (2000), and *Partnerships* (2001). *Making Partnerships Work* was published by Capstone/Wiley in 2002. For more information, see www.shape-shifters.com.

Managing 21st Century Financials

Terry Carroll

Corporate purpose, for most companies, is to create and sustain long-term share-holder value. However, markets are increasingly driven by fear, as the emergence of traded indicators such as "VXN" (and QQV) has shown in the United States. Stuck in the middle are top managers, especially the C.F.O.s. They have to balance long-term planning with "short-termist" behavior in the markets. How can this be achieved? What are the new metrics for survival and sustainable prosperity?

For both quoted and private companies, it's about having a clear understandable business model that works; being able to explain it easily and consistently; understanding strategic business risk and making it work for you; generating sustainable revenues, income, and especially cash; and rapid, reliable reporting. It starts and ends with shareholder value creation.

MANAGING INVESTORS' EXPECTATIONS

It's not so much about managing shareholder value as expectations. The major long-term players (institutions, pension, investment, and insurance funds) are advised by analysts. Short-term investors, traders, and the public are more influenced by news-flow and market movements. How can we reconcile these forces? First, timely financial information; second, "no surprises"; third, always having cash; finally, having a credible, understandable business model.

FINANCIAL REPORTING IN THE COMMUNICATION AGE

Great companies produce rapid, reliable, succinct, simple, usable financial information. Internally, more than three days to report is too long. The Internet or intranets can provide "always-on," real-time connection for the whole company. Management and financial reporting tools and technology allow fast collection, collation, interpretation, and distribution of results. Now, three factors are converging internal with external reporting: urgency, transparency, and consistency.

Global markets and the pace of change mean management needs reliable financial feedback, fast. Meanwhile, external reporting periods are shortening. This is spilling into Europe. Information is a global property, especially when it "leaks." Global brand management demands control of your own destiny. The market wants information as fast as you get it. Too much conversion for external consumption takes time, unsettling management and investor alike. Meanwhile, market regulation requires transparency and "equality" of distribution.

Shareholders and investors want financial information consistent with expectations. The more frequently it is released, the smaller the mismatch. Regular, progressive business and financial newsflow, augmented by rational enhancements to the business model can lead to out-performance. "No surprises" please, because markets wonder if management is competent.

Uneven information flow; profit warnings or their lack; information released to analyst briefings before the market; lack of comment on speculation . . . all these unsettle investors and regulators, often causing sharp movements in share prices. News and specialist market services supply corporate information 24 hours a day. Analysts interpret it as fast as it is produced.

Some C.F.O.s may need to wake up to the new paradigm. Others will see it as an opportunity for skilled relationship management, making the financial information systems work for the company as another weapon in the public relations armory. Brand is everything. Failing this new challenge can seriously damage yours. The right way will please both short- and long-term investors.

CASH IS KING

Investors will demand that companies report quicker. This is a challenge for accounting standards and governance. Historic price/earnings multiples are being replaced by forecast revenues and EBITDA (earnings before interest, tax, depreciation, and amortization) as the currency of decisions. The new metric is cash. How much cash was generated last period; how much remains in the balance sheet; what is the NPV of sustainable future cash flows?

EVERYBODY NEEDS A BUSINESS MODEL

Apart from cash, the other factor that brings together short- and long-term interests is a credible, explainable business model. If you don't have one, analysts will create their own (or worse still, transport it from another company unlike your own). For example, good TMT stocks have floated up and down with bad on the waves of market volatility. Some values are absurd, for good or ill.

Both Nortel (U.S.) and Bookham (U.K.) have been a top 100 stock in their own market. They are both high-tech companies linked to building communications networks. Nortel has been around for 25 years and its market capitalization peaked at around $260 billion in 2000. It has not been immune from recession or the ebbing dot-com tide, falling 90% in the 18 months since.

Bookham Technology, on the other hand, was floated in July 2000 at $16. Its shares rocketed to $85 in a few months, based on the NPV of forecast revenues, for a business model that few people understood. The price was driven by over-optimistic analyst estimates, blind faith, and greed. In a year it fell to $1.19. Its market capitalization fell from $10.5 billion to less than $160 million (the $320 million cash in the balance sheet supported the growing stream of losses). Despite the disparity, its price fall correlated with Nortel, buffeted by fear and optimism.

In the TMT market in general, fear overtook logic as, for example, some telecoms companies which were quasi-utilities were lumped with their busted cousins. In a starved market, some companies ran out of cash because of oversupply to the cash-hungry cuckoos in their nest.

So it's the financial model that really counts, especially generating and sustaining cash. It's lack of cash that busts companies, not lack of capital. When you don't have enough cash to survive a recession and the market isn't receptive to new issues, you have to start slashing costs—"eating yourself"—to stay alive. This can damage the business model, undermine the share price, and become a vicious spiral towards expiry, or at best consumption by a sounder business model.

VALUING THE BUSINESS
There has been much theoretical talk in the past about "value added." What we really mean is that every company should be focused on protecting, creating, and sustaining value. Failure could mean stock price falls, cash calls, unwelcome bids, or business failure.

So the C.E.O., C.F.O., and colleagues need vision and courage. Value creation is top of the agenda. It involves generating the value and protecting it. Brand, fear, technical and fundamental analysis of markets have assumed more significance than the internal business plan, budgets, and the annual report. When investors are frightened or lose faith, they can destroy value much faster than you can create it.

This is why cash generation is critical. Share prices already eroding due to poor results or loss of confidence in a business model fall dramatically faster when you have to raise cash in an unreceptive market. Investors share your wish to sleep easy at night.

Some C.F.O.s cite short-termism as the real driver of value, therefore. They castigate "teenage scribblers" and analysts for not understanding their business. Some make errors of judgment, not only in their handling of such relationships, but also in silence or, worse still, nasty surprises.

Marconi was a case in point. For months investors expected a profit warning. The company continued to make reassuring noises. Investors continued to sell against an expectation of bad news. Eventually the share price was suspended. Dreadful news was released. Returning from suspension the price was savaged. It had fallen from over $19.30 to under 32 cents in a year. Trust evaporated as investors tried to decide whether concealment or incompetence had been to blame. Marconi may never again be a FTSE 100 company.

MESSAGES FOR MANAGERS
Creating and protecting shareholder value are even more important in the 21st century. Volatility, expectations, speed of reporting, and a hungry investor demand for "real-time" information have changed the dynamics. The C.F.O. needs new skills. These include strategic thinking, proactive risk management, and communication and interpersonal skills of a high order.

Value creation is about having a clear strategic and business focus, flexible and adaptable as appropriate. The C.F.O. and executive colleagues must recognize the importance of having a sound, understandable business model. The financial model must be based on value creation, ideally measured in sustainable revenues, income, and especially cash. Reporting should be rapid and transparent, using the speed of technology, with no surprises.

You can create long-term value, but investors can take it away in the short term when fear overrides faith, if you don't heed these messages. Relationship management with analysts, investors, and the media is the critical skill that wasn't mentioned when the C.F.O. trained as an accountant. When you understand and manage strategic business risk and the macro-economic factors, you may at least anticipate the challenge of analysts, whether or not they understand your own unique business model. If the unforeseen intervenes, report it rapidly and accurately, with a clear understanding of the factors and a plan to manage the consequences.

All companies can follow this best practice to prosper in the 21st century:

- fast, reliable reporting
- proactively anticipating and managing investor interest
- investing in relationships
- being clear, informed and consistent
- creating and sustaining long-term corporate value

Finally, much of this message relates to private companies also. Investment of private capital is accelerating. A clear business model is fundamental to accessing the cash for investment and growth, especially if you plan eventually to come to market.

After a 20-year career in financial and public services, Terry Carroll "reinvented" himself as a motivational speaker and performance coach. Working at the leading edge of personal growth technologies, he integrates NLP (neurolinguistic programming), emotional intelligence, accelerated learning, and other proven techniques into the "best of the best" for personal and group change. An established author, his books cover subjects ranging from personal growth to finance, risk, and the psychology of markets.

Managing by the Open Book

John Case

Companies in the 21st century are groping for new ways of helping people work together effectively. This is hardly surprising: the old hierarchical, command-and-control management systems were devised for industrial enterprises, where most people's jobs consisted purely of doing what they were told. Today's knowledge-intensive companies ask employees not only to do their assigned jobs, but also to take responsibility for world-class quality, impeccable service, and continuous improvement and innovation. Thus employees find themselves in cross-functional groups and self-managing teams, charged with running their own projects or work areas as well as with solving their own problems.

But this situation presents a series of difficulties. Most employees don't really understand the business that they're in. They can't read a financial statement or a budget. They have never learned to understand the connections between operational performance and financial results. They don't have a good handle on the costs they incur (and must somehow manage) every day. They lack business acumen, because they have never had the occasion to acquire it.

The approach known as "open-book management," pioneered and developed over the past 20 years primarily by small and midsized companies is designed to solve this problem. Open-book companies teach *and expect* their employees to think and act like businesspeople, and to manage themselves accordingly.

THE ESSENTIALS OF OPEN-BOOK MANAGEMENT

"Open book" is a way of running a business; it means far more than just communicating financial results to employees. The following elements are essential:

Determine the critical numbers. Every businessperson—every manager—has a few key numbers that he or she always keeps a close eye on. In small companies the critical numbers are usually financial: sales, margins, cashflow. In departments or divisions of larger companies, some key numbers are operational—they may include metrics such as units shipped, defect rates, machine uptime, and customer acquisition costs. Savvy managers and business owners know their critical numbers intuitively, and track them from week to week and quarter to quarter. They also understand the relationship between operational metrics and financial performance. Hotel executives know they make money when revenue per available room crosses a certain threshold. Seasoned plant managers estimate profitability simply by watching the number of trucks at the loading dock. Listen to J. Robert Beyster, C.E.O. of Science Applications International Corp. (SAIC), the big global research and engineering firm based in San Diego, California: "What are SAIC's critical numbers? . . . Time sold, or what is more commonly called labor utilization, drives our business . . . If our time-sold targets are not met, we face staff reductions."

Communicate these numbers, and teach people what they mean. SAIC—one of a handful of large companies that practices open-book management—sends out biweekly reports on each division's time-sold performance. SRC Holdings Corp., a midsized remanufacturing company headquartered in Missouri, puts charts on the wall. For example, at an SRC subsidiary that rebuilds electrical equipment, a green chart shows plant-wide efficiency, and a red one shows how much of the finished product was composed of used parts (a larger percentage means more savings).

Teaching the "meaning" of the numbers essentially means explaining the connection between operational indicators and financial performance, and that, in turn, means providing people with a grounding in the basics of business. Employees of SRC, which has practiced open-book management since 1983, actually learn to read an income statement and a balance sheet; wall charts at the company show income and expense breakdowns as well as the operational indicators. A New York City marketing communications firm asks its employees to be "C.F.O. for a day," not only to learn the financial numbers but also to explain them to fellow employees. A Massachusetts manufacturer prepares profit-and-loss statements for each team of production employees, so they can learn to track their contribution to company profits, day in and day out.

Give employees the power and responsibility to manage the critical numbers. Many companies these days claim to "empower" people. But empowerment for what? It doesn't do any good to empower people to halt an assembly line or solve a customer's problem unless they understand the business costs and benefits involved. Indeed, empowerment without such understanding can be counterproductive. One manufacturer empowered employees to do "whatever it took" to ensure on-time delivery of product. It wasn't long before managers discovered that the company's margins were being destroyed by expediting costs and overnight-delivery expenses.

For most companies, the best system of empowerment is regular unit meetings to review and discuss key numbers. If the numbers aren't moving in the right direction, what needs to happen? Who has an idea? At least some of the numbers discussed at these meetings must be financial, precisely to avoid the kind of problem created by the all-out effort for on-time delivery. Indeed, veteran open-book companies such as SRC actually build rudimentary income statements at such meetings: unit representatives report their results for the previous time period and discuss how to correct any unfavorable variances from plan.

Establish (or communicate) appropriate rewards for outstanding business performance. Open-book management asks employees to learn new skills and take on new responsibilities. Employees naturally ask "what's in it for me?" and if the answer is "nothing," the system won't work. Small and midsized companies committed to open-book management typically establish substantial bonus programs pegged to targets on key numbers. These targets can vary from year to year, since any business's priorities vary from year to year (for example, sales growth one year, profitability the next, quality improvements in a third). Whatever the target, the bonus must be transparent, equitable, and nondiscretionary. Employees must be able to see how they're doing on the key indicators over time. They must know that they will be paid the bonus if they make the targets.

Units of large companies may have to plead with the human resources department for flexible compensation plans, and unionized companies may need to negotiate bonus terms with the union. (The difficulties of both are one reason why relatively few large companies have been able to capitalize on the open-book approach.) Another useful tool for open-book management is an employee stock ownership plan or broad stock-option program. Insofar as employees *are* owners, they have a built-in incentive to think and act like owners, which is exactly what open-book management requires. The job for managers then is to spell out the connections between financial performance and the stock price.

OBSTACLES AND PAYOFFS

Open-book management makes a good deal of sense on paper, but so far it has been adopted by a minority of small companies and only a few big ones. The reasons stem from both intrinsic difficulties and institutional obstacles. To "go open book" is a big change for a company. Managers, remembering the maxim that information is power, are accustomed to keeping what they know to themselves, and sharing it only when it suits them to do so. Many employees, for their part, still expect to come to work and do only what they're told; they don't want more responsibility or involvement. Open book is a system that must be learned, and changing people's expectations and behavior requires time and patience. In a large company, moreover, it involves change on many fronts—new training, new compensation arrangements, and new procedures for sharing and discussing information. Unit managers often must navigate a thicket of corporate policies and procedures just to reward employees for hitting a business target they all agree on.

And yet open-book management continues to spread, without much help from consultants or professors, primarily among new, growth-oriented companies. For example, a remarkable 53% of the companies on *Inc* magazine's year-2000 list of the 500 fastest-growing private companies in the United States practice open-book management. The reason is simply that the payoffs are substantial:

- It focuses employees' attention on the basics of the business
- It builds a collaborative environment—open-book companies report less of an "us versus them" attitude and less office politics
- It taps the wisdom and experience of employees at every level
- It helps create a more fun, more satisfying atmosphere in which everyone is working toward common goals.

Most of all it produces results. "By opening the books," writes Fay Wu, chief financial officer of Toronto-based Castek Software Factory, "we focused everyone's attention on business performance ... Castek has successfully doubled its size every year by moving the 'numbers' in the right direction."

MAKING IT HAPPEN

These are some first action steps you can take towards achieving open book:

- Determine your business's critical numbers. Chart the relationship between changes in these numbers and financial indicators (margins, costs, and so on)

- Put key numbers up on a chart or on your company's intranet. Hold lunchtime discussions to explain why these numbers are important to financial performance
- Set short-term targets for key numbers, and review progress at weekly meetings. Begin to involve employees in establishing longer-term targets
- Investigate your company's compensation plan to see how much flexibility you have. Meantime, see whether you can pay small bonuses or rewards out of your budget—and if so, set up a short-term, unit-wide "game" to hit a certain business goal. Pay the bonus if the goal is attained.

Companies searching for a new way of managing people in the knowledge economy can learn much from the small, entrepreneurial companies that have developed open-book management. Open book can be challenging to implement, particularly in a large corporation, but the payoffs are substantial.

John Case is a veteran observer and analyst of the business world and an internationally-known expert on the subject of open-book management. He is the author of five books, including *The Open-book Experience: Lessons from over 100 Companies Who Successfully Transformed Themselves* (Perseus, 1999), and collaborator on three others. He has also written for a wide variety of periodicals, including *Inc.* magazine.

Why EVA Is the Best Measurement Tool for Creating Shareholder Value

Erik Stern

Financial measuring tools are many and varied. The media and equity analysts focus on financial accounting metrics such as sales and sales growth, margin, operating profit and operating profit growth, bottom-line earnings and its partner earnings per share (EPS), market value, return on equity, and return on assets or cash flow.

Each of these metrics is flawed. Neither sales nor operating profit accounts for the financial requirements necessary to achieve them, in terms of either annual expenses or capital invested. Bottom-line profits and EPS take no account of the fact that equity has a cost. Market value ignores the capital employed to create it—invest more, and of course market value rises, without necessarily creating value. And yet each is popular.

Why is so fundamental a series of misapprehensions so widespread? The answer lies in the past. Accounting operating profit is conservative—literally. It focuses on collateral, or at least what would be left of a company after bankruptcy. This is a more than adequate measure for a bank, but it is misleading for an investor. The theory of modern business is founded on the blindingly simple insight that business is primarily about economics, not accounting.

THE PROBLEMS WITH EXISTING CORPORATE FINANCE MEASURES

Debt-inspired measures are misleading because they *expense*—write off as expenses—aspects of business that are becoming increasingly important. Long-term intangible investments (training, brand building, and so on), in particular, create much of the value of companies today. Yet traditional accounting procedures expense these rather than treating them as investments. Additionally, investments in acquisitions (goodwill) and in restructuring (extraordinary items) are expensed. This is a mistake. A focus on value demands that long-term investments should appear on the balance sheet for the current year, taking the cost of capital into account.

Unless they take into account the cost of capital, return measures can become inflated. Furthermore, concentrating on percentages can lead to a misguided focus—for example, reducing capital investments (especially intangibles) calculated to create profits in the future.

If the hurdle rate for returns is very high, increases may discourage optimal creation of value. If the hurdle for returns is very low, increases may destroy value. If return objectives are above the required returns of investors—the right benchmark—then managers may forgo investments that create value. If returns are the objective and an increase fails to meet this required return, value destruction results.

Of other measures, cash flow will not provide the right answers in growing businesses. When Wal-Mart was growing rapidly, new stores cost more than the existing cash flow, yet no one demanded that the company stop investing and growing. Furthermore, the net present value of free cash flow emphasizes success in the terminal value of the equation rather than the horizon that managers can visualize and experience. Free cash flow, in other words, is not a flow measure.

MVA

The best measure of corporate performance is market value added (MVA), because this measure differentiates between the total market value, including debt and equity, and the total capital invested: MVA is the difference. (MVA may also be viewed as management value added—the value managers have added to a company.)

The problem is that MVA is strongly affected by share price, which is notoriously independent of senior executives. This makes MVA less useful for encouraging the creation of value, since it has limited operational use.

THE NEED FOR A MEANINGFUL FINANCIAL MEASURE

An alternative is necessary, one that focuses on what managers can influence rather than what they cannot. The measure should differentiate between financial inputs— what enters a company over time—and outputs—the value created. Clearly our choice should not be a driver of value such as the financial accounting metrics that managers can influence. Consider instead output, on an annual basis, as operating profit after tax, with certain adjustments for intangible and other long-term investments and other accounting anomalies, and input as the annual rental charge on the total capital employed, both debt and equity. The rental charge or required return, known alternatively as the hurdle rate for investments or the weighted average cost of capital, is the true benchmark against which all investments and management should be measured. This is economic value added (EVA).

UNDERSTANDING EVA

EVA covers all that managers can influence, all drivers of value. This is seen more easily if we view EVA as the capital investment multiplied by the difference between the actual return and the required return. If we think in addition about the required return as a mix of business risk and financial risk (where financial risk, or debt level, has a potential benefit also), then we have four of the major components of market value as defined by Merton Miller and Franco Modigliani. These are:

- the cost of capital for business risk;
- the amount of debt;
- the current level of operating profit;
- capital expenditure.

The other components look at future EVA (investor expectations for future growth) in the current level of EVA, what we call FGV, or future growth value: they are the expected return on new investment, and the time horizon for excess growth in profitability or EVA. Managers can influence more or less imperfectly the debt, operating profit, capital expenditure, and future returns. They influence the horizon and business risk little, if at all.

The Value and Scope of EVA. EVA covers profit and loss and the balance sheet, differentiating intangibles and growth, and thus covering all factors of production. Growing or improving EVA is the goal, with historic investments viewed as sunk. Hence, managers should focus on growing when the returns are greater than the cost of capital, redeploying capital when the returns are less than the cost, and improving returns on existing capital, as well as having an optimal capital structure (debt versus equity).

If value creation is key, then EVA is the answer, and EVA improvement is the goal. How managers achieve this or choose to accomplish this depends on what they think is victory for their business. Of course the answer may depend on the state of the economy. In reality, investing and containing costs are crucial everywhere in the economic cycle. However, criticism thrives in a falling market and falters in a rising one. A falling market puts failing companies under the microscope, and a rising market forgives all but the worst performers.

In other words, containing costs increases current and near-term EVA, and is always crucial. But investing determines near-term and future EVA and is also always crucial, if the cash is available.

Performance measurement is the bedrock of business. Since people manage what they measure, EVA can form the foundation for a more transparent and accountable management system, especially when combined with powerful incentives to improve EVA at every level, in every activity, across all functions, and independent of geography. With rights to make decisions accurately allocated, a fair system of transfer pricing in place, information flowing freely, and the appropriate tools and training offered, responsibility joins transparency and accountability through robust control and performance evaluation. Pay for the right performance, and value-based management results.

Under EVA, budgeting gives way to long-term planning. Control of the ends and the means is relinquished respectively to externally and objectively determined investor expectations and to management choice and opportunity that allow managers to bet their own success on their meeting or beating shareholder requirements.

MAKING IT HAPPEN

EVA is, in short, the best measurement tool for creating shareholder value. A balanced scorecard of metrics allows for a big-picture view, but what is the balancing mechanism? If value creation over the long term is the goal—and if it isn't, shareholders should run—then EVA must be the balancing mechanism. Sales, margin, operating profit, and bottom-line profit simply fall short. Market value lacks levers. Return measures give the wrong answers. Only EVA can change companies.

Indeed, EVA correlates better with share price than any other measure: by 50%, compared with up to 30% for other metrics. Since EVA charges for all the factors of production, continuous improvement in EVA always furnishes investors with an increase in value.

- Start using EVA as the key financial measure: subtract input (annual rental charge on the total capital employed) from output (adjusted operating profit after tax).
- Employ EVA as the foundation of a more transparent, responsible, and accountable management system, with robust control and performance evaluation.
- With the right to make decisions accurately allocated, put a fair EVA-based system of transfer pricing in place.
- Couple continuous restructuring of existing businesses to milk value with cautious investing in future businesses.
- Focus managers on growing where returns exceed cost of capital and on redeploying capital where returns are less than its cost.
- Insist on improving returns on existing capital as well as on having an optimal capital structure (debt versus equity).

Clearly if an organization pays lip service to EVA and blindly measures it without thinking about the behavioral consequences and the need to balance simplicity and accuracy, or else provides poorly considered or misguided incentives to create EVA, the outcome will disappoint. However, a robust system adhered to in times of boom and bust will provide the foundation of sound decision making and business practices.

Erik Stern is senior vice president and managing director of Stern Stewart Europe, a global consulting firm that specializes in helping client companies to create and measure shareholder wealth through the application of tools based on modern financial theory. Stern pioneered the development of the EVA® (Economic Value Added) framework and has implemented EVA programs for companies in several industries in the United States and Europe. He has written articles for a variety of publications, including the *Financial Times*, and has appeared frequently on TV, including Sky Business News and Bloomberg.

The Case against the Long Run

Peter L. Bernstein

The author of eight books in economics and finance, Peter Bernstein is a preeminent authority on capital markets and the real economy. His journal, *Economics and Portfolio Strategy*, is read by managers and owners of assets with a combined value of more than five trillion dollars.

Bernstein was the founding editor of *The Journal of Portfolio Management*, launched in 1974. After graduating from Harvard and doing research for the Federal Reserve Bank of New York, he taught at Williams College and was on the faculty of the New School in New York.

Bernstein has been cited numerous times for his work and his thinking. In 1997, he received the Award for Professional Excellence from the Association for Investment Management & Research, AIMR's highest honor. In 1998 he was chosen to receive the annual Graham and Dodd Award for Excellence in Financial Writing. That same year, he was given the Clarence Arthur Kelp/Elizur Wright Memorial Award from The American Risk and Insurance Association (ARIA) in recognition of an outstanding original contribution to the literature of risk and insurance.

"In the long run" is one of the most popular phrases in business and finance. It is also one of the most elusive, and has been used with contradictory meanings. Although many people assume the long run to be an essential part of both business and investment decisions, perhaps it deserves to be tossed into the dustbin.

Sometimes it shows up as a bad-weather friend. When business is rotten or the stock market is depressed, we hear reassuring reminders that things always get better over the long run. Yet when business is great and the market is booming, emphasis on the temporary character of the short run is anathema. Everyone wants good business to last forever. The frequency with which people refer to the long run is a reliable measure of business and investor sentiment.

There is a more important meaning to the long run. Business decisions, where the rubber meets the road, also distinguish between the short run and the long run. Short-run decisions are those we can reverse without much difficulty. When we are locked into something, we are entering the deep waters of the long run. Accumulating inventory, executing a repo, or hiring a temp are clearly short-run decisions. Launching a new product, issuing a 30-year bond, building a new plant, and opening an office in Thailand are clearly long-run commitments.

The two uses of the concept of the long run appear to have nothing in common. The first says "This, too, shall pass." The second says "We are locking ourselves in to this situation." Yet a common thread runs between the long run as a nostrum against bad news and the long run as a policy move reaching out in time: the key word is reversibility. This simple word reveals a great deal about the long run and how to put it to good use in shaping the future. It is important to expose each of these faces of the long run, how they interact, and how to employ them to focus on the doughnut rather than the hole. A close examination reveals that evoking the long run as a security blanket in hard times makes far less sense than its application to strategic business decisions— and even then the concept is mushy.

It is a truism to say that bad times will not last forever. Nothing lasts forever, including good times. Such a statement is little more than incantation, useless for forecasting or planning. John Maynard Keynes well understood this. He was not being facetious when he uttered his famous aphorism: "In the long run we are all dead. Economists set themselves too easy, too useless a task if, in the tempestuous seasons, they can only tell us that when the storm is long past the ocean will be flat." In a naturally volatile system characterized by uncertainty, we are inevitably trapped into the short run. Or, to put it another way, the long run is nothing more than a sequence of short runs.

Much of the appeal of the long run is in its resemblance to an average—the notion of regression to the mean over the long run appears to promise us that the good times will somehow come along after a while and bail us out of the bad times. But averages are dangerous things, useful in decision making only when they summarize a random sequence of events, like dice throws or spins of the roulette wheel. In games of chance, the dice and the roulette wheel have no memory. On the other hand, what happens today is the consequence of yesterday's decision, and what we do today determines what is going to happen tomorrow; hence, passive dependence on averages to hoist us out of trouble can lead to a perilous trap.

This little theoretical digression contains the moral of the whole story. History is notable for the fluctuations from good times to bad, but history is not a random sequence of events. Nothing in the past happened without a cause. The great prosperity of the 1990s developed out of the 1980s—widespread deregulation combined with the flood of restructurings, takeovers, shutdowns, consolidations, layoffs, and, most of all, the revolution in the boardroom and the new emphasis on shareholder values. The impact of the high-tech revolution of the 1990s has been great, but I would argue that the dynamic of innovation would never have taken a grip on the economy without the intensely competitive environment created by the 1980s. Those profound changes in both government and business in the 1980s were necessitated by the terrible errors of the 1970s, errors of both public policy and heedless overexpansion on the side of business. And so on and so on, all the way back to the beginning of time.

Which of these past heterogeneous states of the world are the ones we will have to confront over the long run that lies ahead? No one knows. Have we learned so little that we will replay the horrors of World War I, the 1930s, or the 1970s? Is the unique experience of the glorious 1990s likely to lead to anything that would closely resemble one of the eras of the past? But if the long-run past consists of nothing but experiences with no significance for today's world, then the long-run average derived from past events is also without significance.

We can learn from the past, but the experience of the 1990s is the launching pad of the future. Do not depend on the ocean being flat one day. Equilibrium is an economist's construct, effective on the textbook page but irrelevant for executive planning. Even though nothing goes up or down forever, there is no predictable point, in space or time, to which matters will regress.

When we enter the sacred precincts of the corporate boardroom, the context of the long run changes. Corporate leaders specialize in the search for empty space and disequilibrium, because that is where opportunity lies: undeveloped markets, products, or production and marketing techniques waiting to be exploited. Great economic changes result in displacement, not more of the same.

Once taken, the commitment to spend money filling empty spaces or capitalizing on disequilibrium does not readily lend itself to second thoughts. It is a scary business to decide to build a new factory, open a new market in a foreign land, launch a new drug, acquire a major company in another line, or redesign an entire production process. If you are wrong, embarrassing write-offs will confront you. People who cannot stand the heat of such largely irrevocable decisions tend to go to work on Wall Street or in the City, where assets are liquid and decisions more easily reversed.

Seen from this vantage point, long-run business decisions look a lot riskier than the reversible ones. Yet, from other vantage points, the long-run moves may be less risky than the short-run moves. It all depends on how we manage the risks of irreversibility. Two elements are involved in that process: information and control. Both are essential in making the long run our servant.

The long run would be riskless if the future were known. And if the future were known, irreversibility would be irrelevant. But that is fantasy—we never have complete information. More information, however, is always better than less. Furthermore, we almost always have the option of postponing action while awaiting further information. Up to the point where we start actually writing checks, the arrival of new information has more value than the same information would have after the die has been cast. Decisiveness is admirable, but so is a sense of when to procrastinate before striding into the long run.

What is procrastination worth? Think of procrastination as an option to wait, or even not to act at all. The primary determinant of the value of an option is the volatility in the possible outcomes. Highly volatile outcomes add value to an option because a bad outcome would cost no more than the time spent waiting for information, while a good outcome could have enormous benefit. Consequently, the value of the option to procrastinate is a function of the uncertainty surrounding an irreversible decision. As the option expires at the moment when the corporation sinks its money into the new project, waiting for more information may often be preferable to a "damn-the-torpedoes-full-speed-ahead" approach. Indeed, the option of procrastination is properly part of the cost of capital or hurdle rate, justifying careful estimation of the long-run outlook.

The second element of risk management in long-run decisions is—rather, must be—control. In the typical investment in a reversible asset like a stock or bond, the owners or creditors play a passive role, in reality having no say over the management of the corporation involved. In contrast, the management of the corporation itself has the power after the fact to vary the fundamental parameters of irreversible decisions and illiquid assets for which they carry responsibility. For example, they can change their prices, redesign the product line, or replace executive personnel, among other options.

There are few decisions whose outcomes are so ironclad they are totally immune to revision. That matters. The ability to make revisions in essence means the ability to break the long run into a series of short runs. The greater the control, the shorter the run.

Despite its irrepressible popularity, the concept of "the long run" is in many ways misleading and without substance. The long run of the past tells us almost nothing about the long run facing us in the years ahead. But the long run clearly matters in business decisions. Even here, however, we should not overestimate the apparently risky character of the sunk costs and irreversibility looming over long-range plans to build new facilities, open new markets, or launch new products. Given sophisticated employment of information and control, such moves will almost always open up opportunities to crack that long run into shorter time periods, providing enhanced flexibility and reduced risk to the ultimate outcome.

The Invisible Advantage

Jonathan Low and Pam Cohen Kalafut

In 1995 Sir John Browne took over the struggling oil giant BP and launched a series of dramatic moves that catapulted BP into a leadership position in the oil industry. He acquired Amoco and Atlantic-Richfield Co. and invested in innovative deepwater drilling which enabled BP to bring wells online faster.* Finally, Browne has actively managed BP's brand and reputation by taking a strong environmental position—focusing on reducing emissions and investing in cleaner forms of gasoline.†

Procter and Gamble has beaten Wall Street's revised expectations eight quarters in a row by instituting a "going back to basics" strategy. Instead of developing and marketing new products, P&G is focusing on the top twelve brands it already produces. A series of budget cuts and project realignment have yielded two billion dollars in savings in just over two years.‡

In 1989 Toyota challenged the luxury automobile business by introducing the Lexus. Just five months after its introduction, the Lexus LS 400 was named Best Imported Car of the Year by the Motoring Press Association. Lexus has garnered nearly every excellence award in the auto industry several times over. It has built a brand name synonymous with superior quality, performance, and customer satisfaction, and has experienced 13 consecutive months of record sales. §

The $40 billion French company LVMH Moet-Hennessey Louis Vuitton S.A. has used a multicultural approach to procure ideas and talent. The firm ventures outside France to cultivate and attract the best and brightest human capital and institutes a value system approach to indoctrinate employees. It even hired an orchestra director to show managers how to gather many different talents into one cohesive group. LVMH has developed a climate that encourages bold and innovative leadership. It has also partnered with a school in France that focuses on training individuals in luxury brands and serves as an incubator for the company.¶

Leadership, strategy execution, brand, human capital: these are the currencies in today's marketplace. Value is no longer created solely or even primarily by the corporate behemoths of the industrial era. People and their ideas are the most significant

---

* See Daniel Fisher, "How Sir John Browne Turned BP Amoco into the Hottest Prospect in the Oil Patch," *Forbes*, April 2, 2001.

† See Janet Guyon, "A Big-Oil Man Gets Religion," *Fortune*, March 6, 2000.

‡ See Katrina Brooker and Julie Schlosser, "The Un-C.E.O.; A. G. Lafley Doesn't Over Promise. He Doesn't Believe in the Vision Thing. All He's Done Is Turn Around P&G in 27 months," *Fortune*, September 16, 2002.

§ Jean Halliday and Alice Z. Cuneo. "Lexus Eyes Brand I.D. Consultant," *Advertising Age*, July 9, 2001.

¶ See Concetta Lanciaux, "Building Brand Through People: LVMH's Luxury Talent," *The Cap Gemini Ernst & Young Center for Business Innovation Perspective on Business Innovation: Valuing Intangibles*, November 2001.

drivers of wealth creation in the new global economy. While the dot-com bubble may have fueled false hopes and the dream of easy money proved illusory, an important underlying trend remains: traditional measures of success tied to such factors as value of assets and number of employees, like other standards of size or quantity, may, in fact, signal weakness rather than strength. Whether it is an Internet startup or a *Fortune* 500 corporation, a company's intangible assets are essential to its success.

"Intangibles" comprise the human, intellectual, social, and structural capital of an organization. They include the people, ideas, networks, processes, and their offshoots that are not traditionally accounted for on the balance sheet. Intangibles are legitimate sources of worth in the global business context. The savviest investors rely heavily on intangibles in order to evaluate a company's performance and prospects. In fact, research at the Cap Gemini Ernst and Young Center for Business Innovation (CBI) shows that 35% of portfolio managers base their decisions about where to allocate their investment dollars on intangible assets and not on information in the balance sheet.

In *Decisions That Matter**, a study conducted by the CBI, 81% of respondents said that they got poor information on the value drivers that were most important to them as managers. The study also pointed out that 71% of senior executives were not giving or getting the kind of information that they and their subordinates needed to manage their companies effectively.

What we found was unambiguous. A majority of executives in every industry we studied believed that there were disconnects between the drivers they felt were critical to the company's success and what was actually being measured and reported.

WHAT ARE THE KEY INTANGIBLE MEASURES?

In the not too distant past, a professional investor or investment analyst looked at a company's size, its market share, its debt-to-equity ratio, and other easy-to-measure indicators of financial strength. Then they crunched the numbers and based their earnings estimates and their buy-or-sell recommendations mostly on the tangible and the countable.

In the 1990s, academics realized that intangible assets were increasingly the source of value creation for most public companies and that financial statements alone were no longer adequate as a guide to a company's future. Wall Street, and the financial professionals and analysts, questioned whether they really had the needed information.

Recent events such as the Enron debacle have reinforced the degree to which intangible factors influence corporate value. Financial statements, despite the precision with which they are prepared, are sometimes illusory. Enron's swift destruction at the hands of the markets was driven relentlessly by the failure of its leaders to consider the impact of their actions on the capital markets' assessment of intangibles like leadership, brand, human capital and, of course, reputation.

In order to understand the growing importance of intangibles for Wall Street analysts and investors, the CBI conducted a 6-year research project—*Measures that*

---

* *Decisions That Matter*, Cap Gemini Ernst & Young Center for Business Innovation, 1999.

Matter Value Creation Index* —that involved examining existing material on intangibles as well as interviewing hundreds of portfolio managers and examining about 300 investment reports. There are 12 key measures that we identified from our research and that consistently came up both in our own research and that of others:

1. Leadership: Management capabilities and experience, and the leadership's vision for the future.

2. Strategy Execution: Does management do what it says it will do?

3. Communication and Transparency: Does management communicate honestly and openly? Are its communications believed and trusted? Does it hold itself accountable?

4. Brand Equity: Strength of market position. The ability to expand the market and develop customer relationships, satisfaction, and loyalty.

5. Reputation: How is the company viewed globally? Where does it stand with regard to such things as environmental concerns, community concerns, regulators' concerns, inclusion in "most admired company" lists, and the triple bottom line (a framework for corporate performance measurement based on economic, social, and environmental factors).

6. Alliances and Networks: Supply chain relationships; strategic alliances; partnerships. In a technologically driven global economy, few, if any, companies can afford to go at it alone.

7. Technology and Processes: IT capabilities; inventory management; turnaround times; flexibility; reengineering; quality; internal transparency.

8. Human Capital: Talent acquisition; workforce retention; employee relations; compensation.

9. Workplace Organization and Culture: What makes a company a "great place to work." Teams, employee involvement, etc.

10. Innovation: Ability to innovate; the R&D pipeline; flexibility; effectiveness of new-product development; knowledge creation and use.

11. Intellectual Capital: Patents; know-how; business secrets: the value of ideas in the intangibles economy.

12. Adaptability: The ability to evolve with the marketplace and change in order to prevail over those that cannot.

It is important to understand that the market is already measuring intangible assets whether you like it or not. Now, it is necessary to understand and manage these intangibles on an industry level as well as a company level.

INTANGIBLES AT THE INDUSTRY LEVEL

In order to examine intangible assets on an industry level, the CBI created a statistical measure called the Value Creation Index (VCI)† The VCI takes data from public and proprietary sources (such as company and industry reports, expert ratings, and

---

* Cap Gemini Ernst & Young Center for Business Innovation, 1999.

† *Value Creation Index*. Cap Gemini Ernst & Young Center for Business Innovation, 1999.

government filings). Through a regression analysis and other statistical techniques, it is possible to quantify the impact of intangibles on market value beyond what would traditionally be captured in financial performance reports.

INTANGIBLES AT THE COMPANY LEVEL: WHAT CAN MANAGERS DO?

Intangibles can be very influential at the company level if businesses create a company-wide commitment to managing their intangibles. Managing intangibles involves identifying, assessing, and learning to improve them. While every organization is different, there are five broad steps to consider.

1. Determine the critical intangibles for your business. Virtually every industry has three or four intangibles that are the most important. Some key questions leadership should examine are: What are the real drivers of value in our business? If we could gain a competitive advantage by improving our performance in two or three key areas, what would they be? It is also important not only to rely on three or four senior leaders, but also to incorporate insight from all levels.

2. Decide on metrics for the key intangibles. Examine already existing data collection (e.g. statistics about customers' satisfactions and dissatisfactions) and figure out how you can get other pieces of information that you do not have. Some intangibles are relatively easy to measure while others are more challenging. Where appropriate, poll your customers, suppliers, investors, employees, and other stakeholders.

3. Create a baseline—and benchmark it against your competition. Ultimately, you want a "movie" of your management of intangibles; you want to see whether and how they are improving. Determine where you stand in comparison to your competitors' strengths and weaknesses are and gauge them against your own.

4. Undertake initiatives to improve your performance on key intangibles. Intangibles can be *managed*. Performance can be improved. Assessing and measuring your intangibles helps you determine where to invest time and resources. Undertaking initiatives to improve performance helps you build value.

5. Communicate what you're doing—far and wide. The returns to transparency exceed the returns to secrecy. Share your insights into intangibles with employees, customers, suppliers, industry groups, investors, and Wall Street analysts. Show metrics and targets as well as the importance of specific intangibles. If you can then improve your company's performance, you will gain credibility—and the market will reward you for it.

PARTING THOUGHTS

There is considerable unseen and unrecognized value—an invisible advantage—in the ideas and people who make up an organization. Many different establishments can benefit from the identification, measurement, and management of the kinds of intangibles we have highlighted. A growing acknowledgement of the beneficial power of good corporate governance has stimulated this movement, and will continue to do so. People at all levels can contribute to the understanding and management of the intangibles that, increasingly, will determine their organization's future.

We recognize that there are no easy or final answers. But we believe that whatever you do in this realm will be an improvement on the incomplete and frequently misleading picture painted by traditional financial measures. The legendary economist John Maynard Keynes once said, "I would rather be vaguely right than precisely wrong." We agree.

Jonathan Low and Pam Cohen Kalafut are leading researchers and experts on intangible value. Under the auspices of Cap Gemini Ernst & Young, they have conducted four major research initiatives on the topic, published numerous articles and reports, and spoken to industry and government groups around the world. Jonathan Low is currently a consultant on intangibles to Cap Gemini Ernst & Young and Pam Cohen Kalafut leads CGE & Y's intangibles service offering. They are the authors of *Invisible Advantage* (Perseus, 2002).

Governing the Corporation

Hugh Parker

" Whenever an institution malfunctions as consistently as boards of directors have in nearly every major fiasco of the last forty or fifty years, it is futile to blame men. It is the institution that malfunctions." (Peter Drucker)

While it is difficult to prove conclusively that there is a direct causal relationship between the effectiveness of a company's board of directors and that company's performance in the marketplace, there is plenty of evidence to show that a weak and ineffectual board—especially one dominated by a powerful C.E.O.—will sooner or later commit strategic or other errors that will seriously damage the company's performance, and in some cases bring it to the brink of ruin.

Partly as a result of such well-publicized shipwrecks, and partly as the result of persistent initiatives by Robert Monks and other so-called shareholder activists, steps have been taken by some companies to obviate some of the more egregious board-room malpractices. But many of these, like the 1994 "General Motors Board Guide-lines of Significant Governance Issues," have been largely cosmetic changes aimed at improving the public perception of a board's effectiveness rather than attacking the problem at its root.

The real problem is that in most U.S. companies today there is a huge imbalance between the effective power of the C.E.O. on the one hand, and the nominal authority on the other hand of the board by which the C.E.O. is appointed and to which he or she is legally accountable. The C.E.O.'s delegated authority becomes absolute power, and the board's authority—vested in it by statute and bylaws—becomes effectively powerless.

WHY BOARDS ARE NOT INCREASING THEIR EFFECTIVENESS

In spite of all the attention focused in recent years on the quality of corporate govern-ance—i.e., on the effectiveness (or not) of public company boards of directors—and in spite of efforts made to improve them, most boards are today only marginally more effective than they were ten years ago. There are several causes for this systematic weakness:

1 **For a long time—and largely by custom—boards have not been in a position to really govern the business.** Boards of directors on both sides of the Atlantic have almost never fully performed the trustee role for which they are legally accountable to the shareholders by whom they are elected. By tradition and long habit, boards of directors have always been more or less honorary bodies of which little action has either been expected or wanted. Board meetings have typically consisted of routine rituals through which members are led by a chair/ C.E.O. who is equipped with information, inside knowledge, and staff support so that he or she can, and generally does, control the agenda absolutely. So while boards have the legal authority, it is the C.E.O.s who have the effective power.

2 **Combining the offices of chair and C.E.O. reduces effectiveness.** Combining the offices of board chair and C.E.O. in one person virtually guarantees that the board will be ineffectual. A board can only be as independent and effective as its chair wants it to be and is capable of making it. An independent chair must be able to look his or her C.E.O. in the eye and say "this is my board and I do not agree with you and your management on this issue." But clearly this will never happen if the two offices are combined. Yet this combination is still the norm in over 80% of U.S. companies (but less than 20% of U.K. companies).

3 **Most U.S. boards are simply too big.** In 1998, 70% of the *Fortune* 500 companies had boards with 12 or more members, and 20% had 15 or more. There are several reasons for these high numbers, not least being the realization by some C.E.O.s that the larger the board the less effective it will be in monitoring and controlling his or her performance. Experience has shown that beyond a total of about seven or eight members, a board's effectiveness tends to become inversely proportional to its size.

4 **Too many supposedly "independent" directors are just not qualified to do the job properly.** They often lack the experience, character, and basic financial and other skills required in today's environment. Even worse, although they are elected by the shareholders, in practice they have almost always been selected and nominated by the C.E.O. and rubber-stamped by the board and shareholders. So the wrong people get on corporate boards for the wrong reasons, and their supposed independence is a myth.

5 **Most external directors lack the motivation and/or the time to do the job properly.** Annual fees for directors tend to cluster around $50,000. For an active C.E.O. earning $500,000 or more (plus options) in another company this is too little to justify more than a day or two per month. But for an academic or retired admiral with an income of $100,000 or less, it is too much to put at risk by being too independent, so they tend to support the chair who appointed them.

6 **Lack of relevant information.** Nearly all outsider directors have less information and knowledge about the company and its problems than the C.E.O. whom they are supposed to monitor and judge, and they are entirely dependent on that C.E.O. and his or her management for what information they do have. Thus these outsider directors often only learn about critical strategic and policy issues when things go seriously wrong, by which time it is too late for anything but crisis management and damage limitation. This usually takes the form of replacing the C.E.O., whose successor must then do whatever he or she can to salvage the company.

REEMPOWERING THE LEADERSHIP OF THE BOARD
Corporate governance has evolved differently in each of the major OECD countries. The governance system in each reflects the history, culture, economics, social values, and legal system in that country. One of these variables can be called the degree of "shareholder primacy"—i.e., putting the shareholders' interest first—which today ranges from very high in the United States, moderate in Germany, low in France, and

virtually nil in Japan. In the United States and United Kingdom especially, there are growing pressures from shareholders—which nowadays means the institutional investors—to make the boards of their portfolio companies more responsive and accountable to their shareholders. Hence the current interest in improving corporate governance.

If there is one lesson to be learned by U.S. boards from recent British experience it is the emergence of the independent nonexecutive chair. During the 1970s and 1980s a number of corporate shipwrecks of some highly respected U.K. companies—e.g., Burmah Oil and Rolls Royce—raised serious questions about the competence of company boards in general, which in turn led to the appointment in 1991 of Sir Adrian Cadbury's "Committee on the Financial Aspects of Corporate Governance." In 1992 this Committee published its "Code of Best Practice" which proposed, among other things, that "There should be a clearly accepted division of responsibilities at the head of a company which will ensure a balance of power and authority, with no individual having unfettered powers."

The Cadbury "Code of Best Practice" was adopted by the London Stock Exchange. Companies listed on the Exchange are now required to state in their annual reports the extent to which they have complied with each of the code's provisions, and non-compliance must be explained. The growing practice in the United Kingdom of separating the roles of chair and C.E.O. has restored a better balance between them. It is time for more U.S. companies to adopt this practice.

The most common objection in the United States to this separation of roles is that it is "divisive": that it will lead to indecision and political infighting in the boardroom, that this will undermine the authority of the C.E.O., and that this in turn will weaken the leadership of the company. This view fails to understand that there are two quite different and distinct roles: one managing the board of directors, the other managing the company. The chair is responsible for the former and his or her jurisdiction is confined to the boardroom. The C.E.O. bears full responsibility for managing the company with the authority and powers delegated by the board to which he or she is accountable.

MAKING IT HAPPEN

There are common issues on which the board needs now to focus its attention, and there is widespread agreement that the board needs to set the framework for action. Specifically, this involves the board in eight key activities:
- focusing on core activities and being pragmatic;
- adding value and reducing cost;
- building a business culture that embraces change;
- moving with the market, but not changing faster than the market;
- leading the business;
- integrating e-business activities, aligning and optimizing resources;
- managing risk;
- establishing and maintaining good corporate governance.

To help in considering how best to improve the effectiveness of the board, these activities can be grouped into three main areas:

1 The board needs to consider how best to **set the strategy and direction**. This needs to be more than an emphasis on cost-cutting or focusing on the core business. It needs to outline how the enterprise will create value and improve.

2 Recent developments mean that **managing financial performance** now requires an emphasis on cost reduction, but it also needs to be supplemented with an approach that will steady the share price. A critical issue that seems to be gathering in value and acceptance is that of measurement.

3 Crucially, it needs to be recognized that the role of the board in **ensuring operational effectiveness** is central to the business.

In short, the board must drive the company, and not the other way around.

Hugh Parker is a former managing partner of McKinsey, where he worked from 1951 to 1986. For the last 15 of those years he specialized in corporate governance—effective boardroom management, in other words. Parker wrote what was probably the first book on this subject, *Letters to a New Chairman*, published originally in 1970 by the Institute of Directors in London. He is generally credited in the United Kingdom with having pioneered the field of corporate governance.

What's a Director to Do?

Michael C. Jensen and Joe Fuller

Every wave of corporate turmoil or malfeasance inevitably leads to a discussion about the role of the board. So it is not surprising that the current wave of scandals has set off yet another maelstrom about corporate governance. It was, after all, only a few decades ago that shareholder advocates took boards to task for being asleep at the wheel when the Japanese overtook American industry in the 1970s. They pilloried boards again in the late 1980s for letting managers live high on the hog on the shareholders' dollars—remember the 24 country club memberships the shareholders bought for RJR Nabisco's C.E.O., Ross Johnson.*

And so it comes as no surprise that the current wave of accounting scandals has once again dragged an otherwise fairly anonymous group of people—corporate directors—into the spotlight. Indeed, in the wake of these scandals, a barrage of regulations and new legislation has rolled over corporate directors. These new requirements, including the recently passed Sarbanes-Oxley bill and new regulations by the SEC and the NYSE, Nasdaq, and Amex securities exchanges, all attempt to address corporate abuses and boost confidence in U.S. securities markets. The new rules focus on more timely and transparent financial disclosure; greater accountability for financial reporting; increased oversight and independence of the audit function; enhanced SEC review of financial statements and enforcement of regulation, and broader remedies for violations.

Not surprisingly, these new regulations create potential additional personal liability for directors. In the past, directors had to focus their attention only on ensuring the company's *compliance* with procedural rules to protect themselves. That is, they had to act with reasonable care to safeguard what they believed to be the company's best interests, and they had to ensure that management did not perpetrate fraud, act in bad faith, or harbor personal conflicts of interest with the company. Under most circumstances, the courts applied what is generally known as the business judgment rule, which protects boards by prohibiting the courts from hearing cases in which outsiders, including shareholders, questioned the business judgment of the board.†

If a company followed the letter of the rules, board members could serve in relative safety. They could lay all but the most egregious failures at the feet of others such as managers, lawyers, investment bankers, consultants, and auditors. However, merely complying with the rules won't pass muster any more. In fact, the new legislation requires senior managers to certify that they have implemented procedures to gather all "material" information about the business. Moreover, management must

---

* Bryan Burrough and John Helyar, *Barbarians at the Gate: The Fall of RJR Nabisco.* (New York: Harper Perennial, 1991), p. 93.

† See www.socialinvest.org/areas/research/tobacco and www.corp-gov.org/glossary

have either the audit committee or the independent members of the board valid-
ate that attestation. The legislation also stipulates that every board should have at
least one "financial expert" who—through education and experience as a public
accountant or auditor, or a principal financial officer, comptroller, or principal accounting officer of a company, or from a position involving the performance of similar
functions—has:

- an understanding of generally accepted accounting principles and financial
  statements;
- experience in (i) the preparation or auditing of financial statements of generally
  comparable companies, and (ii) the application of such principles in connection
  with the accounting for estimates, accruals, and reserves;
- experience with internal accounting controls;
- an understanding of audit committee functions.

Clearly, the bill's authors intend to render mute any future defense predicated on a
board's lack of oversight responsibility, or of technical skill.

In addition, the legislation calls for new processes to collect and disseminate information on corporate performance; new, faster reporting cycles, and a clear obligation
to certify that financial reports "fairly present in all material respects the financial
condition and results of operations of the issuer."* Yet, it is fair to say that few, if any,
boards can satisfy these conditions as currently constituted. We know now that even
boards lauded in the past for their work failed to meet the emerging expectations.
Ironically enough, *Chief Executive* magazine voted Enron's board among the best
ever in 2000,† and the business press frequently quoted Tyco's C.E.O., Dennis
Kozlowski—who now stands indicted on charges of racketeering, fraud, tax evasion,
grand larceny, and misuse of company funds‡—as a strong advocate of good corporate governance, strong boards, and directors with backbone. In his words: "We are
offended most by the perception that we would waste the resources of a company that
is a major part of our life and livelihood, and that we would be happy with directors
who would permit that waste . . . So as a C.E.O., I want a strong, competent board; one
that can advise me and my staff how to continue succeeding." Indeed, he served as a
literal poster boy for good governance when he was featured in a cover story in the
Spring 2000 edition of *Directors & Boards*. He also adorned the cover of *Business
Week* in the spring of 2001.§

---

* Sarbanes-Oxley Act of 2002, Pub.L. 107–204, 116 Stat. 745 (July 30, 2002), p. 33
† Robert Lear and Boris Yavitz, "The Five Best and Five Worst Boards of 2000," *Chief Executive*,
October 2000
‡ Stephanie Strom, "In Charity, Where Does a C.E.O. End and a Company Start?" September 22,
2002, *New York Times on the Web*
§ "This C.E.O. Wants Strong Directors," excerpted in "The Way It Was: 1995," *Directors & Boards*,
26:1, September 22, 2001, p.107. See also William C. Symonds, "The Most Aggressive C.E.O." *Business
Week*, May 28, 2001

However, rather than wring our hands and wonder what went wrong in any particular case, we would do well to listen to the wisdom of Peter Drucker when he said: "Whenever an institution malfunctions as consistently as boards of directors have in nearly every major fiasco of the last 40 or 50 years, it is futile to blame men, it is the institution that malfunctions."*. Indeed it is. As long-time observers of boards, we are optimistic that some of the unfortunate scandals that have wracked American business of late can serve as stepping stones to better and more effective governance reforms.

We believe, for example, that small changes in board composition or committee membership are unlikely to bring the kind of change that the current environment demands. Boards instead would do well to change fundamentally their approach to the job at hand. Wise C.E.O.s will want their boards to do so, not only to soothe restive institutional shareholders and regulators, but also to reduce the probability of some future problems in their companies.

How can boards fulfill these new mandates? They should focus on the following areas:

BE CLEAR ABOUT THE DECISION RIGHTS AND ROLE OF THE BOARD

Many years ago Eugene Fama and Michael Jensen suggested a compelling framework for understanding the proper role of the board.† The foundations of this structure lie in an understanding of the inherent nature of agency costs—the costs which arise any time human beings attempt to engage in cooperative effort, including the cooperation inherent in the modern corporation. When people (including managers) make decisions for which they do not personally bear the full costs or benefits, the organization and society are at risk of poor decisions. That risk arises less from the prospect of malfeasance or fraud, but rather from self-interest and the prospect of failure bred of introspection and the human tendency to avoid blame.

We can deconstruct any major decision into a sequence of subdecisions in the decision process. They are:

- the right to *initiate* recommendations for resource allocations or contracts;
- the right to *ratify* those initiatives;
- the right to *implement* the ratified initiatives;
- the right to *monitor* those decisions.

Monitoring rights includes not only the right to measure and evaluate, but also the right to reward and punish performance. We use organizational design to assign the initiation and implementation rights to the same party, and, hence, we call these the

---

* Peter Drucker, "The Bored Board" in *Toward the Next Economics and Other Essays* (New York: Harper & Row, 1981), p.110.
† See E. F. Fama and M.C. Jensen, "Separation of Ownership and Control,," *Journal of Law and Economics* 26 (1983): pp.301–325.

"management rights," while simultaneously assigning to a separate party the ratification and monitoring rights, the "control rights," essential to disciplining managerial behavior.

When control is effective in an organization, the management rights for a decision are separated from the control rights for that decision. In this situation, the typical manager will be exercising both management rights and control rights—control rights over decisions made by subordinates, and management rights for decisions for which their superiors hold the control rights.

We must separate the management rights from the control rights at all levels in the organization to reduce aberrant behavior. This is especially true at the board level. Doing so will bring a new level of stability and oversight to corporate governance. This proposition thus generalizes to the governance structure the long-standing separation principle of controllership: that one should not allow a person receiving cash to be the same person who records its receipt.

Applying this formula to the board would yield the following decision-making model. The board must hold the top-level control rights in the organization, and these include: the rights to initiate and implement certain decisions, such as the right to hire, evaluate, compensate, and fire the top management team, board members, and the company's auditor. The board must also hold the right to ratify and monitor other major decisions, such as those pertaining to changes in fundamental strategic direction. This implies that the Chairman of the Board cannot be the C.E.O., because a Chairman's main job is to set the agenda of the board and to oversee the hiring, firing, and evaluation of the top management team—and no C.E.O. can effectively run the process that evaluates himself. The annual election of directors by shareholders accomplishes the same principal of separation for the board of directors.

Similarly, applying this formula to the board might lead some to adopt the model of nonexecutive chairmen used by some European companies. Academics and students of corporate governance have long debated the respective merits of executive and nonexecutive chairmen. Recent events will undoubtedly rekindle that debate and may decisively tip the balance in favor of the nonexecutive model. The attractiveness of that approach stems less from any hope that nonexecutive chairmen would have interdicted the cycles of managerial self-delusion, hubris and, in some cases, outright fraud that destroyed some prominent companies and undermined trust in the capital markets. Admittedly, a more informed, independent perspective might have helped prevent some of the abuses. But, as we look to the future, the logic for a nonexecutive C.E.O. becomes compelling, simply as a function of the workload responsible board chairmen will bear. Chairmen will have to ensure that each of several committees fulfills its statutory responsibilities under the Sarbanes-Oxley Act and additional administrative responsibility as stipulated by the SEC. New requirements from the European Union and other jurisdictions will undoubtedly follow. Moreover, the capital markets will certainly welcome, if not demand, more mechanisms to assuage anxieties over the potential for future abuses. Companies that chose to take the lead in this regard might well enjoy the type of plaudits that Coca-Cola earned by assuming a leadership stance on the expensing of options.

FOCUS ON CHANGING THE STRUCTURAL, SOCIAL, PSYCHOLOGICAL, AND POWER ENVIRONMENT OF THE BOARD

For all intents and purposes, the directors at most companies are employees of the C.E.O. The C.E.O. does most of the recruiting for the board and extends the offer to join the board. And, except in unusual cases, board members serve at the pleasure of the C.E.O. Moreover, it is rare that the board meets outside of the C.E.O.'s presence or without his explicit permission. Finally, virtually all information board members receive from the company originates from the C.E.O., except in highly controlled or unusual circumstances. A change in these practices will require a major change in the power relationship between the board and the C.E.O., perhaps going as far as a structural separation between the Chairman's and C.E.O.'s positions. Companies can implement several practical steps immediately to infuse more balance into the board's deliberations. They include:

- **The board should have its own budget for purchasing advice from outside experts of various sorts—consultants, lawyers, financial, and other experts.** The Audit and Compensation Committees must become the true clients of the auditors and compensation consultants. That suggests locating the decision rights for choices previously made by management, and the associated budget authority, to boards.

- **The board should have regular, planned meetings with the entire top management team and frequent opportunities to interact privately with key managers.** Boards must create opportunities to come to know, on a personal basis, the individuals on whose abilities and judgment the shareholders rely. The carefully choreographed and often perfunctory board "grand performances" of the past must be replaced by selective, but nonetheless substantial, dialogue. Management must not only expect, but also encourage more frequent dialogue between directors and key operating and functional managers on key elements of the strategy. The board, in its duty to evaluate the C.E.O. and other top managers, can productively implement the principle of 360-degree evaluation, and it should not happen by accident through back-channel conversations.

- **The board must take firm control over not only its own processes, but also its own composition.** That requires employing the newly required Nominating Committee as a vehicle for building the board's ability to exercise its expanding role effectively. Just as auditors and compensation consultants should treat company boards as their clients, so should the executive search firms that identify board candidates. The C.E.O. should become a participant in a board-sponsored process of recruitment, rather than serving as the chief recruiter. One straightforward implication—the Chairman of the Nominating Committee or the non-executive chairman of the board should extend the invitation to serve to new board members, not the C.E.O. This will help avoid the situation in which board members feel indebted to the C.E.O. Moreover, the composition and performance of the board should become an active topic of conversation during executive sessions and between the board and management.*

REMEMBER THAT BEYOND THIS STRUCTURAL AND CULTURAL SHIFT, TWO IMPORTANT PHILOSOPHICAL SHIFTS ARE NECESSARY

First, the mindsets of boards must move from one of careful review to one of insatiable curiosity.† The duty to care has long stood as the principal legal hurdle for directors. We must now add to that a new duty—one of informed inquisitiveness. Question assumptions. Make note of and probe anomalies. If the company's expectations lie outside those that experts generally view as plausible for the firm's industry in terms of growth, profit margin, or return on assets, its board must investigate the assumptions underlying such projections. Directors must answer a fundamental question about such a company—what observable sources of competitive advantage allow it to outperform its market so consistently? Directors must not be content to conclude that growth rates arising from "stretch" goals designed to stimulate the organization to excellent performance will lead ineluctably to outstanding performance. Indeed, that constitutes little more than wishful thinking. Moreover, boards should take personal responsibility for understanding how traditional budget processes and stretch goals frequently inculcate a lack of integrity in an organization and destroy value.* They must play a role in reforming these systems.

Second, directors must move beyond a single-minded, legalistic focus on compliance and focus on clarity. This represents more than getting the footnotes right or engaging the right auditors. Instead, the current situation requires setting forth a truly accurate picture of the company and communicating that picture to shareholders. Rarely do board members have the kind of information they need to assess accurately the progress of the corporation. Getting that information requires boards to overhaul the process by which they get substantive information about corporate performance from one controlled by the C.E.O. to one in which the board has ready access to relevant information from unimpeachable sources. Board members must understand the key strategic dimensions that determine the company's competitive position, the factors that drive the logic of value creation, review progress against those drivers regularly, and audit the company's performance against relevant measurements across those dimensions from year to year.

Individual directors have tried in the past to do the things we have suggested, either in whole or in part. And yet, few ever succeeded consistently. Consider the case of former Supreme Court Justice Arthur Goldberg, a member of the board of TWA,

---

* Charan, Ram. *Boards at Work: How Corporate Boards Create Competitive Advantage.* (San Francisco: Jossey-Bass, 1998), 240pp.
† "The duty of curiosity," is a phrase used by Gwendolyn S. King, director of the National Association of Corporate Directors. See that trade group's publication, *DM Extra*, January 31, 2002 at www.nacdonline.org

who asked to form a committee on operations.* He intended this committee to get periodic reports on the company's progress and receive support from a cadre of outside experts, including scientists, economists, public relations people, and financial engineers. Management denied his request, and he subsequently left the board. Presumably, he had realized that he didn't have the necessary information to do the job, and preferred to maintain his intellectual integrity at the expense of his position.†

Indeed, it is our belief and our great hope that ruined reputations, corporate value destruction, and new laws will do more than force directors to do the job they have long been employed to do. Rather, they will encourage them to do that job more confidently and competently, as well as cause management to support them unreservedly in that work.

HONESTY AND INTEGRITY: EASY TO ASSERT, DIFFICULT TO IMPLEMENT

In the end, honesty and integrity constitute matters of human behavior and human choice. No combination of rules, punishments, and threats can substitute for men and women of integrity who bring principles to the boardroom and apply them. High stakes characterize the boardroom environment, as does pressure not to rock the boat and, when in the slightest doubt, to support management and board colleagues. Laws and regulations can establish an environment that encourages principled behavior and discourages turning a blind eye to problems by punishing violations. But human choice and allegiance to these principles remain critical attributes of any system of governance and, ultimately, for the principled and productive society that they enable. If we expect companies to behave with more integrity than we have recently observed, the people who populate them, from the Board of Directors on down, must confront the nature of these choices and help ensure that they each make them appropriately.

Everyone espouses allegiance to principles such as honesty and integrity. Yet evidence from human behavior indicates that when it really matters, people often choose to abandon the very standards they espouse. And this includes not only C.E.O.s and directors, but also government and religious officials. It is now time that corporate directors think carefully about how to restore integrity in corporate governance. This is not an easy task. It will only come when men and women of principle confront not only substantive, difficult business questions honestly, but also change inbred behaviors which encourage many of them to avoid painful confrontations and difficult trade-offs. The current tragic circumstances make this transition easier, as the consequences of unethical or illegal behavior, including ruined reputations, ruined

---

* See Michael C. Jensen, "Corporate Budgeting Is Broken: Let's Fix It," *Harvard Business Review*, November, 2001, pp. 94–101, available at http://papers.ssrn.com/paper=321520, and Michael C. Jensen, "Paying People To Lie: The Truth About the Budgeting Process," September 2001, available at http://papers.ssrn.com/paper=267651

† Lorsch, J., and E. MacIver (contributor). *Pawns or Potentates: The Reality of America's Corporate Boards.* (Cambridge, MA: Harvard Business School Press, p. 57–58, 1989). See also Monks, Robert A. G., and Nell Minow. "Power and Accountability," New York: HarperCollins, 1992

companies, and criminal prosecutions for once-feted executives, are unambiguous to even the most cavalier and insouciant directors.

Honesty and integrity in our actions and words are most valuable to *others* when it costs *us* something to adhere to them. When it costs us nothing, it follows that the associated actions are worth little or nothing to those who depend on us. Yet, it is in those circumstances in which values count the most to those with whom we deal (that is, situations in which it is costly for us to be honest) that people inevitably prove most willing to suspend those qualities and forgive themselves those obligations. Indeed, in granting ourselves such forgiveness, we assuage our guilt by finding ways to blame others. The speed with which boards, analysts, auditors, investment bankers, lawyers, and banks have moved to lay the blame for every corporate misdeed at the feet of C.E.O.s and others reflects both a measure of truth and a degree of guilt. And, in the ultimate corruption of principle, we abandon these principles not only to lower the costs on ourselves and others, but also to "protect" the reputation of the institutions we serve. Consider, for example, the current troubles that many corporations, auditors, investment banks, and other institutions in which those responsible appear to have overstepped ethical bounds to protect their organization from "short run" damage. These tendencies—to avoid short-term pain at the cost of far greater long-term harm and to lose one's sense of personal responsibility in favor of institutional interest—is far more prevalent and dangerous than most observers care to admit. Sadly, such actions usually end up imposing far greater cost on these organizations than those that would have been incurred by straightforward and early confrontation with the pain.

In the end, legislators will pass new laws, regulators will promulgate new rules, and the climate of capital markets will change. But restoring integrity to the system will, ultimately, occur one step, one director, one audit committee, one board, and one organization at a time. It will require men and women of courage and conviction on boards and in management teams to incur costs in the short run, in order to preserve their reputations and fulfill their duty—the preservation of the value of the organizations they serve.

Michael C. Jensen is managing director of organizational strategy at Monitor. Professor emeritus at the Harvard Business School, Jensen is the author of *Foundations of Organizational Strategy* and *Theory of the Firm: Governance, Residual Claims, and Organizational Forms*, both published by Harvard University Press. Jensen was elected to the American Academy of Arts and Sciences in 1996. Joe Fuller is C.E.O. of the Monitor Group, a family of professional firms located in Cambridge, MA.

Heeding Marley's Ghost:
"Mankind's Business" Is Our Business

Gerald L. Pepper

In Charles Dickens's *A Christmas Carol*, Ebenezer Scrooge is confronted by the ghost of his deceased business partner, Jacob Marley. Scrooge is confused as to why Marley is weighted down with such heavy chains and burdens in his afterlife when, during his life on earth, he did "nothing worse" than tend to his business. At this point Marley screams at Scrooge, "Mankind was my business!" Marley laments his short-sightedness when he had the opportunity to make a difference in the lives of men and women, for now his chance has passed. He implores Scrooge to avoid making the same mistakes and sends him the ghosts of Christmases past, present, and future to help Scrooge become a responsible citizen.

A more contemporary spin on Dickens's classic might ask: Do people who aren't employees or direct customers care about your company's success? Is your company acting like a good corporate citizen making a difference in people's lives? Has your company made mankind's business its business? If you can't answer yes, then pre-pare yourself for some sleepless nights. Heed Marley's ghost: make bettering the human condition part of your business conduct, not just your business plan. It's your company's duty, it makes good business sense, and it's easy to do. Consumers care, and making your business a better corporate citizen can secure competitive advantage.

MARLEY'S CASE: THE CITIZENSHIP OBLIGATION

Marley's case is straightforward: members of a society are morally obliged to help each other, this is what citizenship means. For corporate citizens, meeting this moral obligation includes relatively obvious means such as protecting the environment, paying wages, making profits, and guaranteeing workplace safety. But these are organ-izational survival concerns as much as anything else, and citizenship isn't defined by self-interest. A less self-centered technique for meeting the moral obligation of citi-zenship is contributing money. This option is crucial to the survival of many cultural and service beneficiaries. But it falls short of Marley's plea. Marley didn't visit Scrooge to encourage him to give a donation. He visited Scrooge to tell him to become a participant in the city, someone who understood his fellow men and women so that he could help them, so that they could help each other.

Like Scrooge, organizations need to be full and recognizable participants in the life of the community, and that participation isn't simply accomplished through dona-tions. Full community membership is accomplished only through real people partici-pating in real community activities. For the corporate citizen the moral obligations of citizenship are met most practically via workplace volunteer programs. "Workplace volunteerism" refers to formalized efforts by organizations' members to donate their time and talents to community service. Programs are investments, sanctioned and coordinated by workplaces as the active demonstration of concern. They take compassion out of the business plan and give it a face.

MARLEY'S ARGUMENT: CORPORATE CITIZENSHIP IS GOOD BUSINESS

Corporate philanthropy is not a new idea, although the ways in which philanthropy is accomplished have changed dramatically. In the past, generosity was a product of individual benevolence. Prominent people, not organizations, gave money to social causes, generally those least associated with the individual's business so that no hint of impropriety could be charged. This position evolved dramatically over the years until it became common for companies (for example, Levi Strauss, Cummins, Ben & Jerry's) to give away a percentage of their pretax income to selected causes.

In the 1970s, organizations began to use philanthropy strategically to build community goodwill and alliances. By the 1980s, many companies had built volunteerism into their human-resources strategies, finding ways to engage employees in outreach initiatives and using their community activism as both a recruiting and a retention tool. Today, communities and organizations recognize that separating business and community needs is artificial. Society expects organizations to lend a hand, and organizations, sometimes motivated by benevolence, sometimes by image management, have responded.

In return the public rewards such civic-mindedness by contributing to the success of these organizations. This is the business point of view that justifies the effort. Companies develop a reputation for being concerned about the greater good, and this reputation helps attract customers, employees, partners, and vendors. Confidence in new products is enhanced, trust in the company increases, and organizations that do contribute beyond themselves stand in stark contrast to those that do not. Conducting business in a socially responsible fashion is a reason for customers to come to a business, not stay away. Surveys conducted in the United States, Canada, and the United Kingdom all confirm this.

People (including employees) want organizations to make an effort to address social problems, and reward those that do.

- A 2000 survey of 25,000 people in 23 different countries found that corporate citizenship had more impact on public perception of companies than either brand quality or business fundamentals.
- When price and quality are equal, 81% of consumers are more likely to purchase a product associated with a cause.
- Studies by the Conference Board and IBM report that companies with high community involvement show improved employee morale (by as much as 300%), increased productivity, and stronger partnerships with suppliers, customers, and the general public.

MARLEY'S EXAMPLES: MONEY'S NICE, BUT COULD YOU LEND A HAND INSTEAD?

Giving money is good; making donations matters. But, in the long run, money is far less important to corporate citizenship than volunteerism. Volunteer programs are

- a direct statement by the company: We care, all of us;
- a direct reflection of the company's values: We are a small community within a larger community;
- a direct action: Here is what we are doing today to make a difference.

Volunteering humanizes workers. It puts them closer to real life, real impacts. The volunteer learns and begins to appreciate the level of need; volunteers come together in unity and determination; and volunteer efforts generate results that are often far more generous than those an organization would be able to produce by donations. For example, local executives volunteering to serve on the board of the Health Museum of Cleveland, Ohio, were able to turn the failing organization into a healthy, nonprofit business, largely through their strategic planning and resource capabilities.

An organization may want to encourage its employees to volunteer because doing so makes those employees feel better about themselves and their employer. When workers make a difference in their communities they enjoy fulfillment. It's the difference between giving money to finance a local playground and picking up a hammer and helping to build it. Money matters, but ultimately it's people who change the world. Effort associates a responsible organization to the good it is doing—do not simply rely on donations.

Pioneers in corporate responsibility include the following:

- Matsushita Electric of Japan demonstrates its commitment to the community through projects like traffic-safety courses, visitation programs in which employees take time to visit senior citizens living alone, environmental cleanup projects, equipment donations, charity bazaars, and sponsorship of folk festivals.
- Employees of First Union Bank in Charlotte, North Carolina, have donated more than 1.5 million hours of time as tutors, mentors, chaperones, teachers' aides, and readers. The company allows employees up to four hours per month of paid time to donate to local school and related programs.
- Verizon employees worldwide donate 10 million hours a year to community causes, and in 2000 the company matched $8 million worth of employee contributions to various educational, arts, health and human services, and environmental concerns.
- More than 25% of Glaxo Wellcome's 4,500 employees in the Research Triangle area around Raleigh-Durham, North Carolina, donate time tutoring underprivileged youth. Employees and their families are encouraged to donate time to causes in which they are interested, with the company donating $500 to nonprofit organizations to which its employees or their spouses have donated 50 or more hours.
- More than 1,000 employees of Bayer Corporation donate time to the company's program, Making Science Make Sense. The program is aimed at increasing

science literacy across the United States by offering hands-on, inquiry-based science education.

- About 20 executives make up Avon's global Corporate Social Responsibility Committee, which helps to ensure that the company keeps its commitment to civic responsibility. The committee helps coordinate the community enrichment activities of Avon's 2.3 million representatives in 113 countries around the world.
- For over 30 years Fuji Bank Group has cosponsored an annual traffic safety campaign in Japan that has reached over 41 million children. Additionally, the company has given over $16 million in charitable donations of items such as wheelchairs and books translated into Braille.
- In Ukraine, MEEST Corporation is an example of targeted corporate responsibility, devoting both volunteer and financial support to the Children of Chernobyl Fund, as well as supporting political candidates dedicated to bringing democratic ideals to the nation's politics.

MAKING IT HAPPEN

Companies need to encourage their employees to be involved in social issues. The reasons are clear: societies benefit, organizations benefit, and employees benefit. But it isn't enough just to encourage employees in the newsletter or at quarterly meetings. A successful program of corporate citizenry should be planned and executed with the same care that any other important organizational objective receives. The following represent a cross section of the primary issues involved in creating a credible and successful corporate-wide initiative.

- Analyze needs and priorities. Ask: What sorts of charitable causes will our people work for?
- Assign the coordination effort to a person or an office.
- Promote the program—internally and externally.
- Network with other organizations and learn from best practices.
- Show the community impact. One reason for doing all this work is because it increases customer loyalty and the organization's image. Community action will do neither if the community at large doesn't know about it.
- Get C.E.O. buy-in. Without it you're wasting your time.
- Recognize that making an impact will cost time, but that it will not necessarily entail huge actual costs. And even if it does, the cost is an investment.
- Don't reinvent the wheel. Find good sources of information and follow their advice. For example, the Conference Board of Canada produced a report listing 18 benchmarks to use in developing broad, effective programs to promote social responsibility. The report even includes a corporate social responsibility "benchmark assessment tool" for use by both large and small companies.

Organizations are community members. Like individuals, businesses may have the right to remain distanced from social causes, but their obligation is to be involved. Business survival is incumbent upon a healthy community and the goodwill of its customers, and both of these are influenced by the corporation's efforts at being socially responsible. Accomplishing corporate citizenry takes a combination of resources, commitment, and effort. But mostly it takes genuine belief. If citizenship is a core organizational value, the rest will follow. Heed Marley's ghost before it's too late. Let your business make a difference today.

———

Gerald L. Pepper is an associate professor of communication at the University of Minnesota Duluth, teaching, lecturing, and researching in the areas of organizational culture, communication and creativity, conflict management, group process, and employee identification. He has provided consulting to many organizations and lectured widely. Pepper is the author of *Communicating in Organizations: A Cultural Approach* (McGraw-Hill, 1995).

Improving Corporate Profitability Through Accountability

Marc J. Epstein and Priscilla S. Wisner

Improved governance requires the right employees, the right culture and values, and the right systems, information, and decision making. Unfortunately, most organizations are attempting to steer their information-age businesses using industrial-age measurements. Managers have struggled for decades with accounting systems that fail to measure many of the variables that drive long-term value. The historical lagging indicators of performance that are commonly used by accountants are of limited value in determining the value of businesses for external stakeholders, and are of little use in guiding the business internally. Financial data on profitability and return on investment are valuable measures of corporate performance, but they are lagging indicators that measure past performance. A broader set of financial measures is necessary (for example, measurement of intangible assets such as intellectual capital and research-and-development value), in addition to an expanded set relating to customers, internal processes, and organizational measures.

The metrics must include the *leading* financial and nonfinancial indicators of performance that are the drivers and predictors of future financial performance. For example, fines and penalties may be a leading indicator of corporate reputation, employee turnover is a leading measure of future recruitment and training costs, and product quality is a leading measure of customer satisfaction, which in turn is a leading measure of market share.

IMPROVED INTERNAL AND EXTERNAL REPORTING

Just as companies expand their performance measurement parameters, they must also expand their performance reporting models. Employees, shareholders, financial analysts, activists, customers, suppliers, government regulators, and others increasingly demand detailed information about corporate activities, and the Internet has made the dissemination of that information easier and faster. No longer can managers claim they don't have the information. The data are easy to collect, and it's essential to have broader and more forward-looking information to effectively manage the diverse issues that managers now confront daily. Managers should collect this broader array of information on activities and impacts both inside and outside the company and select a set of data to provide adequate disclosure to their various stakeholders. External stakeholders need a broader set of information to effectively evaluate corporate performance, and voluntary disclosure of this information is critical for corporate accountability. This accountability, both inside and outside the firm, through an effective corporate communications strategy, is an essential element of effective and responsible corporate governance.

Proactively managing external disclosures should be a fundamental part of corporate communications strategy. By externally disclosing a more comprehensive set of measures, company executives are seizing the initiative to describe the company's strategy, set expectations, increase transparency, and ensure goal alignment between the company and a broad set of stakeholders. Disclosing performance measures allows investors and other stakeholders to view the company through the eyes of management. A clear, comprehensive communications strategy is highly valued by shareholders and analysts alike.

CASES IN POINT

The Campbell Soup Company has continually improved corporate governance.

Changes undertaken in the early 1990s required a majority of directors to come from outside the organization. All directors must stand for election every year and must own at least 6,000 shares of stock within three years of election. Among other provisions, interlocking directorships are not allowed and insiders are banned from certain key committees.

In 1995, the board began a rotating yearly performance evaluation of directors, board committees, and the board as a whole.

In 2000, the board approved a new director compensation program to closely link director compensation to the creation of shareholder value; only 20% is paid in cash (tied to attendance at meetings). The full set of Campbell Soup's governance standards and current performance review are disclosed in the annual proxy statement to shareholders.

The Cooperative Bank, based in the United Kingdom and with 4,000 employees, has won numerous awards for the high degree of transparency and accountability the company has exhibited. The bank has identified seven partners in its quest for corporate value: shareholders, customers, staff and their families, suppliers, local communities, national and international society at large, and past and future generations of cooperators. The company surveys all these stakeholder groups to determine the critical elements in creating value for each, and performance targets are set on the basis of this information. In 2000, 68 targets were established. The Cooperative Bank 2000 Partnership Report states that 47 targets were fully achieved, acceptable progress was made on 11, and 10 were not achieved. The bank reports progress on each target, providing data and management commentary, and establishes targets for the coming year. During 2000, the Cooperative Bank significantly improved ethical and ecological performance while achieving strong profitability.

MAKING IT HAPPEN

The rewards from building the accountable organization are much like those from building the quality organization—the more committed the managers and workers and the better integrated the concept with company line operations, the greater the benefit. As a first step, managers must build accountable systems and practices within the company. Then they can build bridges to the outside. As they move toward full accountability—well-governed, measured, managed, and publicly responsive—they will position themselves to reap many benefits:

- Improving decision making: the accountable organization generates a wealth of information on performance, which in turn informs decision making with facts, not intuition. People inside and outside the company can make more effective decisions to further company strategy and goals.
- Accelerating learning: the accountable organization installs feedback systems that yield rapid-fire learning from people both across and outside the company. The company with the most feedback loops—internal and external—is the most successful.
- Empowering people: the accountable organization thins the ranks of middle managers that distill and convey information and apportions new decision-making authority to the front lines. As management articulates what it wants with concrete quantitative measures, workers have unmistakable guidance as they figure out how to deliver it.
- Communicating the story: the accountable organization delivers its story of value with credible financial and nonfinancial numbers. As senior managers report more numbers externally, exposing performance transparently, shareholders and analysts have less reason to undervalue their stock.
- Executing strategy: the accountable organization communicates each strategy and tactic with specific measures that align direction in ways that written objectives cannot. The hard measures then give managers a month-to-month reading on whether the strategy is working.
- Inspiring loyalty: the accountable organization markets its value on a basis of reliable performance measures. The no-smoke-and-mirrors approach spurs cooperation and inspires the loyalty of investors, customers, suppliers, employees, business partners, and communities.

Once a company has decided to improve corporate governance, measure a broader set of indicators of past and future success, and report internally and externally, managers must develop systems to drive these decisions through the organization. Leading companies are developing integrated closed-loop planning, budgeting, and feedback systems to help align strategy implementation with corporate performance. While leadership at the top is critical, buy-in at the shop floor is essential for the success of any system implementation. Metrics must be linked to strategy and must be consistent throughout the organization. Companies are increasingly stating a desire to become more customer focused, yet many are still basing employee rewards on meeting revenue and profit goals. If companies expect employees to be more customer focused or more socially or environmentally responsible, part of overall performance evaluations and rewards should be on customer focus or social responsibility.

Accountable managers encourage not only continuous judgment, but continuous improvement. They insist that everyone in the organization participate in decision making. They implement a culture of constant learning and insist on building learning organizations. Accountable managers communicate constantly, setting a tone of forthright feedback and transparency.

Full accountability comes only when a company combines a strong governance structure, improved and broad measurement of relevant performance impacts, timely and full internal and external reporting, and comprehensive management systems to drive the accountability model throughout the organization. By combining these elements companies are creating value for the stakeholders whose support they need in order to prosper—customers, investors, employees, suppliers, communities, the public, regulators, and other government officials.

Marc J. Epstein is currently distinguished research professor of management at Jones Graduate School of Management at Rice University in Houston, Texas. He has completed extensive academic research and has considerable practical experience in the implementation of corporate strategies, and the development of performance metrics for use in these implementations. Epstein is author of a dozen books and over 100 professional papers. He also provides seminars, executive courses, and lectures to senior managerial audiences throughout the world. Priscilla S. Wisner is a professor of global business at Thunderbird, The American Graduate School of International Management, in Arizona. Her research interests are focused on the implementation of corporate strategy to improve social, environmental, and economic performance. She teaches graduate business and executive education classes in managerial accounting, decision analysis, and profit planning and control.

Toward Global Governance:
The Paradox of Legitimacy

Francis Fukuyama

Francis Fukuyama of the John Hopkins School of Advanced International Studies is renowned for his insightful, provocative, and ground-breaking views on the development of international politics, economics, and commerce. His book *The End of History and the Last Man* (Penguin, 1993)—developed from an article of the same name—ignited debate about the future of the world political order in the post-Cold War era. In recent years, Francis Fukuyama has focused on the role of culture and social capital in modern economic life and on the social consequences of the transition into an information economy. In this article, he argues that civil societies, through a variety of channels, are becoming much more involved in setting global norms of behavior for corporations. The result is an informal system of global governance that is emerging alongside official institutions such as the World Trade Organisation, and this has significant implications for the way that global corporations do business.

The most obvious development regarding global-level policy in the last few years has been the direct participation of civil society in establishing things like corporate codes of conduct. A good example is the Nike sweatshop issue. Instead of legislating labor policy through the World Trade Organization, change was brought about by grassroots efforts in Honduras, where a nongovernmental organization (NGO) supporting workers' rights staged a protest and Nike accepted a new code of conduct.

The idea that companies can do well by doing good is at the heart of Peter Schwartz's book *When Good Companies Do Bad Things*. Companies have an interest in protecting their reputations, and none want to be vilified in the way that Shell was, for example, for dumping oil into the North Sea. However, the consequences of this need careful thought. Nobody wants overt international regulation because no one has figured out how to do it in a way that is remotely responsive and flexible, avoiding excessive bureaucracy. On the other hand, more informal kinds of self-regulation by the private sector have problems because in many areas it is hard to bring pressure on companies to improve their conduct. In other cases it is not clear that the NGOs that are pressuring the companies to adopt new codes of conduct actually represent the real interests of the people. This is the paradox of legitimacy.

For example, Ethan Kapstein points out in an article in *Foreign Affairs* that it's not clear whether the anti-child-labor code adopted by Nike is actually doing these countries any good. Nike promises not to hire anyone under the age of 17, but mandatory schooling in most of Central America ends at about age 12. In effect, Nike is saying that it will no longer employ these out-of-school kids who were supporting their families by working for a Western multinational. It's a complicated issue. It may be appealing to say that we have alternative ways of effecting global governance, but how to do it equitably and legitimately is something that is still unclear.

We have democratic institutions like Congress, elections, and political parties that have evolved over a long period of time because they were the best way anyone could figure out to represent all of the different societal interests and at the same time make the representatives accountable. You can unelect your representative if you don't like what he or she is saying in your name. The NGO sector doesn't have that kind of accountability. Perhaps you could make them accountable, but then you start regulating them, and they become part of the problem rather than part of the solution.

It is difficult to balance the need for a system that is flexible and participatory against the need for one that is legitimate and representative. Often the two are enemies. The reason we have formal, hierarchical, well-established institutions is to make them transparent and legitimate. But once they become formalized and hierarchical, they also become slow, inflexible, and hard to modify. There's not an easy way to reconcile those kinds of competing demands.

From the standpoint of any multinational corporation, global governance will be a central issue in the next few years. They are going to have to spend a lot of time worrying about how to deal with NGOs, how to deal with the backlash against globalization, and how to make their activities seem legitimate in all sorts of different markets.

COEXISTING IN A FRAGMENTING WORLD: THE NEW DIFFICULTY IN FINDING CONSENSUS

It has always been the case that culture and social norms are more difficult and slower to change than technology, so it's not as if dealing with technological change is a new problem. In many ways, the kinds of social changes that took place in the United States between 1850 and 1900 were more momentous than the changes that took place between 1950 and 2000. That is when everybody essentially moved from the family farm to the city to work in factories. I don't think that the Internet even compares to that kind of change in people's lives, or the kinds of norms that accompany this different kind of urbanized, industrialized life.

What's new is that we have more cultural diversity and a bigger and more complex society. That makes it extremely difficult to generalize about what is going on. You can get pockets of cultural adaptations or cultural stasis that all coexist in the same society. People who don't like change will simply wall themselves off and live in a community where they don't have to deal with it.

Getting society-wide consensus on certain issues is therefore much less likely now than in earlier generations. On the other hand, it may not be necessary in many cases. From a business technology standpoint, for example, you can have a high level of innovation, diversity, and social change in the San Francisco Bay Area while other parts of the country are virtually left out of it, and the latter don't hinder the former. This is also highlighted with the example of India, with a top tier that is world class, absolutely competitive in a globalized world in IT, and then you've got half the country that are failing basic literacy.

One of the reasons that this is significant is, of course, because it does pose a major problem with social justice. I've always thought that "cyberpunk" novelist Neal Stephenson's dystopias were really very apt, because what he describes is a world that is extremely fragmented. The old dystopia used to be an Orwellian vision where everything was regimented. In Stephenson's world everything is fragmented, and you get pockets with high degrees of social order next to very chaotic communities. They all somehow coexist with each other. I think that's a more accurate vision of where the world is actually going.

———•◦•———

This essay was adapted from an interview undertaken with Mr. Fukuyama by Peter Leyden, Knowledge Developer at Global Business Network (www.gbn.com). The publishers gratefully acknowledge the support of Global Business Network in making these ideas and insights available.

Enterprise Information Systems

Thomas H. Davenport

Information systems have become an integral part of how organizations work and compete. They now support every business objective and process. Those systems that support core business activities for the entire organization are known as enterprise information systems or enterprise resource planning systems. Without them, no organization could easily take orders from customers, procure goods from suppliers, make sure that there is sufficient inventory, or keep track of employee compensation and vacation balances. Enterprise information systems consist of some of the following types of system, many of which are linked in the contemporary organization's technology architecture:

- accounting and financial
- human resource management
- sales and order management
- logistics and supply chain
- manufacturing
- inventory management
- customer relationship management

Enterprise information systems do not include those systems that serve only a small part of an organization—say, a standalone system to manage the legal department. They also would not generally include systems for analyzing data or supporting decisions, or for sharing knowledge within an organization. Enterprise systems are primarily focused on core business transactions. Because of their importance and complexity, enterprise systems have turned the usual formula for business change on its head. It used to be that firms decided what they wanted to do, then built systems to accomplish it. Now they must think first about what they can accomplish with systems, and then they proceed to do it. Of course this raises significant issues for how companies manage and compete.

GETTING THEM IN AND GETTING VALUE

Almost all firms that implement enterprise systems do so by buying and installing a package. Firms such as SAP, Oracle, and PeopleSoft (in descending order of current market share) supply application packages that are an integrated collection of modules—one for accounting, one for human resources, and so on. Firms attempt to configure the packages to fit their particular organizational situations. Because of the complexity of the packages, it is not generally advisable to modify them beyond the limits of the configuration process—hence the constraints that these systems impose on organizational flexibility. Some organizations, however, develop their own proprietary modules and interface them with their packages, although this can be a difficult undertaking as well.

The configuration process has been challenging historically, since both the packages and the organizations they support are complex. Vendors often provide a preconfigured set of choices that a particular organization can select from—for example, what currency to use, or whether revenue will be recognized across geographical units or product groups. The choices are complex, and deciding what options a particular company needs to fit its organization and way of doing business requires both business and technical decision making, and a high level of communication between technical and business managers. Many business executives do not understand these systems or the importance of not modifying them substantially. The idea that they should change their way of doing business to suit the limitations of an information system is often hard for them to understand. But for business people to withdraw from the configuration process almost guarantees that a system will not meet business objectives.

One of the key challenges with such systems is to achieve real business value in the implementation process. These systems are capable of delivering such benefits as radically improved business processes, reductions in inventory, increased sales (through one-stop ordering and prevention of stockouts), and better management of financial and physical assets. Most organizations, however, fail to achieve these benefits—in part because simply installing the system often becomes the overriding objective. This was particularly true for the organizations attempting to install enterprise systems before the Y2K bug took effect. Yet these systems are expensive—usually costing in the tens or hundreds of millions of dollars to implement for a large organization—and managers of the projects must not lose sight of the potential benefits. The key to achieving benefit is to view the project not as a technical initiative, but as a business change project with clear objectives and measures.

CHANGING EVERYTHING AT ONCE

The secret to both the opportunity and the difficulty of enterprise information systems is their tight integration with the business they support. Enterprise systems, to be effective, must be closely aligned to a company's business processes, information, organizational structure, and strategy. While this integration is positive in the sense that businesses can get higher-quality information than ever before, it is also challenging to deal with, both at the time of implementation and thereafter.

During implementation, the integrated nature of these systems means that organizations must "change everything at once." That is, they must make sure that all aspects of the organization that will be affected by the system are consistent with their objectives for them, and that the system fits each aspect. For example, most companies will have objectives for process improvement and for greater consistency of key processes across the organization. In most cases, some change is desired from the current state. An organization may wish or need in the course of its enterprise system project to develop greater consistency in definitions of key information across different business units, for example. At the same time it may want different units to share the same process for reporting financial matters. Identifying and bringing about these changes in the business may be much more difficult than simply configuring and installing a new system, but it is the system project and its managers that get saddled with the responsibility for making the changes happen.

Because the project involves business change as well as a new system, many organizations put a senior business executive in charge of the project, such as the chief operations officer or chief financial officer. If the desired changes primarily involve a single functional area, it may make sense to put a functional executive in charge, such as the head of logistics or manufacturing. Putting an IT executive in charge is a good way to ensure that little business change gets accomplished, even if the system gets installed.

THE IMPLICATIONS FOR COMPETITIVE ADVANTAGE

It has been estimated that an enterprise systems package can support up to 70% of an organization's information needs. Since these systems come as packages and are similar from one company to another—even after the configuration process—the question arises how firms can obtain competitive advantage from their systems and the processes they support, if they are all essentially alike. The answer is that competitive advantage can still be achieved, but it is difficult.

Some companies tailor their enterprise systems to fit the needs of their business, and rely on being the first to install the systems in their industry. Reebok, for example, added size and color information to the basic SAP system, and was the first company in the athletic shoe industry to implement a package with these capabilities. Its rival Nike also installed SAP, but completed its implementation several years later.

Another alternative is to implement enterprise systems only in those "commodity" business functions that are not associated with competitive advantage. Intel, for example, believes that its primary advantages over competitors come from its product design and manufacturing processes. When implementing an enterprise package, it did not use any package capabilities in these business functions, but rather developed its own systems internally.

WHAT'S NEXT FOR ENTERPRISE SYSTEMS?

Enterprise systems have thus far been implemented primarily to support internal operations. In the future, it is likely that systems will be integrated across organizations. If a supplier's systems can interface with a customer's without human intervention, firms could better coordinate their logistical and production processes, and the costs of supply chains could be reduced. Some firms are already beginning to work on this integration, either on a one-to-one basis or with multiple other firms through an intermediary.

Given the similarities across businesses in areas supported by enterprise systems, it is likely that we will begin to see new business arrangements wherein several firms collaborate on common business transactions and enterprise systems. For example, six oil exploration firms in the North Sea, including BP and Conoco, have combined their accounting and financial processes and enterprise information systems in a joint effort to share services. They have outsourced the operation of these services to an external professional services firm.

The other key direction for enterprise systems is for vendors and implementing firms to add increasing amounts of functionality to their systems. Today, for example, many firms are working at adding customer relationship management (CRM) and supply chain management (SCM) capabilities to their base enterprise systems. They have integrated their enterprise systems with the Internet, so that core transaction systems can be employed in electronic commerce. They are also making enterprise systems information more easily available through portals and data warehouses. It is also likely that many firms will eventually add product life-cycle management functions to their core systems. The tight grip that enterprise packages have on business information systems is likely only to increase.

For an organization that has yet to implement a system, the following steps will help it get under way in the most effective fashion:

- Create the project as a business change initiative, not a systems project—and start by identifying the business objectives that the new system will enable.
- Select a package from a well-established vendor that has all the functionality your organization needs, and limit the changes to the configuration options provided.
- Don't put off the changes in business processes and organizational structure until after the system is installed.
- Tie incentive compensation of the project team, sponsoring executives, and any consultants used to the successful accomplishment of business objectives.

For companies that have already installed enterprise systems but did not receive sufficient value, it's not too late to organize a project to optimize the system and deliver more benefits. The steps for this type of project include:

- Identify the areas of the business in which value from the system should have been achieved, but was not.
- Create a process improvement or reorganization initiative to bring about the desired business changes.
- Reset the configuration of the system to fit the new process and organization.

———•———

Thomas H. Davenport is director of the Accenture Institute for Strategic Change, a research center in Cambridge, Massachusetts, and also distinguished scholar in residence at Babson College. He is a widely-published author and acclaimed speaker on the topics of information and knowledge management, reengineering, enterprise systems, and the use of information technology in business. His books include *Mission Critical: Realizing the Promise of Enterprise Systems* (Harvard Business School Press, 2000), and he is coauthor of *The Attention Economy* (with John Beck; Harvard Business School Press, 2001) and *Working Knowledge* (with Laurence Prusak; Harvard Business School Press, 2000).

Integrating Real and Virtual Strategies

David Stauffer

Not long ago experts predicted the demise of long-established companies as relics of the Industrial Age. Then, as high-tech firms faltered, observers concluded that digital outfits weren't such world-beaters after all.

Today corporations young and old are demonstrating that success in the 21st century may most likely spring not from either old virtues or new technologies, but from a potent blend of the two. The ways in which any business effectively intertwines its real and virtual strategies—its bricks and clicks—uniquely reflect its history and its strengths. But an examination of companies that have successfully married clicks to bricks suggests that the key elements of a blissful union are:

- early and unflagging support from the top of the organization;
- meticulous strategic planning based in part on what other organizations have done;
- a clicks-side operation that strives to boost bricks-side business—and vice versa;
- technology employed not to replace workers, but to empower them;
- a structuring of products, services, and functionalities that allows customers to switch from clicks to bricks and back again at will.

How can you make each of these elements part of your powerfully integrated bricks and clicks strategies? Here are the essentials.

Taking It from the Top. Integrating bricks and clicks involves hard work, insight, and more than a few frustrations. Your effort won't necessarily succeed with the strong backing of corporate leaders. But it will certainly fail without that backing. Someone at the next level can, and probably should, be put in charge of implementing bricks and clicks integration. But the continuous, driving impetus must be exerted from the top.

One company with the right leadership chemistry is Eastman Chemical Company of Kingsport, Tennessee. Eastman has been one of the manufacturing sector's most prolific adopters of digital technologies, with an e-effort led by chairman and C.E.O. Earnest W. Deavenport, Jr. and chief information officer Roger K. Mowen, Jr. Both are career-long Eastman employees, with chemical engineering and sales and marketing backgrounds respectively. Yet Deavenport thinks way outside the chemical engineer's box. "Do you want to step back and wait until technology kills you?" he asks. "Or do you want to be out there on the leading edge?" And Mowen says his nontech background means that "business managers don't see me as the IT guy with wildly impractical ideas."

This high-tech odd couple implemented a bricks and clicks strategy by making a highly visible commitment to the effort. If managers—particularly those of the old school—don't see the top honchos leading the way, they're sure to play safe and stay where they are today.

Benchmarking and Best Practices. You've probably been advised more times than you can count not to reinvent the wheel. That's in part because it's sound advice endorsed by super-successful C.E.O.s. Ford C.E.O. Jacques Nasser has borrowed best practices from other industries in leading his organization's bricks and clicks integration. Among his initiatives was setting his managers' sights on emulating the build-to-order business model that made Dell successful. The Net-based enterprise FordDirect.com is structured along lines of Dell's build-to-order concept.

Do some exploring in business publications—on the Web and by networking. Which companies are marrying clicks and bricks in a way you might emulate? Who's strongest where you may be weakest? What opportunities can you offer for a fair exchange of best practices? How can you encourage internal units to exchange their best ideas? Someone has already invented the wheel that's right for you. Find it.

A Virtuous Spiral of Mutual Aid. Provide incentives for your virtual-realm people to drive business to traditional outlets and for facility-based folks to generate online traffic. That's what Office Depot has accomplished. This Delray Beach, Florida office products retailer achieved its bricks and clicks synergy by getting things right when it first went online.

- *Office Depot made its Web unit an integral and equal part of its overall organization.* "That meant we weren't fighting over who got which customer or made which sales," says Monica Luechtefeld, the firm's e-commerce chief. By providing online access to information about store locations and inventory, Office Depot's Web sites have increased store traffic. The stores, in turn, promote the Web sites.
- *Office Depot committed additional time and expense to fully integrate Web functionality with its existing information infrastructure.* Luechtefeld asserts that this is a largely unseen and often neglected strategy that can aid Net success. Now an Office Depot customer, even one new to Web purchasing, has online access to the past 18 months of purchasing history, from bricks as well as clicks.

Office Depot's experience suggests these strategies:

- Provide incentives for extending clicks efforts to the bricks side and vice versa. For example, tie part of sales reps' incentive pay to customer use of e-commerce.
- Make Net-based sales channels equivalent in structure and status to traditional channels.
- Tie Web functionality fully into existing systems as it's introduced.

Technology: It's a People Thing. New technology is often viewed as a way to reduce manpower. Some dot-coms even trumpeted the fact that they needed no employees at all (other than a few geniuses at the top). But some corporations that have achieved the most from emerging technologies view new capabilities as ways to further empower their people.

One of these is Inditex SA of La Coruña, Spain, a manufacturer and global retailer of hip clothes for fashion-conscious young people. Best known for its Zara stores, Inditex employs the clicks of digital technologies to link its people and operations worldwide and thereby boost sales from its bricks—some 1,000 stores on four continents.

Inditex starts with computers in every store, into which managers and sales reps enter notes on their sales-floor observations, not just on what's selling, but on the when, how, and why of selling. Fashion consultants similarly report from the favorite haunts of target customers. All of the input is analyzed in La Coruña by designers and production managers. They're empowered to make decisions on what to make, how to make it, and where to send it. Result: an incredibly short four-week lag between field observations and delivery of new fashions based on those observations.

Instant global communication is the enabler of Inditex's speed. But the key to its success is trusting and empowering employees.

Corporate leaders must provide their people with the technological capabilities that transform them from order takers or bean counters into experts with a stake in contributing to the company's success.

Customers See Only Seamlessness. Do you see new technologies as strange and different channels for conducting business, channels used by strange and different people? If so, you're right—at least in the early stages of a digital initiative.

But experience has increasingly shown that companies make distinctions between bricks-customers and clicks-customers at their peril. For one thing, few customers now dwell in only one of these worlds. And even those who do deal with a corporation through only one channel want the same products and prices offered in the other.

Charles Schwab learned that lesson after it set up its first online unit, e.Schwab, as a separate unit. Online customers got a break on stock-trading fees, but paid for that saving by having access to fewer services than those available to branch-office customers. E.Schwab succeeded at first, but soon stalled. Chairman Charles Schwab told *Forbes*, "Customers didn't feel good about the nonintegrated services."

So Schwab took a gamble by terminating e.Schwab and recognizing the online and offline customer as a single individual. That meant offering the lower online trading fee on the bricks side and extending enhanced services to the clicks world. Revenues plunged initially, but the gamble eventually paid off in new customers, new assets, and rocketing revenues.

The way to view customers, Schwab's experience shows, is holistically. Whether a customer interfaces with you by bricks, clicks, or both, that customer wants to be equally valued and get equal value. Make sure you provide it.

COMBINATIONS THAT SOAR
Consider the following examples:

- Cemex SA, a Monterrey, Mexico, cement maker that uses global positioning system (GPS) satellite technology to overcome the once-intractable obstacles of traffic and weather, delivering cement to construction sites within a 20-minute window.
- Rosenbluth International, a Philadelphia corporate travel manager that used technology to pioneer the call-center concept. It has since incessantly applied

technological innovations to automate the tedious aspects of workers' jobs and simultaneously serve customers better.

- Snap-on Incorporated, a Kenosha, Wisconsin, manufacturer and distributor of mechanics' tools that uses the Internet to make its dealers the main focus of digital initiatives. Its online catalog recruits new customers for dealers and provides dealer commissions on most sales.
- Tesco, the United Kingdom's #1 supermarket chain, which is the world's sole example of a profitable purveyor of foods to customers who place orders online. It's simultaneously growing its bricks side by building ultramodern hypermarkets in Asia and Eastern Europe.

To follow their principles:
- Launch your bricks and clicks integration with an enthusiastic, ongoing commitment from the top of the organization.
- Explore what other firms have done to make clicks work with bricks. Avoid their missteps; adapt their successes.
- Insist that bricks and clicks become mutually supportive, with incentives on each side to boost business on the other.
- Implement new technologies, not to replace employees but as a means of benefiting from their ground-level expertise and judgment.
- Blur customers' perceived distinctions between your bricks and clicks channels until they see no distinction.

We tend to view technological capabilities as something quite apart from the physical environment of factories, warehouses, trucks, and stores. Accordingly, most companies at first managed their clicks and bricks as nonintersecting universes. We know now that this distinction is not only incorrect, but it misses out on synergies. As bricks and clicks are treated as occupying one world, they can boost each other—and your business—to unprecedented success.

David Stauffer heads Stauffer Bury Inc., a business writing firm that compiles management information and produces business publications for corporate clients. He is the author of several books including *D2D—Dinosaur to Dynamo* (Capstone, 2001) and *Big Shot: Business the Cisco Way* (Capstone, 2001). His numerous articles have been published in journals such as the *Harvard Management Update* and the *Wall Street Journal*. He also teaches business writing as an adjunct professor at Rocky Mountain College in Billings, Montana.

Marketspaces

Jeffrey F. Rayport

From the Athenian agora to the mall of America, the places where buyers and sellers negotiate their transactions have for thousands of years been just that: places. But over the past two centuries, and especially since the advent of the Internet and the World Wide Web, technology has given rise to an alternative to the marketplace: the virtual market*space*.

More and more transactions that once took place only in the marketplace now occur in the marketspace, largely free from the bonds of space and time. As a result, there are exponentially greater opportunities—and expectations—for deeper, more frequent interactions between companies and customers. With the growth of a service-based economy in which products are increasingly commoditized and differentiation ever-harder to achieve, successfully managing company-to-customer interactions is not just advisable—it's critical. Indeed, there is a dialectic between the rise of the marketspace and the growth of the service-based economy: each feeds, and feeds off of, the other and they must be considered together.

Thus, the marketspace presents both challenges and opportunities. Companies that either underestimate (the Internet is overhyped; nothing much has changed) or overestimate (technology changes everything; all the old rules of business are obsolete) its significance stand to suffer. On the other hand, firms that understand that the marketspace demands creative new strategies, yet relentlessly test those strategies against fundamental principles of service management, are likely to prosper. Even in the technology-enabled marketspace, using service to manage relationships with customers will only become a greater virtue.

FROM MARKETPLACE TO MARKETSPACE

A marketplace consists of three basic components:
- sellers, offering something of value (goods, services, or information);
- buyers, offering something of value in return (cash or any of the above);
- a physical location (store, exchange) where the two come together.

In the marketspace, buyers, sellers, and the value they exchange remain the same, but the time and space constraints disappear. In the marketspace, their transactions take place virtually any time, anywhere, thanks to a variety of technology-mediated interfaces (not just the Web) such as the telephone, wireless device, and personal computer. If a transaction takes place and you cannot say with confidence *where* it occurred, it happened in the marketspace.

One could say that the marketspace was born more than 150 years ago, the first time that a lone Morse code operator telegraphed an order to a supplier. Succeeding generations of communications technology—telephone, fax, pager, mobile phone, even fast-food drive-through microphone—expanded the universe of transactions that could take place outside of the marketplace.

The marketspace as we know it today is chiefly enabled by the kind of "screen-to-face" interactions offered by the Internet in general and the Web in particular. It should be noted, however, that the first (and still one of the most successful) screen-to-face technology predates the Web by more than a decade in the form of the humble ATM. In spitting out cash at more and more locales around the world, the automated teller machine performed first, on a widespread basis, what many marketspace interfaces are doing today: it represented a substitute of capital for labor, thus threatening to make bank tellers an endangered species.

Banks originally positioned ATMs as a service channel for their least profitable customers, assuming that account holders with substantial means would continue to talk with live tellers. They soon discovered, however, that customers of all stripes enjoyed banking at the machines—and the number of machines, networks linking them, and services they provided mushroomed. The result of retail banking's shift from marketplace to marketspace was nothing less than a transformation of the entire industry's competitive dynamics. As the ATM became the dominant interface between customer and company, consumer loyalty to individual bank brands eroded. The network trumped the brand as the locus of both customer relationships and economic value, which is why we are more interested in spotting Cirrus or NYCE on the side of an ATM than a placard for our particular bank.

By the early 1990s, even before the emergence of the Web, virtual channels were beginning to transform businesses and industries and create significant new sources of value. This is why, in 1992, fellow Harvard Business School professor John Sviokla and I, convinced that the old paradigms for teaching the first-year marketing course were increasingly outmoded, sat down and hatched a new term (and a new course) to describe the brave new business world: marketspace.

Since that afternoon, bubble economies and Wall Street manias have come and gone. But today, I have no doubt that the marketspace is a very real and powerful phenomenon—one that is here to stay.

THE MARKETSPACE *IS* TRANSFORMING BUSINESS

Just as the ATM changed the competitive dynamics of the banking industry, the emergence of the (so far) ultimate screen-to-face interactive medium—the Internet—represented an opportunity for radical reengineering and productivity gains across the full breadth of the economy. Today, it is the Internet that is the key technology enabling and propelling the explosive growth of the marketspace.

The Impact of the Internet and Technology. The Internet allows millions of customers to interact with a firm at any hour, from any place, via millions of distributed digital interfaces, on devices such as the PC. At any given moment, for example, thousands of people from around the world are simultaneously logged on to Amazon.com, buying CDs, selling food processors, browsing books, comparing prices, applying for credit cards, downloading music, registering for wedding gifts, sending electronic greeting cards . . . Much like the back-office reengineering revolution of the

1980s, the Internet represents a front-office reengineering revolution. It allows—in fact, it *mandates*—a ground-up rethinking of how companies interact with and create experiences for their customers. What drives this rethinking is clear from the success of automated-interface businesses, from banking with ATMs to bidding on auctions at eBay. It's no longer frontline service workers who have a monopoly on management of customer relationships in the service sector—it's machines that are increasingly doing the managing.

The widespread deployment of technology makes deep insight into customer experience possible, and necessary. Literally and figuratively, screen-to-face interactions augment the value of service, making it possible for companies to deliver service at lower cost and at higher quality. In a sector that has long been characterized by diseconomies of scale, machine-mediated interactions make scale economies possible. Given the importance of the service sector in the world's economies—it represents more than 80% of gross domestic product output in the United States, for example—this is a revolution of real magnitude and scope. Moreover, customer relationship management via machine gives businesses around the world a competitive weapon at a time in economic history when service is more crucial than ever.

The Rise of Mass Personalization. With the accelerating commoditization of products and brands, it is not supply, but customer demand, that is the scarcest and most valuable resource. As we continue to move toward a service-centered economy, firms are increasingly dependent on the quality of their customer relationships. Even for product-based businesses, service, more and more, is the key differentiator. Such iconic brands as IBM and Xerox that once made their money selling boxes (mainframe computers and copying machines) now sell those boxes at a loss; they rely almost exclusively on follow-on service, maintenance plans, financing, and even consulting services for their margins (indeed, the lion's share of IBM revenue is derived from services). Even Microsoft, famous for its ruthless pursuit of profit, has launched its game console, the Xbox, with a business plan for our times. Analysts estimate that every Xbox sold will cost Microsoft nearly $200 in negative margin, but that Microsoft will make up the difference—and ultimately reach profitability on the platform—by selling games, upgrades, and networking services.

That's why personalization has become such a hot concept; it's the ultimate frontier in the delivery of human-mediated or technology-mediated services. And, once again, technology can help marketers defy commoditization by enabling deeper and richer relationships with customers than ever before. For example, technology known as collaborative filtering allows online retailers to predict the products and services their customers may want to buy, based on their previous choices and on the preferences of other like-minded consumers. Or take Ritz-Carlton: the upscale hotelier can elevate its renowned personal service to new heights through its online customer database. A consumer who has stayed only at the Ritz in San Francisco, for example, can walk into its Washington, D.C., property to find that her credit-card and frequent-flier numbers, preference for non-smoking rooms, and desire for an extra chocolate on her pillow have preceded her. Can other high-end hotel chains afford not to follow suit? Clearly, companies that fail to exploit the power of marketspace technology to make them more customer-centric are forfeiting a key competitive advantage.

... But Success in the Marketspace Means Paying Attention to the Fundamentals. The advent of the marketspace has already had a significant impact on business—particularly on the way that companies interact with their customers. However, that does not mean (as was famously proclaimed about the Web not long ago) that the marketspace exists independently of the fundamental laws of economics. In the end, the marketspace is not about new rules for a new economy, nor even about the Internet or the Web; it is about using the tools of digital technology to achieve a fundamental goal that is as old as the marketplace itself: the creation and nurturing of profitable customer relationships.

In the marketspace, just like the marketplace, the name of the game is providing value to customers; if anything, the marketspace makes the age-old business axiom "serve the customer" even more paramount. Technology must be used to create customer interfaces that deliver higher levels of customer-perceived value (relative to competitive offerings), thus driving rising levels of satisfaction and loyalty. The challenge for managers is to understand the full spectrum of interfaces available to them—both screen-to-face (online) and face-to-face (offline)—as well as how to manipulate those interfaces to optimize the customer's experience.

Technology, in other words, is simply another, albeit immensely powerful, business tool. Successful managers will seek out new and creative ways to integrate it into their firm's overall strategy to build and manage strong, loyal customer relationships in a high-impact yet cost-effective manner.

CASES IN POINT

By bringing together buyers and sellers who would likely never meet in a physical place, the auction Web site eBay has become one of the best-known and most successful marketspace enterprises. Sellers list their wares in eBay's databases, which are then searched by prospective buyers. Technology facilitates the transactions: would-be buyers can sign up to be notified by e-mail when the object of desire comes up for auction, and they can have their bids automatically set (and reset and reset, as the bidding warrants). It makes little difference whether seller and buyer live across town or across the globe; they are linked by the electronic network of the Internet. In the end, eBay connects physical entities (people and products), but it does so in a highly efficient manner. It outsources to customers all the physical aspects of doing business—merchandising, inventory management, inventory carrying costs, shipping and handling, and logistics—thus keeping its margins extremely high. Moreover, eBay's reach and efficiency would be impractical, or even impossible, to realize in the physical world.

With the launch of Schwab.com in January 1998, discount broker Charles Schwab became one of the first companies in the brokerage sector—or in the general retailing sector—to create integrated online and offline offerings. When it did so, it kept its eye squarely on the customer, not the technology. Its Web site, for example, was designed not to showcase technological bells and whistles, but to provide easy-to-find, quick-to-download information to its core customer segment: the investor who wants to make fast, informed investment decisions without paying for advice. Ultimately, by embracing the Internet while staying focused on its customers, Schwab was able to use technology to offer superior service at lower prices to its target segment. Moreover, Schwab was the first to demonstrate unequivocally that the marketspace extends and augments the marketplace, but seldom replaces it. A case in point: Schwab's success online was real, but research showed that two-thirds of new accounts, which would be accessed largely online, were nonetheless opened offline. As a result, even at the height of the Internet boom, when retail banks were closing branch offices by the dozen, Schwab was building new offices in key locations. Schwab drew the blueprint for the integration of the physical and the virtual—offline and online—for consumer-facing businesses.

MAKING IT HAPPEN

As we have outlined, building and managing customer relationships is at the same time increasingly important, reliant on technology, and complex. Some of the issues to consider may include:

- **How the Internet is shifting the balance of power to your customers.** It is important to realize that customers are now much more able than ever before to choose from a global marketspace, and as a result are often much more demanding in their expectations for service. The Internet offers customers richness and reach at the same time. E-commerce blurs the traditional trade-off between reaching large sections of customers with limited information, and only a few customers with large amounts of information.
- **The Internet is revolutionizing sales techniques and perceptions of established brands**—what are the consequences, either risks or opportunities, for your business in terms of such issues as the ability to sense customer needs and to build brand loyalty?
- **Modern marketspaces are now open 24/7.** The pace of business activity and change is rapidly accelerating, and the need to be flexible, adaptive, customer-focused, and innovative is now at a premium. The Internet compresses time and it is useful to consider how well-prepared and configured your business is. First, the Internet is always available and working; second, there is a culture of urgency and the ability to elicit immediate feedback, if required; and finally, the issue of immediacy means that issues, both trivial and important, need to be actioned swiftly as the trivial can fast become urgent.
- **There is a premium on managing knowledge.** Now more than ever, managing and leveraging knowledge is a key skill, and knowledge is a vital strategic resource that needs to be nurtured and developed.
- **Is it possible to extend the business in order to add value for current and potential customers?** Many organizations are now able to reevaluate factors as fundamental as their objectives, markets, and competencies, all of which may have been altered by the new marketspace opportunities and realities.

- **The Internet is increasing interactivity among people, customers, companies and industries.** It may help to assess the extent to which your business can—and could—forge new, valuable links with key groups.

Today, the traditional marketplace has a virtual counterpart: the marketspace. The advent of the marketspace fundamentally alters the ways firms can interact with, and manage, their customers. Companies must refine their corporate strategy accordingly. The proliferation of technology-mediated or "screen-to-face" service interfaces offers myriad opportunities for companies to manage customer relationships both more efficiently and more effectively. In this era of ever-accelerating competition and commoditization, service is the ultimate weapon.

———◆———

Jeffrey F. Rayport is C.E.O. of Marketspace, a consulting and information firm that helps executives craft strategies for the networked economy. Before founding Marketspace, a Monitor Group company, Rayport was a professor at Harvard Business School, where he created the first course in e-commerce at a top-tier business school. He has also written and cowritten a number of books on e-commerce, including *An Introduction to e-Commerce* and *Cases in e-Commerce* (both with Bernard Jaworski; McGraw-Hill Higher Education, 2001).

The Next Scientific Revolution Is Now

Peter Schwartz and Peter Leyden

Peter Schwartz is a cofounder and chairman of Global Business Network, a futurist think tank and strategic consulting firm specializing in scenario planning. He wrote the best-seller *The Art of the Long View* (Doubleday, 1996). Peter Leyden is knowledge developer at Global Business Network, working with the firm's network of scientists, technologists, and future-oriented thinkers in many different fields. Leyden, the former managing editor of *Wired* magazine, is a coauthor of *What's Next: Exploring the New Terrain for Business* (Perseus, 2002), as well as *The Long Boom* (Perseus, 1999), now published in eight languages.

The 1990s proved once again that new technologies can drive fundamental economic changes and that businesses need to tune in to these developments early in order to thrive, if not survive. But before the technologies appear, the basic science must emerge. Given the accelerating pace of change, a business person should not only keep an eye out for emerging technologies, but track key developments in science as well. As it happens, the scientific world is on the cusp of some revolutionary breakthroughs—particularly in the fields of biology, physics, and chemistry. Transformative technologies are sure to follow. The following conversation lays out what to expect in the next decade and beyond.

Leyden: How would you describe the state of science right now?

Schwartz: We are in a period of a major scientific and technological revolution akin to what happened at the beginning of the 20th century. In physics, chemistry, and biology we are seeing really revolutionary change, both theoretically and in terms of our capabilities. And as a result, we are going to see enormous advances in technology.

Significantly, the three sciences converge at the very small scale, the molecular and atomic scale. As a result, what we're seeing are developments in these realms coming together and creating revolutionary ideas and capabilities. And the ultimate form is nanotechnology, or molecular engineering, manufacturing at the atomic level.

Leyden: Could you give us a better time frame about where we are in this revolution?

Schwartz: It's different in the three disciplines. In many ways biology is further along, because we really have had a scientific revolution that began 20 years ago—in genetics and molecular biology. The clearest expression of it is the decoding of the human genome. But there are many other elements of it. They've given us a deep understanding of how biology works at a very fundamental level. We have new power over biology that was never imaginable—let alone doable.

Leyden: Like with recent stem cell research that points towards our eventual ability to grow replacement organs?

Schwartz: Stem cell work is a perfect example. And there are many, many others. The new drug Glivec is designed as a molecule targeting a particular molecule in a cancer cell. You just couldn't do that, you simply didn't have the technical means to even dream of that, and you didn't even understand the notion of how one molecule connected to another molecule. So in biology, we're very far along in the revolution. That's why it'll have such large effects in the near future, because a lot of the conceptual revolution has already happened.

Leyden: So then where are we in physics?

Schwartz: In physics we're about to go through a big conceptual revolution, just as relativity and quantum theory were a huge conceptual revolution over the Newtonian physics that came before.

Scientific revolutions are always preceded by two phenomena. One is that the old model gets weirder and weirder and weirder. That's what happened with the old model of the sun going around the earth. You could make the math work but, boy, it was hard, and it got weirder and weirder over time as we learned more. And then it got real simple when somebody said: "Well, suppose the earth goes around the sun?" Ah! Yes! All the weirdness in the math went away. So today our models of both the very big and the very small have gotten weirder and weirder and weirder, and nobody seems to understand them. There was a great quote at a recent scientific meeting: "We live in a preposterous universe." And I want to say: "No, we have preposterous models in the simple universe."

The other phenomenon preceding a scientific revolution is that we find data that simply doesn't fit the old model. A perfect example of that was the recent discovery that the universe is expanding at an accelerating rate. That means there's another big force out there overcoming gravity—by a lot. This is a whole new form of energy we never even imagined. In fact, Einstein had a hint of it in his early work, but he said "Naw, that's too crazy," and got rid of it. He called it the cosmological constant. The data now says he was actually right.

Leyden: Are you talking about "dark matter," the missing mass of the universe that scientists calculate must be out there but that we still can't see?

Schwartz: That's another whole weirdness. I'm talking about dark energy. Why do we call these things "dark?" It's because we can't see them, find them, or imagine them. But then we didn't know there were radio waves out there until we invented this device called a radio. We haven't invented the "radio" for dark matter energy, though actually we have gotten little hints. We had a tweak of reception of dark matter recently. And we have huge evidence now that there is dark energy in the data on the accelerating expansion of the universe.

So in physics we are ripe for a new model. Does that mean we will necessarily get one? No. Because, of course, this requires a great leap of imagination: and rigor. There are candidates out there already who might turn out to prove string theory, or other variations on the theme. So it isn't that we don't have some potential Einsteins out there.

Leyden: Could it be that the breakthrough is beyond humans, at least in this century?

Schwartz: No. The field is supersaturated; it's ready to break. But it might be 20 years. It might not be five years. But I think we're ripe. The world is ripe. One of the things that has to happen, and it was true with relativity and quantum mechanics: the mathematics has to advance and be able to support the new fields. Einstein had to learn Riemannian geometry and Riemann had to invent it, which happened just as Einstein was doing special relativity. Einstein's friend showed the new math to Einstein in 1912, and on the basis of Riemannian geometry he could come up with general relativity.

So higher-dimensional mathematics, computational abilities, simulation abilities need to continue to develop for us to be able to push these physics fronts. So, where we are in physics is that we are ready to give birth to a new model. But we don't have it yet.

Leyden: What should we expect when the new model does pop out?

Schwartz: When it happens, two things are likely, one really big and the other almost really big. First of all, we'll re-perceive the universe. Relativity had a huge impact on people's perception of human life and the human condition. What our re-perception will be this time, I don't know. But it's clearly going to shake things up again.

Secondly, it will create new technological capabilities. A good example that is very likely, but again unpredictable, is with energy. Suppose there is dark energy out there. Suppose there is a way to overcome gravity using that energy. Well, suddenly we could be in a world of completely new sources of energy, and maybe even antigravity vehicles. Now, I'm not saying that's likely. Don't misunderstand me. But it's not at all implausible to speculate about that class of outcome coming about—after all, you couldn't have solid-state physics and television and all that kind of stuff without quantum theory and relativity. If I had said to you in 1875: "We will someday have pictures flying through the air in color and motion," you would have thought I was crazy. Is it magic? How can you send that over the air? Of course, today we do it every day, every second, all over the planet. But it required new physics.

And so all I'm saying is that because we know that one of the things that has to be explained is dark energy, and that dark energy is about overcoming gravity, then it is not implausible that the technological expression of this could be some combination of new energy sources or antigravity devices.

Leyden: What about the third field, chemistry?

Schwartz: In chemistry the real issue is that the fundamental basis of chemistry has been thermodynamics. We have an understanding at a theoretical level of how molecules are formed, but the real world of chemistry is millions and billions of molecules bumping into each other under various conditions. We may apply catalysts or heat or cold, but what we're dealing with are statistical processes of very large numbers of things. So what applies here are the laws of very large numbers and statistics and thermodynamics.

What we're now talking about is understanding and getting control of individual bonds, individual molecules, individual connections between them. Not only do we understand these at a more fine-grained level, but our level of control is gaining enormously at a fine-grained level. We can't do this yet, but we're close to it. And this will almost certainly come—the ability in the very near future, the next few years, to use very small electric fields to disassociate an individual bond in a molecule and realign it around another electron.

So it is the movement of chemistry from the realm of many large numbers of things bumping into each other to finite numbers of objects being controlled individually. This changes both our understanding and our capability fundamentally—for designing new materials, for example.

Leyden: Now, you're making a distinction between this molecular level chemistry and what lay people think of as nanotechnology.

Schwartz: Yes, nanotechnology is about machines, this is more about materials. But these then begin to overlap in the realm of nanotechnology, because you'll need to be able to do this kind of new materials manipulation to get to nanotechnology. And even before you get to nanotechnology, you get to new materials, new kinds of chemical processes.

Here's an example of something that has already been done, though it's just a step on the way. Today, if I want to take a rod of steel, put it onto a copper sheet, and weld the two together, I have a choice between the old welding techniques and new kinds of welding. I can use a hot welder and some metal that bonds the steel and copper together. Or I can take a superfine powder of the steel and the copper—and there's a way to align these molecules electrostatically so that one actually flows into the other. What you then have is steel, copper, and then a kind of flow between them of copper and steel merging into one. You are actually creating a new layer of metal in between the two, but it is a layer that at the top is steel and at the bottom is copper, and it transitions in between.

Leyden: So you could imagine whole new classes of materials?

Schwartz: Exactly. So we might see new materials, new methods of manufacturing materials, new chemicals, and new kinds of chemical processes.

Leyden: What's your time frame here?

Schwartz: The next five years. Chemistry is closer because a lot of the theoretical work is far along, but the physical capabilities are hard to do, and there's a feedback between the theory and the technical capabilities that has to happen. There's still some more theoretical work that has to be done. So chemistry is further away than the biology, nearer than the physics. But all of this is in the span of the next 20 years. And even in the next 10 for a lot of the science. Almost all of it.

Leyden: That grounds us in time. How relevant are these developments to business?

Schwartz: I think they're huge. The implications are that we are moving fast toward a world of new science and technology. Just take a good example: energy. We're making all kinds of assumptions about the future of energy. These could turn out to be fundamentally wrong because we have really radical leaps in technology. Environmental issues are another. On the other side of these revolutions, the technical capabilities to deliver clean technologies would be very different. Manufacturing processes are another. All the different ways we make stuff—make cars, make semiconductors, make furniture—could change. The new materials and the new manufacturing methods could be extremely significant.

Leyden: So businesses should be watching these scientific developments today even if they have a 10- or 20-year tail?

Schwartz: If you think about R&D, it has a 5- to 10-year time horizon. So in terms of R&D activities, it means you've got to be pushing the frontiers of science and technology now.

Intellectual Capital

Thomas A. Stewart

Intellectual capital is just that: a capital asset consisting of intellectual material. As such, it is one of three forms of capital: financial capital, that is, money; tangible or fixed assets, which include land, buildings, machinery, and other long-lived equipment; and knowledge.

To be considered intellectual capital, knowledge must be an asset—able to be used to create wealth. Thus intellectual capital includes: the talents and skills of individuals and groups; technological and social networks and the software and culture that connect them; and intellectual property such as patents, copyrights, methods, procedures, archives, etc. It excludes knowledge or information not involved in production or wealth creation. Just as raw material such as iron ore should not be confused with an asset such as a steel mill, so knowledge materials such as data or miscellaneous facts ought not to be confused with knowledge assets.

INTELLECTUAL CAPITAL AS AN ASSET

From the standpoint of traditional accounting, intellectual capital frequently does not fit the definition of an asset. Generally, under accounting rules, an asset must be tangible; it must have been acquired in one or more transactions, so that it has a known cost or a market value, and it must be under the control of the party whose asset it is said to be. Thus scientific skill is not an accounting asset, but laboratory equipment is.

Intellectual capital theory argues that this definition is too narrow and hinders businesses from seeing, managing, or building knowledge assets. This in turn inhibits companies' ability to compete and prosper in an economy in which knowledge has become an important source of profits. The intellectual capitalists use a looser definition: an asset is something that transforms raw material into something more valuable. It is a magician's black box. Inputs get put in—a few handkerchiefs, say; the asset does something to transform them; and out come outputs worth more than the inputs—rabbits, maybe. The question of ownership and control matters less than the question of access. A corporation might not own scientific expertise (in the form of a cadre of employees, for example), but it has the use of it and can exert a quasi-proprietary influence over how it is used.

Intellectual capital, then, is knowledge that transforms raw materials and makes them more valuable. The raw materials might be physical—knowledge of the formula for Coca-Cola is an intellectual asset that transforms a few cents' worth of sugar, water, carbon dioxide, and flavorings into a dollar's worth of refreshment. The raw material might be intangible, like information. Knowledge of the law is an intellectual asset; a lawyer takes the facts of a dispute (raw material), transforms them through his or her knowledge of the law (an intellectual asset), to produce an opinion or a legal brief (an output of higher value than the facts by themselves).

282

Though financial accounting does not measure intellectual capital, markets clearly do. Shares of companies in the pharmaceutical industry, for example, generally trade at a high premium over the book value of their assets, and the companies' return on net assets is abnormally high; but if their spending on research and development is added to their capital, both their market-to-book ratios and their returns on assets come to resemble those of less knowledge-intensive companies. (There is a slowly growing movement to find ways to account for intellectual capital and report it to shareholders. Scandinavian countries, particularly Denmark, are leaders in the field.)

Indeed, it was the unusual behavior of the equities of knowledge-intensive companies that first drew the attention of analysts to intellectual capital. The term seems to have been employed first in 1958, when two financial analysts, describing the stock-market valuations of several small, science-based companies, concluded that "The intellectual capital of such companies is perhaps their single most important element," and noted that their high stock valuations might be termed an "intellectual premium." (Morris Kronfeld and Arthur Rock, "Some Considerations of the Infinite," *The Analyst's Journal*, November 1958, p. 6.) The idea lay dormant for a quarter of a century. In the 1980s, Walter Wriston, the former chairman of Citicorp, noted that his bank and other corporations possessed valuable intellectual capital that accountants (and bank regulators) did not measure.

INTELLECTUAL CAPITAL ANALYZED

Karl-Erik Sveiby, a Swede, intrigued by the anomalous stock-market behavior of knowledge-intensive companies, began an investigation that produced the first analysis of the nature of intellectual capital. Sveiby, his colleagues, and *Affärsvärlden*, Sweden's oldest business magazine, noticed that the magazine's proprietary model for valuing initial public offerings broke down for high-tech companies. Sveiby concluded that these companies possessed assets not described in financial documents or included in the magazine's model. With a likeminded group of associates, he sat down to puzzle out what these might be. In "Den Osynliga Balansräkningen Ledarskap" ("The Invisible Balance Sheet"), 1989, they laid the foundation stone for much of what has come after by coming up with a taxonomy for intellectual capital. Knowledge assets, they proposed, could be found in three places: the competencies of a company's people, its internal structure (patents, models, computer and administrative systems), and its external structure (brands, reputation, relationships with customers and suppliers).

After some tinkering by others—the pieces are now usually called human capital, structural (or organizational) capital, and customer (or relationship) capital—Sveiby's model still stands. It has made managing intellectual capital possible by naming its component parts. Shortly thereafter, Leif Edvinsson, an executive at the Swedish financial services company Skandia, persuaded his management to appoint him "Director, Intellectual Capital"; Skandia became the business world's most conspicuous laboratory for intellectual capital studies.

Ideas whose time has come flower everywhere at once. Ikujiro Nonaka and Hirotaka Takeuchi in Japan began investigations of how knowledge is produced that resulted in

"The Knowledge-creating Company" (*Harvard Business Review*, November-December 1991) and Thomas A. Stewart synthesized U.S. research in intellectual capital in "Brainpower: How Intellectual Capital Is Becoming America's Most Important Asset" (*Fortune*, June 3, 1991).

Every company or organization possesses all three forms of intellectual capital. Human capital consists of the skills, competencies, and abilities of individuals and groups. These range from specific technical skills to "softer" skills, like salesmanship or the ability to work effectively in a team. An individual's human capital cannot, in a legal sense, be owned by a corporation; the term thus refers not only to individual talent but also to the collective skills and aptitudes of a workforce. Indeed, one challenge faced by executives is how to manage the talent of truly outstanding members of their staff: how to use it to the utmost without becoming overdependent on a few star performers, or how to encourage stars to share their skills with others. Skills that are irrelevant to a company's business—the fine tenor voice of an actuary, for example—may be part of the individual's human capital, but not of his employer's.

Structural capital comprises knowledge assets that are indeed company property: intellectual property such as patents, copyrights, and trademarks; processes, methodologies, models; documents and other knowledge artifacts; computer networks and software; administrative systems; and so forth. A data warehouse is structural capital; so is the decision-support software that helps people use the data. One knowledge-management process is converting human capital—which is usually available to just a few people—into structural capital, so it becomes shareable. This happens, for example, when a team writes up the "lessons learned" from a project so that others can apply them.

Customer capital is the value of relationships with suppliers, allies, and customers. Two common forms are brand equity and customer loyalty. The former is a promise of quality (or some other attribute) for which a customer agrees to pay a premium price; the value of brands is measurable in financial terms. The loyalty of a base of customers is also measurable, using discounted cash-flow analysis. Both are frequently calculated when companies are bought and sold. In a sense, all customer capital should eventually reflect itself either in a premium price or a sticky buyer-seller relationship.

Every organization possesses intellectual capital in all three manifestations, but with varying emphasis, depending on its history and strategy. For example, a chemical company might have as a knowledge asset the ability to concoct custom chemical compounds that precisely match its customer's needs. That asset might be people-based, residing in the tacit knowledge of dozens of skilled chemists; it might be structural, found in an extensive library of patents and manuals, or databases and expert systems; it might be relationship-based, found in the company's intimate ties to customers, suppliers, universities, etc. Most likely, of course, the asset—skill at making custom chemicals—is a combination of the three.

At least three characteristics of intellectual capital give it extraordinary power to add value. First, companies that use knowledge assets deftly can reduce the expense and burden of carrying physical assets, or maximize their return on them. For example, transportation companies can use information networks and skill in logistics and load management to maximize their utilization of assets like rail cars and containers. Second, it can be possible to get enormous leverage or gearage from knowledge assets. The value of an aircraft can be realized over just one route at a time, whereas that of an airline's reservation system is limited only by the number of people in the world. In a study of the chemical industry that examined 83 companies over 25 years, Baruch Lev, professor of accounting at New York University, found that R&D spending (one form of investment in intellectual capital) returned 25.9% pretax, whereas capital spending earned just 15% (about 10% after tax, approximately the cost of capital).

Third, human and customer capital are the primary sources of innovation and customization. The increasing sophistication of machinery and information technology has led to the automation of more and more repetitive tasks. These manufacturing economies of scale are sources of competitive advantage in industrial processes. At a certain point, however, their value diminishes: the more it is possible to do a task the same way twice, the harder it is for one company to differentiate its offerings from its competitors'. When this happens the value of innovation, customization, and service increases; all are highly dependent on intellectual capital.

Thomas A. Stewart is editorial director of *Business 2.0* magazine and a member of the board of editors of *Fortune* magazine. He is the author of the bestseller *Intellectual Capital: The New Wealth of Organizations* (Currency/Doubleday, 1997) and *The Wealth of Knowledge: Intellectual Capital and the Twenty-First Century Organization* (Currency/Doubleday, 2002). In 2002 Stewart was appointed editor of the *Harvard Business Review*. For more information, see www.members.aol.com/thosstew.

Explaining the Passion That Powers the Web

David Weinberger

Businesses make plenty of mistakes on the Web. They make users click 15 times to buy a single item. They get into price wars and cut prices below the profitability point. They put up sloppily secured sites that get hacked by teenagers with too much time on their hands. But the big mistake that businesses make isn't economic or technical. It's psychological or (dare I say it?) spiritual. They're not getting the biggest "it" there is to get: the Web isn't theirs. The Web is *ours*.

It's easy not to get this point—although, in another sense, you have to have your head inserted pretty far up a dark place to miss it. This is perhaps the biggest way businesses confuse the real world with the Web. In the real world, an unowned space, such as a new continent, is divided into owned parcels. If I own a piece of land, I build what I want on it and you may enter it only with my sufferance. So, companies assume that their Web sites are theirs in the same way. They think that visitors are entering the company's property. But, while that may be true legally, it's not true in any other way. Companies, typically, even make the Copernican mistake of thinking that the Web is about them. But it's not. The Web is ours. Profoundly ours. Ours in ways that transcend ownership. That is what gives the Web its power and appeal. Miss that fact and your Web presence will be worse than ineffective. It will alienate your customers. Heck, it's probably alienating them right now.

For example, I recently bought a washing machine. I went to some consumer review sites that confirmed my preference for a front loader and let me narrow the choices to Kenmore and Maytag. I checked some more customer sites and then at www.thathomesite.com stumbled on discussion boards devoted to the merits of these machines. The owners seemed to like both, so I was leaning towards Kenmore since it's considerably cheaper. But then I read a complaint about the Kenmore. It seems that the "done" buzzer is so loud that it wakes up the neighbors. There followed a flurry of messages confirming the complaint and suggesting various workarounds, including snipping the wires. Still, I decided to purchase the Kenmore because we'd be keeping it in the back corner of our basement. So, I went to our local store and bought it. (New models, by the way, have a volume control.)

If you were reading closely, you will have noticed that in my buying process I skipped a step: I completed the entire sales decision process without ever going to the Kenmore site. But why would I go there? I was getting great information from other customers. They were telling me the truth as they saw it. They were talking like real human beings, exaggerating this, boasting about that, making jokes left and right. And I got from them not just honest reviews but information that I would never have gotten from the Kenmore site or store. It would never have occurred to me to ask how loud the buzzer is.

I then visited the Kenmore site, just out of curiosity. And it lived up to expectations: clean, crisp, professional . . . and totally boring and almost completely worthless. In other words, it was like the vast majority of corporate sites on the Web.

Boring and worthless would be bad enough. But it gets worse. The Kenmore site opens with a flash animation that portentously tells us that it is "introducing a revolutionary new washer that will change the way you think about laundry." Only then do you get to see the oh-so-professional home page that tells us in big print that Kenmore is "Smart. Stylish. Simple." This goes all the way beyond boring to off-putting. It's so unconnected with our interests and our way of talking that it alienates us. Alienating your customers is just about the worst thing you can do, far more damaging than sending them irrelevant marketing circulars or even annoying them to the point of having them call you to protest. Alienating them puts a gulf between you and them that is deep and is not only emotional, but intellectual. Alienated customers not only don't like you, they don't have the slightest idea what you're talking about and don't want to understand. Think about how you felt when your parents made you bring a rubber sheet to a sleep-over. That's alienation.

Alienation is an interesting phenomenon. It implies a sense of belonging that's been violated. But if the Web is a club, it's the least exclusive one since the People Who Type Society. What is this sense of belonging on the Web? Where does it come from?

In part it comes from the Web's origins in the minds of geeks. This antiauthoritarian subclass of humanity came to the Internet with a sense of "us against them," with the "us" being a set of rational contributors to a better world and the "they" perceived as a set of greedy, money-grabbing, technically inept morons. But the Web has spread far beyond the geeks, and their influence now is much more marginal. There is something about the Web itself that generates this sense of belonging, of shared community. The Web is a new persistent public place—a world that isn't made of atoms and isn't really just made of bits; you could string all the bits together that you wanted and you still wouldn't have the Web as we experience it. This new world is made of pages and links, both of which are expressions of human interest. We're on the Web because we have something to say or because we're interested in what other people say about an interest we share; we build the Web page by page and chat by chat because of this. The stuff of the Web is quite literally human passion.

This gives us a hint about the nature of the "ours." The Web isn't ours in most of the usual senses of the term. It is not ours legally. We don't own the Web the way we own our house. We don't own the contents of the Web the way we own what we have written. It would be closer to say that the Web is ours in the way that term is used in the Woody Guthrie song "This Land is Your Land." Guthrie's song is a statement about the proper balance of values in a democracy—this land is not primarily about lining the pockets of the landed gentry but was established for the good of the everyone God created.

I think, however, there is a further sense of "ours" that helps explain the deeper sense of alienation that we feel from the millions of sites like www.Kenmore.com. The real world, as it is affectionately known, is the one into which we are born. It existed before we were conceived and after we die we will be buried in it. It consists of atoms that form the landscape within which we are constrained to build our lives. If we were born near water and fig trees, we will have one type of life; if we were born into a land of ice-crusted caves, we'll have another type of life. The real world gives us distances and a geography spread out among those distances, and tells us to do the best that we can. Thus, the real world is fundamentally not human, although we humans take it up and transform it into livable lands—tilled, watered, leveled, planted, at times even exploded and remade. The Web, on the other hand, is made up of words and other forms of significance. It is human through and through. This is the sense in which the Web is ours. It is ours the way language is ours. It is *of* us.

Most businesses are too busy trying to sell us stuff to think even for a moment about why we are on the Web. We are there for lots of reasons, starting with gathering information, and including everything from downloading pornography to learning how to tie our Boy Scout neckerchiefs. But the palpable excitement about the Web comes not from a sudden desire of our species to become research librarians or Eagle Scouts, but from our excitement simply about being connected one to another. We are making this new human place—the Web—out of nothing but words and passion. We are sharing interests, an act as fundamental to humanity as breaking bread together. Then we go on to the typical business site and suddenly a pitch man is yelling at us. All he wants to do is transfer money from our wallet to his. There's no recognition that we're on the Web to talk with other people who care about the same things as we do.

You don't have to be a psychologist to see that most sites are insultingly wrong about why you are visiting them. You can just listen to the language they use. It's the language of marketing, an arcane cant never uttered by script-free human mouths, written by professionals feeding on one another in committees. The boasting, the inability to admit any flaws in their products, the slickness of the words designed to penetrate our defenses without ever actually being heard or thought about . . . the jargon tells us that the site has only one thing on its mind. To these sites we are nothing but targets.

You can't fix this simply by changing your rhetoric. Focus groups may tell you that a homier-sounding jargon will increase your sell-through rates by 1.4%, but you're still faking it and you will be discovered, chastised, and abandoned . . . just as you deserve to be. Instead you have to do the hardest thing for a business to do: give up the attempt to control your customers. Discover within your own borders the employees who still care about the products they're building. Those employees are already out on the Web, talking with your market, telling them the truth about your products, and doing so in the excited high-pitched tone of voice that conveys genuine enthusiasm. Build your Web presence around those people. Get used to the idea that the most important conversations about your products will occur among customers (and some of your employees) not on your own site. Learn how to take that as the most positive of signs; if people aren't talking about your product, then no one cares about it. And if you can't trust your employees to tell the truth and still run a viable business, then in fact you don't have a viable business.

The very worst thing you can do is to build a site that you view as yours, a place that you imagine people come to in order to hear your marketing messages. It's bad marketing, and worse it commits the spiritual mistake of thinking that the Web is a place to be divided into lots and owned by individuals, rather than as a new world made of the human stuff, a world that is fundamentally ours.

David Weinberger is coauthor of the bestselling book *The Cluetrain Manifesto* (with Christopher Locke, Rick Levine, and Doc Searls; Perseus, 2000) and author of *Small Pieces Loosely Joined* (Perseus, 2002). He is a frequent commentator on National Public Radio's *All Things Considered*, a columnist for several magazines, and writes a highly-regarded e-zine (www.hyperorg.com) about how the Web is changing the way businesses run. He is also the one-person strategic marketing company, Evident Marketing, helping high-tech companies decide what their products can be and how they can talk about them.

Managing What We Know

Laurence Prusak

Laurence Prusak is a leading knowledge manager, specializing in issues of corporate knowledge management. He is the author of many articles on knowledge and information management and coauthor of several books, including *Working Knowledge* with Tom Davenport, and *In Good Company*. He has worked with organizations renowned for their expertise and approach to knowledge management, including IBM and Ernst & Young, as well as working as a researcher at the Harvard Business School, and as a teacher of social and economic history at several universities. In this essay, he addresses some of the most significant questions about how to manage knowledge effectively, and also how knowledge, people, and technology interact. He explains the view that while technology does not create knowledge, it is providing real and potential benefits for organizations.

The most common misperception about knowledge management is that it's not about knowledge! People conflate "knowledge" with data, information, judgment, creativity, and perception. These are related subjects, but each one is distinct. Information, for example, is a static message; it's frozen, one-way. There's a sender and a user. Information can be a concert, a painting, a poem, or a memo from the person in the next cubicle. Knowledge is "what people know." If I had to pick two things that exemplify the quality of "knowing," one would be "rules," and the other "pattern recognition" around a bounded domain, for example, publishing, management research, chemistry, or chess.

Let's take this idea further. Wittgenstein and other philosophers would argue that individual knowledge does not exist. There are individual *experiences*, but all knowledge is social or collective because the very vocabularies and frames in which we develop our knowledge are socially constructed. People know things collectively—in practice. I can't stress this point enough. If I told you that I was a chemist, for example, there is a legitimized practice of chemistry, so all chemists have the same points of reference. An individual cannot know a chemistry that is apart from the *practice* of chemistry. So in many ways, you can certainly have very diverse individual experiences, and individual people may know different things. But that knowledge is meaningful only in its social or collective context—especially in organizations.

How do organizations keep track of what they know? The best approach is by mapping or visualization. Since most firms are large, diffuse, and geographically and cognitively dispersed, it is hard to visualize where everyone is, what they are doing, and what they know. There are some excellent resources on how to create maps and other graphic depictions of people, practices, and knowledge; see, for example, *The Visual Display of Quantitative Information* by Edward Tufte and *Mapping Strategic Knowledge* by Anne Huff and Mark Jenkins. Mapping knowledge networks is something quite distinct from the typical organizational chart, which reflects power and coordination, but not knowledge. Job titles and hierarchical matrices have very little to do with what people actually know and do. You're not an IT manager; you specialize in IT strategy, or outsourcing, or customer information analysis. It's important in mapping your organization to focus on the practices, not the individuals. Focusing on individuals is valueless, because it's not important what individuals know.

The best way to *share* knowledge is by sharing work, learning from others who know what they're doing. If I wanted to learn about publishing, for example, I could read some books. But a better way is to hang around a publishing house, watch what publishers do, and then try it out yourself. The same principle applies to chemists in labs, consultants with clients, and athletes on a field. Learning by doing is about *adaptation* (adapting to your environment) and *assimilation* (you assimilate all the signals). You learn by doing things and reflecting on what you've done. You draw heuristic lessons from your actions—rules and patterns that you recognize and develop in practice. Consider a person just graduating college with B.S. in chemistry versus a 50-year-old chemist in a large firm. What's the difference? The younger person may remember more of the formal rules, but they couldn't know the emotional experience of *doing* chemistry.

Contrary to popular belief, technology doesn't have much to do with knowledge acquisition at all. Americans, in particular, are technophiles; we think everything can be improved through technology. Technology is a great tool for information management; there's nothing better than IT for managing systems and processes. But there is no substitute for experience. Remember that it takes the same amount of time to learn French now as it did in the year 1000!

Ultimately, I'd argue that apprenticeship is the best possible model for learning. However, it's not always practical. In many organizations, there's a lot of resistance because management does not see the direct payoff from the investment. But apprenticeship programs can be no more expensive to launch than an ERP system—and you'd learn more. The best thing an executive can do it is to give people *time* to talk to each other and the *freedom* to seek each other out.

How do you motivate people to share what they know? When people hoard knowledge, one of two things is happening: they are either unable to share or unwilling to share. *Unable* usually implies that the costs (in time or other resources) are just too great to justify the investment. But then there's *unwilling*; this means the culture and the incentive systems are at odds with sharing real knowledge (as opposed to data or information). There are many factors to overcome, because we live in a very individualistic culture. First, you need to provide incentives: most social expectations are reinforced in groups, such as teams, departments, and business units. At IBM, for example, 90% of my bonus used to be based on *my* performance; 5 years later, 80% of my bonus is based on *group* performance. Tangible metrics like this signal that sharing knowledge is rewarded. When you have gigantic disparities in compensation between executives and the front line, it sends the message to the front line that "we up here couldn't possibly care about what you know." People internalize that message if they are paid low wages, especially when executives are paid 400 times as much as they are!

Another approach that can foster knowledge flow is to have "knowledge inter-mediaries." You can appoint people to look around the firm for people doing new things and bring them to other people's attention. Apple used to call these people "evangelicals." People will do this anyway; usually, organizations will have people with a natural gift, but you can formalize the process—give people incentives and roles to do it. Sometimes executives choose them, other times people choose themselves. Japanese firms have "talk rooms," where people come every day to talk about what they're doing and what they've learned. Remember that people veer toward learning live and through stories. All people—and it's not a generational or gender issue—learn directly from their peers. Whether formalized or not, knowledge sharing needs to be the real deal, and not perceived as corporate PR or a politicized program to showcase some groups or projects at the expense of others.

A lot of research shows that new knowledge comes from the fusion of old knowledge in new ways. Many books on this topic, including Nonaka and Takeuchi's *The Knowledge-creating Company* and Dorothy Leonard's *Wellsprings of Knowledge*, explore the dynamics of tacit knowledge. What happens when you put together hard-core marketers and R&D folks? That's when you see the sparks fly! When you just get marketing people together they'll simply reinforce their shared knowledge. Unusual combinations of people can help each other see old things in new ways and unleash innovation in many dimensions.

How can knowledge management help organizations make decisions in a turbulent, unpredictable, and volatile environment? Let's take a look at hospitals. A huge study was conducted in which the researchers determined that hospitals with more nurses have higher survival rates. This positive correlation was not attributed to the way they perform their formal nursing duties. The nurses become the eyes and the ears of the doctors. They can detect and sense subtle changes in patients just by being around them, much more so than any measuring technology. The point is that the same lesson applies in business enterprises. If you have people working directly with customers, out in the field, give them a place where they can be heard without recrimination. This is without a doubt the best way to proceed in a very turbulent world. Listen to those on the front lines of the action. Of course, it's easy to say this, but very, very few firms do it.

Is all knowledge useful? There's a difference between knowledge and truth. Knowledge is socially constructed. Consider three Massachusetts-based firms: Wang, Polaroid, and DEC. All of them had "official" knowledge about market trends and their own competitive capabilities, but it was flawed. It wasn't true. Firms need to apply the rule of falsification. This is what philosopher Karl Popper talked about. If I tell you that lowering the price of your product will increase sales—this is falsifiable. Either it's true or not. For individuals and organizations alike, either nature or the markets will correct false knowledge. If you think that you can fly out the window, nature will correct you. If you think the PC will never fly, the markets will correct you.

Getting back to technology, there is one way in which technology is having a direct effect on knowledge, and that is *transparency*. Technology is making knowledge transparent. Chat rooms, mobile wireless devices, weblogs—it's much easier to get a stronger sense of who knows what. It's all out in the open. This creates tensions between those who have power and those who have knowledge. For example, how come Team X seems to know a lot about Y, while Team Z seems to get the rewards? Ubiquitous computing reveals who has knowledge and who is willing to share. So, while technology doesn't create knowledge, it is helping to democratize the process by which it is generated and shared.

The New Service Economy

Paul Saffo

Paul Saffo is a writer, business adviser, and technology forecaster, studying long-term information technology trends and their impact on business and society. Author of *Dreams in Silicon Valley* and *The Road from Trinity*, his essays have appeared in numerous publications, including *The Harvard Business Review*, *Wired Magazine*, *Civilization Magazine*, the *Los Angeles Times*, the *New York Times*, and *Fortune*. He also serves on a variety of boards and advisory panels, including the AT&T Technology Advisory Board, the World Economic Forum Global Issues Group, and the Stanford Law School Advisory Council on Science, Technology, and Society. Here, Paul Saffo assesses the profound social and economic effects resulting from the convergence of communications and technology. He argues that the real impact of computing is the blurring of products and services, with significant implications for producers and consumers alike.

THE NEXT BIG SHIFTS IN COMMUNICATIONS

So far, the Internet has barely touched our lives. The Internet arrived on the one piece of real estate we've been trying to get away from for the last 20 years: our desktops. It has not gone much further. This is what makes wireless and broadband so important, because both put us in an always-on world, unlike dialup. For example, wireless devices, such as cellphones and personal digital assistants, deliver the Internet to where we actually live, work, and play. That has profound implications for our life and also for the medium. So far, the Internet has barely touched our lives.

The other big shift is in the *nature* of communications. Before deregulation in the 1980s, communications was synonymous with people talking to other people. The symbol was a telephone handset on a desk. Along came the Internet in the 1990s, and the leading edge of communications was no longer simply people talking to people; it was people accessing information, and people accessing other people in information-rich environments. We have saturated those activities. Would you like to receive *more* phone calls? Do you feel like you don't have enough Web pages to surf? These are saturated for the people who have them today. The only growth in delivering the Internet lies in getting it to people who don't already have it.

The *real* growth is not going to come from people talking to other people or people accessing other information—it's going to come from machines talking to other machines on people's behalf. I think what we're going to start seeing in ten years, and really visibly in 20, is an enormous drop in the total communications traffic on the planet attributed to humans. The vast bulk of communication will be machine to machine. In two decades, the amount of communications traffic attributable to human beings will be below the rounding error of your average corporate telecommunications accountant.

CHEAP SENSORS WILL CONNECT CYBERSPACE
TO THE REAL WORLD

So far, we have two parallel universes: the physical reality that each one of us occupies, and cyberspace, where our machines live. The two worlds barely touch. In fact, the place they touch is so constrained that it is literally a piece of glass called an interface. We peer through the portal of our computer-screen interfaces into cyberspace, but we don't immerse ourselves in it. We look through the window at stuff, and for the most part, the computers don't look out at all. They have no idea that there is anything on the other side of the glass.

Now, do something as simple as putting a video camera on the computer, and make it aware that there are people in the room. Put a GPS (Global Positioning System) chip into a cellphone and make the cellphone aware of where it is in the world, and it can do interesting things for you. When you call emergency, they don't have to ask where you are because your phone will have already told them. A cellphone that knows where it is isn't just a good safety device, it is also a candidate for interesting location-based marketing, certain to delight advertisers but drive the rest of us crazy.

The revolution in geographic information systems (GIS) is happening because of cheap sensors. We're about to connect GIS to ordinary consumer life. Consider this example. It's 4:45pm on Friday, you're walking down Sutter Street in San Francisco and your phone chirps at you. It's an e-mail chirp. You look at the screen and it's not an e-mail—it's an electronic coupon from a Chinese restaurant a block and a half away in your direction of travel. They know you like Tsingtao Beer, and it says, "Get in here in 15 minutes and you get half off Tsingtao, and free appetizers!" Whether or not that is something that we want is another story, but I can assure you that it will be offered to you.

Another example: You're driving up U.S. Highway 101 and discover that your car, unbeknownst to you, has been sending telemetry on its operating condition back and forth to the manufacturer. Just south of Redwood Shores, your screen lights up and a voice comes on and says, "Hey, dude. Your car is 2,000 miles past its oil change. If you get off at the next exit, there is a mechanic standing by at Autobahn Motors. They will have you in and out in 15 minutes. Oh, by the way, we know you like Starbuck's eggnog lattes. It's November, and, though it's a little early for it, we've taken the liberty of brewing up an eggnog latte, and it is waiting for you while your oil is being changed."

In the long term, the car ceases to be a product—it's a *vehicle for service*. One can easily imagine, at the extreme, people selling you a car at or below cost because they know they'll make it up in service.

Let's consider what's happening in the area of white goods. For the last couple of years, every white-goods manufacturer on the planet has had a top-secret program to put Internet connectivity into their washers, dryers, and refrigerators. Why? Well, they didn't quite know why, but it was cheap to do and they were desperate for product differentiation. Your washing machine craps out, and you've got to buy a new one. You go down to the store and the high-end model has a big sign on it that says,

"Internet ready." You say under your breath, "Do I look like Bill Gates? I don't need my washing machine to talk to the Internet."

But, in fact, you buy that washing machine because it has some other feature you want. So they install it. As the delivery people are carrying out the cardboard box, your washing machine wakes up. Unbeknownst to you, there's a little radio transponder in it that is listening for 802.11 and a couple of other frequencies, and it picks up the radio signal from the 802.11 box on the side of your house that you've already put in for your wireless computer network. It establishes communications and says, "Hi, I'm a washing machine. Would you mind if I borrowed some of your bandwidth from time to time to talk to my manufacturer?"

So your washing machine is now regularly talking to your manufacturer. One morning, you're late to work. You swing open the door and almost knock over the Maytag repair person who is about to knock on your door. You say, "What are you doing here?" They reply, "Gosh, your washing machine didn't tell you? It's got a flat bearing. It sent me an e-mail last night screaming for help. Would you mind if I drop in and fix it?"

Companies like Electrolux did tests a couple of years ago. They said, "Gee, young people don't want to go down to the wash-o-mat unless they want to socialize, but they don't want to buy a washing machine and carry it through life either. We're going to use this to transform the nature of the experience, almost like the car. Instead of selling you a washing machine, we will loan you a washing machine. We retain title, and the machine will tell us every time you use it. At the end of the month, we'll put a charge on your credit card based on the number of uses. It will either be the same price or slightly less than the wash-o-mat that you go to." That's an oversimplified scenario, but that is where things are headed.

THE SERVICE ECONOMY FINALLY ARRIVES

This is where the real transformations come. I'm a technology forecaster, but my interest is in what technology does to society. In general, even the most anticipated of futures tends to arrive late and in completely unexpected ways—if it ever arrives at all. It's what makes us all so humble as forecasters.

For example, in the 1970s, everybody was writing about the leisure society. What were we going to do with all of our time after robots took over our jobs and computers took over our paperwork? I can't wait. I would love for someone to deliver a leisure society. In the 1980s, there was this thing called the service economy. The forecast was basically that everybody would either be flipping hamburgers at McDonald's or they would be consultants—which, of course, didn't happen.

Now, pull a thread through all these themes: wireless, bandwidth, sensors, increasingly autonomous smart effects. Pull that through, and suddenly the service economy just arrived in a completely strange and unexpected way. We're still buying physical products, but those products are actually concealed services. When you buy a cellphone, you think you're buying an artifact. In fact, you're buying the point of service for the thing that's truly valuable, which is communications. The car ceases to become a product; rather, it's a transportation service. So the service economy finally does arrive, hidden in physical products.

Why should we care? Now I shift from being an observer to an advocate—suddenly it puts wheels on the goals of issues like closed-loop recycling, a green economy, and design for disassembly.

For example, the car dealer wants to retain title to the car in the same way Interface Carpet retains title to the carpets it sells. I have a box full of old cellphones in my garage because I get a new one every nine months. I really want to send the old phone back to the manufacturers and have them send me a new one. I don't even want to own the darn thing. You guys keep it; you dispose of it. The same goes for a car or a washing machine. Look what has happened with disposable cameras. You buy the camera, you shoot the roll, you send the camera back with the film. Kodak actually recycles a huge percentage of the pieces of that camera. They basically just peel off the paper and repackage the thing.

It gives us a chance to change the stream of commerce. The thing that persists is the service, and the thing that is transitory is the physical object, which goes back and gets reused in the stream.

This essay was adapted from an interview undertaken with Mr. Saffo by Peter Leyden, Knowledge Developer at Global Business Network (www.gbn.com). The publishers gratefully acknowledge the support of Global Business Network in making these ideas and insights available.

Social Entrepreneurship:
A Model for Sustainable Growth

Paul Hawken

Paul Hawken is an environmentalist, entrepreneur, and best-selling author, widely respected for his ideas on how corporations can achieve sustainable, ecologically-sound development. His latest book, written with Amory and Hunter Lovins, is *Natural Capitalism: Creating the Next Industrial Revolution*. In it, Paul Hawken highlights the costs and consequences of 200 hundred years of industrial development, introducing four strategies necessary to perpetuate abundance, avert scarcity, and deliver a solid basis for social development. In this article, he argues that a whole range of natural resources and heritage—from the human genome to water and the airwaves—are being dominated by corporations, and he outlines the consequences of this development.

THE ANTIGLOBALIZATION MOVEMENT IS REALLY THE FIGHT AGAINST THE CORPORATIZATION OF THE COMMONS

The people who are arguing most articulately and vociferously against globalization are protesting the "corporatization of the commons." These commons that are being corporatized include the human genome, seeds, water, food, airwaves, media, and if the draft agendas of the World Trade Organization and other bodies are passed, much more. The commons include stories, music, and culture as well. They include place and self-determination. They include the ability for people to decide what is and what isn't acceptable as a product in a certain locality or region or place. They include tradition. All these areas are being taken over or corrupted by corporations.

Corporatization is caused by the unending and pressing mandate for corporations to grow their capital. If a corporation doesn't grow its capital, there is no change in value—in fact, there would be a loss of value. Furthermore, if financial capital and shareholder value does not grow, then the leaders of a corporation are replaced. Managing a large corporation is like being on a gerbil wheel. As soon as the wheel slows down to a certain level, a new gerbil with fresh legs is brought in.

Not so long ago, if a C.E.O. led a company with a 7 or 8% return on investment, that was considered to be a creditable performance, and they could keep their job. Now, 7 or 8% is seen as unsatisfactory, often leading to a C.E.O. being quickly replaced by someone who promises greater returns. What kind of world is it where, in the words of Hazel Henderson, "capital is divine?" It's a world where capital has the right to grow, and it's a higher right than those of people, cultures, places, and qualities that historically have been our commons. What happens is you have an enormously overdeveloped corporate sector.

Corporations are seeking new areas in which they can grow, and they're going into areas that just weren't imagined before. Corporations are continuing to colonize, whether they realize it or not, and this is an extension of Western cultural exploitation that goes back 500 years. This new weight of colonization is having disastrous results. For example, many major multinational utilities want to effectively privatize water supply in many parts of the world. Similarly, three of the world's largest biotechnology corporations want to control 90% of the germplasm of 90% of the caloric food intake of the world. Ted Turner said that in the end there will only be two media companies in the world, and he wants to have a stake in one of them. Rupert Murdoch thinks the same way. McDonald's opens up 2,400 restaurants a year. Right now, one out of every five meals in the United States is fast food, and McDonald's wants that to be the case everywhere in the world. Coke says that it has 10% of the total liquid intake of the world, and its goal is to go to 20%. Or is it 30%? These are absurd and devastating goals for corporations.

These challenges are being answered by people who are suffering, not simply by white middle-class protestors in Quebec, Genoa, and Seattle. In many places in the world where corporations are trying to implement their visions of how to grow capital, they are meeting resistance. They will continue to meet resistance from the world as long as they try to colonize what people have held in common throughout the history of humankind.

THE CORPORATIZATION OF THE WORLD IS
THE DISASTROUS LOSS OF DIVERSITY

The way to create healthy, vibrant economies and societies is through diversity. We know that scientifically. Any system that loses its diversity loses its resiliency and is more subject to sudden shocks and changes from which it can't recover. The corporatization of the world is the loss of diversity—it's forcing uniformity upon people. As Arnold Toynbee said, the sign of a civilization in decay is the institution of uniformity and the lack of diversity.

And that's exactly what we're seeing, only it is called "harmonization." The degree to which a company or a corporation honors diversity and then allows it to emerge from a place, a country, locale, culture, tribe, or city is a good thing. The degree to which it tries to enforce a one-size-fits-all formulaic solution to diet or media or agriculture is, in my opinion, going to be seen in hindsight as just as much a criminal act as the deracination of indigenous people by the Spaniards, the genocide of Native Americans, or the enslavement of African Americans. We look back at those things now and feel ashamed. We will look back at what we are doing right now to the world and see it as a violation of humanity.

The economic principle of subsidiarity says that decisions, whether they be economic or political, should always be made at the smallest or closest unit relevant to the issue at hand, because those are the people who not only have the most at stake but who also have the experience and knowledge with which to make an intelligent decision. Of course there are problems with subsidiarity when there's a breakdown like in the Congo or Rwanda. Nevertheless, subsidiarity within a true democratic system is the proper way to make economic decisions.

Rather than talking about globalization, we should be talking about the localization and interdependence of economies. Those corporations that help with localization should do very well. For example, energy companies should introduce technologies to create local sufficiency with respect to energy, to the degree that it is possible. Whether it is a global company or not, it is a company that is helping a region, a locale, a city, or a village. A company that introduces the means to increase self-sufficiency is doing even better. A company that seeks to dominate local economies—to buy out, take over, or make that economy or country dependent on them—is violating humane economic principles.

WE'LL REMEMBER THE SOCIAL ENTREPRENEURS AND NOT THE BUSINESS PEOPLE

It is true that this view of the corporation is not a very charitable assessment. Can I imagine corporations as brilliantly adaptive and helpful? I don't have to imagine it: there are 70,000 or 80,000 companies in the United States alone that are doing fantastic work with respect to society, the environment, energy, agriculture, and water. And there are more companies all over the world that are acting similarly. It's just that I can't think of any that are listed on the New York Stock Exchange or appear in the *Fortune* 500. I don't think real solutions scale up in the way that large corporations do.

The truly innovative acts of entrepreneurship that are occurring now and will continue to occur are no longer in business. Social entrepreneurship: that's where the action is. That's where the real innovators are. That's where you'll find the people who will be remembered 50 to 100 years from now. We won't remember a single person who's in business except as a footnote.

Apple says, "Think different." Who are they talking about? People like Gandhi, Einstein, Muhammad Ali. They're talking about people who actually took care of other people, who cared and were compassionate. I've asked myself, when will the Rosa Parks of the business world step up and sit at the front of the bus? It would take an amazing person to do that. Essentially, that person would say that we have marched too long in lockstep with policies and assumptions that are harmful. It's time that we spoke the truth about what we do, about what happens to us as people, about the enormous polarization of wealth, about how we treat people, and about how globalization is a race to the bottom, enforced by rules that nobody agreed to. We'll remember that person, but I don't think they'd have a job for very long.

This essay was adapted from an interview undertaken with Mr. Hawken by Peter Leyden, Knowledge Developer at Global Business Network (www.gbn.com). The publishers gratefully acknowledge the support of Global Business Network in making these ideas and insights available.

X-engineering Success

James Champy

An example of the joint venture is Concert, formed by AT&T and British Telecom to provide communications services to large multinational companies. The venture made sense on paper. Neither AT&T nor British Telecom had the global coverage that its big customers required. Rather than try to build this capability—at a cost of billions of dollars—and bang heads in competition, it made more sense for these companies to create a jointly owned company out of their combined resources. But in the end, these giants did bang heads, taking the venture apart. It would seem that someone forgot to put terms into the deal about what to do with assets and customers in the event that the alliance failed. About the only thing that the partners seemed to be able to agree on was that it hadn't worked. As Concert wound up its business, it was losing about $200 m each quarter.

What happened? Most observers attribute Concert's failure to a difference in cultures between the two partners. That's certainly plausible. The management styles of both companies are different, and each company has been distracted with its own struggle to maintain share in its local markets. A similar alliance formed by France Telecom and a number of other telecommunications companies also failed after much effort and millions of Euros. In fact, the business landscape is littered with alliance failures.

Research into these failures confirms that differing cultures and management styles are the principal causes for break-ups. But I believe that the problems go beyond different management breeding. Often alliances are the brainchild of sales organizations that are just looking to get access to each other's customers. The word *synergy* is freely used to justify a deal without much appreciation for what it will take to make the alliance work. Simply agreeing to jointly market products or services isn't enough to sustain an alliance. There is not enough value created for the partners or for their customers.

Even when an alliance is initially successful, it can fall apart when one partner becomes dominant and tries to exercise too much power. This often happens in the information technology industry when large software publishers or hardware manufacturers try to assert control over their smaller channel partners, the systems integrators and consultancies that use their products in delivering services. The big guys just assume that they know more and have superior processes. That behavior causes two problems:

1 Arrogance creeps into the relationship, forcing out the trust and good will needed to make it work.
2 Knowledge is lost.

There is a good chance that a smaller channel partner is closer to customers, knowing what they really want, and having a better process. When one alliance partner starts to assert power over another, the alliance is near its end. Recently I spoke with one large technology company that admitted that only 10 of its 400 alliances produced any significant business.

WHY BOTHER AND WHAT'S CHANGED?

The case for making alliances work goes beyond increasing a company's product offering or virtual size. Alliances can address the enormous inefficiencies that exist in many industries. Companies keep large and depreciating inventories because they don't have visibility into each other's operations. And because companies don't have processes that connect well together—such as your selling process not working well with my buying process—lots of unnecessary work and paper is produced. For example, it takes 26 separate electronic and paper documents to make many trans-oceanic shipments. Supply chain reengineering is just scratching the surface of what's possible if companies could work more closely together.

Up to now, it has been difficult to do the kind of collaborative work that a powerful alliance requires. Many economists have argued that the management and transaction costs outweigh the benefits, but that balance may well have shifted with the advent of the Internet. This ubiquitous network is not just about a new channel to market or a place to advertise. Its principal corporate benefit will be as an enabler of a new breed of cross-organizational processes that will dramatically improve business performance. To achieve this benefit will require what I call *X-engineering*. The "X" connotes the organizational boundaries that you will cross.

MAKING ALLIANCES WORK

Making alliances work requires that the partners are culturally compatible. But the partners must do more than be polite to each other and throw resources, processes, people, and customers into a venture. A venture must be thoughtfully designed and implemented and the principles of X-engineering applied. Here's what to do.

Do conduct an open assessment of cultures and management styles. Studies that show cultural and management style differences to be contributors to failure are right. Probe each other's beliefs and values. Ask some simple questions, such as how will your partner handle a breakdown of relations with a customer? How do you both deal with issues of breach of integrity? How will you think about quality, innovation, profitability? Remember, there is no single company culture that is "right." The issue here is compatibility, and hopefully you and your partner will value the same things.

In the end, you must choose your partners carefully. Trust your intuition, and don't fool yourself into thinking that you can influence what your partner fundamentally believes. Company cultures, like country cultures, don't change easily.

Make your processes transparent. Most companies operate under the premise that their processes are unique and should be kept secret. Just the opposite is true. There are very few processes within a company that are unique. Maybe you have a secret formula or a proprietary manufacturing technique, but most of your and your competitor's processes are the same. To operate an alliance, companies must be open so that process relationships can develop. You cannot intimately connect unless you understand how each other operates.

A corollary principle is that you must share good ideas. Forget about who gets the credit. Just put good ideas into the alliance and go on and develop new ones. Just like any business, an alliance cannot be starved—especially by its partners. It may need innovation to maintain its competitiveness.

Harmonize your processes. Being transparent isn't enough. Chances are that your processes and the processes of your partners won't connect easily. For example, if one partner contributes the sales processes to a venture and another partner the service processes, work will have to be done so customers experience these processes in a seamless way. Lots of problems occur in hand-offs. All the processes of an alliance have to be examined to be sure that they are harmonized—that is, that they act in concert with one another. In some cases, totally new processes will have to be developed.

Create a powerful business proposition for your customers. An alliance is only worth doing if it can make one plus one equal three. The partners have to create a business proposition for their customers that neither could offer on its own. An alliance cannot be sustained because it's convenient for its partners. It requires steady revenues, and that will only happen if it offers a compelling business proposition for customers.

An improved business proposition can take many forms. It could be reduced costs and lower prices. That's what Dell and its product partners are doing in Dell's electronic marketplace. Alliances can offer variety and choice. Amazon.com is now a retail channel for Toys-R-Us. An alliance can make service more robust. Many computer hardware manufacturers partner with service providers to handle service problems. Unfortunately, customers don't always experience the benefits of such combinations because the partners haven't harmonized their processes.

THE IDEAL IS POSSIBLE

What does a great alliance look like? It's one that builds on the strengths of its partners, meets a customer need, and avoids the replication of resources or the redundancy of work. Yes, the venture must also make money, but I believe profits will come if the earlier three conditions are met.

The Star Alliance was formed by a number of major airlines. The Alliance members share few overlapping routes, but they do share information about their customers' travel preferences. This means that they can act as complementors, not competitors. They can offer the intelligent routes that their passengers want. The Alliance also wisely allows passengers to interchange and pool frequent-flier miles from individual member airlines. There is something in the deal for everyone. And because these airlines act as complementors, they will avoid spending billions of dollars on redundant jumbo jets to compete for routes. If the members can find ways to share more processes and eliminate redundant work, even more benefits will result.

More than ever, businesses need alliances to reduce costs, improve service, and feed innovation. Customers now expect that you can deliver anything, anytime, anywhere;

but few companies can do that on their own. The Internet now enables the fundamental cross-organizational change required to reduce costs and create customer value. But relationships must be X-engineered—partners carefully selected, operations made transparent, and processes harmonized. Otherwise, relationships will consume enormous amounts of management time and yield little for companies and their customers. Enter alliances with your eyes and company wide open and expect that they will require an active, continuing negotiation between the partners. Only then will they be worth the effort.

———•·•———

James Champy is chairman and head of strategy of Perot Systems consulting practice, providing strategic direction to the company's team of business and management consultants. He is an authority on management issues surrounding organizational change and corporate renewal. He wrote the bestsellers *Reengineering the Corporation* (with Michael Hammer; HarperBusiness, 2001) and *Reengineering Management* (HarperBusiness, 1996). His latest books include *The Arc of Ambition* (with Nitin Nohria; Perseus, 2001) and *X-engineering the Corporation* (Warner, 2002). He has moderated programs for the PBS Business Channel and writes frequently for a variety of publications, including *Forbes* and *Computer World*.

Turnaround Strategies

Sir John Harvey-Jones

The area of business which, mercifully, few of us have any experience of is turning a business around before it goes under—but when the rocks ahead are clearly visible. In these situations, the first casualty tends to be the current leader. He or she is usually replaced by a hired "hard man" to do the dirty work. The result is all too often far below what could be achieved by someone already within the organization, who would have been aware of the culture which has led to the decline in the first place.

The in-house candidate (a role I have personally filled) is desirable because he or she has the best chance of saving the largest proportion of what may be salvageable. After all, insolvency practitioners, or at least the good ones, could be described as managing turnarounds, but at a cost which most of us would attempt to avoid. The greatest difficulty the in-house employee faces is the problem of analyzing the causes of the downfall with sufficient clarity and over a long enough time. The elapsed time from the first business mistake to eventual collapse varies enormously. Very large organizations can carry on for a surprising time before events overwhelm them, while in the case of the small business, retribution tends to strike much more quickly. What is certain is that both the stock market and the banks have less and less tolerance of business mistakes, and the time available to demonstrate an effective recovery plan is becoming ever shorter. Moreover, the judgment of the chances of success is made by business analysts and the press, who probably have very little knowledge of the real situation which has led to the visible signs of failure. In reality, these are all too often symptoms rather than causes.

It is the people within the organization itself who know the myriad problems which must be overcome and the actions to be taken. Therefore the turnaround problem becomes one of pointing out the new direction. This is where being able to call on the knowledge, drive, and enthusiam of existing employees can be so valuable. This is obviously far more difficult when all of your employees are worrying about the future, and the best and most self-confident are voting with their feet for a safer environment. The reason many companies find themselves in trouble is almost always due to problems right at the top. I have yet to meet such a situation which was caused by the employees. Employee dissatisfaction is largely caused by mismanagement or frustration. No employee actually wants to do a bad job, or to be seen to be doing one. Obviously no employee actually wants the company to fail or to find themselves faced with enforced redundancy on minimal terms.

DIAGNOSIS AND SOLUTION

If you find yourself managing a turnaround, the first two points on which you have to concentrate are your diagnosis of the problem and endeavoring to ensure that you have a reasonable time gap in which to carry out your chosen solution. For the diagnosis, you need every scrap of information, opinion, and statistical analysis you can lay your hands on. The views and openness of those on the shop floor are as important—or in some cases, more important—than those at the top. Individuals in these situations are astonishingly honest with themselves, and it is from this apparently inchoate mass of opinion and fact that a first "rough cut" analysis will appear. The strategy has to be concise and simple, for it is essential that everyone inside or outside the company should understand the objectives. The detail is best left to those who will have to deliver it.

Self-evidently you cannot turn around a company by doing more of what has already landed you in trouble, although it is extraordinary how often the existing management blame their own ineffectiveness and not the strategy which has so obviously failed.

Few individuals are so closed-minded that they won't give you a chance if you explain your thinking, and in any case, no recovery plan is a single unique solution. The eventual solution you decide upon can, and must, be one to which all parties (particularly within the company) can offer their support.

Remember that your advent has kindled hope in those who work for you, coupled with probably unrealistic assumptions of a miraculous and speedy change in the situation.

WHERE DOES EVERYBODY STAND?

A positive strategy with clear delegation for action and a lot of trust in your employees can change things surprisingly quickly. The next, and very difficult, action is entirely within your own outfit. It is absolutely vital that everyone knows where they stand. Start with the key 10–20%, who you are sure need to be on board. Make clear that as long as you have a business, you need them and they are as secure as anyone in these times can be. Then address the 10–15% most at risk. It is almost certain you will have to reduce cash, but generally a pay-out of under 20% will do the trick. Remember that starting at the top involves fewer people and releases more money. Those most at risk deserve the earliest warning and the most help. Sharing the task of helping them to find alternatives eases the pain, as does the maximum affordable financial aid.

The remainder should be told that they are not at immediate risk, and that the risk to them depends almost entirely on the success of the turnaround.

The financial state of the company should be known to everyone, as should the direction and amount of change that will be required. Don't be trapped by the fear of lack of security on data. Bad news travels like lightning and all too often is far exceeded by the rumors and ill-concealed "schadenfreude" of those in the outside world. You only get one shot at trying to turn around a business, and concealment of the reality is not a help.

DELEGATION AND TRUST

Once you have decided the strategy, the objective, and the team, delegate furiously. People have to know they are trusted and that all depends upon them.

Do not allow the inevitable attempts to "delegate upward." You must keep on pushing the problem back to employees, while reiterating your commitment and support for their actions. The world is littered with examples of individuals who have achieved what you and others felt was impossible. Problems are only, and can only be, solved by those who "own" them, and your leadership role is to reinforce that ownership.

LEADING BY EXAMPLE

You now enter what is probably the most personally difficult phase of all. Both inside and outside the company, you have to radiate confidence and realism while encouraging people to increase their speed of activity. This is helped by removing the brakes, simplifying the structure, reducing the senior management numbers and levels, and increasing the tempo.

Example is all. You cannot expect everyone else to throw themselves at the problem if you turn up late and go off early to enjoy a liquid lunch. The drum beat is taken from the top. In my own case, I have reduced my pay level and given back money I had been awarded until the business results had turned. You need a few dramatic examples from the top. Don't expect that stopping tea and biscuits will be greeted with anything other than cynicism. Selling the headquarters or the board cars is more likely to hit a responsive chord.

It is the board that has led the business into the mess, and it is the board who must be seen to take the medicine and be totally committed to the change. In my own case, a 50% reduction in the number of executive board members and a refusal to allow deputies both increased our speed of response and demonstrated that there were no sacred cows.

Everything has to be up for grabs, and fear and tradition must not be allowed to inhibit action.

- Act in the certainty that people within the organization itself know the myriad problems which must be overcome and the actions to be taken.
- Concentrate first on your diagnosis of the problem and ensure a reasonable time to execute your chosen solution.
- Ensure that the solution is one which all parties, particularly within the company, can support.
- Start your program by telling the key 10–20% that you need them on board. Then address the 10–15% whose jobs are most at risk.
- Once you have decided the strategy, the aim, and the team, delegate intensively to people who know they are trusted and that all depends upon them.
- Remove the brakes, simplify the structure, reduce senior management numbers and levels, increase the tempo—and implement a few dramatic examples from the top.

The whole problem is to achieve ownership of a new plan and a new pace of action—and all must be results oriented. Turnarounds are difficult, and test the imagination and courage, but once it is evident you have started on the way up again there is no limit to how far and how fast you can go.

———————

Sir John Harvey-Jones joined ICI as a work study officer in 1956, after 19 years in the navy. He rose to be chairman in 1982, and was largely responsible for reshaping the company, doubling the price of ICI shares, and turning a loss into a billion-pound profit after only 30 months in the job. Since receiving his knighthood in 1985, Sir John has written several books, including the bestsellers *Making It Happen* (HarperCollins, new edition, 1994) and *Getting It Together* (Ulverscroft, 1992). He also took part in a TV series entitled *Troubleshooter*, where he was invited to visit and advise businesses.

Core Versus Context:
Managing Resources in a Downturn

Geoffrey A. Moore

E xecutives well understand the value of focusing on core business issues and activities, although they sometimes fail to distinguish between core as competitive advantage versus core competence. The former is what the market rewards, the latter what the company is good at. One of the toughest challenges in business occurs when core competence is no longer core. Competition has caught up with you to such an extent that what was once core has now become context. The market still demands the process, but it's no longer willing to pay a premium for it.

Companies thus find themselves with an increasing portion of their asset base—sometimes in equipment, always in personnel—that no longer generates attractive returns. What was once differentiated and at a premium has now been commoditized. This in turn causes investors to bid down the value of their stock, since they see an increasingly large portion of their capital going to fund processes that are at best financially inert and are potentially a financial sinkhole.

Every company is subject to erosion of core into context; the very nature of competitive markets works to neutralize differentiation over time as competitors find ways to mimic or substitute for the value created. The knee-jerk response of most management teams is to make or find new core, which is necessary but insufficient. What they must also do is systematically work to shed themselves of context or face a perpetually deteriorating core/context ratio, with loss of attractiveness to investors and, ultimately, an uncompetitive cost of capital. In this section we will outline the impact of core versus context, and the actions that companies must take.

THE IMPACT ON COMPANIES

Companies get trapped by context from various causes, many attributable to organizational inertia. Such processes were once their bread and butter, making it hard to abandon them. Moreover, if the alternative is to outsource the work (the fundamental domain in which context shedding is accomplished), there are inevitable concerns about cost. Rarely do in-house teams *not* assert that they can perform a given function cheaper, faster, and better than outsourcers.

Long-term, however, this is not the case. Where one company's context is another company's core, market dynamics ultimately favor the latter's position. That company can invest in productivity-improving systems and processes with full support of its investors, whereas the other company cannot. Moreover, it can attract the best people because it can provide them an upwardly mobile career path, whereas the latter company cannot. Finally, it can amortize investments across a broad base of customers, whereas the other company cannot.

Thus, in the long term, failing to outsource is a losing game. Only in the short term—specifically, in the current quarter—is it often more expensive, in part for reasons of transition costs, in part because prices and offerings are not as competitive as one would want until market forces have a chance to work. The end result: unless the outsourcer makes a short-term sacrifice, it's unlikely the deal goes forward.

Most executives are wise to this game, but few appreciate how pernicious it is to accede to it. They don't see how every context process not outsourced creates a tax on the asset base of the company. Worse, they don't see how failure to manage context aggressively leads necessarily to a loss of agility in their corporate culture and a corresponding rise in stifling administration. Why?

Context processes have no upside, but they do have downside. Context carries liability just as core does. The difference is that core also transfers competitive advantage, which context does not. Thus, if you're managing core, you're always in search of the efficient frontier of risk versus reward. But what is the best strategy for managing context?

Darwinian natural selection will drive context managers to increasingly risk-averse strategies, those being the most suitable for managing processes that have a downside but no upside. As a company's core/context ratio deteriorates, its population of managers will thus become increasingly risk-averse. They are happy for other people to take risks, but not themselves (and not others if that's going to put their area in the line of fire). The result? Large corporations become stultified and unresponsive.

SUCCESSFULLY MANAGING THE CORE/CONTEXT RATIO

The proving ground for outsourcing context today is contract manufacturing in the electronics industry, with companies like Cisco and Dell, and outsourcers like Solectron and Flextronics, leading the way. What these companies are exploiting is the premise that whatever is one company's context can be another company's core. In this relationship, whenever a business process is transferred from one to the other, the investors of both companies applaud, one because it went off their balance sheet, and the other because it went on to theirs.

Drill down into the systems investments that have enabled these early adopters to steal a march on their competitors and we see that they focus on two critical issues: *control* and *visibility*. The following cases provide examples.

Beyond manufacturing, more companies are looking to outsource IT and financial and human resources services. Payroll has long been a function considered outsourceable. For example, a visible departmental outsourcing deal has been struck by British Petroleum with PricewaterhouseCoopers for human resources. Here, the best strategy is to determine for each function what is still core and what is legitimately context, (particularly critical in the case of IT).

Early outsourcing relationships between EDS and General Motors and between IBM and Kodak provide some important lessons. In both cases, the corporations were fed up with their in-house organization and wanted a better substitute at a fixed price. They made no attempt to segregate core from context. Instead they focused on price, which was negotiated as low as possible. This in turn motivated the outsourcers to cut corners or nickel-and-dime the end users on change requests, leading to bad relationships and bad outcomes. The end result was annoying when it came to context processes, but it was devastating when it ended up holding core projects hostage.

Conversely, outsourcing IT infrastructure looks to be a major growth market, as companies like Exodus attest on the server farm side. Moreover, specialized services like 24/7 performance monitoring and security management both lend themselves to third-party provisioning. These functions, although frequently mission-critical, are almost never core. This is where outsourcing shines.

KEY POINTS WHEN MANAGING THE CORE/CONTEXT RATIO

1 **Be prepared to delegate core activities.** Top management can delegate core to middle management. Of course, it rarely wants to, because this is the fun stuff. The truth is that the middle of the organization has a better view of emerging market trends; if you empower it, it will do a better job than you.

2 **Outsource and manage context.** Top management's most powerful lever is the outsourcing of context. This is not the fun stuff. But middle management is never positioned to act on this directive, as it can't afford to put its political capital at risk. Only top management can drive these initiatives, always with an eye toward repurposing reclaimed resources into the next generation of core work.

3 **Distinguish between mission-critical and supporting activities.** To the distinction between core and context needs, we need to add the distinction between *mission-critical* and *supporting*. The former applies to processes that can directly damage customer outcomes or corporate capabilities. These must be kept under managerial control. The latter, by contrast, can be readily outsourced with only modest controls.

   The big challenge in core/context ratio management comes with the need to outsource mission-critical context. Indeed, executives often confuse mission-critical with core because they're sure they *can't* outsource such processes. But to manage their core/context ratio, they must. This demands new best practices in outsourcing, enabling customers to retain control and visibility while transferring the bulk of work to another organization.

4 **Harness the benefit of technology.** The technology key to the new best practices is for the company and its outsourcer to create information systems that give the company short-term adaptive controls and long-term visibility into its risk positions. The Internet provides a backbone for enabling such systems. The business logic that must ride on that backbone is just now coming to market. Early adopters may well have to write their own systems in order to get ahead of their competition.

Dell has used IT to develop end-to-end visibility into their inventory positions and used their market power to force suppliers to hold that inventory until the last second. This would be intolerable for the supplier were it not for Dell giving them near-real-time visibility into the emerging order mix, which is made possible by con-figuration software, now Web-enabled, that funnels customer demand from an infinite array of selections into a finite and manageable set of options.

MAKING IT HAPPEN

1 First, start with a questioning analysis of core and context activities, at three levels:
   - **Top level**: which of our businesses are still core? Which have become context?
   - **Business unit level**: which of our line functions are the real basis for our competitive differentiation? Which are not?
   - **Function level**: which of our processes are the source of differentiation? Which are driven by more compliance?
   - **Departmental and, if useful, individual levels**: how much time is spent on context activities?

2 Next, consider two key ideas to help guide this process, asking the questions:
   - If we were entirely free of current obligations, what could we do to increase the competitive advantage of our company? This helps people to see the possible sources and types of core activity, and may help start the journey to get there. It also identifies the task work that should be passed on or left alone.
   - What work would we be willing to surrender if we were assured that someone else would handle it appropriately? This becomes a lightning rod to attract context processes that, once aggregated, can be analyzed for disposal.

3 Finally, implement and monitor the results. It helps to understand from the outset that the process of detailed implementation will invariably result in a course correction later. Also, not only does the process of implementation need to be monitored to ensure that it remains on track, but the core/context ratio needs to be regularly assessed, as competitive markets are far from static. One of the keys to successful implementation is to assemble a sufficient amount of work to motivate an outsourcer to put their best efforts into the work.

Executives must learn to manage the core/context ratio. Regardless of how superior their core is, eventually its impact will be dwarfed by an ever-expanding context. It's like cholesterol: if you do not manage context, it will finish you.

———•———

Geoffrey Moore is managing director of The Chasm Group, a consulting practice based in California that provides market development and business strategy services to high-technology companies. He is also a partner with Mohr Davidow Ventures, a venture capital firm specializing in specific technology markets including e-commerce, Internet, enterprise software, networking, and semiconductors. Moore is a frequent speaker at industry conferences and his books are required reading at leading business schools. These books include *Crossing the Chasm* (revised edition, 1999), *The Gorilla Game* (revised edition, 1999), and *Living on the Fault Line* (2002), published by HarperBusiness.

Snapping Managerial Inertia

Jeffrey Pfeffer and Robert I. Sutton

Why do so many managers understand so much about employee and organizational performance and work so hard, yet do so much to undermine performance? Why do so many companies sponsor training programs and knowledge-management initiatives, yet see no impact from those efforts? Knowing what to do isn't enough. Companies must inspire action to turn all of that individual and collective knowledge into achievements that affect the company's business results.

What happens in many companies is that managers spend so much time fighting internal battles that they have little time left to fight the company's competitors. In too many companies points are scored on the elaborateness of internal presentations (meaning that people spend inordinate amounts of time preparing those presentations to impress their bosses and peers) instead of tangible business results. In many other companies the penalty for failure is so great that managers spend their time preserving the status quo rather than trying to find new and better ways of affecting business results. Further, the "not invented here" (NIH) syndrome prevents people from learning from each other for fear that they'll give credit to some other person in the company who has developed a better method—for fear they'll admit the other person deserves more recognition and, perhaps, a greater share of the available rewards.

It doesn't have to be this way. Many companies are finding ways of overcoming the knowing–doing gap. Knowing how to bridge this gap will make a positive difference in your company's business results, your employee's morale and performance, and your effectiveness as a manager.

GUIDELINES FOR ACTION

The following principles serve as a framework for overcoming obstacles and guiding organizational innovation:

Recognize the Importance of Philosophy. Many companies have undertaken experiments in one division or location to implement high-performance work teams. While many such efforts have shown outstanding results, few of these companies have been successful in transferring these new work methods to other plants, divisions, or locations. A prime example of this is that few of the innovations from Saturn and NUMMI have ever been adopted by other parts of the General Motors organization. What's missing is a company-wide understanding of the basic philosophy of the new methods and a frank and open discussion of why the new methods are important and must be replicated throughout the company.

Companies that don't accept talk as a substitute for action often do one or more of the following:

- promote people who have developed a real-world understanding of the organization's work processes because they have performed them themselves;

- build a culture that values simplicity (and doesn't reward complexity), uses simple, clear, and direct language, and values common sense;
- use action-oriented language and follow up to ensure that decisions are implemented;
- refuse to accept excuses for why things won't work, instead encouraging employees to reframe objections into challenges to be overcome.

Act and Teach Others How to Act.   Too many companies place great value on conceptual frameworks, fancy graphic presentations, and lots of words, but little value on action. Why are so many change efforts approved in the boardroom and never implemented? Honda puts employees into suppliers' organizations so they can see how the suppliers make parts and what work methods they use. Being closely involved with the supplier is imperative for real understanding and learning.

At IDEO Product Development, C.E.O. David Kelley walks the talk of learning through trial and error. Kelley and other top managers teach employees their method and students enact it by designing, building, demonstrating, and pitching their inventions to each other.

Plans and Concepts Count Less Than Action.   Too many companies are stymied by analysis paralysis, the feeling that plans must be complete and bulletproof before any action is taken. The more successful companies encourage action to foster learning by doing. In many of these companies it is believed that an 80% solution today is better than a 100% solution months or years from now. Continental Airlines C.O.O. Greg Brenneman speaks of the airline's turnaround in this way: "If you sit around devising elegant and complex strategies and then try to execute them through a series of flawless decisions, you're doomed. We saved Continental because we acted and we never looked back."

Tolerate Errors As a Sign That Learning Is Taking Place.   Does your company treat mistakes so harshly that people continuously analyze and discuss plans instead of taking action? Thomas Edison tried thousands of materials for light-bulb filaments before discovering tungsten. When someone asked him how he overcame so many failures, he said that he never failed—he just learned. Roger Sant, cofounder and chairman of AES, fosters a culture of forgiveness, noting, "You would be amazed at how quickly people support and forgive one another here."

Drive Fear out of Your Organization.   If employees fear that any new idea that doesn't work perfectly at the first attempt will result in punishment or dismissal, they'll never try anything new. Rapid prototyping is a manufacturing design method in which new ideas can be tried out quickly and relatively inexpensively and plans modified based on results. Failure of a new idea is viewed as part of the learning process, not as something to be feared. Successful companies encourage risk-taking and encourage employees to try new ideas without an overwhelming fear of retribution should they fail.

Companies that work to drive fear out of their organization often try some of these approaches:

- Rather than shooting the messenger, reward employees who deliver bad news. If the company doesn't know about a problem, it can't solve it.
- Punish inaction, not unsuccessful actions. An unsuccessful action should be viewed as a learning experience.
- Share failures. When leaders share their failures, they give permission to others to fail and encourage them to try.
- Banish anyone, at any level, who humiliates others.
- Learn from, and even celebrate, mistakes—especially when trying something new.

Fight the Competition, Not Each Other. Because competitive free enterprise has triumphed as an economic system, many companies have adopted internal competition as a way of life. This is typified by such practices as normal-curve performance rating systems, recognition for relatively few employees, and individual measurements and rewards that set people against each other. These practices take the focus away from the real opposition: external competitors. There are exceptions, however.

Measure Action and What Turns Knowledge into Action. Many companies are awash with data measuring every conceivable action. Amid so many measures employees spend far too much time focused on the numbers and how they'll look, instead of on actions that can help improve the business and meet overall goals. More successful companies focus on a few key measures of company performance, believing that if those key measures are met, everything else will fall into line.

Leadership Is the Key. Successful leaders create a positive learning environment that not only helps employees learn but also helps them apply that learning to their work to make a positive difference in business results. They lead by their own example and teach others how to act.

MAKING IT HAPPEN

At Men's Wearhouse the emphasis is on team selling; employees succeed only as their colleagues succeed. Customers don't care who gets the commission, they want great service from every employee.

The SAS Institute has a very low turnover rate, based partly on employees' preference not to have to constantly look over their shoulder to see which colleague is getting ready to subvert their work in order to look better themselves.

Southwest Airlines focuses on key measures such as lost bags, customer complaints, and on-time performance.

AES focuses on uptime of their power plants, new business development, and environmental and safety factors.

Measurements that can help turn knowledge into action include those that are:

- focused on organizational success rather than individual success. This encourages teamwork and interdependence.
- focused more on processes and means to ends, not on end products and final outcomes. This helps to facilitate learning and provides data that can better guide action and decision making.

- focused on the business model, culture, and philosophy of the firm. This means that measurements will vary from firm to firm and will generally depart from traditional accounting-based indicators.
- focused on a mindful, ongoing process of learning from experience and experimentation. No process is ever viewed as complete or final.

When David Kearns was C.E.O. at Xerox, he applied quality principles to the top management team as he encouraged their implementation throughout the company.

The C.E.O. of General Motors teaches in GM University, demonstrating his personal commitment to knowledge building and sharing.

Many readers will finish this article and start nodding: How did they know what's happening in my company? But recognizing that the problems exist isn't enough. Going back 20 years, Peters and Waterman, in their book *In Search of Excellence*, recognized that the most successful companies have a "bias for action." And that's what you need to snap your company's managerial inertia. Start right now!

Jeffrey Pfeffer is the Thomas D. Dee II professor of organizational behavior in the Graduate School of Business at Stanford University, and author of numerous books, including *The Human Equation: Building Profits by Putting People First* (Harvard Business School Press, 1998). Robert I. Sutton is professor of management science and engineering at Stanford University and author of *Weird Ideas That Work: 11 and ½ Practices for Promoting, Managing and Sustaining Innovation* (Free Press, 2001). Together, they wrote *The Knowing-Doing Gap* (Harvard Business School Press, 2000).

Now!—The Role of Urgency in Creating Positive Change

John Reh

The speed and extent of changes in the dot-com space, while highly visible, are not unique. The Pony Express was forced out of business in only 18 months because of competition from the telegraph. Japanese automakers almost destroyed several U.S. giants in that industry. And the popularity of the PC pushed Dell and Microsoft past IBM, the company that developed it.

The strengths that got you to the top won't keep you there. Others are always pushing to move past you, to dominate your market, to steal your best customers. You need to stay ahead of them. You need to change with the times—or ahead of them. And that need is urgent.

Business organizations have always had to deal with change. That change now is simply coming faster. Change that occurred in the automobile industry over a period of 20 years starting in the 1960s occurred within less than 20 months in the Internet industry. Change will occur; management must make it as positive as possible.

Businesses are living organisms. Like animals they have certain characteristics that enable them to survive in their environment. When that environment changes the organism must evolve too, or it will die. If the organism is not able or willing to change fast enough, it will be unable to survive in the new environment. Those organisms that can change quickly can survive, however.

CHANGE IS NEVER UNANNOUNCED

Changes always give signs they're coming. Sometimes signs are obvious and we all see them. The more sensitive you are to your environment, the more likely you are to notice the changes. But being aware that change is coming is not enough: you have to be able to react in time.

The environment in which a business operates can change in innumerable ways. Some of the changes are obvious and happen over a long time. For instance, new government regulations that govern your industry are publicly announced, go through a public comment period, and are likely to be revised and republished before they take effect. Few are caught off guard by such changes. We begin to prepare changes to our operations so that we can perform in compliance with the coming regulations.

Other changes can happen more quickly. A competitor may release a new product that captures significant market share almost overnight. A key supplier may suddenly go bankrupt. One of our facilities may be destroyed by a natural disaster. Our latest product may be more popular than expected and our plants unable to keep up with the demand. We develop contingency plans to cover such occurrences.

The better you are at tracking your markets and your competitors, the less likely you are to be surprised by a new product rollout. The more closely integrated you are with your supply chain, the less likely you are to be caught unprepared for a supplier's financial difficulties. The better attuned you are to your customers, the more likely it is that your product demand forecasts will be accurate.

SUCCESS BUILDS COMPLACENCY

Some companies are more sensitive to their environment and better equipped to deal with changes in that environment than their competitors. Sometimes it's an issue of size, sometimes an issue of longevity. Always it's an issue of leadership.

Success can breed complacency, dulling the sense of urgency around the need for change. Procedures that have outlived their usefulness survive because "that's how we've always done it." It's hard to let go of methods of doing things that have contributed to past successes, even though they now waste time and no longer create value.

As a manager, you know change will occur. You saw, for example, how quickly the Internet became an essential part of business and how much more quickly businesses that had not properly understood it failed. You also know people have a natural tendency to resist change, a tendency you have to overcome. You have to act to initiate the process of change.

URGENCY: YOUR BEST WEAPON

Nothing is more important in creating positive change than a sense of urgency. It must start at the top, be communicated throughout the organization, and it must be felt by the entire organization.

Urgent in the American Heritage Dictionary is defined as "compelling immediate action; conveying a sense of pressing importance." If you want to blast people and organizations out of their inertia you have to get their attention, give them a compelling reason to act outside their comfort zone, and keep them moving. The sense of pressing importance helps you move ahead, and that gives you time to recover from mistakes or to change direction early enough, so that only minor corrections are required later.

Once you know a change is needed, urgency keeps you from wasting precious resources on the wrong choices. Failing to communicate a sense of urgency to your organization leaves an avenue open to continue with the status quo. This not only delays the implementation of the needed changes, it consumes resources that will be needed to make them. The most critical of these resources is time.

Those responsible for change must focus on the roles of the leader, not on the tasks of the manager. Leaders set direction, communicate the vision, and empower people to do what has to be done for the change to succeed. Managers plan how to make the changes happen. They organize, allocate resources, and help people perform more efficiently. Managers are necessary if a change is going to succeed, but the leader is critical.

URGENCY AT WORK

In the summer of 1999, Carlos Ghosn, new C.O.O. of Nissan, set a goal of profitability by 2001. Saying that a sense of urgency was key—"you should come to headquarters and the walls should be on fire"—he set in motion his Nissan Revival Plan (NRP). On May 17, 2001, Nissan announced its best financial results in a decade.

Wal-Mart has a Sundown Rule, founder Sam Walton's twist on the old adage, "Don't put off until tomorrow what you can do today." Observing that rule means striving to answer requests the day they're received. It's one reason that Wal-Mart associates are famous for their customer service.

AsiaTrak (Tianjin) is a joint venture of Caterpillar, Itochu, and SNT that provides undercarriage products to the excavator and tractor industries. The company culture recognizes time as a competitive advantage and aims to err on the side of moving too fast rather than too slowly.

Few industries are as time-sensitive as floral retailing. 1–800-FLOWERS.COM uses a Web-based system for transmitting orders and scheduling deliveries. The system, called BloomLink, incorporates real-time chat capability so florists can ask questions about an order as they receive it.

MAKING IT HAPPEN

Laying the groundwork for change requires leaders to:

- recognize that change isn't easy;
- determine what you want to change and what benefits change will create. Plan how you will communicate the change and the reasons it is necessary.
- communicate that message to the entire organization, in plain language, using enough different media to reach everyone;
- impress on everyone the urgency of making the change happen;
- share as much as you can, as early as you can, with as many as you can;
- insider-trading restrictions may limit your actions, but don't hide behind them;
- pushing people out of their comfort zone is high-risk, but can yield high reward;
- help people be brave. Brave people move faster;
- dare to dream. Planning change means visualizing a present that doesn't yet exist;
- reinforce the message by repeating it often and keeping it fresh in people's minds.

People do what they think is in their best interests. You need both positive and negative tactics to create a sense of urgency around your desired change. Show people why the status quo is bad for them. Then show them your vision of the future and why that will be better.

First:

- manufacture a crisis to start the ball rolling;
- allow a very visible (but not deadly) problem to blow up out of control;
- widely publish internal reports that support your position that the status quo is unacceptable;
- make information available that shows how quickly the situation is going from bad to worse.

Then:

- show people the significantly better state that will exist for them after the change;
- reinforce the need for urgency with a good slogan, like the UPS tag line, "Moving at the Speed of Business";
- use time-based metrics to keep up the sense of urgency;
- set targets that are unreachable without the change.

If your goal is to centralize the customer service staff in a single location to reduce costs, build and post graphs so people can track their progress toward the goal. A weekly step chart showing the savings planned from closing smaller facilities, for example, can help people visualize the goal. Superimposing actual savings on the same chart can vividly illustrate the value of closing one office a couple of weeks early and can help keep the sense of urgency high.

For business strategies to work in practice, organizations need to develop and change: business strategy is not about preserving the status quo, it is concerned with making progress, and this requires change. Combined with this is the fact that, whether it is welcome or not, change is the only constant in business: it is inevitable and needs to be harnessed. If it is not proactively managed, then the effects can be overwhelming.

Leading change is a vital aspect of leadership in general, because it requires dynamic, focused action. Without this proactive leadership, change will fail—or fail even to get started. Leadership is essential to delivering effective change as it provides vision—a clear idea of purpose and direction. Leadership and a sense of urgency are also important to communicate, facilitate, guide, and focus activity; to solve problems; to coordinate and make decisions. In general, to provide a framework that ensures success, the leader must create a sense of urgency and provide the necessary motivation and support.

Change is happening more often and more quickly. The leader's job is to manage that change to create a positive outcome for the organization. Creating a sense of urgency is the best tool for making that happen.

John Reh is an Internet management consultant (www.peoplearecapital.com) with over 20 years of hands-on management experience in a variety of industries. He has published more than a hundred best practice articles and believes management is as much art as science, but a skill that can be learned. His Web site www.management.about.com includes a resource library of the best management information on the Internet.

Value Innovation

W. Chan Kim and Renée Mauborgne

There are two traditional schools of thought on how to compete and achieve growth. First there is the positioning school, which suggests that companies need to choose an attractive industry and then position themselves within it. This approach takes an industry's conditions as given. It also encourages companies to allow the competition to determine the parameters of their strategic thinking. Competitiveness is based on perceived advantages over the competition.

Then there is the capabilities school, which works from the inside out. This approach takes a resource-based view. Companies identify what they have, and think of what they can do best with it.

These two schools of thought are no longer sufficient. Despite their strengths, neither systematically addresses the strategic challenge of innovation, new demand creation, and—with it—the creation of new business space. Value innovation is an attempt to start to build this third school of thought.

UNDERSTANDING VALUE AND INNOVATION

Value and innovation are—or should be—inseparable. Value innovation places equal emphasis on value and innovation. Value without innovation can include value creation that simply improves the buyers' existing benefits. On the other hand, innovation without value may lead to bleeding-edge technology or innovation for innovation's sake. But it will not lend itself to mass-market commercial opportunities.

In classical economics, innovation is about random choice; it happens, and so companies tend to rely on people who are very intuitive. However, because innovation is seen as random, strategy has not addressed the challenge of how systematically to build new market spaces and new wealth. Value innovation challenges these assumptions. Value innovation doesn't have to be totally random. Value innovation is the crux of strategy, not the result of one genius.

Another problem is that innovation has been mistakenly equated with advances in technology. There are plenty of examples of companies that developed technology and then failed to capitalize on it. In video-recording technology, for instance, Ampex Corporation led the way technologically in the 1950s—but value innovators like JVC and Sony brought the technology to the mass market. There are also many examples of true value innovation occurring without new technology. Look at Starbucks coffee shops, the furniture retailer IKEA, the fashion house of Ralph Lauren, or Southwest Airlines. They are in traditional businesses, but each is able to offer new and superior value through innovative ideas and knowledge.

Value innovation can be defined as creating an unprecedented set of utilities at a lower cost. It is not about making tradeoffs, but about simultaneously pursuing both exceptional value and lower costs. It is distinct from either value creation or technology innovation. The power of value innovation is in engaging people to build collective wisdom in a constructive manner.

Value innovation is fundamentally concerned with redefining the established boundaries of a market. If you offer buyers hugely improved value, or create an unprecedented set of utilities in order to give birth to new markets, then the competition becomes unimportant. Instead of playing on the same field, you've created a new one.

Value improvements only get you so far. Value innovation enables companies to shift the productivity frontier to a new terrain. Value innovation is concerned with challenging accepted assumptions about particular markets, changing the way managers frame the strategic possibilities.

CREATING NEW MARKET SPACE

The driving force behind value innovation is the willingness of companies to create new market space.

Innovation occurs across industries, countries, and companies. These are universal forces. It is therefore less relevant to categorize organizations by their sector or geographical location. Yet if you look at strategy literature, industry boundaries are usually regarded as central—think of SWOT analysis or Michael Porter's Five Forces Framework.

To explain further, companies have tended to concentrate on differences between groups of customers. They have divided them into ever smaller and neater segments so they can customize their offerings to meet the needs of those segments.

Value innovators take a different approach. Instead of looking at differences between customers, they focus on the basic commonalities across customers. When companies create unprecedented value on those commonalities, the core of the market is pulled toward them as customers are willing to forgo their individual preferences. Value innovation desegments and collapses established market boundaries by challenging accepted and assumed market order. Unlike the strategy framework built on environmental determinism driven by competition, value innovation takes a reconstructionist view of the market, where its focus is on shaping the market by cognitive reorderings in managers' strategic thinking.

The challenge is to create new demand—what we call *market space*. New market space is about creating a company's future. Companies can continue to mine their wealth from an existing market space—that's maintenance. They can concentrate on market share. But there is something more—the act of creation. Creating new market space will become increasingly vital.

Creating new market space provides growth. There are two paths to growth. One is the mergers and acquisition path, which often leads to growth, but rarely to profitable growth. The other is organic growth, cultivated by creating new businesses. While this path is profitable and necessary, in markets where supply exceeds demand companies are often hesitant because they find it difficult to believe that they can succeed in changing things. Our research on new market space, however, has revealed six patterns or paths that companies can apply to achieve this end. They are:

- looking across alternative industries;
- looking across strategic groups within an industry;
- looking across the chain of buyers;
- looking across the buyer experience cycle;
- shifting the functional-emotional appeal of an industry;
- looking across time.

FAIR PROCESS

Another element is our concept of *fair process*. This has to do with people. Transformation requires that companies earn the intellectual and emotional commitment of their employees. To do this requires a degree of fairness in making and executing decisions. All a company's plans will come to nothing if they are not supported by employees.

If a company violates fair process, it can be devastating. British Airways lost significant ground in employee morale and customer service after it announced a cost-cutting program at a time when its profits were high and its planes were full. There was no engagement, explanation, or clarifying of expectations.

Fair process is based on the simple human need for intellectual and emotional recognition. Without fair process it can be difficult for companies to achieve even goals their people generally support.

To embrace fair process, companies must first ask themselves whether they engage people in decisions that affect them. Do they ask for input and allow people to discuss the merit of one another's ideas? Do they explain why decisions are made, and why some opinions have been overridden? And, after a decision is made, is it clearly stated so that people understand the new standards, targets, responsibilities, and penalties? The big U.S. automakers have a history of violating fair process and have paid the penalty many times over.

CASES IN POINT

The Bert Claeys Group built new market space around Belgium's movie theaters by refusing to accept common perceptions about what was a declining industry. Bert Claeys ignored long-term decline and created the world's first megaplex, with 25 screens and seating for 7,600.

Other value innovators can be largely unknown. Two examples are the Hungarian bus company NABI, which is rapidly dominating the U.S. bus market by changing the value curve of the industry, and Cirque du Soleil, the Canadian circus that has led to a redefinition of the circus industry. Cirque du Soleil collapses the two industries of theater and circus, and in doing so it leapfrogs Ringling Brothers and Barnum and Bailey circuses, opening up the entire adult audience to circus at a price several times more expensive than that of a traditional circus.

There is also the French company JCDecaux, which is the leading provider of outdoor advertising space. JCDecaux created an entirely new industry space by converting bus stops and metro stations into very desirable advertising space. Municipalities win by getting outdoor furniture that is stylish and free, while JCDecaux wins by selling the advertising spaces in these desirable prime-location city stops.

MAKING IT HAPPEN

We have created three analytical tools to help managers identify a winning business idea, whatever the market space it occupies or creates.

The *Buyer Utility Map* indicates the likelihood that customers will be attracted to a new idea. This is a matrix based on six stages of buyer experience—from how easy it is to find a product to how easy it is eventually to dispose of it—and six *customer utility levers*—from environmental friendliness to improved customer productivity. Innovations should occupy as many squares on the matrix as possible, although it is unlikely to be more than three or four.

The *Price Corridor of the Mass* identifies which price will unlock the greatest number of customers. It does this by benchmarking prices not just against similar products, but different products that fulfill the same function. For example, short-haul airlines compete not just against other airlines, but against buses, trains, and cars.

The *Business Model Guide* is a framework for calculating whether, and how, a company can deliver an innovative product or service at the targeted price. It includes options such as cost targeting and opportunities for outsourcing and partnering.

W. Chan Kim, born in Korea, and Renée Mauborgne, an American, are based at INSEAD in Fontainebleau, France. Kim is the Boston Consulting Group's Bruce D. Henderson Chair Professor of International Management, and Mauborgne is the INSEAD Distinguished Fellow and Affiliate Professor of Strategy and Management. Both previously studied and taught at the University of Michigan Business School.

Creating an Entrepreneurial Mindset

Rita Gunther McGrath and Ian C. MacMillan

Although uncertainty might cause many to freeze, it can be used to your benefit. Uncertain situations are full of new opportunities. Your task is to continuously identify high-potential business opportunities and exploit these opportunities with speed and confidence. Thus, uncertainty can become your ally, not your enemy.

ENTREPRENEURIAL LEADERSHIP: THE MOST IMPORTANT JOB

Entrepreneurial leaders are distinguished from other managers by their personal practices. These fall into three categories: setting the work climate, orchestrating opportunity-seeking, and moving particular ventures forward personally.

Climate-setting practices create a pervasive sense of urgency for everyone to work on new business initiatives. Dedicate a disproportionate share of your own time, attention, and discretionary resources to finding and supporting new business models. Gary Wendt, who drove massive growth at GE Capital, demonstrated this principle. He consistently made new business development his top priority agenda item—at every meeting and chance encounter.

Orchestrating opportunity-seeking involves removing uncertainty from your staff by clearly specifying what type of entrepreneurial opportunities are wanted. We call this "ballparking." A Swedish entrepreneur whose small company excelled at CAD/CAM technology defined his company's entrepreneurial playing field as "50 to the power of 4." This meant he was interested in proposals that had the potential to deliver 50 million Swedish kroner ($5 million) in profits, by capturing 50% market share, with 50% margins in at least 50 countries. The logic was to seek opportunities where he solved a real problem for enough customers so that he could capture the lion's share of a defensible global market without having to deal with competition from multinational firms. This gave his people scope, but also kept them focused on those opportunities where he felt that his company could build a strong position.

Specific hands-on management practices recognize that the quest for insight is the single most important source of competitive differentiation a management team can bring to an organization. For example, Robert Brown and Linda Mason, founders of Bright Horizons child care centers, capitalized on an insight that allowed them to create an attractive business model in a traditionally unattractive industry. Instead of focusing on individual families' needs for child care, the couple instead redefined their customer as corporations. In 15 years, the venture grew from a concept to a thriving business with over 340 centers.

ESTABLISHING THE ENTREPRENEURIAL FRAME

The entrepreneurial frame defines your goals. The idea is to push you and your team to undertake those initiatives that go beyond mere incremental improvement to really make a difference. Framing has two parts: first, a definition of success; and second, an articulation of strategic direction.

The process for establishing a frame involves working through the following questions:

1 If you were to do something in the next three to five years that you, your boss, and your company's investors would regard as a major win, what would this look like?

2 What is the minimum amount of profit you need from your new ventures (at maturity) to make a difference to your business? What rate of growth must you sustain?

3 What is the increase in profitability you need to achieve in the next three to five years?

4 What return on investment are you seeking?

Next, articulate strategic direction by establishing screening criteria that are consistent with your ballparking definition. Any proposal that has "screen-out" criteria results in "dropping it dead." "Screen-in" criteria represent characteristics that can be described as "the more the merrier"—the more of these characteristics, the more attractive the opportunity. Think through the following questions:

1 What were the least desirable businesses that you have been involved with? What characteristics made them undesirable? What does this tell you about areas to avoid in the future?

2 What made a particular opportunity very rewarding for you? What does this tell you about areas to pursue in the future?

3 Integrate these statements into a list of (about) ten screen-out statements and ten screen-in statements that capture your experience. A screen out might be: "The opportunity would consume too much time from our key people." A screen-in might be: "This is an attractive market in which we already have a strong position." Try to make your screening statements as specific to your business as possible.

Eventually, your goal is to have about ten screen-in and ten screen-out statements that the organization can agree accurately reflect the types of businesses that are desired and not desired.

CREATING A WELL-STOCKED OPPORTUNITY REGISTER

An opportunity register is an inventory of potentially attractive new business opportunities. The idea is that at any point in time you'll have a rich set of potential opportunities to choose from, rather than having only the choice of those that managed to survive a corporate winnowing process.

Two techniques are useful here. The first is called consumption chain analysis. The consumption chain is used to map the customer's entire set of experiences with your product or service offering. It begins with the trigger event or circumstance that leads a customer to be aware of a need, and continues through all the steps involved in their being a customer of yours. Any link in the chain has differentiation potential which you can uncover by probing into the customer's experiences at each link.

The second technique is attribute mapping. This captures how well your offering is appealing to customers' needs at the moment. Start simply, by identifying an offering and an important customer segment. Then analyze the data to see where you could enhance positive attributes and eliminate negative ones.

By using these two techniques, you will typically discover more good ideas than you can execute with the resources you have. The challenge then is to winnow them down to the very best, while bearing in mind that you don't want to overemphasize either existing businesses or new ones.

CREATING FOCUS USING REAL OPTIONS REASONING

Like investing in a financial option, real options reasoning involves making small investments that give you the right to make a decision later. The idea is to limit your downside exposure until the upside potential of the opportunity is demonstrated. In conjunction with limiting risk, an options approach allows you to create focus and strategic alignment across your portfolio of initiatives. The portfolio addresses whether the market is certain or not, and whether the technological environment is certain or not.

Map the initiatives that your firm is pursuing on the chart. The mapping should reflect your strategy. If your strategy is to grow the existing business you will want more emphasis on the lower left hand section. If your strategy is exploration, you'll want more options. Firms usually learn from this exercise that they are taking on too many projects and that the projects that are in the pipeline are not consistent with their strategies. One way to fix this is to allocate resources to different sections of the map before projects are approved, then make them compete with similar projects for resources.

PROMOTING ADAPTIVE EXECUTION BY DISCOVERY-DRIVEN PLANNING

Discovery-driven planning is a plan to learn, not to show that you had all the answers when you wrote the plan. The technique requires the interaction of five processes:
1 determining the frame (objectives) at the level of a project;
2 establishing competitive and market benchmarks;
3 defining operating specifications;
4 documenting assumptions;
5 establishing key milestones.

In uncertain environments, conventional planning makes no sense. Instead, plan with discipline to the next major milestone, then pause and re-plan as new information becomes available.

- Dedicate a disproportionate share of time, attention, and discretionary resources to finding and supporting new business.
- Push yourself and your team to launch initiatives that go beyond mere incremental improvement to really make a difference.
- Seek ten screen-in and ten screen-out statements to accurately reflect types of businesses desired (screened-in) and not desired (screened-out).
- Use the "consumption chain" to map the customer's entire set of experiences with your product or service offering.
- Use "attribute mapping" to capture how well your offering is appealing to customers' needs at the moment.
- Limit your downside exposure to a new initiative until the upside potential of the opportunity is demonstrated.

In all these techniques, the emphasis is on the twin activities of pursuing opportunity while remaining focused.

—•—

Rita Gunther McGrath is an associate professor at Columbia Business School, formerly a senior technology manager for the City of New York. Her research focuses on economic transformations through entrepreneurship and new technologies. She publishes widely in both scholarly and practitioner publications and has won several awards, including the Academy of Management Review "best paper" award. She teaches and provides consulting to a variety of organizations.

Ian C. MacMillan is academic director of the Sol C. Snider entrepreneurial research programs at the Wharton School, University of Pennsylvania, and also the Fred Sullivan professor of management. He was previously a chemical engineer and gained wide experience in everything from gold and uranium mines to the South African Atomic Energy Board. His articles have appeared in many prestigious journals such as the *Harvard Business Review*. Together, they coauthored *The Entrepreneurial Mindset* (Harvard Business School Press, 2000).

Using New Scientific Thinking to Create a New Society

Margaret J. Wheatley

What I noticed early on, was that—for all the great efforts, for all the human energy expended, and for all the money spent—true organization change rarely succeeded.

I'd ask top consultants to tell me what their major successes were. It took a long time to get any kind of response, and their replies were quite shallow. That told me the paradigm about managing major organizations was dead; I was convinced that I did not want to spend my career doing more of the same kind of work that others in the field of management were doing. Then I read James Gleick's book about chaos (*Chaos: Making a New Science*) around 1989; it triggered whole new thoughts in me. I started connecting my liberal arts background—my interest in combining history, philosophy, and science—to the field of management. By 1990 I was writing *Leadership and the New Science*, and, upon its publication, I found that people were very receptive to my ideas. Their interest continues and grows.

If we don't change the way we manage business in the next ten years, we're dead.

The terrorist attacks that started in September 2001 are really "kindergarten," in terms of the kinds of changes we'll have to deal with in the future. It forces a major question: How do you behave as a leader when you don't have control over your own business? Think of it: the airline/hotel/car rental/travel industries have been socked— no matter how well they were managed in the past—by terrorists! Who had that prospect in their current business plans? More and more changes of this magnitude will affect managers in the future; we will all be facing extreme uncertainty and vulnerability. And it will not matter how good your planning systems are; you will have to lead under conditions of mega-change.

So the issue to focus on, to learn how to adjust to, is *change*. Managers are going to have to learn how to deal with exponential change, with cataclysmic events that affect all aspects of their work world.

Managers traditionally thought that understanding and managing systems was a luxury field of study. Not any more. Managers will only survive—their businesses will only survive—if they have developed, top to bottom, a trusting and cohesive workforce, people who can rapidly adjust organizational systems to unpredicted events. This means that everyone in the enterprise will need new levels of independence, flexibility, adaptability; and everyone must enrich their comprehension that every organization is part of an interconnected world. If you look at what's happening to businesses in light of recent terrorism and its mammoth impact, it's not surprising that a recent news story noted that companies were now preparing five different annual budgets, with the suggestion that (depending on events) one of those budgets might only be 40% accurate. *And that may be the best any business can do!* For those in management, business schools and corporate trainers will have to come up with courses which plainly don't exist today. We need courses with titles like "How to Lead When You Can't Be a Hero" or "How to Lead in Complete Uncertainty." Those are the new skills for managing in the next century.

How can companies best promote enterprises that are profitable and good places for people to work? Even the question isn't quite right.

That question comes from a simpler time. Wouldn't it be great if that were the *only* major problem we faced in this new century? We must face the fact that we are living in an age where people can do great work, generate profits, and be quite pleased with the overall corporate culture—and *still* be critically challenged by enormous uncertainty. Managing a business is no longer like managing chess, even three-dimensional chess. You can't anticipate all the moves you are going to have to make in the future; there will be too much change. If anything, the game for tomorrow's manager is the Asian game of "Go!", where you can only determine your next move based on what your opponent has just done, and the range of options is limitless.

Yet this new reality presents managers with both challenge and opportunity. One need not become permanently depressed, because what exponential and unpredictable change demands is a greater appreciation of the human spirit and a greater reliance on human creativity. Managers need to focus on this and never forget it.

Look at any organization today and it's *people* who matter the most. I was touched when the C.E.O. of the Morgan Stanley financial powerhouse said, quite emotionally, that he was awestruck after the demise of the World Trade Center buildings on September 11, 2001. Unbelievably, out of 3,700 employees who occupied 25 floors of one of the buildings, only *six* were lost in the disaster. The C.E.O., realizing what true and permanent loss his firm might have had if more had perished, exclaimed, "This is a miracle!" He went on to extol how important the human element is to the management of the global financial services firm. To me, this is a new dimension to Morgan Stanley—and a new dimension to management, a new *emphasis* in management. Machines and computers are great for what they do, but they are linear by design; they can deal with mega-change in one way. Only the human element, spirited and creative, can face change head-on—*and adapt*. Managers who willingly acknowledge this and enhance their mastery of human systems have the best chance of surviving and prospering in the future.

Margaret J. Wheatley is a graduate of the University of Rochester, New York, and University College, London). A Peace Corps volunteer in Korea, she was an educator and administrator from 1966–1973 before earning a doctorate at Harvard. She worked as a consultant in Cambridge, Massachusetts, until 1989.

Placing Bets in a World of Uncertainty

W. Brian Arthur

W. Brian Arthur is Citibank Professor at the Santa Fe Institute, and currently serves on its board. From 1983 to 1996 he was Dean and Virginia Morrison Professor of Economics and Population Studies at Stanford University. His work on increasing returns won him a Guggenheim Fellowship in 1987 and the Schumpeter Prize in Economics in 1990. Arthur is also one of the pioneers of the new science of complexity. His main interests are the economics of high technology; how business evolves in an era of high technology; cognition in the economy; and financial markets. In this article, he discusses the tension between complexity and uncertainty in our world today.

For about 300 years we've had a reductionist version of science. We've been looking in finer and finer detail—organisms, then organs, then cells, then organelles, and DNA—each time understanding mechanisms. At the same time, there have always been people curious about how some of these elements come together to make patterns. Rather than taking larger patterns and saying that they are made of elements, it means looking from the bottom up, not the top down, and asking how these elements make a difference.

In the early 1980s we all got desktop workstations, and it turned out for the first time that in physics or mathematics, or for that matter economics, we could start to look at these elements coming together and forming patterns. The elements might be dipoles or atoms or stars and galaxies, but each element is reacting to the aggregate pattern that those elements together create.

Most earlier science, and certainly economics in particular, just looked at static equilibrium patterns—for example, what prices and quantities of goods on the market would be held in equilibrium by the other prices and quantities of goods?; what strategies could you or I adopt if we're running companies?; where can I change my strategy and improve against the pattern your strategies are creating?

Complexity is about patterns coming into existence. It's not about equilibria. If you just drop water in a tray, you're only going to get one outcome. But if you polish the tray and put a thin film of water on it, you get a known linearity, or positive feedback, because some molecules under surface tension attract others, but gravity will tend to pull them apart again. Conduct that experiment again under identical conditions and the beads may gather in a slightly different pattern. What makes complexity interesting is that these interacting elements may settle into different patterns. In complexity theory, we're interested in the whole idea of how patterns come into being.

THE EL FAROL PROBLEM

In my own area, economics, I began to apply this pattern formation approach to forecasting models. There are a lot of examples in economic systems. The stock market is one where your behavior—whether you buy or sell Intel or Cisco—depends very much on what you think Intel or Cisco stock will be worth in three days' or three months' or in a year's time. Similarly, you buy a house based partly on what you think it might be worth in 10 years' time.

There's a bar in Santa Fe called El Farol. On Wednesday nights they used to have Irish music, but the bar gets terribly stuffy and crowded if too many people go. Imagine that 100 people are thinking about going to El Farol. The bar only holds 60 comfortably, so each person is trying to forecast how many other people will be there that evening. You have 100 people separately and without communication trying to figure out if they are going to go to El Farol that evening. If each one of them thinks it will be fewer than 60, then they will show up. If each one is expecting more than 60, then they will not go.

Now let's imagine that nearly everybody is forecasting that it will be crowded tonight. Nearly everyone won't go, so that will negate that forecast. Let's say that 85 people are expecting fewer than 40 to show up. Then those 85 will show up, which will negate the fewer than 40. So, if people have similar forecasts—and economics is built on this notion: that we all will do the same thing under the same circumstances— those similar forecasts will negate each other. For me, the theoretical problem was: How does one form forecasts in a situation where, if we all form the same forecast, that forecast would be immediately negated?

NAVIGATING THROUGH THE FOG

Now apply this line of thinking to business. Imagine all the C.E.O.s in a certain area are all going into wireless technologies or proteomics or genomics—something trendy. All 20 of these people are on the prow of the ship. There is a kind of fog of technology into which they are heading. No one knows how well the technology is going to work, or who else is going to be in the game or who their competitors are going to be. They don't know how their technology is going to work. They don't know whether the public or other businesses will be interested. They don't quite know what the regulatory atmosphere will be. Each has ideas about all of these factors, but none of these is particularly well known. All of that creates a fog of technology. This is the world of indeterminacy in which all high-tech entrepreneurs live.

If technology C.E.O.s are *not* confused they aren't being truly smart. The El Farol problem comes into play when the problem gets serious and it's about more than going to a bar at night. When you're talking high-tech the problem can be whether or not to build a fabrication plant at $4 billion a go.

As the ship moves forward through the fog the C.E.O.s can start to see the outlines of a city. But actually the city is created, or the future is created, by the actions the other C.E.O.s are going to take, and those are predicated on their beliefs. Each C.E.O. is trying to form beliefs, forecasts, or, more generally, a guiding vision about a situation that is, in turn, forming from the visions of others.

PLACE YOUR BETS

To illustrate the dynamics of decision making in this context of uncertainty I created a metaphor I called "the casino of technology." Imagine that all technology strategizing takes place in a big casino. There are gaming tables everywhere, and the Larry Ellisons and Bill Haseltines of the world are all wandering from table to table wondering which game to join.

Imagine there is a new game forming. Let's say it's "broadband" or "digital banking." Bill Haseltine runs Human Genome Sciences. Suppose he's the first to the table and he says, "I want to play this game." The croupier says, "Fine, Mr. Haseltine. You can play."

Haseltine says, "Well, how much will it be to ante up?" The croupier says, "For you it will be $4 billion." Haseltine replies, "Fine, who else will be playing?" The croupier says, "We do not know until they arrive." So Haseltine says, "OK. What products are we going to be playing with?" The croupier says, "We do not know until we see them." Haseltine asks, "How well will they work?" The croupier says, "No one knows that until the future." Haseltine replies, "What are the rules?" The croupier says, "The rules will be formed when people sit down."

Haseltine has to decide whether to play or not. If he waits until the game is fully in progress, it will be too late. Under a condition like that, whether you take very smart people like Haseltine or Bill Gates or Craig Barrett or anyone else, there is no correct answer. So what a C.E.O. in a high-tech venture has to do is figure out scenarios or figure out backup strategies.

I think the reason I am so interested in the El Farol problem is that it's starting to make sense. El Farol turned out to be the simplest situation that I could cook up that had that kind of diabolical twist to it—everyone thinking the same way and therefore negating each other.

One theme that emerges from this line of thought is that any economy is driven a great deal by what economists call expectations—somewhere in between forecasts and visions, if you like, or notions about the future. Sometimes these visions can be self-fulfilling; at other times they can be self-negating. Self-fulfilling could be positive or negative. If everybody is open, the system stays open and free trade flows. Then we're expecting that to keep going and it becomes self-fulfilling. But if something goes badly wrong, people then are expecting bad times, and then things get closed and shut down and that can become self-fulfilling. You can switch between those two regimes.

This essay was adapted from an interview undertaken with Mr. Arthur by Peter Leyden, Knowledge Developer at Global Business Network (www.gbn.com). The publishers gratefully acknowledge the support of Global Business Network in making these ideas and insights available.

Leading Managers to Adapt and Grow

Warren Bennis

Warren Bennis is practically synonymous with leadership. A student and protégé of Douglas McGregor, he was invited by McGregor in 1959 to establish a department of organization studies at MIT's Sloan School of Management. After serving in administrative positions in the 1960s and 1970s—as provost of SUNY Buffalo and president of the University of Cincinnati—he returned to research and teaching in 1979, joining the faculty at the University of Southern California, where he continues to pursue his groundbreaking work on learning, leadership, organizational life, and personal development. He is the author of dozens of articles and over 30 books on leadership, including *Leaders*, *Greeks and Geezers*, *Managing the Dream*, and *On Becoming a Leader*. Here he reflects on the factors that have most profoundly influenced this thinking, as well as on the qualities that people and organizations must nurture in order to create meaningful work.

Like everyone else, I'd have to say that there's no one thing that has influenced my thinking. And that's probably true of life. In my own case, I think there were several factors that came out along the way and that, in looking back, seem like a set of eccentric precursors instead of kind of a singular willful, purposeful, I-know-what-I-want-to-do path. I'll start off from how I grew up. There were giants in the air. It was during World War II and these iconic figures dominated the world—some for great evil and some for great good. We happened to be on the side of great good, when you think about Churchill and Roosevelt. I'm reminded of how grateful we should be for their examples of leadership and how wary we should be of dictators and demagogues like the Hitlers and Mussolinis. In those days, very like as recently as September 11, 2001, we turned our eyes to public figures.

This was true when I was a young person. As I was born in 1925, it was very clear that the Depression and World War II were influential in my development. Those of us growing up in those formative years saw horrors with Mussolini, Hitler and, later on, with Stalin. Listening to Hitler giving his speeches during the 1930s before World War II was very, very scary.

So, I grew up at a time when you saw how influential leaders could be and how influential their activities, their political entities, their organizations could be—potentially virulent and toxic; how much pathogen could be spread by one person and how many healthy white cells by the other. That was just part of it, part of the zeitgeist, part of the era. It was very important, though largely unconscious to us.

There were other things—of a more "micro," interpersonal nature. I happened to go to a college where the president was one of the men who laid the foundation for our field of organizational behavior and leadership. That was Douglas McGregor, who was the president of the college that I went to and had come from MIT. Well, it was no accident that I also became a college president and also did my Ph.D. at MIT. He was very interested in group dynamics and leadership—wrote a lot about it—and certainly the "McGregorian chants," as I called them, were very influential. Being at MIT, being in Cambridge, Massachusetts, during the 1950s and 1960s certainly influenced my thinking. I was fascinated by how, under certain conditions, groups can do the most creative, the most spectacular things and reach the most extraordinary heights of achievement—if they can create the right conditions for it. *Organizing Genius*, for example, was really the fruit, the result of those early years of thinking about groups. I became very interested to see how organizations, where we spend at least a third of our life, if not more, can be less toxic, more healthy, and provide more opportunities for people's growth, so that they can reach the frontiers of human possibility.

Three words leaders have trouble dealing with: "I don't know." I think good leadership will often start with questions whose answer is: "I don't know, but we're going to find out."

Even before September 11, we were living in a world characterized by mystery, doubt, complexity, uncertainty, and chaos. Think about the transformation from an analog to a digital society. In 1989, for example, there were only 400 users of the Web; now, as Shakespeare wrote in the 16th century, "we are a girdled globe." Before September 11 there were something like forty ongoing border disputes around the world. Globalization. Disruptive technologies. People are going to have to deal with doubt and uncertainty.

Organizations, organizational leadership, and organizational culture will have to be people factories—generating, nourishing, and nurturing terrific talent. They have to be education factories where that talent will be continually going to school. They will have to be led by leaders with enough emotional intelligence and cognitive capacity to be able to hold two divergent ideas in their heads at one time. I think those are going to be the critical aspects.

I'm going to add from my own work what I consider to be four critical aspects of leadership, which came out of a study about leadership and learning. I think they're important. And I want to argue that these four factors, which I think are critical for leading in this new world, are context- and culture-free. One is the adaptive capacity, which I think is probably the *sine qua non*, absolutely the most essential and central aspect of leadership in this environment of complexity and turbo-change. The adaptive capacity has a lot of things under it. It means a sense of resilience, hardiness, and creativity. It means seizing opportunities. It means learning learning. The second critical ingredient is the capacity to engage followers in shared meaning—to align the stars around a common, meaningful goal. Not just any old goal. Think Henry V at Agincourt: "a mission from God." Third, leaders are really going to have to spend a long time—and it's a continual process—finding out who they themselves are: learning their own voice, learning how they affect other people, learning a great deal about emotional intelligence. And finally, leaders will have to rely on a moral compass, a set of principles, a belief system, a set of convictions. Every good leader is going to have to—one way or another—learn these capacities. Now, I do think there are contextual and cultural factors, but I'm saying that, regardless of culture and context, these four factors are essential. They are necessary, but not sufficient. For example, if you're interested in leading a ballet company, you must know something about choreography and about the art world. There's a whole ecology around ballet, around science, around being a baseball manager. Nevertheless, these four factors are, across the board, essential, whether talking about Shakespeare or the failure of Ivester at Coca-Cola.

Managers need to ask themselves: Do you really want to lead? Are you aware of the sacrifices, the time demands, the complexity? Do you have a true commitment to abandon your ego to the talents of others? Do you love what you're doing? Do you enjoy trying to understand the social etiquette of bureaucracy? Do you really enjoy engaging others?

Any great place to work can be profitable. In fact, the most profitable *are* great places to work. I remember a former president of MIT once said to me, without a trace of grandiosity, that MIT "has had the habits of success." There's something about being successful that tends to perpetuate itself. I think that what will make a workplace great is when people really feel down deep that the company is on their side, that they will be treated equitably and fairly, that they are being given many opportunities for self-development and organizational development, where people are encouraged to "talk truth to power." If they're going to be putting in a lot of work at a place, not only do people need to have a license to tell the truth, they want to be in a place where they really feel they're going to be learning. People want to feel nurtured, that they're growing, and that there are enormous developmental opportunities available to them. To use my friend, Charles Handy's, book title, I think we're all "hungry spirits." Deep down, we all want to make a difference; if there's no meaning at work, people will check their hearts at the door.

Really Leading: Leadership That Is Authentic, Conscious, and Effective

Debashis Chatterjee

The leadership crisis is a crisis of perception. Imagine that you have to lead in a world that is vastly different not only from what you think it is, but also from what you think it can be. This world is changing faster than our thoughts can grasp. Consider that by 2037 only eight of the top 100 of the world's corporations are likely to be based in the United States. Today our timeworn notions are being seriously challenged. Consider what three corporate leaders have to say on the nature of the changing business environment:

- Leo Burke, former director of Motorola University, believes that "the future has already happened. However, this future is unevenly distributed."
- Michael Eisner, the C.E.O. of Disney, claims his organization brings a new product to the market every five minutes!
- Goran Lindahl, former president and C.E.O. of ABB, says, "Space is intellectual, space is not just physical space. Space is an environment that cultivates strong and useful ideas."

Reality as we know it is reshaping itself in countless nonlinear ways. Our thought-based linear models and plans are inadequate to contain this complex reality. What we need today are leaders with a quality of consciousness that can find coherence in this complexity. We need leaders with greater capability as well as "cope-ability."

THE THREE PARADOXES OF LEADERSHIP

Pursuing Stability at a Time of Increasing Change. The first great paradox of leadership is that leaders must provide for stability in times of change. Change can be perceived only against an unchanging background.. Each epoch of change has its unyielding frameworks, paradigms, and world-views.

Leaders shape reality. They do so by combining change and stability. This involves the synthesis of two innate human competencies: creation and construction. Whereas creation is a living and changing process, construction is a structure of stability that controls this process. Creation is multidimensional and dynamic; construction is sequential, progressing step by step. Any human organization has both a creative and a constructive aspect. Whereas the energy and vision of its members constitute the creative element of an organization, the functional division of the organization into design, manufacturing, and marketing constitutes the constructive element. Creation provides the organization with its core impulse, or the spirit of enterprise. Construction provides the tools and mechanisms for channeling impulse into activity.

During change, leaders have to challenge obsolete constructs, structures, systems, and procedures that sap the vital creative spirit of societies and organizations.

Paradoxically, leaders have to clarify a consistent set of values or principles to make the process of change sustainable. Leaders have to ground themselves in certainty before they can lead people to an uncertain world of possibilities.

How do organizations on the bleeding edge of change maintain the integrity of a vital and creative organization while juggling with fleeting forms? The consulting firm, McKinsey, binds the unique spirit of enterprise of individual consultants with the integral purpose of the organization. McKinsey partners have developed "T-shaped" consultants. The vertical spike symbolizes the unique depth of expertise that each consultant brings, whereas the horizontal bar of the T stands for the need to integrate their expertise with the generalist perspective of the entire organization. Rajat Gupta, the managing director of McKinsey, says he builds a culture of flexibility and change without undermining the strong set of values governing McKinsey's ethos.

Handling and Combining Urgent and Emerging Issues. The second great paradox of leadership is that leaders must develop the capacity to engage the urgent with the emergent. Change forces us to allow the urgent to dominate us: quarterly reports, market share, and tangible return on investment become paramount. In this paranoia, the emergent is often lost. Yet the emergent is the invisible face of a corporation's current reality. Roberto Goizueta, the former (and significant) C.E.O. of Coca-Cola, always believed that the future of the soft-drinks industry could be conceived as an emergent reality of infinite openings and possibilities. When the former Soviet Union was in political turmoil, Coke sent marketing experts to configure the country's emergent reality. Ed McCracken, the chairman and C.E.O. of Silicon Graphics, views emergence through the metaphor of farming. He says, "I grew up on a farm in Iowa, and I really appreciate the farming mentality, because you work really hard—and then you let the weather happen."

The urgent presents itself in tangible shape and form, whereas the emergent is subtler in its appearance. Leaders need to pre-sense emergent reality. In times of information overload leaders suffer from acute attention deficiency. They need to cultivate reflective moments in their work lives in order to restore the quality of attentiveness and see reality with greater clarity. A story from the Zen Buddhist tradition illustrates the point:

> Three Zen masters are walking across a field. The youngest among them notices a flag tied to a pole. He draws the attention of his two companions and says, "Look how the flag moves." The middle-aged master pats the younger one on the back and says, "My boy, can't you see it is not the flag that moves, it is the wind that moves." The old master who has been listening in silence softly says, "If you have attention enough you will see that it is neither the flag nor the wind that moves, it is the mind that moves."

Mutually Reinferring Knowledge and Action. The third great paradox of leader-ship is that leaders have to hold the tension of knowledge and action at the same time. The contemporary explosion of knowledge has far outstripped our capacity for action. Leaders today have to ask two fundamental questions:

1 Is this knowledge relevant?
2 Can this knowledge be put into practice and, if so, how?

Leaders need to operate through a framework of consistent values by which they can capture relevant knowledge and provide appropriate structures and tools to convert knowledge into action.

Knowledge is internal motion; action is external motion. Traditionally, organizations could rely on the knowledge of the few at the top, who would strategize and plan for the actions of those below. Today an organization needs to be omniscient to be omnipotent. Organizational intelligence, which is simply knowledge-processing capacity, now needs to be distributed all along the organization's network in order for the organization to grow capacity for action. Ed McCracken of Silicon Graphics thinks that an Information Age company has to get as much connection as possible up to the nodes of the organization. This enables the company to have faster access to organizational intelligence and greater capacity for decision making at the grassroots.

MAKING IT HAPPEN

How do conscious leaders make things happen? First, consciousness is not just about being aware of reality, it's also about influencing reality. This is truly an effective and integral view of leadership. Conscious leadership is a process that rests on two fundamental principles:

1 the principle of integration;
2 the principle of transformation.

Integration in the current climate of change implies *making the complex coherent.* Much of the complexity in the workplace comes from two sources: lack of attention and the loss of meaning. Leaders can restore lost attention through engagement with the minds and hearts of people they choose to serve. True integration is the orchestration of thought, feeling, and action. It is the process of connecting strategic intent with tools and techniques that evolve from people's own ingenuity and innovation. Loss of meaning occurs when leaders are unable to connect between the values of the organization and values-in-action, between knowledge infrastructure of the organization and its performance system.

As a leader, it can help to consider how the competing needs of the task, team, and individual overlap.

- Achieving the **task** builds the team and satisfies the individuals.
- **If the team needs are not met** then the team lacks cohesiveness and efficiency, performance of the task is impaired and individual satisfaction is reduced.
- **If individual needs are not met** the team will lack cohesiveness and performance of the task can again be impaired.

Often leaders see charisma as being the defining skill of leadership. The difficulty is that charisma is frequently ineffective or inappropriate: it often dominates people and creates a reliance on the leader, instead of breeding initiative. Developing a successful workforce requires *empowering* leadership. This can be developed by fostering:

- a belief in constant learning rather than assumed mastery;
- the development of high self-esteem in others;
- a willingness to ask questions, admit weaknesses, and listen to answers;
- strong interpersonal skills, including an appreciation of other people and sensitivity to individuals;
- an ability to engender trust, build relationships, and inspire others; and the capacity to trust others;
- the ability and desire to develop leadership in others;
- the capacity to handle criticism by listening and drawing out people's concerns;
- a capacity to develop an effective vision for the future;
- an approach that possesses, values, and nurtures innovation and initiative;
- the ability to communicate well at every level;
- integrity and trustworthiness;
- mentoring, coaching, and counseling skills.

Transformation happens through sustained and sustainable change. It is a principle that creates so much synergy in a system that change happens spontaneously. Imagine an organization that captures relevant information from a swarming sea of data and quickly converts it into knowledge, creating one seamless flow of intelligence. That kind of organization must have the integrity and fluidity of a conscious system like the human body. When a certain part of the human body is in distress, the entire body's intelligence is activated to meet the contingency. Transformation happens through the unity of intelligence. In a human system leaders can bring about such unity of intelligence by trusting and acknowledging the essential magnificence of the human factor. A human being is a creation of life and not a construction of a machine-world. Conscious leaders therefore know that a human performs best as a factor of creation rather than as a factor of production. In this pursuit conscious leaders can do no more to lead people to their essential wholeness.

Conscious leaders learn to hold together the coordinates of stability and change, the urgent with the emergent, and knowledge with action. Authentic leadership is about restoring people to their full potential. Leaders accomplish this through the principles of integration and transformation. Conscious leaders lead people toward themselves.

Debashis Chatterjee is a professor of business at the Indian Institute of Management in Lucknow. He is the author of the internationally acclaimed book, *Leading Consciously* (Butterworth Heinemann, 1998). A Fulbright Scholar and Harvard Business School's thought leader, Chatterjee has taken his revolutionary leadership insights into four continents of the world. He has been a trainer in several *Fortune* 100 Companies and has taught at the Center for Public Leadership at Harvard University.

How to Walk on the Leading Edge without Falling off the Cliff

Judith A. Neal

The complexity of the business world today is astounding. Nothing is predictable. The rules of the game are changing. Just when you think you've figured out how to have a competitive advantage, a competitor develops a new technology. Just when you think you've found the right motivation tool, the values in your workforce seem to shift. Just when you think you've found the right geographical area for the expansion of your internationalization efforts, political turmoil erupts.

Yet some people seem to have an uncanny knack for knowing what's going to happen before it unfolds. They're able to create new rules for the game instead of following the rules everyone else follows. They're able to plan a strategy that seems absurd to most people at first, and is later called brilliant when it's successful. They are a part of an unusual breed of leaders called edgewalkers.

An edgewalker is someone who walks between two worlds. In ancient cultures each tribe or village had a shaman or medicine man. This was the person who walked into the invisible world to get information, guidance, and healing for members of the tribe. This was one of the most important roles in the village. Without a shaman the tribe would be at the mercy of unseen gods and spirits, the vagaries of the cosmos. The skill of walking between the worlds hasn't died out, in fact it's even more relevant today. Organizations that will thrive in the 21st century will embrace and nurture edgewalkers. Because of their unique skills, they are the bridge-builders linking and facilitating different approaches, strategies, and techniques.

WALKING ON THE LEADING EDGE
Five key skills form the hallmark of an edgewalker:
- visionary consciousness
- multicultural responsiveness
- intuitive sensitivity
- risk-taking confidence
- self-awareness

Visionary Consciousness. Edgewalkers begin with *visionary consciousness*. All their other skills are in service of a sense of mission about something greater than themselves. They feel called to make a difference in the world. The visionary skills arise out of a strong sense of values and integrity. Often these values are developed through some kind of painful experience or loss, and the edgewalker becomes committed to helping other people who may be going through similar kinds of experiences. Typically, the edgewalkers have gone through a major personal or career change that requires them to develop new skills that were never needed previously.

Edgewalkers are the consummate integrators of seemingly unrelated ideas, skills, and fields.

Multicultural Responsiveness. Edgewalkers must have strong *multicultural responsiveness.* They're bilingual in the sense that they can understand the nuances of different worlds or cultures. They span conventional boundaries and act as translators. Edgewalkers know how to pick up on subtle cues that are different from their own. They pay minute attention to people different from themselves and have an open, warm curiosity about people from other cultures. They look for commonalities more than differences, and they want to know more about the worlds of others.

Intuitive Sensitivity. Edgewalkers have strong *intuitive sensitivity.* They're natural futurists. Because they're avid readers they are constantly integrating information from many sources and looking for underlying themes and patterns. Like the shamans of old, they've learned to pay attention to subtle, perhaps invisible, signs of potential change. They have an uncanny knack of making the right decisions, often taking action that seems counterintuitive to others. But when asked how they knew what to do in a particular situation, they have difficulty explaining. They reply, "I just 'knew'." Intuitive skills are gained through the practice of deep listening. When listening to others, edgewalkers listen as much for the unsaid as the said. They also look for coincidences, patterns, or synchronicities that might provide clues to guide them in their decision making.

Risk-taking Confidence. Another strong skill that edgewalkers display is the skill of calculated *risk-taking confidence.* Edgewalkers have a strong sense of adventure and experimentation. They're always attracted to the next new thing. Like entrepreneurs, edgewalkers are easily bored with stability and are attracted to what's over the horizon. They're constantly asking what's next and trying to figure out how to be part of it. Because they're able to walk in two worlds, the world of practicality and the world of creativity, the risks they take to jump into the next new thing are based on information and intuition. Having a clear vision guided by strong values helps the edgewalker take risks that might not make sense to others.

Self-awareness. The most important edgewalker skill is that of *self-awareness.* A principle that edgewalkers understand is that each person is a microcosm of the whole. Leaders who are edgewalkers know that if they're experiencing a vision or dream or hunger, it's most likely arising in others as well. The challenge for the edgewalker is to find others who have the same passion and to work together to make a difference. Leaders who are edgewalkers have a strong sense of being connected to something greater than themselves.

These five skills can be taught. However, the leaders who tend to learn best strongly value their own personal development and have low control needs.

AVOIDING POTENTIAL PITFALLS

Edgewalkers can often get too far ahead of the pack. If this happens, they lose their credibility and the opportunity to influence others to do creative work. It's nice to have someone say you're ahead of your time, but there are few rewards for being too far out there. The most successful edgewalkers can remain in the real world and can remember established language and values so they can be a bridge to new ideas. For this reason, you should:

1 Watch for signs that you may be getting too far out on the edge; if this seems to be happening, revisit your own past experience, current priorities, and future aspirations.
2 When you have a new idea that you want to implement, talk to people who are likely to disagree with you or try to block you.
3 Create relationships with people who may provide a good reality check.
4 Have patience with people who don't want to move as fast as you do; take time to build relationships with them and specifically ask for their support.
5 Cultivate the skill of honoring people who disagree with you; listen for any pearls of wisdom they have to offer.

If you feel blocked at every turn by people committed to the status quo, consider finding a different organization to work for, or even going out on your own. Being an edgewalker can feel very lonely. Connect with other edgewalkers for support and inspiration.

EDGEWALKERS IN ACTION

There are many interesting examples of people that successfully walk the leading edge.

Tom Aageson, the former executive director of Aid to Artisans, is now an independent museum consultant. When Tom turned 50 he was a highly successful executive at the Mystic Museum in Connecticut. For his birthday he went on a week's retreat to contemplate the rest of his life. He realized that his mission was to do whatever he could to eradicate poverty in the world. That led him to a position as the executive director at Aid to Artisans, which helps artists and craftspeople in developing countries to design and market products that respect their cultures and improve their economic situation.

Bill Catucci is the executive vice president and group executive for Equifax and former C.E.O. of AT&T Canada. When Bill first came to work for AT&T Canada, the company was losing a significant amount of money. His first act was to send a check for $75 to the home of every employee, saying that this wasn't much, but it was a token of appreciation for what they had already contributed to the company, he looked forward to working with them to turn the company around, and there would be more where that came from if they were successful. The company became successful and people were rewarded well.

John Lumsden is the C.E.O. of Metserve in New Zealand. John is originally from Scotland and served as an executive in Canada for a number of years; he's truly learned how to walk in different cultural worlds. Each month at Metserve there's an orientation for new employees that begins with a Maori welcoming ceremony. John holds regular "advances" (as opposed to retreats) for his management team, at which people spend time reflecting on deeper questions of life and work.

Jennifer Cash O'Donnell is director of organizational strategy and professional development for AT&T's Asia-Pacific group in China. Walking between the worlds of operations and organizational development, she helps AT&T achieve great results through a focus on human relationships and team-building, using Barry Heerman's Team Spirit process. Her success at AT&T Solutions with this team-based program led to her promotion to the directorship in Asia. This provides her with yet another opportunity to be an edgewalker.

To make your journey:

- Write mission and values statements for the work you want to do in the world.
- Read professional material in fields that are unfamiliar to you.
- Listen carefully to what people and the world have to say.
- Trust your instincts about ways you can make a difference.
- Remember to take time to nurture your inner being and to pay attention to the signs you receive.
- Master practicality and common sense, as well as commanding the creative and visionary skills.
- Bring creative skills to scientific problems.
- Involve others in your ideas, recognizing different approaches and perspectives.

Edgewalkers are the leaders of the future. They are the corporate shamans who bring wisdom and guidance for their organizations. It's not an easy role to play, but it's one that's essential to the success of your organization—and one that can make you feel fully alive.

———•‹•›•———

Judith A. Neal is the executive director of the Association for Spirit at Work (www.spiritatwork.com), which offers networking, publications, research, courses, and consulting to individuals and organizations seeking a greater integration of spirituality and work. Prior to this, she spent some years as manager of organizational development at Honeywell, after which she ran her own consulting firm, Neal and Associates, and became management professor at The University of New Haven. She is working on her book *The Four Gateways to Spirit at Work*, which can be found online at www.fourgateways.com.

Creating the Vision of Managers Growing from Good to Great

Jim Collins

Jim Collins's career, since the publication of *Built to Last*, which he coauthored with Jerry Porras, has been meteoric. Since 1995, he has operated a management laboratory in Boulder, Colorado, where he conducts multiyear research and works with senior executives. More recently, Collins's book, *Good to Great*, has garnered an even wider audience. "Good is the enemy of great," Collins believes. But how a company achieves greatness is a lesson too few managers have taken the time to learn. Collins has dedicated the rest of his career to teaching that lesson to everyone he can.

What we have to keep in mind, when we think of what is "state-of-the-art" in management, is that this field is much more science than art. The conditions and the nature of business may change, but the principles of management really do not. So, if you want to think about the world in 2050, it's a sure thing that business will be different, but it's also a sure thing that many of the basic truths of management won't.

Think about the managers—that's what they were, whatever name they used—who built the pyramids. Given the tools and technology they had (and leaving aside labor relations practices we might frown on today!), those Egyptians were using sound management principles to get the work done. You could pick numerous events or personalities throughout history to make this same point. There was a great deal of management required of Christopher Columbus in his daunting expedition involving those three tiny ships, and he managed the challenge admirably. Sure, the scope and complexity of the challenge may be dramatically different, but, essentially, the people managing NASA today are doing the same basic kinds of things that Columbus had to do. So, while the marketplace and organizational conditions under which you manage a group or a process may change, most of the fundamentals that define the superb manager remain the same, at heart, in 1350 and in 2050.

Why this is incredibly important to me is that my own mission in this field of study is to define what's immutable about management and leadership. Perhaps that's why many see my work as different from that of the many other authors who are writing today. Many management thinkers see themselves as engineers; I guess they see management as a form of engineering. Management, to many, is a series of "wheels and pulleys"—and people—that, if configured *just* right, will work! I'm much more of a physicist. I'm striving to research and write about the eternal laws, the unyielding principles, that inform sound management thinking.

I am indebted to Jerry Porras in so many ways, not only as a coauthor, but as a mentor. More than anyone else, he set me on a path that I hope to stay on as long as I can continue to make a contribution. But I am indebted to him in one fundamental way, in particular. What Jerry gave me was a lifelong gift—and it wasn't a set of ideas, a list of bullet points, or a point of view. Jerry didn't give me content; he gave me *method*.

Once I discovered the importance of method in the field of management, my career horizons changed. Jerry stressed the importance of taking on a big question and then using the right tool kit to go about answering that question! He stressed—time after time, year after year—that the world will accept the answer to a truly major question only if one has a rock-solid method. So, on *Built to Last*, where Jerry and I spent years trying to outline the immutable laws of visionary leadership, it was the utilization of controlled comparisons that was the breakthrough.

Prior to *Built to Last*, no other piece of management research that I'm aware of tried to look at two sets of companies, one set visionary and the other could-have-beens. Each company under study was matched to a "peer" within its own industry, and we studied what they did and didn't do over their entire life span. What was truly great about the approach was that it developed a new kind of scientific method of inquiry in the field of management, in order to tackle major questions. And, as we all now know, the approach yields insights that can be breathtaking. So, the approach I now have used for years and that I am trying to hone each day is quantitative and qualitative—but, most of all, it's scientific. It is a process that leads to true insights, and there is simply no way to cut the cycle time to arrive at compelling, confirmable insights about how to manage and lead.

What, then are the most important management "truths" today that people should be thinking about, reading about, and acting upon?

To answer that, let me go back to 1998. A group of people like me, authors and others who give a lot of thought to the world and leadership in general, came together to talk about our commonly held ideas, if any—or, at least, our commonly held concerns. As so often happens at these events, the discussion turned to what the future would be like 50 years out. When it came my turn to comment, I apologized and said that I really didn't know what the world would be like in 2050, but I also said that I had a wish. Wouldn't it be fascinating, I asked the group, if we could know what another group of thinkers—meeting in perhaps these very same chairs in this very same room in 50 years—would smile and shake their heads at when they thought about what we, today, hold to be truths about the world? Putting it a different way, I asked this: "What do we, today, take for granted, that in just 50 years our successors will marvel that we actually believed to be true?"

That meeting was held on the top floor of one of the towers of the World Trade Center in New York.

Now, think about that. In just three years, the assumption has been completely shattered that it would be risk-free to hold a meeting (any kind of meeting!) in the United States, because the United States is, after all, a safe cocoon. That's a world view that has been irreversibly changed. The United States now sees the world as those who live in Europe or Israel do or those in Brazil, who have to hire armed guards to surround their houses so they can sleep at night. But all this underscores the need for managers to be ever mindful of the value of adaptability: while you're operating at full tilt, you still have to be ready to confront new and perhaps quite unexpected (and, even, sometimes unwelcome) challenges.

If there is a new key management question for all of us to focus on, it might be this. How does one run—how does one lead—any business, government, company, university in an unsafe and terribly chaotic world? I believe the answer to that question inevitably brings leaders to address two priorities that are much closer to home and are, therefore, much more manageable.

In an unsafe and uncertain world, managers must determine what their organization has to contribute to the world that no other institution can. It is terribly important for managers to be emphatically clear about what it is that their enterprise can (1) be deeply passionate about, (2) be the best in the world at doing, and (3) have as a sufficient economic engine to keep the business going forward. I derived this viewpoint after thinking long about Isaiah Berlin's famous essay, *The Hedgehog and the Fox*. Too many businesses are fox-like (fast, sleek, beautiful), but they miss the very essence of greatness because, unlike the hedgehog, they do not understand what it is that makes them unique, powerful, and altogether unassailable.

But there's another point to make. In an unsafe and uncertain world, managers must find the right people to help them make that special and unique contribution to the world. I commented once, and I meant it, that too many companies spend too much time trying to motivate the right behaviors in the wrong people, rather than getting the right people in the first place. In my most recent book, *Good to Great*, a team of researchers and I searched through 1,435 companies to find the small number that made the leap from average (or worse) results to truly great results and that sustained those results for at least 15 years. The good-to-great companies did not just hire anyone, then try to train them. Instead, they looked, and waited, and looked some more, in order to find the exact caliber of people they needed to make the company operationally strong and financially profitable.

Only then, when they had "the right people on the bus," did they start to fine-tune things like vision, strategy, and structure. It's an important lesson. By concentrating on finding only the right people for your organization and by giving those people liberal access to capitalize on your organization's best opportunities, you create an enterprise which can weather storms of uncertainty because the right people are, in general, focused on what your company does the best—and they are working at their own personal best. It's not an insurance policy against occasional setbacks, but it's the closest thing there is. Study any great company, and you'll find the pattern distinctly clear.

You cannot make the world either safe or certain. No one can. But what you can do is to make sure that you, and the people you hire to work with you, commit to being the very best at what you do. Don't settle for just being good. There's too much of that already. We have good schools, because people aren't committed to having great ones. There's good government, because people don't want to invest themselves in establishing great government. And too many companies miss the chance to be great simply because they sanction the attitude that "being good is good enough."

I fervently believe that nearly *any* company can become a great one. How greatness is achieved in the organizational world is the scientific breakthrough that I have been privileged to study and write about after investing more than a decade in research and thinking about what separates great from good. But greatness is not conferred, nor does it come by luck or through an inheritance. Greatness comes when leaders commit themselves and all who work with them to becoming the very best at what they collectively do. Deep, personal commitment precedes greatness. There is no other way.

Ethical Ambition

Derrick Bell

Derrick Bell is one of the most forthright and best-known commentators on race and ethics in the United States. A prolific author, his autobiography is entitled *Confronting Authority: Reflections of an Ardent Protestor* and his latest book, *Ethical Ambition* (Bloomsbury, 2002). Bell, now visiting professor at New York University's School of Law, attracted headlines when he became the first tenured black professor at Harvard Law School in 1971, only to leave in protest about the lack of black women on the faculty. He also resigned as dean of Oregon Law School after the School refused to hire a qualified Asian American woman.

In this interview with Stuart Crainer, Derrick Bell talks about the ethical questions now facing the corporate world in the wake of Enron, Worldcom, and other scandals.

As a lawyer and academic, people might question your credentials to talk about business ethics.

True. It's one thing to preach about living an ethical life in the world of academia—sure there's some power plays there and politics—but it's nothing like business. People might ask what do I know about this slug-it-out, beat-to-the-bottom-line, winner-takes-all world. I have avoided working within it. But it seems to me that the principles are similar. You won't succeed unless your primary concern is keeping hold of your integrity.

So you're right to think that the field of business is different, but I don't think it is possible to live a life without an ethical code. You need to look in the mirror.

So how can ambition be ethical? Aren't ambition and ethics mutually exclusive?

Ethics can be an integral part of your ambition. There is no lasting success that isn't ethically founded.

Ethical ambition means simultaneously honoring our values, our dreams, and our needs. It requires critical compassion and honesty toward ourselves and others. It can be achieved only by thoughtfully and candidly assessing who we are, what we believe, what we value, and what we desire. It also involves sacrifice—not only of time and energy, but of inaccurate or outdated perceptions of ourselves and our lives. Many of us are thwarted in achieving our goals because when our values and desires clash, we are paralyzed. Others are disappointed with their lives because they surrender things—like hopes and convictions—that seemed to stand in the way of more material goals.

There are no universal codes of ethics are there? Nepotism, for example, is acceptable in Mexico but not in the United States.

That's a good example because nepotism inevitably leads to its own difficulties, even if no laws are broken and some of it works out okay. I guess the Ford family is a good example, though there are always exceptions. Basically, if you bring people in and shoot them up to the top, there are negative reverberations all the way down.

Looking back at your career, have you always looked in the mirror?
Of course, when I look back I see there were times when I thought I was doing right. At one point, for example, I was handling hundreds of school segregation suits and my marriage was probably a little shaky because my family hardly ever saw me. I was saving the world so far as I could see.

As I look back over those years I think, why didn't I recognize that I wasn't the white knight riding into town filing these suits? What I was doing was taking away leadership opportunities from people who were pretty much sidetracked waiting for this litigation to happen.

If some of the executives who are in so much trouble now had been able to look in the mirror, they might have sensed that what they were doing was not only wrong but would lead to disaster.

But isn't greed central to capitalism?
Perhaps we should use a word which is a little subtler! There was a guy, who I talk about in my book, who was determined to avoid the rat race of the big law firms—even though he had spectacular credentials and he joined a firm which had a reputation for treating people well. He did well there but he realized that, although he hadn't intended it, over time his primary goal became making money. That was the measure. He warned people about this.

It is the subtle things. You're doing the same job each time and you can do it in 15 minutes rather than an hour, but still bill an hour. Little things like that build up and build up. It's impressive but discouraging. It happens all the time. The secretaries who help themselves to stamps and paper. A small thing. But you'd really feel better about yourself buying your own goddamned pencils!

The question is good and my answer, though not very satisfying, is my answer. You don't have to sacrifice your integrity. When you do, even if it works and no-one catches you, there is a price to pay.

Is too much emphasis now given to shareholder value?
Placing a high priority on shareholder value, while seemingly a valid basis for corporate policymaking, all too frequently serves as a shield for actions that, at best, are unethical and, at worst, criminal.

Such dealings include mergers like the hotly contested combining of Hewlett Packard and Compaq, the principal benefits of which, according to opponents, will be increased profit through the dismissal of thousands of employees, and exorbitant payments to the top executives of the merging companies. With no apparent shame or remorse, businesses are setting up headquarters in Bermuda and other off-shore locales, as the toolmaker Stanley Works is attempting to do, so as to avoid U.S. taxes. To compete effectively, we are told, corporate America must move its manufacturing plants to third-world countries to exploit low labor rates and, coincidentally, take advantage of lax health and environmental laws.

But don't such measures benefit shareholders?

These and far more complicated tactics often serve to benefit company executives while placing shareholders at risk. The various maneuvers of Enron, aided and abetted by a major accounting company, Arthur Andersen, are examples of strategies that are hugely profitable for a time and then, when uncovered, are devastating to both employees and shareholders. The executives, unless indicted and convicted (quite difficult under U.S. laws) walk away, perhaps chastened, but still very rich.

So shareholder value is more a diversionary mantra than a guiding principle for many American corporations. Rather, the guiding principle is profit—however gained—that by the very nature of our free enterprise system, transforms reasonably honest business leaders into unbridled money grubbers . . . particularly when government supervision is deregulated or rendered ineffective by political inaction, and inadequate funding of regulatory agencies. Business executives of great intelligence, substantial business experience, and great wealth involve themselves in financial schemes that are not only unethical, but downright stupid.

Could you give me an example?

Consider former Alco International executive, L. Dennis Kozlowski—successful and rich beyond the wildest dreams of the average citizen, who now faces criminal prosecution for shipping expensive art objects intended for his Fifth Avenue apartment to New Hampshire, to avoid the New York state sales tax. Then there is Martha Stewart, an icon of success and propriety, who has seen the stock in her business lose 39% of its value in the wake of charges that she, a former stockbroker, used insider information to sell 4,000 shares of ImClone stock, one day before the company made an announcement that sent its share price plummeting.

What can be done?

As the scandals grow in number and in their blatant character, it is reasonable to ask whether anything can and should be done to clean up corporate America. The answer, beyond disgrace for those apprehended and small reforms in regulatory laws, is very little. Major corporations control the lives of ordinary citizens far more than the officials they elect, and those officials, with very few exceptions, are beholden to corporations for the funds that keep them in office—a goal evidently far more important to most of them than either personal integrity or making good on promises made when they were running for office. Aware that elections apparently have little to do with the important aspects of their lives, most people don't vote, and those who do are likely to be influenced more by TV ads—sponsored indirectly by major corporations—than by any careful and independent assessment of the candidates' records.

And truth be told, many working class Americans—themselves caught up in the hope that, through the lottery or some other similarly unlikely scheme, they will become rich—tend to admire as much as despise corporate corruption. When even the death of John Gotti, a notorious crime boss, captures the headlines, and the interest and—let us say it—the admiration of the masses, public anger at wrongdoing in the executive suites is likely to be both minimal and brief.

And the solution?
There is no easy solution to an economic system that—while encouraging hard work, innovation, and risk-taking in the quest for financial success—develops in some the sense that becoming number one is more important than how you get there.

There is, though, a challenge for those who view the maintenance of ethical standards for themselves and their companies as not only the prudent course, but the only means of achieving a success unburdened by lies, cover-ups, and the continuing fear that structures built with greed as the glue will come undone. For the rest of us, we can speak out against corporate corruption, encourage those reforms that can be enacted, and support those who find the courage to reveal what they know is wrong.

If, despite the best efforts of expensive lawyers, friendly politicians, and high-powered public relations experts, the corporate scandals manage to generate widespread disgust and a demand for action, perhaps reform advocates can establish a corporate truth and reconciliation commission. In lieu of prosecution, business executives might be offered the chance to explain in detail how they evolved from ambitious and perhaps ethical young business people to the persons capable of the acts of which they are charged. If the testimony is forthright, society may gain an understanding of how success comes to be measured by wealth, power, and influence, rather than the commitment to integrity based on respect for self and others, that at some point gets jettisoned as the price of getting ahead.

Has the world become overly materialistic?
Material success has replaced justice and equality as the overarching social goal. On one hand, because many obvious barriers to outsider success—overt and legally-sanctioned prejudice—have been lifted or broken, material success *is* possible for those who only a generation or two ago might have had to put most of their energy into merely surviving. On the other hand, we still live in a society where racism, sexism, homophobia, and other group prejudices remain viable despite public rhetoric to the contrary. In fact, huge disparities in income and opportunity are generally accepted because we believe that those who work hard make it, and those who don't, do not. We even believe this to some degree when we're working hard and not making it! All of this creates profound stress, because those of us who survive those challenges often feel that we must constantly choose between our beliefs and our goals, and end up either feeling guilty for succeeding, or morally intact but personally unfulfilled.

People have been talking about ethics and codes of behavior for decades. There is greater awareness, but it isn't necessarily practiced.
I have no doubt we are going to have some stronger rules. But the ideal set of rules, to keep money out of politics and so on, isn't going to be developed in a few days. Those who feel strongly need to campaign for reform.

The major beneficiaries of instituting higher ethical standards would be businesses, because it would build confidence and what have you, but they do not see that.

So in the short term, the number of abuses and examples of whistle blowing is likely to grow?
Yes. With whistle blowing, people tend to remember the guys who come out looking great and are heralded, but the overall record is not good. Whistle blowers get fired, don't get much recompense, can't prove their case, and then can't then find another job very easily.

Are you optimistic that progress will continue to be made, or have things stalled?
Many of these things start off in a dramatic way of black and white but then evolve into other groups. Corporations now embrace diversity in its larger definition. White women have been the real beneficiaries of affirmative action in our country.

There is dramatic change in some areas. Things kind of go in waves, and that's true in the racial diversity issue. The waves are not necessarily motivated by the highest principles, but they're cyclical.

Leading in Interesting Times

Chris Turner

There is an old Chinese saying that is considered both a blessing and a curse: "May you live in interesting times."

And that is where we find ourselves—in a world that is messy, unpredictable, often incomprehensible, and incredibly interesting; a world where old ideas of leadership and management no longer serve us; a world that calls for a rethinking of all our assumptions about the nature of organizations and our roles within them.

Most agree that new technologies have affected us in profound ways. Just a few years ago, the Internet was merely a playground for techies. And despite the fact that many dot-coms have folded, the Internet has permanently shifted the way we live and work. Its very existence challenges the fundamental operating assumptions of many organizations.

The Internet originally sprang from people's need to communicate and share information. It is a network of relationships and conversations: dynamic, emergent, adaptive, complex, collaborative, and self-organizing. Nobody is in charge. By nature, the Internet is an organic and feminine phenomenon.

Most business enterprises, by contrast, have roots in the Industrial Age. The mindset leans toward the mechanistic: control, predictability, and internal competition are valued. Even in flattened organizations, reporting lines and hierarchy are carefully defined. These companies are laced with masculine norms and values.

Yet ask any C.E.O. what's required to succeed in the future and he or she will inevitably say that the ability to innovate, to change direction on a dime, and to manage across cultures are imperative. They will talk of tapping the power of the Internet; but many fail to recognize the dissonance created when systems with very different operating assumptions converge: masculine versus feminine; controlled versus messy; engineered versus self-organizing; convergent versus divergent. Michael Lewis's book, *Next*, illustrates how the very existence of the Internet challenges institutions as we have known them.

Neither the Industrial Age model nor the Web model is right or wrong. This is not an either–or proposition. To be successful in the future, we must think and act in ways that recognize the paradoxical nature of converging approaches.

MAKING IT HAPPEN

Because I work in many companies, I have the opportunity to observe individuals who navigate this paradoxical world quite well, who are leading effectively in these interesting times. Some lead from powerful positions; others lead informally and have huge influence on their organizations—yet all of them share certain mindsets and practices that are worth noting.

Leaders don't take themselves too seriously. Sometimes I ask people "Did you ever feel like a big sham?" Leaders inevitably have hilarious stories about such moments.

One friend tells about being invited to a very prestigious conference. When he mentioned the meeting to friends and family, their responses were maddeningly similar, "How did *you* get invited?"

He recalled that during the big gathering he kept waiting for everyone to turn to him and say, "You don't belong here. You're nothing but a big sham. Please leave."

Leaders sometimes manage grudgingly. These leaders are imaginative, visionary, and have active intellectual lives. They will often say that managing is both the most rewarding and the toughest part of the job, and they tend, over a career, to move between management and nonmanagement positions.

One of the finest leaders I know recently sold his enterprise for big bucks but has agreed to stay around for four to five years to ensure success. I asked him what he wants to do next. He put his head in his hands and said, "Anything where I don't have a bunch of people reporting to me." It was one of those days.

Leaders are good at conversations and relationships. These leaders have mastered the art of hanging out. They make opportunities for casual conversation. They do lunch. They nurture relationships. They aren't all extroverts, nor do they walk around slapping people on the back. On the contrary, many seem quiet when you first meet them. Their approach is often gentle, sometimes even deferential. But because they are great listeners, people gravitate to them.

An organization is really nothing more than a network of conversations and relationships, so it is unsurprising that these "hanger-outers" become the go-to people in enterprises. They know what's up, they know how to make things happen, they can get things done. They move comfortably through chaos.

Leaders don't hang onto their own assumptions and beliefs. Despite the fact that these leaders are powerful, either formally or informally, they don't get overly attached to their own assumptions about "the way things are."

Recently in a meeting with a C.E.O. and his senior staff, the C.E.O. was under incredible pressure. When his colleagues suggested that a planning process would take several weeks, he snapped, "We can finish that in fifteen minutes." A soft-spoken staffer commented, "Well, it's just not that easy." The C.E.O. retreated and within moments was laughing at the absurdity of his statement. He is a person of strong opinions with a powerful job; yet people are not afraid to challenge him because he is down-to-earth, self aware, and really smart. He listens—even when he doesn't like the message.

Leaders are politely tenacious. These new leaders are quietly upbeat. That's not to say they don't get discouraged, even depressed at times. But their funks are brief. If they think an organizational approach is misguided, they either figure out how to work around the craziness or they focus on how to present their viewpoints more convincingly. They ask questions like, "Help me understand why you think this strategy will be successful." They probe the assumptions that have led the organization to a certain place and remain open to seeing things differently. At the same time, they are not afraid to challenge the status quo or to accept responsibility for their own mistakes.

Leaders thrive on ambiguity. Although many of these leaders have grown up in organizations that are obsessed with control and prediction, they themselves tolerate ambiguity quite well. They analyze; they look at data; they study the situation; they pick people's brains; they solicit feedback. If they need approval, they are masterful at selling their ideas—even within risk-averse organizations. They understand that most decisions are about playing the odds—that nothing is a sure thing.

Leaders are curious, always learning. The next time you take a trip, notice the person across the aisle madly tearing articles out of newspapers and quizzing the flight attendants on the airline survey. The odds are that this person is one of these new leaders I'm talking about. These people are hugely curious and ever in search of new information, new points of view. Walk into their offices and you'll see stacks of books and publications; prepare yourself to hear stories about their latest discoveries. They are ever learning.

Many of these leaders seem to have minds that are more divergent than convergent. Engineers are often convergent. They work to connect all the dots. Artists are more commonly divergent. If they even see the dots, they figure that trying to connect them perfectly is a waste of time. In one of Gore Vidal's essays, republished in his most recent book, *Empire*, he contrasts the convergent mind of Jimmy Carter with the divergent minds of Kennedy and Clinton. He suggests that Carter's obsession with connecting all the dots contributed to his ineffectiveness in a dynamic role. Whatever a leader's style, he or she is careful to surround himself or herself with and listen to colleagues with diverse points of view. He or she understands the value of balance.

Leaders understand that fear is corrosive. Leaders are never punitive. The Chilean biologist, Humberto Maturana, says that "love is the only emotion that expands human intelligence." Leaders understand this at a gut level—although some might hesitate to use the word love.

As managers, these folks are careful about the way compensation policies are designed. They understand that sharing the wealth creates more wealth, not less. If someone is in the wrong job or underperforming, these leaders help the person find another position or figure out a way for them to depart gracefully with a generous package. They recognize that punitive behavior creates fear that, in turn, stifles the creativity they so value.

Leaders talk like real people. Companies are like families; they each have their own language, their own acronyms, their own shorthand. Sometimes people in organizations become so steeped in buzzwords and jargon that, to the uninitiated, they sound like soulless droids from outer space.

These new leaders have a knack for avoiding institutional language. They talk in plain speak. This is part of their appeal, part of the reason that people gravitate to them. They are accessible. They have no need to impress others with insider words. They understand this quote from *The Cluetrain Manifesto* (Perseus, 2001): "In just a few years, the current homogenized 'voice' of business—the sounds of mission statements and brochures—will seem as contrived and artificial as the language of the 18th century French court."

Leaders understand the power of context.   Workplaces are embedded with messages. I'm always amazed to hear people say they want their organization to be more innovative while working in offices that are absolutely dismal. To inspire innovation, these companies typically schedule creativity workshops.

If we think of an organization as a fish tank, many efforts to improve enterprises focus on the fish and ignore the water. The true power for change resides in the water, the environment in which the fish live. The water is the context.

I was recently with a group who were ruminating about leadership, wishing for discipline in their organization. When their lunchtime meeting was over, they all departed leaving their lunch mess behind. With this particular group, their leadership efforts need to start with cleaning up after themselves. Their lack of discipline in caring for the physical environment sends signals that affect the organization exponentially.

As Malcolm Gladwell points out in his great book, *The Tipping Point*, "we are all more than just sensitive to changes in context. We're exquisitely sensitive to them." Alan Kay, one of the original innovators in Silicon Valley, says, "Context is worth 50 IQ points." Leaders pay attention to environmental details. They invest in making the workplace more inviting, whether by painting it in bright colors, putting good art on the walls, or taking interior desks so the windows can be shared by everyone. They are attentive to how meetings are conducted, the forms their communications take, the culture's graphic identity. They tell stories and encourage storytelling because stories contribute to context. They tinker with the environment constantly. Recently a C.E.O. showing me around her facility paused to pick up a scrap of paper on the stairs. She didn't see the paper as paper; she understood it to be a message about the organization.

I don't have a neat seven-step approach to cultivating the attributes and behaviors detailed here; but what I notice about these leaders is that they are acutely self-aware and very present. They think. They recognize their own strengths and weaknesses. They constantly look for ways to improve themselves—not so they'll be more professionally successful, but because they subscribe to the discipline of personal mastery. Their leadership comes from who they are as much as what they know.

Chris Turner partners with a wide variety of organizations to create sustainable learning environments that nurture creative thinking, learning, innovation, energy, fun, and meaning. A native Texan, she spent 16 years at Xerox Business Services, both as a line manager and as the designer and leader of a breakthrough transformation strategy. She recently published *All Hat and No Cattle: Tales of a Corporate Outlaw* (Perseus, 2000). She has also been featured in *The Dance of Change* by Peter Senge (Doubleday, 1999), and *The Circle of Innovation* by Tom Peters (Vintage, 1999).

Current Lessons in Business Leadership

Stan Davis

Stan Davis is an independent author, speaker, and consultant best known for linking the fundamentals of science and technology to likely futures in business and management. He is Senior Research Fellow of the Center for Business Innovation in Cambridge, Massachusetts. A widely-read author, Davis has written three books with Christopher Meyer: *Blur: The Speed of Change in the Connected Economy* (Perseus, 1998), *Future Wealth* (Harvard Business School Press, 2000), and *It's Alive* (Crown Business, 2003). In this article, Davis reflects on the challenges facing leadership in the face of global terrorist threats and recession.

In the past year we've experienced powerful economic recession, the bubble bursting on the dot-com boom, the terrorism of 9/11, a raft of major corporate scandals, and a pervasive financial panic in the stock markets. If ever there was a time for leadership, it's now.

Ask around the business world, however, and what you get is something different from our usual approach to leading. What's striking is the general lack of answers and direction, much more pervasive than creative new approaches to the problems at hand. No major new theme, strategy, or technique has captured the imagination of the business world. No one is leading us to a great leap forward. Leadership is taking one step back to take two steps forward—but we're still at the one-step-back point.

What we hear is a return to focusing on fundamentals. In our search for answers to allay our discomfort, we go back as far as necessary to find solid beliefs we feel we can trust. Paradoxically, this has "led" us back to the past: the only motif that has currency now is the retro-theme "back to basics."

The focus on basics is meaningful and true. It is a retrenchment, a falling back to someplace where we feel a solid footing, so we can lead ourselves back to a better state.

THE "REAL" ECONOMY

A healthy example of this is our renewed appreciation for the "real" economy. The real economy is measured by jobs and production, the market economy by financial performance and the stock market. Most commentary says that the real economy is strong but is being dragged down by the financial economy. The good news is that "back to basics" has us focusing on the real more than the purely financial aspects of our businesses. The bad news is that this focus will do little to improve companies' stock prices. remedial back to basics in our financial accounting—for example, expensing executive stock options and C.E.O.-signed responsibility for what the books say—will also have salutary effects. In time the net effect should be a healthier balance between the two economies.

MOVING FORWARD

The temporary mantra, "one step back to basics," should put us back on track, readying us to take those two steps forward. As a necessary corrective it is not misguided. It positions us for moving ahead, but it doesn't tell us what those forward steps need to be. Here are some suggestions.

First, companies are simultaneously both businesses and organizations. A business is what you do, and an organization is how you do it. Businesses are about resources, products and services, customers and markets, and they are about competition. Organizations, on the other hand, are about things like chains of command, departments and committees, structures and processes. Business leadership should focus on business at least as much as on organization, if not more.

Second, while you're taking a business focus: Which is more important to your company, innovation and growth or efficiency and productivity? The current emphasis on fundamentals is more closely tied to efficiencies than to growth. As we go forward, a key element in business leadership will involve knowing which one to emphasize and knowing when to shift focus. Long-term health will require corporate leadership that can innovate and grow companies.

Third, businesses exist out there in the marketplace, while organizations focus their attention internally. The major events of the past year are what economists call "externalities," whereas most steps business leaders have taken are internal organizational ones. A select few business leaders create policies to deal with the externalities and the systemic issues they raise. The majority of us, however, fail to resolve this contradiction. We are constrained to lead from within our organizations, while our companies would fare better if more internal employees would lead with an external focus on the business. Even if we're terrific leaders for the people around us, at best we affect the 30 or 40% of corporate problems that reside inside the organization, while not touching the 60 or 70% of our problems that lie outside, external and beyond the reach of individual actions.

Fourth, leadership isn't the exclusive preserve of those at the top. On 9/11 the firefighters embodied leadership as much as New York Mayor Giuliani did. Too much of the stuff on leadership is about C.E.O.s, presidents, and generals. I wonder how an ordinary person is supposed to apply what they learn from them to their own lives and work. Jack Welch, for example, was probably the greatest business leader in the second half of the last century, and he was also very vocal about leadership. But how many of his leadership skills get applied outside of GE by ordinary people like a local sales manager in Kansas City or a plant supervisor in Milwaukee? So another leadership lesson from the past year should be to focus more on leadership by ordinary people.

Fifth, new forms of management and organization spawned by the information age are just beginning to take root in corporate America. These include shifts in organization from hierarchy to network, from centralization to decentralization, and from independence to interdependence. September 11 taught us the uncomfortable truth that terrorists have embraced these new forms more completely than has our own private sector.

The negative events of the past year knocked the hubris and confidence out of us. So there's plenty of room for leadership: leadership by ordinary people, leadership that focuses both externally and internally, leadership that balances business growth and productivity, and leadership that builds new forms of organization.

Meaningful Leadership

Kjell Nordström

Employees no longer snap to attention when ordered to do so. They don't passively fall into line, and intimidation and threats do not work. The fact that the work force is no longer subservient doesn't mean that leadership is redundant, however. On the contrary, the new world of work requires even more thoughtful and meaningful leadership.

Leaders must challenge people to depart from the patterns of the past and to create new ones. This new form of leadership is about stirring the pot instead of putting on the lid. The new leaders are creators of chaos as much as originators of order. It is the job of great leaders to support the organization in combining order and chaos.

DIRECTION

Direction is not a matter of command and control, but of focusing—allowing and encouraging people to focus on what really matters. It is spiritual management rather than micromanagement. In a chaotic world, people cry out for individuals who can provide meaning to their private and professional lives.

All organizations need a shared idea of why they exist, who they are, and where they're going. In modern businesses this is usually expressed through a vision. The problem is that most companies don't have an operationally potent vision. Most so-called vision statements are generic wish lists whose length is matched only by their emptiness. Visions should be unique. They should differentiate.

To provide direction, a vision should be clear, continuous, and consistent. It should inspire commitment and be continually communicated. Scott McNealy of Sun Microsystems has a favorite formula: 0.6L. Every time information reaches a layer in the organization, only 60% gets through to the next layer. This quickly adds up—especially in hierarchical firms.

With the onus on communication, leaders must distill the company direction into the most potent capsule. At Disney the vision is to "make people happy." 3M focuses on "solving unsolved problems," while AT&T talks about IM&M—"information movement and management." These statements are simple enough to be shared by all employees, and clear in saying what the companies should *not* be doing.

In addition to visionary bullets, companies need short-term goals that inspire change and that themselves change over time. Jim Collins and Jerry Porras, in their book *Built to Last*, call these "big hairy audacious goals (BHAGs)." They come in many shapes and forms, and can be quantitative or qualitative. In the early 1990s, Wal-Mart set its sights on "becoming a $125-billion company by the year 2000." Almost a hundred years ago, Ford decided to "democratize the automobile." BHAGs can be geared toward a common enemy, as was Nike's "Crush Adidas" in the 1960s, or they can use role models as a benchmark. In the 1940s, for example, Stanford University decided to try to "become the Harvard of the West." General Electric adopted a more inwardly oriented focus in its 1980s goal to "become number one or two in every market we serve, and revolutionize this company to have the strengths of a big company combined with the agility of a small company."

Besides being the distilled essence of what a company is and what it stands for, visions and goals should ignite and inspire commitment. People must want to belong.

Communicating a vision not only involves repetition and a carefully distilled message, it demands the ability to tell a story. True leaders realize that metaphors and language are incredibly powerful. Stories and myths contain a built-in tension that draws people in and ensures that the message sticks. Stories are adaptable and open to an array of interpretations; they are universal and eternal. They communicate more than mere facts. Leaders should give rise to and spread stories.

EXPERIMENTATION

Business life has until now been built around spurts of creation and extended periods of exploitation. Companies exploited natural resources, technologies, and people. We are good at exploitation because we have hundreds, perhaps thousands, of years of experience. We know exactly what to do when we find a gold mine. We put structures and systems in place and get to work. When it is exhausted, we look for the next gold mine.

In contrast, we're not very good at creation. Our societies are not built for it, our organizations are not designed for it, and most people are not trained for it.

By its very nature, creation involves a departure from traditional structures and frames. In a world of creativity-sucking board meetings, past structures have ruled the roost. Now we have to be prepared to depart from the agenda. Exploring routes other than the one most traveled can prove worthwhile. After all, Viagra was discovered when scientists were looking to develop a drug to relieve high blood pressure, Columbus was actually trying to reach India rather than America, and Fleming's penicillin was the result of a "failed" experiment.

Innovation requires experimentation, and experiments are risky. So an innovative environment must have an exceptionally high tolerance for mistakes. The trouble is that traditional organizations are not the most forgiving of environments. This not only stops people from failing—it stops them from trying. It leads to the building of systems that act against innovation instead of nurturing it.

The challenge for leaders is to make it less risky to take risks. Work at Decision Research, a company based in Eugene, Oregon, studying risk-management strategies, suggests that people are more likely to accept risks that they perceive as voluntarily undertaken, controllable, understandable, and equally distributed. Conversely, people are less willing to take on risks that they don't understand and that are unfairly distributed.

EDUCATION

Education is a competitive weapon—for individuals as well as firms. If you want to attract and retain the best people, you have to train them.

Already companies are setting up their own universities to train tomorrow's executives. There are now 1,200 corporate universities worldwide, covering virtually every industry. Amid this welcome, and overdue, maelstrom of activity, the nature of education has fundamentally changed, and it will continue to do so.

Since a lot of knowledge is tacit and difficult to communicate, learning can by no means be restricted to the classroom. We must learn also on the job. Education is as much about improving the processes in which we work and getting to know the people around us, as it is about reading yet another book or listening to yet another lecture. Development is about mentoring, training disciples, and coaching. It is the job of leaders to create new leaders. The distinction between learning, working, and living is gone.

PERSONALIZATION
To attract and retain good men and women, we have to treat them as individuals. The word "individual" originates from Latin and literally means indivisible. We are moving toward one-on-one leadership. The consequence is that every little system needs to be personalized. People can be approached, evaluated, rewarded, and inspired in a number of different ways.

Motivation is increasingly based on values rather than cash. The challenge for organizations is that values are more complex than mere money. By having and communicating a clear set of values, the organization becomes self-selecting—it primarily attracts people who share that attitude.

If people and their motivations differ, rewards must differ. We are used to differentiated contracts in every other market, but not in the labor market. While standard contracts are acceptable in a mass-production context, they are hardly applicable to a building full of highly charged brains with widely different reasons for being there. Working contracts are increasingly individual and individualistic. People express themselves through their contracts. You are your contract, and your contract is you.

Today's employees are more questioning and demanding. They are confident enough to air their concerns, grievances, and aspirations. If they were customers, we would call them sophisticated. It is perhaps significant that we tend not to. Maybe we should. Perhaps we must.

MEANINGFUL LEADERSHIP IN ACTION
Telling Stories. Ikea's founder Ingvar Kamprad uses storytelling. Many people know how Kamprad travels by bus to and from airports to save money. It's a simple story, but its ramifications and message are very powerful. Here is a rich man who is still in touch with reality, who is concerned with value, who is the same as us. Kamprad's bus journeys are a metaphor of the values embodied by Ikea.

Encouraging Innovation. 3M is famed for its 15% policy—researchers can spend up to 15% of their time on their own projects. This is called, among other things, "the bootleg policy." It may also be called a competitive advantage, because it's helped foster so many good ideas—most notably the Post-it Note.

"The object is to spur as many ideas as possible, because perhaps one in a thousand will turn out to fit," explains Post-it Note developer, Art Fry. "An idea might be perfectly good for another company, but not for yours. Putting together a new product is like putting together a jigsaw puzzle of pieces such as raw material suppliers, distributors, government regulations, the amount of capital you have to spend. If one part doesn't fit, the whole project can fail."

Caring for Human Capital.   The highly successful software company SAS Institute in Cary, North Carolina, has no limits on sick days. You can even stay home to take care of sick family members. The firm is responsible for the largest daycare operation in the state. People work a 35-hour week, and there are baby seats in the lunchroom. Pampering? Sure, but if you can't pamper your own people, you're hardly likely to pamper your customers and go that extra mile to enhance their experience.

Kjell Nordström is based at the Institute of International Business at the Stockholm School of Economics, where he received his Ph.D. He runs the School's International Business course, and helped to found the prestigious Advanced Management Program—a five-week, top-management program that attracts the elite among Scandinavian business leaders. He is the coauthor of *Funky Business: Talent Makes Capital Dance* with Jonas Ridderstråle (Financial Times Prentice Hall, 2000).

Who's Guiding Your Corporate Destiny?

Don Blohowiak

Organizations worldwide face a troubling demographic challenge. In blunt, politically incorrect plain talk: too many entrenched, old-style views, too few young leaders.

Population trends conspire to leave a huge hole in managerial ranks. Baby boomers, those born between 1946 and 1964, will soon retire from the full-time labor force, leaving a huge talent vacuum, with the greatest impact likely to be felt about 2010.

Throughout industrialized nations boomers have failed to replace themselves with a baby boomette. The 1970s pop-culture mantra of zero population growth apparently took root in fertile soil. The birthrate for nearly all developed countries continues to decline below the replacement rate of 2.1. This shrinking labor pool comes just as many nations see their economies cranking along at near-full throttle, straining the means of production to meet demand. Most companies already sense the coming shortage. McKinsey & Company surveyed nearly 7,000 executives and managers in 2000 and found only 7% who could strongly agree with the statement, "Our company has enough talented managers to pursue all or most of its promising opportunities."

DEBOSSED CAN'T MEAN AN END TO LEADERSHIP

But wait, isn't the "flat" organization, delayered of paper-shuffling, non-value-adding middle managers, solving the shortage problem? In short, no. Expectations for high performance results from customers and the financial markets alike mean that leadership is in increasing demand just as the labor pool evaporates.

Team- or process-oriented organizations may need fewer bosses, but they depend on bountiful cadres of *leaderful* people to make their teams and task forces productive. As Tom Peters recently opined, "We're going to see leadership emerge as the most important element of business—the attribute that is highest in demand and shortest in supply."

THE NEED FOR LEADERSHIP

A quick scan of the business landscape reveals a loud cry for leadership. Today's market decrees that an organization can survive only by consistently demonstrating increasing capacity for such hard-earned virtues as speed, innovation, responsiveness, value, productivity, quality, and teamwork.

The means to achieve such virtues lies in the province of leadership. They include:

- clarity of direction and priorities
- decisiveness
- adaptability to changes in technology, customer expectations, and society at large
- proficiency of the workforce
- consistency of execution

Leadership sustains life in an organization struggling to endure in a cruel market of demanding customers and ruthless competitors. Weak leadership condemns an organization to death.

LEADERSHIP VOID
This obvious need for leadership comes at a time when C.E.O. tenure is increasingly measured in months as impatient investors look for substantial results instantly and then constantly.

The irony, of course, is that results actually derive from leadership and competent execution by people who toil far from the executive suite. Most of them were sweating in the trenches before the latest C.E.O.'s arrival, and most will still be there when this one is replaced by yet another water-walking hopeful.

An organization that's going to be consistently successful must be led consistently well throughout its ranks. That means cultivating leadership skills deeply and broadly in the work force at large so that the whole organization can amplify, bring to life, and continuously make real the inspired musings of its visionary top leader. With fewer titular leaders at the very time that organizations need more leadership, the gap must be closed by more people, many without rank, being *leaderful*. And that means going beyond empowerment. It is not enough to empower employees; it may even be dangerous to do so. If empowered employees are not adequately prepared to exercise the rudiments of leadership as requisite underpinnings for their conferred power, they're tantamount to fully authorized but unguided missiles.

DEEP LEADERSHIP IN THE REAL WORLD
Some organizations grasp that leadership can't be the sole province of the executive suite, or even vested in the shrinking ranks of its heavily burdened middle managers. Others are beginning to uncouple the false relationship between position and leadership.

We may never live in a bossless world—and that surely isn't the goal—but, as these organizations demonstrate, we should strive to create a world where more people act leaderfully regardless of the hierarchy's depth.

With a leadership tradition spanning more than two centuries, the Marine Corps, operating in relatively small numbers, usually under hostile conditions, understands that its formal leaders can be lost just when they're needed most. So, while vesting official authority in top ranks, the Marines make leadership development at all levels a priority. Personal leadership by all Marines is an ethic that is constantly on the agenda. It is reflected in continual training, in the culture of daily life, and in formal celebrations to mark what the Corps values most: honor, initiative, and accomplishment by the *team*. The Marines do not aggrandize their formal bosses. (Just try to name a famous Marine Corps general.)

Far removed from the Marines' frontline artillery, the finance organization of Motorola has put personal leadership on its agenda. It encourages its accountants, analysts, and other professionals at all levels to be leaderful in their work regardless of whether they have any personnel management responsibility.

Likewise, CUNA Mutual Group, the financial services giant that supports credit unions worldwide, has created training and assessments to engage individual contributors in developing leaderful competencies. CUNA Mutual requires all its employees to understand its current challenges and opportunities and to know and apply the company's mission and vision to their own work. In addition, the company makes it clear that contributors can't merely be passive recipients of orders from their managers. "All employees are required to work with their manager and others to set goals and plan their workload—and to apply sound reasoning to make effective decisions and suggest process improvements where appropriate."

BUILDING LEADERSHIP IN YOUR COMPANY

Because every individual works and learns differently, there is no universal leadership development panacea. And no one becomes a better leader instantaneously as the result of a singular event or experience, no matter how intense, memorable, or expensive.

But the author's experience, and studies conducted by Linkage, the Center for Creative Leadership, and Development Dimensions International, indicate that the following methods are most likely to build more leaderful associates from well-meaning people regardless of rank:

- opportunities to practice leading. Surgery, swimming, and leading are all developed by supplementing instruction and coaching with actual practice.
- evaluations (objective, from validated instruments; and subjective, through feedback from colleagues);
- instruction from credible leadership teachers, ideally including respected senior executives.

A program for making it happen includes the following steps:

- **Identify the leadership capabilities you need to accomplish your organization's business objectives.** They may vary from those typically considered standard leadership competencies. If your organization doesn't truly value teamwork, preaching its virtues will ring hollow. Don't ask the middle to be better than the top, or you'll get two sure results: demoralized would-be leaders, and departing talent.
- **Secure senior management support of, and participation in, the leadership development process.** If you can't readily point to the leadership qualities you're advocating in your company's own senior ranks, reconsider the development effort until it has registered an impact at the most visible level of management.

  Get top managers to put leadership development on their priority agenda and to become involved in the design and delivery of the leadership curriculum—not to talk about leadership theories, but to share their own very personal experiences with leadership challenges in their careers, especially their darkest and lowest moments. If you can't get senior managers to actively participate in the development program, it's not important. Save everyone a lot of time, energy, and money and avoid putting ambitious, hopeful people into a process that is bound to disappointment them.

- **Craft a uniquely tailored leadership development program.** It should:
  - tie in closely with your business needs. Don't try to build an idealized leader based on a pop business guru's overly generalized and unattainable model.
  - integrate multiple coordinated development mechanisms (see below);
  - welcome all interested associates;
  - teach and cultivate appropriate leadership skills. Someone wrestling with decisions about whether to merge with a competitor isn't drawing on the same leadership competencies as someone consumed with making sure a package gets shipped by 6 p.m.
- **Develop leadership capacity in your firm's people.** Use methods to increase the odds of delivering meaningful learning with tangible business results. Provide your associates with opportunities to:
  - participate in special assignments or work on special projects outside their normal work duties to give them exposure to new groups or departments (and most especially to talented senior managers);
  - rotate into new full-time assignments—a fresh view comes from a new vantage point;
  - teach or mentor others; a mentoring or teaching assignment provides great opportunities for people to pay greater attention to and reflect on what they do and why they do it that way;
  - receive coaching or mentoring; this personal, interactive learning experience could be in a one-on-one relationship with a more senior manager or could come through participation with a group of peers;
  - attend external development courses and learning events;
  - go to in-house training courses and leadership development programs;
  - volunteer for service to a charity or nonprofit organization to expose them to other perspectives and nonroutine challenges, some of which may well be bigger in scope than currently offered by their day job.

Leadership, like luck, is a secret ingredient in every successful enterprise. Unlike luck, leadership can be cultivated and grown. But it doesn't happen quickly. Given the growing need for and the shrinking supply of future leaders, smart business-people will give immediate priority to intentionally and programmatically developing leadership skills at all levels of their organization.

The important elements of encouraging leaders at all levels include voicing and demonstrating your expectation for leaderful behavior and providing people with quality instruction, useful feedback, and rewards for practicing leadership. In the very near future a high-performing organization will be a leaderful organization. Build yours now.

Don Blohowiak is executive director of Lead Well, a leadership development firm based in Princeton, New Jersey, which consults worldwide. He is the author of six management books, including *Your People Are Your Product* (Chandler House, 1998) and *The Complete Idiot's Guide to Great Customer Service* (Simon & Schuster, 1997). Blohowiak is also the founder and editor of *The Productive Leader,* a newsletter published by The Economics Press. To find out more, please visit www.leadwell.com.

Helping Managers Measure Up to the Leadership Challenge

Jim Kouzes

Jim Kouzes is the author of numerous books on leadership. He is also the chairman emeritus of the Tom Peters Company as well as an executive Fellow in the Center for Innovation and Entrepreneurship at the Leavy School of Business, Santa Clara University. He is coauthor of several books, including *The Leadership Challenge* (with Barry Posner; 3rd ed., Jossey-Bass Wiley, 2002).

If there is one thing I've learned in over three decades of studying and teaching leadership, and in working with numerous outstanding leaders, it's this: *leadership is a relationship.*

All of us who write and speak and teach on leadership owe a profound debt of gratitude to an extraordinary group of men and women who toiled in the new field of behavioral science. Contemporary research on leadership began during World War II, and while we've learned a great deal since then, most of what we've learned has been built upon the foundations of that early work. So often we treat leadership and team-work as if they were new phenomena, but we know they're not. Serious research has been going on for almost three-quarters of a century. Now, it may be a bit oversim-plistic to try to summarize all of the leadership research in one phrase, but let me be bold enough to give it a try. What we learned in 1946 and what we've learned in the last year is this: leadership is all about how people influence other people to do something. It's all about human relationships.

So I smile when someone asks: "How will leadership be different 50 years from now?" My sense is that the practices of a leader have not been nor will be much different. The *context* will change, but the *content* will be pretty much the same. Our research indicates that leaders engage in five practices to get extraordinary things done in organizations. They "challenge the process," to make sure it's constantly improved. They "inspire a shared vision of the future" that followers deeply believe in and embrace with enthusiasm. They "enable others to act," fostering collaboration and strengthening individual capacity, to make a new vision a new reality. They "walk the talk"—or "model the way" as we call it—setting an example by their own behaviors to show others how the organization can best stay true to its vision and values. And, lastly, they "encourage the heart"—they recognize individuals for their contributions and then celebrate the community of people who care passionately about the destiny of the enterprise.

Each generation, then, has to redefine leadership for its own historical context.

It's so easy to confuse changing times with unchanging fundamentals. For example, today many seem to think that the Internet will change everything. Well, it makes sense in some ways, but not when it comes to leadership. For example, looking back to the time when the telephone was first invented, someone then might have said that bold leadership is connected to using the telephone. Put a phone on everyone's desk! Put a phone in everyone's home! Hook people up to long distance; enable them to converse across the globe, anytime, anywhere. That'll make them higher performers. That sounds silly now, but it's equivalent to what's been going on with the Internet. Are we better off because we have the telephone? Certainly. Are we better off because we have the Internet? Absolutely. Is the telephone or the Internet the secret to better leadership? Not in the slightest. The principles of leadership are the same; only the context is different.

Leadership is about relationships. It's about working with and guiding people in new directions. It's about achieving the most positive interaction between customers, employees, shareholders, vendors—whomever! One serendipitous reminder of this principle was the cover story on the issue of *Time* magazine dated September 10, 2001. It was about U.S. secretary of state Colin Powell, and the general thrust of the story was that he was becoming an afterthought in the leadership of the United States on the world stage. Well, we all know what happened exactly one day after that. Terrorists struck New York, and Washington, D.C., and in the skies over Pennsylvania. Immediately after those tragic events, Colin Powell had to reach out to leaders around the world and marshal a coordinated response to the insidious threat of worldwide terrorism. He had to ask the leaders of many countries (and their people) to do things they had not thought they would have to do, that perhaps they did not want to do. But they took the call from the U.S. secretary of state and then they acted. Why? I'm sure they said something like this (at least to themselves) as they responded to Secretary Powell's requests. "We'll do this," they probably said, "because it's *you*, Colin. We trust you." Leadership is all about relationships that are based on a person's credibility.

Where did I learn this? No one single person taught me my current point of view about leadership, but my father comes close to being the one who influenced me the most.

My father, Tom Kouzes, served the United States for over 30 years. In his final career assignment he was deputy assistant secretary of labor. In addition to his regular job, my dad always loved teaching and training, especially in the field of organizational management. Here I was, growing up in the Washington, D.C. area during my earliest years, and my dad would bring home books by people like Peter Drucker and talk about them. He was also fascinated by short, experiential exercises that would help people in training classes "feel" the leadership lesson and not just think about it. I'll always remember that.

As I think about all this, *both* my mother, Thelma, and my dad strongly influenced me. At home, I would participate in all kinds of discussions about management and political science and world affairs. My mother was a volunteer at the United Nations and, beginning in 1961, we had foreign students live at our home year-round. She also was very active in the civil rights movement, and even took part with Dr. Martin Luther King in the great march on Washington. Now, it's worth noting that all this was happening before the term "diversity" was the hot concept it is now. I'm so thankful that I learned at a young age how important it is to see leadership issues through a global pair of glasses. Because of a combination of influences like the ones my parents provided (and from all the experiences I had becoming an Eagle Scout), I was determined to join the Peace Corps when I was young. There's no question that my service in Turkey helped me to see the critical importance of leaders—how they can improve the world through social action.

There was one other strong influence. Everything that led me to my career followed the path of the applied behavioral sciences. In fact, I think it's safe to say that everything that we read or hear or see today about leadership has its roots in the applied behavioral sciences.

I was especially influenced by David C. McClelland. His work on *The Achieving Society* was seminal. His research and writing definitely tie to the idea that leadership is about relationships. In fact, Daniel Goleman, who popularized the term "emotional intelligence," was a student of McClelland's at Harvard, and Goleman credits McClelland as the taproot of his own work. Here's just another example of what is old is new again. McClelland's work is a wonderful starting point for anyone who hopes to lead in the difficult and chaotic years ahead. A leader who is capable of managing relationships constructively must realize that there are basic skills that have to be mastered.

I have to add one other point, however. Leadership not just about skills, no more than any relationship is just about skills. Credibility is the foundation of all relationships. So, you can have all the skills in the world, but if people don't believe in you as a person, they simply won't want to follow you. We call it the First Law of Leadership: If you don't *believe in* the messenger, you won't believe the message. When we ask people what credibility is behaviorally, the response can always be summed up in the phrase "Do What You Say You Will Do," or DWYSYWD for short. In other words, for people to want to *willingly* follow someone, they have to observe two things: first, the leader has a clear set of values and beliefs, and, second, the leader's behavior is consistent with those beliefs.

Which leads to another practice that too many leaders discount. Leadership requires self-knowledge. This is a much a more significant point than many first assume. It's amazing how few leaders take the time to answer a very simple but key question: "What do I *really* care about?"

When a leader can answer what it is that he or she really cares about, then it's possible to see the actual leadership face that he or she presents to the rest of the world. Many, if not most leaders have some kind of speech about wanting their company to be both profitable and a great place to work. Yet great words in a nice speech are not the same as becoming fully aware of what you really care about. What keeps you awake at night? What ideas or issues grab hold of you and won't let go?

Learn what you really care about and you slowly but surely start to find your leadership voice, to discover your true vision and values.

John Robbins is the son of the co-founder of the Baskin-Robbins ice cream empire. He grew up in a household that sometimes served ice cream for breakfast; he swam in a backyard pool that was shaped like an ice cream cone. But John walked away from all of that. He rejected the lifestyle, and he rejected the production factory approach to how we treat animals. He embraced a whole new lifestyle structured around the profound idea that our diets can help save our lives and our planet. He is also an eloquent and passionate proponent for a saner approach to how we live, eat, and work in our environment. Now, John didn't wake up one morning with the revelation that this was the way his life should go. He spent 10 years after university on an island, in a one-room log cabin that he and his wife, Deo, built. By being with his thoughts and living a very simple life, he emerged with great clarity about his calling.

Now, I am not advocating that all leaders need to spend a decade alone on an island. But the point to stress is that today's work world is full of so much frenzy, so much noise, that it's nearly impossible for anyone to pause and reflect. But you have to! Winston Churchill, despite all the challenges that confronted him, found time to paint. Guess what he was thinking about when he painted? All great leaders find time to reflect: Lincoln, Gandhi, Martin Luther King. I believe this fervently. Any leader who says I don't have time to reflect is crippling his ability to lead. Why?

People who follow you want a leader who stands for a larger purpose. They want meaningful work, and connecting to a larger purpose ennobles and energizes everyone's efforts. Leadership is about relationships. It's about trust. It's about doing what you say you'll do. So I ask: what do *you* really care about? Find the answer to that question and you're on the path to becoming a better leader. Ignore that question, and you're on the road to an empty life. You can't pay people enough to care. People care when they have meaning in their work, when they can connect to a larger purpose. Find a worthy purpose for you and your constituents, and the profits will follow.

"Work" and "Change"

William Bridges

Few grasp how to make sense of life's changes better than William Bridges. His insights and strategies for dealing with difficult, painful, and even scary times are extremely relevant, particularly as we begin a new millennium marred at the outset by enormous adversity and a chilling sense of uncertainty. Indeed, his message is one of hope, compassion, and deep understanding. His book *Transitions*, first published in 1980, continues to be trumpeted as the quintessential resource for understanding the process of surviving and reviving in the face of change. Subsequent books include *Managing Transitions* and *GobShift*.

Americans share many of the nomadic traits of some of their Old World cousins. Yet, these New World pioneers, in particular, have long been regarded as people on the move. Even Alexis de Tocqueville noted in 1831, " . . . the American has no time to tie himself to anything, he grows accustomed only to change . . . regarding it as the natural state of man." With my original training in the field of American civilization and my extensive exposure to history, government, and literature, I have been able to draw from a wealth of resources over the years, like de Tocqueville, whose work, *Democracy in America*, is a brilliant study of the American culture.

Similarly, Edward P. Thompson's *Making of the English Working Class* provides extremely valuable information concerning the development of the historical artifact we call a "job." Originally, a "job" was an invention that could go away as easily as it came into existence. The word was first used as a verb, meaning something comparable to "doing." With the advent of the Industrial Revolution, the work people performed could be dissected into discrete tasks, and "job" came to mean something for which people took responsibility, like a possession. This perspective is useful in understanding why the "job" as we know it today—representing more of a function based on a set of activities—is literally imploding.

While I came to appreciate such *external* analyses of change, I was motivated to examine the thinking of others to formulate my own beliefs with respect to the *internal* experience of it. Those influencing my conclusions included: Arnold J. Toynbee, who helped us understand the process of renewal as it occurs in civilization and in a person; Dutch anthropologist Arnold van Gennep, who first coined the phrase *rites of passage*; and philosopher Mircea Eliade, whose analysis of religion assumed the existence of "the sacred" as the object of worship of religious humanity—providing a source of power, significance, and value.

Peter Drucker and Charles Handy, two organizational writers, and Ralph Waldo Emerson—all helped to enhance my perspective around what van Gennep referred to as the "neutral zone"—that period between the end of one phase and the beginning of the next in which the greatest opportunity for discovery and renewal is present. What I particularly came to appreciate is the absence of "focusing mechanisms" in our lives today that allow people to "know" where the end points and beginnings are. Our "transitions" are becoming all-consuming. They overwhelm everything rather than providing channeled influences that move us consciously in some new direction. Given the changing nature of work—with increased demands for knowledge, the disintegration of large corporations, and an accelerated pace of change—it is no longer appropriate to think of work as "fixed" jobs. To appreciate this, we have only to consider the dramatic example of the *Wall Street Journal*, whose offices were directly across from the World Trade Center in New York. The very next day following the destruction of the towers by terrorists, the publisher was able to go to press, utilizing an extensive network of cell phones, e-mail systems, fax machines, and remote sites of operation. With that magnitude of integrated technology, we can't think in terms of individual workers arranged in fixed work units producing a product. Instead, what we need to envision is whole communities of people agreeing to assume shifting roles in a highly flexible context.

All to say, these influences, combined with my own research, have shaped the way in which I view "work" and "change." You see, change is an *event*, whereas transition is a *process* that is always in flux, always disruptive. It forces people to go into a "neutral" role, and it is in this area that business and management have their most important work cut out.

As we begin the new millennium, I predict a dramatic intensification of the trends of the last 10 years. The pace of change has already given business many new advantages. Flexibility and responsiveness are the preeminent qualities of the new workplace. And, while technology enables us to work faster, with fewer jobs and greater productivity, business also has the ability to use more "outsiders." A new construct is well under way as traditional jobs continue to diminish.

Our work habits and lifestyles will change further. We'll need whole new systems of support for employees. To illustrate this: when Washington officials talk about a "safety net" of retirement security, unemployment benefits, and the like, their model is consistently predicated on the old concept of jobs. In the 21st century, *portability*— which allows workers to accrue benefits as they move from one assignment to another—will be terribly important. Business cannot continue to operate in an environment where health insurance, for example, acts as some huge counterweight to the migration of human capital across the workscape.

These are the *external* realities associated with change that I see. The *internal* realities are that people won't be able to keep pace—assimilating the turbulence of a process that gets protracted *ad infinitum*. They may go through the motions, but they won't be into the new work *emotionally*. They'll still be back in the old job. We're seeing this now, and I predict it will continue—slowed only by an occasional crisis—but it will be an unsustainable position leading to all kinds of meltdowns. At the end of the day, there is no end, as "home"—that safe haven from the world outside—is assaulted by beepers, cell phones, and unsolicited sales calls. Families are melting away. I predict other meltdowns, as well—psychological breakdowns, depression, constant fatigue. Even today, large numbers of people are running on empty.

To break this destructive trend, we must work on how the experience of transition can lead to personal renewal. Of course, in the midst of turbulence, usually the last thing we want is transition, especially when we're looking for renewal; but that's how renewal really takes place. We have to learn how to enjoy the ride more, by going *with* the transition—renewing on the fly, so to speak, without necessarily blowing the whistle for a timeout.

New skills will be needed to cope with these conditions. To begin with, *self-management of change* will be essential for everyone. Individuals, as well as businesses, will need to be able to make quick shifts. Leaders in every organization will have to realize how often the rules change, and they will need to assume hugely more responsibility for getting people through these changes successfully—especially for the well-being of the enterprise as a whole. This will involve every aspect of the change process—communication, timing, training, etc. The old way of "command and control" will be a formula for disaster, particularly if people are allowed to remain stuck in the unfinished mess of transition.

We will also need to reframe the concept of a *career* by incorporating elements that are "change-friendly." We must foster an entrepreneurial spirit that feeds on the change process. Indeed, the *new-style career* will require that everyone know:

- what resources, skills, and abilities they bring to the table;
- where the problems are that are yet to be solved and what the "market" needs;
- what new skills will be needed to bring solutions to these opportunities;
- that we are all "micro-companies," requiring strategic planning, training, financing, etc.;
- that transitions lead to renewal, and we need to be open to traversing many neutral zones.

We will have to find ways to make organizations even more flexible in the future. To do this we will have to facilitate the process by letting go of things that are not servicing us well anymore. We will also have to find ways of getting the most benefit from those who are not in the direct employ of the enterprise. This will involve new forms of recognition and reward sharing. And, finally, management will need to reinvent itself. Instead of assuming responsibility for assigning fixed duties, discrete tasks—like purchasing or human resource management—leaders will do better to shift the focus to cross-functional teams and/or outside workers who, in turn, will assume responsibility for getting work done and adjusting continuously—even more quickly—to change.

In the end, by involving people more in the design of their own work situations and tying rewards to results, people will become more aligned with the goals of the enterprise and more concerned with its welfare. Not only will this approach enable businesses to prosper, it will avert many of the costly meltdowns of human capital. But make no mistake, this will require a major shift from the old-style thinking of one "master" and one "job" to the new reality of *self-managing transitions*.

Emotional Intelligence

Cary Cherniss and Daniel Goleman

Ever since the publication of Daniel Goleman's first book on the topic in 1995, emotional intelligence has become one of the hottest buzz phrases in corporate America. Many business leaders have found compelling the basic idea that success is strongly influenced by personal qualities such as perseverance, self-control, and skill in getting along with others. They point to sales persons who have an uncanny ability to sense what is most important to the customers and to develop a trusting relationship with them. They also point to customer service employees who excel when it comes to helping angry customers calm down and be more reasonable. Conversely, they point to brilliant executives who do everything well except get along with people, and to managers who are technically brilliant but cannot handle stress, and whose careers are stalled because of these deficiencies.

Many studies have confirmed that the so-called "soft skills" are critical for a vital economy. For instance, the influential report of the United States Secretary of Labor's Commission on Achieving Necessary Skills argued that a high-performance workplace requires workers who have a solid foundation not only in literacy and computation, but also in personal qualities such as responsibility, self-esteem, sociability, self-management, integrity, and honesty (Secretary's Commission on Achieving Necessary Skills, 1991). Emotional intelligence is the basis for these competencies.

But what exactly is "emotional intelligence?" What is the link between emotional intelligence and organizational effectiveness? Is it possible for adults to become more socially and emotionally competent? And finally, what is the best way to help individuals to do so?

WHAT IS EMOTIONAL INTELLIGENCE AND WHY IS IT IMPORTANT?

Emotional intelligence is the ability to identify and understand accurately one's own emotional reactions and those of others. It also includes the ability to regulate one's emotions and to use them to make good decisions and act effectively. EI provides the bedrock for many competencies that are critical for effective performance in the workplace. For instance, one's effectiveness in influencing others depends on one's ability to connect with them on an emotional level, and to understand what they are feeling and why. To influence others effectively we also need to be able to manage our own emotions.

CAN ADULTS BECOME MORE EMOTIONALLY INTELLIGENT?

Many managers and executives who accept the notion that emotional intelligence is vital for success are less certain about whether it can be improved. On the other hand, there are consultants and trainers who claim that they can raise the emotional intelligence of a whole group of employees in a day or less. Who is right? The truth lies somewhere in between. A growing body of research suggests that it is possible to help people of any age to become more emotionally adept at work. However, to be effective, programs need to be well designed, and the change effort requires months, not hours or days.

Several examples of effective change programs can be found in the Model Programs section of the CREIO Web site (www.eiconsortium.org). These models, all of which have undergone rigorous evaluation, show that well-designed training and development interventions can produce significant improvements in the so-called "soft skills," and these improvements in turn result in greater productivity and reduced costs. Unfortunately, while it is possible to improve workers' emotional competence, it is not easy to do so. Many programs intended for this purpose fail because they are poorly designed and implemented.

WHAT IS THE BEST WAY TO IMPROVE EMOTIONAL INTELLIGENCE?

To be effective, change efforts need to begin with the realization that emotional learning differs from cognitive and technical learning in some important ways. Emotional capacities like self-confidence and empathy differ from cognitive abilities because they draw on different brain areas. Purely cognitive abilities are based in the neocortex. But with social and emotional competencies, additional brain areas are involved, mainly the circuitry that runs from the emotional centers to the prefrontal lobes. Effective learning for emotional competence has to retune these circuits.

Unfortunately, these particular neural circuits are especially difficult to modify. Emotional incompetence often results from habits learned early in life. These automatic habits are set in place as a normal part of living, as experience shapes the brain. As people acquire their habitual repertoire of thought, feeling, and action, the neural connections that support these are strengthened, becoming dominant pathways for nerve impulses. When these habits have been so heavily learned, the underlying neural circuitry becomes the brain's default option at any moment—what a person does automatically and spontaneously, often with little awareness of choosing to do so.

Because the neural circuits that need to be modified extend deep into the nonverbal parts of the brain, the learning ultimately must be experiential. Learning to control one's temper, for instance, is like learning to ride a bicycle. Understanding what needs to be done on a cognitive level only helps to a limited degree. It is only by getting on a bike and riding it, falling over, and trying again repeatedly, that one ultimately masters the skill. The same is true for most emotional learning. It usually involves a long and sometimes difficult process requiring much practice and support. One-day seminars just won't do it.

IMPLICATIONS FOR TRAINING AND DEVELOPMENT

Because emotional learning differs from cognitive learning in a number of ways, training and development efforts need to incorporate a number of elements. Below are some of the most important ones:

1 **Practice:** There needs to be much more opportunity for practice than one normally sees in the typical work-based training program. Not only do there need to be many opportunities during the training itself, but also the learners need to practice new ways of thinking and acting in other settings—on the job, at home, with friends, etc. And this regimen needs to occur over a period of months.

2 **Ongoing encouragement and reinforcement from others:** Even with ample practice during the training phase, the old neural pathways can reestablish themselves all too easily unless learners are repeatedly encouraged and reinforced to use the new skills on the job. The best change programs continue to help participants to apply what they have learned after the formal training phase ends. They also provide periodic reinforcers and reminders to help the participants maintain the fragile new patterns of behavior that they have so recently learned. And effective programs provide social support to help individuals continue to work at strengthening the new competencies that they acquired in the training.

3 **Support from the boss:** A learner's bosses play an especially critical role in providing the support necessary for successful change. Reinforcement by one's supervisor can be especially powerful in helping new emotional competencies to take root. Also, supervisors influence transfer and maintenance of new competencies indirectly by serving as powerful models.

4 **Experiential learning:** In addition to sustained practice, feedback, reinforcement, and support, effective social and emotional learning needs to be based primarily on experiential activity rather than more intellectual, didactic approaches. Developing a social or emotional competency requires engagement of the emotional, noncognitive parts of the brain.

5 **Emotionally intelligent trainers and coaches:** Because the competencies involved in social and emotional learning are so central to our personal identities, special care and sensitivity is required in the way that training is presented. The personal nature of what is involved in this kind of learning also makes it critical that there be a trusting and supportive relationship between the learners and trainers. Trainers need special skills and more than a little emotional intelligence themselves.

6 **Anticipation and preparation for setbacks:** Even when a training program has all of these elements necessary for successful personal change—ample practice and support, emotionally intelligent trainers, etc.—learners will inevitably encounter setbacks. The old emotional memories and social habits will tend to reassert themselves from time to time, especially when people are under stress. Thus, effective training programs also include "relapse prevention," which refers to a set of techniques that help people to reframe slips as opportunities to learn.

Emotional intelligence can make a big difference for both individual and organizational effectiveness. However, if the current interest in promoting emotional intelligence at work is to be a serious, sustained effort, rather than just another management fad, it is important that practitioners try to utilize practices based on the best available research. Only when the training is based on sound, empirically based methods will its promise be realized.

———◦◦———

Cary Cherniss, Ph.D., is professor of applied psychology at Rutgers University, specializing in emotional intelligence, work stress, management training, organizational change and career development. His six books include *Promoting Emotional Intelligence in Organizations* (with Mitchel Adler; American Society for Training and Development, 2000) and *Beyond Burnout* (Routledge, 1995). He has also consulted widely in both public and private sectors. Psychologist Daniel Goleman, Ph.D., has written several bestsellers, including *Primal Leadership* (Harvard Business School Press, 2002), *Emotional Intelligence* (Bantam, 1997), and *Working with Emotional Intelligence*. He worked for many years for the *New York Times* covering the brain and behavioral sciences; has been a visiting faculty member at Harvard University; helped found the Collaborative for Social and Emotional Learning at the University of Illinois, and speaks on emotional intelligence and leadership worldwide. Cherniss and Goleman cochair Rutgers' Consortium for Research on Emotional Intelligence in Organizations. Together they edited *The Emotionally Intelligent Workplace* (Jossey-Bass, 2001).

Elephants and Fleas

Charles Handy

Now in his 70s, Irish-born Charles Handy remains the genteel, civilized voice of management. Handy worked for Shell before pursuing an academic career as a professor at the London Business School. His first book, *Understanding Organizations* (1976), gave little hint of the wide-ranging, social and philosophical nature of what was to come. In his later books *The Age of Unreason* (1989) and *The Age of Paradox* (1994), Handy coined some of the best known and most useful management concepts of recent years, including "the shamrock organization" and "the portfolio career," and explored federalism in an engagingly accessible way.

For all his gentleness, however, Handy's ideas have a subversive edge. In his latest book, *The Elephant and the Flea* (2001), he returns to the theme of the changing landscape of working life, focusing on the symbiotic relationship between large companies (elephants) and small businesses (fleas), which include free agents, entrepreneurs inside and outside the organization, and firms with fewer than 10 employees. "You will all be fleas one day," he advises, "so enjoy your fleadom."

What is the most important thing and who is the most important person to have influenced your thinking?

I read lots of things and listen to lots of people and absorb them. I take bits and pieces. I like a lot of what Gary Hamel says, for example, but probably because it confirms my own prejudices.

The major influences on my thinking have been my life experiences and my wife Elizabeth. Elizabeth pushed me to step outside organizational life and focus on what I do best—which I think is writing—and to make a business out of that. So I'd say it was the experience of my own life, prodded by my wife, and then influenced by people like Peter Drucker, Gary Hamel, and the American social critic Jeremy Rifkind.

How will business be different in the 21st century?

It will be more shapeless, in the sense that in the past 50 years we had things called companies, and they really were companies—groups of people bound together with roughly the same purpose. Businesses now are much more a collection of globules—partnerships and alliances.

I see business now as much more of a federal creation than it was—a series of autonomous organizations that includes universities, government, and different groupings of people. We are groping toward new ways of thinking about businesses.

What new skills will be needed to cope with these changes?

Key skills will be the ability to win friends and influence people at a personal level, the ability to structure partnerships, and the ability to negotiate and to find compromises. Business will be much more about finding the right people in the right place and negotiating the right deals. So in a funny way the functions that will be the most important are recruitment and purchasing. It's ironic that neither of these has traditionally been seen as the star.

Conceptual skills are also becoming much more important. There used to be a big distinction between managerial and technical skills. The ability to analyze numbers was considered most important then. In the last 20 years, the softer, human skills have become more important. But it is conceptual skills that are now coming to the fore. They are what the federal organization is all about.

The new workforce wants to contribute to humankind in some way as well as earning a livelihood. Finding a way to describe a cause is important and useful. The why is as important as the what and the who.

Does this change the role of leadership?
A good C.E.O. spends at least half his or her time on people. The shift now is to the C.E.O. as teacher and missionary, persuading people that his or her priorities are important to them.

Conceptualizing is increasingly important. I think strategy now is much more to do with defining—or conceptualizing—what your organization is all about. A lot of the old thinking about strategy is out of date.

Look at Jack Welch. He is a great self-publicist. He had great conceptual skills. His strategy in the early days was that he only wanted businesses that were number one or number two in their markets. But he later reversed that. He realized that GE was becoming complacent, so he reframed his message. He said to his people: "Redefine your market so that you only have 10% market share." He forced them numerically to stretch their horizons and broaden their outlook. That sort of conceptualizing is increasingly important. His human skills were also very important. The question now is whether the new C.E.O. will be able to hold it together, or whether without Welch GE will fall apart.

How do you develop these sorts of skills?
I once said that education is experience understood in tranquility, and I think that's true. The only way people learn these conceptual skills is by being pushed into roles that are just beyond their grasp, so they are out of their depth and have to stretch themselves. You need to support them, of course, and forgive them when they get it wrong. I don't like the words mentor and coach. Michael Young has a term "educational companion," which I prefer. Organizational companions could be one way to help managers learn these skills.

Are there new management questions we should be asking?
The new management questions aren't really new but they have a new urgency. In my new book I talk about the disappearing middle. The middles of whole industries are disappearing. Take publishing, which is one I am familiar with. At present there is a long chain of processes and organizations between me as an author and the reader.

Everything in this chain of distribution is now in doubt apart from the beginning and the end—the author and the reader. How the first connects with the second is now open to a wide range of options.

We could dispense with the physical bookstore, the option focused on by Amazon.com and its imitators. Jeff Bezos says I can connect these two points in different ways. The publisher too could choose to bypass wholesalers and bookstores and publish electronically. Or, if I was intrepid enough as the author, I could bypass the lot of them and put my words on a Web site for anyone to download for a fee.

This phenomenon of disappearing middles—disintermediation—allows new-comers to insert themselves into the gaps. The question for managers is: how do we redefine ourselves if we're in the middle?

It's quite hard for elephants to do. That's where fleas come in. Elephants are there to connect the talent to the customer, so the fleas need the elephants. But the elephants need the fleas, too, to create new value and to spur innovation.

What will happen to the concept of the career in the future?

It will be a professional career path and not an organizational one. People increasingly define themselves by their profession, and the definition of profession is much wider. It includes everything from beauty technician to chef and even sanitary engineer. We're all professionals now.

Very few jobs in future will be defined as jobs. Those that are—like checkout cash-ier—will disappear. There will be customer relationship managers or something like that. So people will either be professionals or entrepreneurs—fleas in short.

To promote your career you may work in a large organization—an elephant—for a while to gain skills and expertise. You may go back to elephants periodically to upgrade your skills or credentials. But you will have to take responsibility for your own career and your own life.

It starts as a mental thing. So think customers, not jobs. Think skills, not grades. What can you sell that is useful to other people? One day you will need to do that. One day you will be a flea.

How can companies best promote enterprises which are a) profitable and b) good places for people to work?

Elephants have to become venture capitalists for the people within their own organ-izations. If people come up with a good idea that fits with the brand, the organization should back it with money and time.

Look at what Ricardo Semler has done with Semco. "We don't have a strategy," he says, "it emerges from the initiatives that come up from the front line." For example, the company makes and erects cooling towers. From talking to customers, the Semco people heard lots of complaints that the towers kept breaking down because of main-tenance problems. "We know how to maintain them," they thought. So they said to the customers: "If we take on maintenance we want 60 percent of the saving you'll make from preventing breakdowns". Then they went to the Semco board and said:

"We want to keep 20% of the 60% ourselves". The board said OK. So Semco is acting like a venture capitalist for its own people.

Or look at GE. When Jack Welch said "redefine your market so that you have less than 10%," GE was basically acting as a VC to its people, encouraging them to look for new business opportunities. It's more than just money. It's about persuading people that they can build a business, create something new. People have to believe they can leave a footprint in the sand and all that.

Creating Corporate Creativity

Edward de Bono

In my experience with major multinationals and other organizations, the basic behavior is "maintenance and problem solving." This means running things as they are and solving problems as they arise. A great deal of lip service is paid to creativity but little is done. In surveys I have done at my seminars, 90% of people agree that creativity is important, and 80% claim that little is done in their own organizations.

Three things are becoming commodities in business. Competence is one of those things. If your only hope of survival is that your competitors will continue to be more incompetent than yourselves, you are weak, since there is nothing you can do to stop them from becoming competent. Information has already become a commodity available to anyone willing to pay for it. State-of-the-art technology is a commodity which can be bought or commissioned, with some exceptions such as pharmaceuticals.

When everything is a commodity, what is going to matter is the design and delivery of value created from these commodities. This requires creativity. Six chefs at a cooking competition each have the same ingredients and the same cooking facilities. Who wins? The chef who can create superior value from the basic commodities.

THE USE OF CREATIVITY

Creativity is used to solve problems, design ways forward, resolve conflicts, simplify procedures, cut costs, improve motivation, design new products and services, and fashion strategies. Any situations that require thinking demand creativity. Without it, we are condemned to repeating the standard routines.

In 1971, I suggested at a workshop with Shell Oil in London the concepts of horizontal drilling. Today, most oil wells in the world are drilled this way because the yield is three to six times that of a traditional well. (I am not claiming that this change came about as a result of my suggestion, but the chronological fact remains.) After a seminar to Ingwe Coal in South Africa, the senior engineer told me they had developed a new way of cutting coal—the first new way in 80 years. In both cases, there was not a problem, but applying creativity to the usual way of doing things developed powerful new ideas.

A major Scandinavian company used to spend 30 days on their multinational project discussions. Today they do it in two days through using parallel thinking instead of argument. After training in creative thinking, a U.K. television company said they had had more ideas in two days than they had had in six months before. One afternoon, Carole Ferguson (a certified trainer) put together 130 workshops for a steel company. Using just one of the techniques of lateral thinking, they generated 21,000 ideas that afternoon.

A person tied up with a rope cannot play the violin. If we cut the rope, does that make that person a violinist? If you are inhibited you cannot be creative. If you release yourself from that inhibition, does that make you creative? That is the essential weakness of processes such as brainstorming. Creativity can be a much more structured discipline with specific mental operations that can be used deliberately.

THE BASIS OF CREATIVITY

The purpose of the brain is to be non-creative. Instead, it is supposed to establish routine patterns for dealing with a stable world. If it were otherwise, life would be impossible (there are 39,816,800 ways of getting dressed in the morning with eleven items of clothing). As a self-organizing system the brain allows incoming information to organize itself into routine patterns. We should be grateful for these patterns. But there are side tracks which are suppressed. If, somehow, we manage to move "laterally" to the side track then, in hindsight, the new idea will be logical and obvious. This is why we have never appreciated creativity. Because every valued creative idea is logical in hindsight, we have assumed logic would be sufficient to reach this idea. This is simply not true in the asymmetric nature of self-organizing systems.

DELIBERATE CREATIVE PROCESSES

The techniques of "lateral thinking" are based directly on this understanding of brain behavior. The technique of "random entry" takes us away from the usual starting point to create a new "chance" starting point which allows us to open up tracks we could never have accessed from the usual starting point. That is why the history of science is full of examples of major discoveries that were triggered by an apparently random event.

In any self-organizing system there is a mathematical need for provocation. Otherwise we remain stuck in local equilibria instead of reaching a global equilibrium. The new word "po" signals that something is put forward as a provocation. "Po, you die before you die," sounds illogical but enabled Ron Barbaro of Prudential Insurance, Canada, to develop the concept of "living needs benefits." There are formal ways of setting up provocations. It would be pointless to use "judgment" on provocations. We need to develop the very different mental operation of "movement." There are formal ways of getting "movement" from an idea.

"Challenge" is another aspect of lateral thinking. We challenge accepted concepts and perceptions, and then develop alternatives. This was the process that led to the suggestion of horizontal drilling of oil wells. We challenge traditional, accepted and usual concepts, not because they are wrong or inadequate, but because the adequate can hide the better idea.

Alternatives are generated by extracting the concept that lies behind the existing approach. There follows a search for finding a better way of delivering this concept.

"CASE MAKING" VERSUS CREATIVITY

In a court of law if the prosecuting lawyer thinks of a point which would help the defense case, that point is not going to be made. Conversely the defense lawyer would never mention a point that might help the prosecution case. This is not exploring the subject, but "case making." With parallel thinking, all parties at any one moment are looking and thinking in the same direction. The change in direction is signaled by the symbolic "six hats." Each hat indicates a mode of thinking: for example, white hat for information, red hat for feelings, and green hat for creative possibilities. The result is a much quicker and much fuller exploration of the subject. Every person present is using his or her thinking and experience to the maximum instead of "making a case." This method is now widely used in schools and with senior executives. Why pay someone a large salary if you are not going to use that mind fully?

CREATIVITY IN THE ORGANIZATION

In any organization, creativity is either a risk or an expectation. If it is not an expectation, it is always a risk. In my experience the culture of creativity needs to be set by senior management. That way, creativity becomes an expectation. Executives and workers are now expected to come up with and explore new ideas. They receive "recognition" for doing that. Failure to explore new ideas means you are not doing your job properly. Training in creative methods then follows as part of the culture.

To promote creativity throughout your organization:

- Break out from the trap of "maintenance and problem solving," or running things as they are and tackling problems as they arise.
- Recognize that competence, information, and technology have become commodities, and that only creativity adds value.
- Use creativity to solve problems, design ways forward, resolve conflicts, simplify, cut costs, motivate, design new products and services, and strategize.
- Challenge traditional, accepted, and usual concepts and perceptions, because the adequate can hide the better idea.
- Use the "Six Hats" method for parallel thinking, with everybody looking and thinking in the same direction, and not arguing.
- Lead from the top to create the expectation that executives and other workers will come up with and explore new ideas.

Edward de Bono is the originator of "lateral thinking," and "parallel thinking." He qualified as a doctor, going on to read psychology, and from this basis developed his work in the practical aspect of human thinking. His work in the area of perception provided the basis for the DATT program in business and the CoRT program in schools. His many publications include, *Six Thinking Hats*, (revised edition, Little, Brown, 1999), and *New Thinking for the New Millennium* (New Millennium Press, 2000). For more information, please visit www.edwarddebono.com.

Managing Internal Politics

Kathleen Kelley Reardon

Many of the hurdles managers must face and overcome have little to do with technical competence. Rather, they have to do with politics. Internal politics is a fact of life in organizations, yet many managers and C.E.O.s will tell you their success is largely due to allowing "no politics" in their firms. They'll regale you with stories of how they use and encourage "people skills" to create a desired environment and accomplish organizational goals. What they're really talking about is how they use politics.

In common vernacular, "politics" is used to describe what people do to influence decision makers, accomplish hidden agendas, and surreptitiously advance their careers, often to the detriment of others. But politics is not always so sinister. By its very nature, politics involves going outside usual, formally sanctioned channels to accomplish objectives, but not necessarily in a secretive manner and often to the benefit of all involved. When used to influence people in the service of valid company goals, politics becomes a positive tool indeed. The team leader who makes valuable connections with people who can advance the team's efforts is acting politically.

While a high level of field-based competence is required, given two competent persons, the one who has political savvy, agility in the use of power, and the ability to influence others is more likely to succeed as a senior manager. Indeed, to the successful senior manager in a competitive organization, day-to-day life *is* politics. That's why smart business people think like Caroline Nahas, managing director of Korn/Ferry International, southern California. To be politically astute, you need to "read where the trend lines are" and "be ahead of the game."

Of course, politics is not always positive. Sometimes, people must defend themselves from political maneuvering. When surrounded or targeted by coworkers playing underhanded political games, job survival may require one to act similarly. In organizations where biases or favoritism dictate who gets key assignments and promotions, political maneuvering is required to get into the loop. Here again, there's nothing unethical going on. The organizational political arena merely requires the use of relational strategies to advance oneself. In short, the astute manager must understand how politics functions in organizations and how to advance his or her and the firm's own goals.

SIZING UP THE POLITICAL ARENA

The first step in acquiring political acumen is learning to identify the kind of political arena in which you operate. Without this knowledge, managers operate in the dark, wondering why opportunities were lost. All four primary political arenas—minimal, moderate, highly political, and pathologically political—often coexist inside a large organization.

In a *minimally politicized* arena, the atmosphere is amicable. Conflicts rarely occur and don't usually last long. There's an absence of in- and out-groups, and one person's gain isn't seen as another's loss. Rules may be bent and favors granted, but people treat each other with regard and rarely resort to underhanded political means. These are excellent environments for people uncomfortable with aggressive politics. Unfortunately, such organizations are more the exception than the rule.

Moderately politicized organizations operate on commonly understood and formally sanctioned rules. They often include smaller, fast-moving firms and large ones focused on organizational agility. Where customer focus, results, teamwork, and interpersonal trust are priorities, politics are rarely destructive, and often focus on surfacing worthwhile ideas. Achieving objectives via unsanctioned methods isn't unusual, but tends to be subtle and deniable. When conflicts get out of hand, managers will invoke sanctioned rules or shared mores for resolution.

As a manager, however, when such an arena becomes dysfunctional, you will see considerable denial before unspoken political rules surface to where you can identify and address them constructively.

In a *highly politicized* culture, conflict is pervasive. Instead of applying formal rules consistently, combatants only invoke them when convenient. In-groups and out-groups are clearly defined. Few people dare to communicate directly with senior managers. "Who" is more important than "what" you know, and work is often highly stressful, especially for those in out-groups. When there's conflict, people rely on aggressive political methods and involve others in the dispute. Highly political organizations are usually incapable of resolving conflicts constructively. They place blame and terminate losers. Such quick fixes rarely alter the dysfunctional pattern.

Pathologically politicized organizations are often on the verge of self-destruction. Productivity is suboptimal and information massaging is prevalent. People distrust each other, interactions are often fractious, and conflict is long-lasting and pervasive. People must circumvent formal procedures and structures to achieve objectives. They spend much time covering their backs. Management uses a carrot-and-stick approach to control people. Subordinates are seen as stubborn, willful—even stupid. In the classic *Harvard Business Review* article, "Asinine Attitudes toward Motivation," Harry Levinson described this as the "jackass fallacy."

IDENTIFYING POLITICAL PATHOLOGY

To avoid political pathology, managers must recognize its encroachment. Here are five indicators that it's time to alter the political environment to save it from self-destruction.

1 *Frequent flattery* of persons in power, coupled with abuse of people in weaker positions.
2 *Information massaging.* No one says anything that might rock the boat, and the common means of communication is hint and innuendo.
3 *Malicious gossip* and backstabbing are common, even where little overt conflict appears.
4 *Cold indifference*, where no one is valued and everyone is dispensable, indicates the area has been systemically polluted by people in charge. Survival is based on obsequiousness, and getting others before they get you.

5 *Fake left, go right.* People, even entire departments, purposely mislead others in order to look good when they fail. Teamwork is absent. Managers sacrifice subordinates' careers to avoid looking bad.

MATCHING POLITICAL STYLE TO POLITICAL CULTURE

The second crucial step in learning to manage politics is identifying individual political styles. The mix of styles and their "fit" with the predominant political arena exert considerable influence on goal achievement.

The Purist. The least political are "purists," who believe in getting ahead through hard work. They shun politics, and rely on following sanctioned rules to get things done. Purists are usually honest—sometimes naively so. They believe in getting ahead by doing their job well. Purists trust other people and prefer to work with those who do the same. Behind the scenes grappling for power and prestige is not of interest, hence purists are best suited to minimally political climates.

The Team Player. "Team players" believe you get ahead by working with others and using politics that advance the goals of the group. They rarely put career needs ahead of group needs. Team players prefer to operate by sanctioned rules, but will trade favors or engage in other relatively benign politics to achieve team goals. Focused on doing the job right and creating conditions for team member advancement, team players are best suited to moderately political environments.

The Street Fighter. An individualist, the "street fighter" believes the best way to get ahead is via rough tactics. The street fighter relies more on subliminal politics than the purist and the team player, but is just as likely to invoke sanctioned rules when they serve personal goals. Street fighters watch their backs, push hard to achieve personal goals, and are slow to trust others. They thrive on the "cut and thrust" of business, enjoy intrigue, and derive gratification from working the system. The street fighter is comfortable in highly political arenas and can survive in pathological ones as well.

The Maneuverer. The "maneuverer" is also an individualist, one who believes in getting ahead by playing political games in a skillful, unobtrusive manner. Subtler than the street fighter, but uninhibited about using politics to advance personal objectives and favored team objectives, maneuverers prefer to do so in deniable ways. They look for ulterior motives in others, have little regard for sanctioned rules, and rely largely on subliminal politics. These smooth operators are less committed to hard work than purists, and only operate as team players when it suits their agendas. People get in the way of a maneuverer at their own peril. The maneuverer is best suited to highly political and pathological arenas.

The task of all managers with regard to politics is to assess the arena prevalent in their division, and that of the larger organization. Is it becoming highly political or pathological? If so, is this because opinion leaders are of the street fighter or maneuverer styles? There's nothing inherently wrong with street fighters and the occasional maneuverer may be an asset if he or she brings something valuable to the group. A predominance of these styles, however, can tip a division or organization closer to pathology, a condition that is difficult if not impossible to reverse. Savvy managers familiarize themselves with political warning signs and, as IBM C.E.O. Lou Gerstner did when he implemented a policy of straight talk, they take steps to stem the tide of political self-destruction.

MAKING IT HAPPEN
To navigate politics in your organization:
- Assess the degree to which your organization is politicized. Is the atmosphere amicable or distrustful? Is the workforce productive, or does conflict prevent work getting done?
- Recognize the signs of impending political pathology: flattery of superiors, malicious gossip, information massaging, indifference, and purposeful misleading.
- Take steps to detoxify the workplace: communicate more openly and directly, invoke sanctioned rules or shared mores to resolve conflict, emphasize solving problems over placing blame.

Politics are a reality in the workplace; and, consequently, one must manage the conflicts that arise from political behavior. Politics, in and of itself, is not bad if it works to serve company goals by making sure that the workplace is productive and that morale remains high. Politics must never be allowed to degenerate into a self-destructive process.

Kathleen Kelley Reardon, professor of management and organization at the University of Southern California Marshall School of Business, has served on the faculty of the MBA, Executive MBA, and International MBA Programs. She is a leading authority on persuasion, politics in the workplace, negotiation, and interpersonal communication. She is the author of five books and numerous articles published in communication and business journals, including the 1994–95 *Harvard Business Review* reprint "Bestseller" case "The Memo Every Woman Keeps on Her Desk" and the book following from that, *They Don't Get it, Do They? Communication in the Workplace—Closing the Gap Between Women and Men* (Little, Brown 1995). Her most recent book for Doubleday, *The Secret Handshake: Mastering the Politics of the Business Inner Circle*, released in early 2001, focuses on strategies for working effectively within organizational political climates.

Response Ability—How Managers Stay Up When Times Are Down

Paul Stoltz

Adversity, ranging from annoyance to tragedy, has become the rule in corporate life. Adversity is everything that gets in the way of, or blocks, an organization's quest to fulfill its vision, achieve its goals, and accomplish its strategic plan. To keep these imperatives alive requires greater resilience than most managers possess. Given that managing adversity lies at the heart of management's ability to unleash human capital, how can managers learn to harness adversity to launch new levels of opportunity and momentum? As adversity rises, every manager's and organization's resilience and effectiveness hinges on *Response Ability*, the ability to respond optimally to whatever happens the moment it strikes. Response Able managers thrive amid the same difficulties that paralyze their less Response Able counterparts.

MANAGING IN ADVERSITY

The Silent Toll. While today's workplace is arguably more dynamic and exciting, it is also exacting a growing toll. A Gallup Poll revealed that 19% of workers are "actively disengaged"—they are delivering a small fraction of their talents at work. Furthermore, 61% (or more) are at least partially disengaged. The estimated cost to corporations in the United States alone is $350 billion; multiply that several times over for a worldwide estimate.

As adversity rises, workers feel increasingly stretched. Their work and their lives become more complex, chaotic, uncertain, and demanding. Their entire world tasks them to do more, faster, and better. The physical toll adversity takes upon the majority of the work force includes a multitude of dismal symptoms, including diminished immune functions (with increased sick days), sapped energy, insomnia, and stress. Inside most people, today's levels of adversity create a chronic and toxic biochemical reaction that holistically degrades their performance deeply.

The psychological toll of the adversity trend manifests as depression, restlessness, anxiety, and pessimism—all psychosocial phenomena which are occurring at epidemic levels and growing. These conditions are also symbiotic, feeding off and flourishing in each other's presence. Overall the grand-scale toll of adversity in organizations, their capacity, and human capital is inestimable. Fortunately, it is also largely unnecessary.

The Truth about Motivation. Nearly every manager perceives motivating others as an important and essential duty. Yet, intuitively, we know that we cannot motivate others: authentic motivation originates and is sustained from deep within the self. Attempting to motivate others can be like painting your car red to make it go faster. It may *feel* faster, but very little has happened to strengthen performance.

To fully understand the myth and challenge of motivation, we must consider three forms of capacity. A person's *Required Capacity* is what the world demands of them, or what is required of them to perform their job effectively. As adversity mounts, most people's required capacity is growing at an accelerated rate, making it harder to remain fully engaged and motivated.

When we motivate others, we are striving to help them tap and deliver their *Existing Capacity*—their talents, aptitudes, competencies, experience, knowledge, wisdom, and energy—to the challenge at hand. People are hired for their Existing Capacity under two assumptions: that they will tap most, if not all, of it on a regular basis and that they will grow it to meet or exceed the Required Capacity.

The portion of their capacity that a person actually taps and delivers is called their *Accessed Capacity*. Anyone who has hired someone knows that many people fail to access their best abilities at work. This is a chronic source of frustration among managers and the major source of lost or underutilized human capital. The quest of every manager must be to hire and grow Response Able people who can consistently tap and grow their Existing Capacities. Clearly traditional methods of motivation, screening applicants, and training employees fall critically short of what is required.

ACHIEVING SUCCESS AND RESPONSE ABILITY

Fortunately, there is a way to assess and strengthen how people respond to adversity, or their Response Ability. Beyond your IQ, experience, or skill-set, it is your Adversity Quotient, or AQ, that most directly predicts and determines your ability to weather and harness the current storm for future gains.

AQ is scientifically valid, a reliable measure of your hardwired pattern of response to adversity. More than 100,000 employees in dozens of companies representing a broad range of industries have measured their AQs and learned about how their CORE affects their Response Ability, capacity, and resilience.

A Response Able culture is one in which . . .

1 *People thrive on adversity.* The greater the challenges, the more energized and engaged people become. In fact, people get bored if things are too calm for too long.

2 *Challenges unleash greatness.* People are at their best in trying situations and times. They consistently dig deep and bring out their greatest talents when faced with the impossible.

3 *There's calm in the storm.* There is a norm of cool-headed decision making. People are not easily fazed or thrown off by unexpected turns of events or adversities.

4 *There are stories of overcoming.* There is likely to be a history of resilience, with revered sagas of heroes who faced and overcame adversity to create pivotal advancements.

5 *Managers hire and keep the best.* Self-motivated, fully engaged people are attracted to and are likely to stay with the organization.

A low AQ culture is one in which . . .

1 *People crumble under pressure.* When adversity strikes, people are stunned, angry, resigned, and uninspired.

2 *Situations bring out the worst.* As adversity mounts, people act in selfish, distant, panicked, mean, disengaged, and dispassionate ways. Conflicts arise, panic spreads, helplessness grows, and problems fester.

3 *It seems like a blame game.* Adversity makes people point fingers and sidestep blame. The greater the adversity, the more accountability, trust, and agility suffer.

4 *The bleeding edge moves in.* Despite efforts to reward self-motivated top performers, there is a history of losing these people. Turnover remains a chronic, incalculable loss of human capital and potential.

5 *Excitement reduces to passionless pursuit.* People go through the motions, but the culture lacks passion, excitement, risk-taking, and a compelling sense of purpose. A mere 5–20% of the workforce drives the success of the entire organization.

Adversity Quotient: the CORE of Response Ability. AQ is comprised of four CORE dimensions, which together determine and drive Response Ability. Each dimension plays a unique role in a person's resilience, performance, innovation, and strength.

C = Control: *To what extent do I perceive I can influence the situation at hand?*
This dimension of AQ assesses perceived control, not actual control. It pinpoints your propensity for self-determination on the one hand and helplessness on the other.

O = Ownership: *To what extent can/should I play a role in improving this situation?*
This dimension assesses propensity for inner accountability. In contrast to blame, which is about pinpointing the source of the problem, ownership is about playing even the smallest role in improving the situation, regardless of its cause.

R = Reach: *How far does this adversity reach and affect other areas of work or life?*
This dimension pinpoints the perceived size or magnitude of the adversity, which has a dramatic impact on likelihood to take meaningful action.

E = Endurance: *How long can you continue to confront adversity in a positive way?*
This dimension provides a reading on how you will deal with the next challenge, obstacle, or difficult personality.

When we measure these four characteristics, individually and collectively, basic patterns emerge. A company can be seen as either having a Response Able culture, or not.

ORGANIZATIONS BUILDING RESPONSE ABILITY

ADC Telecommunications successfully positioned itself to provide vital hardware and services to the prominent warriors (Lucent, WorldCom, Sprint, AT&T, etc.). Yet, when the entire sector lost 70% of its market value in a matter of a few months, ADC's stock plummeted, despite record earnings. ADC decided that creating a Response Able, resilient sales force would position them for a superior and quicker comeback against competitors. In classes in Singapore, Spain, China, Canada, and the United States, ADC's global sales force from 16 countries learned new ways to get, keep, and grow people who can thrive in a demanding, dynamic industry.

Marriott International recognized that the defining factor in sustaining their aggressive growth curve while maintaining their high standard of service during an economic downturn would be their associates' and leaders' Response Ability.

Many other organizations—including FedEx, Deloitte & Touche, Palm Pilot, and Qualcomm—have focused on how well their employees and managers handle adversity, resulting in improved performance, retention, agility, innovation, problem solving, resilience, and accelerated change.

MAKING IT HAPPEN

Growing a Response Able workforce that can not only cope with but thrive in adversity-rich times requires a commitment to forgo the comforts of mediocrity and the courage to reinvent existing norms regarding Control, Ownership, Reach, and Endurance—the pattern of response to adversity. To start to build Response Ability, managers must:

- assess the Adversity Quotient of their current workforce;
- hire high AQ people;
- grow high AQ, Response Able leaders;
- pay attention to how people respond to adversity the moment it strikes, assessing Control, Ownership, Reach, and Endurance;
- focus on what facets of a situation can be influenced, no matter how impossible it may seem;
- establish norms of people stepping up to improve and address difficulties the moment they arise;
- contain each adversity in scope immediately;
- be the first to recognize and seize the opportunity embedded in each adversity;
- strategize around worst case scenarios in a matter-of-fact way.

Adversity is on the rise, and that's the *good* news! Great companies and managers are—and increasingly will be—those who can harness the force of adversity to create even greater opportunity. They assess and strengthen their Adversity Quotients to become more Response Able. And they use their growing Response Ability to optimize their human capital and to stay up when times are down.

———————

Paul Stoltz is president and C.E.O. of PEAK Learning Inc., an international performance consulting company that has evolved into the international hub for Adversity Quotient (AQ) related training, consulting, applications, and research. He and the PEAK team are the authors, lead researchers, and architects of the groundbreaking AQ theory, measurement tools, books, and methods. He wrote the bestsellers *Adversity Quotient: Turning Obstacles into Opportunities* (John Wiley, 1999) and *Adversity Quotient @ Work* (William Morrow, 2000).

Preventing Your Work Problems
from Causing You Stress

David Allen

If you're a knowledge worker, manager, or executive, you must constantly think creatively, make decisions, and manage what you and others are doing about it all. Every input triggers these behaviors, every opportunity invites them, and every crisis demands them. And when you avoid the appropriate thinking and decisions, or don't sufficiently manage the resulting actions, you pay a steep internal price—you lie awake at 3 a.m.

The volume of executive choices in a single day can be astonishing; the typical mid- to senior-level professional makes hundreds. Add the weight of several onerous problems—a 20% staff cut, a customer about to cancel a big deal, and a tax audit next week—and you wonder how anyone gets any sleep at all!

Unproductive worrying doesn't have to happen, however. If you apply a certain thought process and manage the results appropriately with good systems and reviewing habits, you can eliminate the distraction. You can get to sleep in the middle of even the most challenging of situations. But we aren't born knowing how to do this, nor is it taught in school or on the job. There is a learned set of behaviors that can be practiced and mastered. As with tennis, golf, skiing, or sailing, you must learn and apply the basic moves of work to play the game well. And you can continually improve how well you do this.

WHAT KEEPS US AWAKE?

You can't eliminate challenging circumstances in life and work. What you can improve on is how you deal with them—and how much stress you're willing to allow and endure. There's a difference between stress and intensity. Intensity is concentrated energy focused on dealing with a situation. You can be intensely involved with something and still sleep five minutes later. Stress (the kind that usually keeps people up at night) is infinitely looping inner conflict caused by unfulfilled commitments to yourself.

The broken-agreement syndrome is subtle, though, and not often conscious. Unhealthy stress occurs when some part of you thinks something should be different, but you aren't yet appropriately engaged in making it happen. This kind of stress occurs when:

- you keep something you're paying attention to completely in your head, without acting on it;
- you don't decide and focus on what you want to be true about the situation;
- you don't decide the next physical actions required to move it forward;
- you don't organize reminders of those actions and outcomes to systematically trigger appropriate progressive motion.

GET IT OUT OF YOUR HEAD

If you keep something only in your mind, you file it in psychic RAM, the short-term memory space that has limited capacity for filing and retrieval and operates with no sense of past and future. (You told yourself to clean your garage six years ago, and some part of you thinks you should have been cleaning your garage every day since then!) As soon as your RAM contains more than one current agenda item, it creates inner failure and stress, because you can only do one thing at a time, and RAM thinks it should all be happening *now*. If that were only two or three things, it might not be very noticeable. But most people have hundreds and sometimes thousands of woulds, coulds, and shoulds piled up internally, forming a kind of free-floating, unproductive tension and overreaction. Capturing something in writing will start to relieve pressure and facilitate intelligent focus.

DEFINE THE GAME AND DECIDE THE NEXT MOVE

Even if you write down something that's bothering you, if you still haven't identified what you really intend to be true about it (the successful outcome), you won't resolve the frustrated feeling. For instance, if you've just found out that a key person on your staff is quitting, just writing down "key person leaving" probably won't make you relax. You must determine what you want to be true, for example, "reorganize staff" or "replace marketing VP." Then you'll have defined the loop that needs to be closed.

This still isn't sufficient, however, to relax your brain. You must also determine the next physical action required to move the situation forward toward closure. What has to happen first to replace your staff person? Send an e-mail? Converse with your partner? Call a recruiting firm? Or wait for someone else to do something?

PUT THE RESULTS INTO A TRUSTED SYSTEM

Once it's clear where you're heading with a situation and how to kick-start forward motion, it will feel much better. But there's one final critical element that has to be in place to allow you to let it go in your mind: you need to entrust the management of the outcome and the action to a system outside your own head. You have to know that you'll actually look at "replace marketing VP" written somewhere and think about it as often as you need to. And if your next action is to call about recruiting firms, you need to know that whenever you find yourself at a telephone with discretionary time, you'll see a reminder of that call as an option for what you need to be doing. Or if you've delegated the whole project to someone else, you must trust that the person will do it without fail, or at least that you have a reliable tracking mechanism to remind you in a progress report.

Even if you can't decide what to do about something, action is inherent in finding out what you need to know to make the decision. In the rare case that you really do simply need to sleep on it, you still need to trust that sometime in the future you'll be reminded about it. "Ready to decide about selling the company yet?" could go on your own calendar on a date you think appropriate, and you could then rest. You really just decided not to decide, and your own agreement with yourself is kept.

If you haven't engaged all these steps, your mind simply cannot let go. You can numb it or try to ignore it, but you can't fool it. Your mind knows whether you've made necessary decisions about a problem or situation and whether you have a system in place to manage the results. With anything less, some part of your psyche retains it.

But your head doesn't usually do a very good job of managing these distractions. That part of your mind hanging onto the issue doesn't seem to have innate intelligence. If it did, it would only remind you of a current issue when you could actually do something about it. (Most likely you remember you need batteries when you're trying to use a flashlight with dead ones, not as you're passing the battery display in a store!)

So when you think something needs to be different, you've implicitly made an agreement with yourself. If it remains unrecorded, undecided, and unmanaged objectively, your mind will not stop trying to get resolution, and it does that rather ineffectively. It can occupy your thoughts and still make no progress: you're awake at 3 a.m.

Carola Endicott, vice president of clinical operations at the 400-bed New England Medical Center in Boston, said: "A specific tool that has become a way of life for me is the simple question: what is the next step? In all of the hundreds of meetings I attend in the course of a year, I have learned the power of asking that simple question. Without it, the worry lingers—was I supposed to do something? Capturing and organizing my own next actions is also critical. By knowing these can be easily tracked and reviewed, I can free up my mind for being open to new ideas—and let it take a rest at night!"

Mike Verville, director of retail operations at L.L. Bean, described the dramatic results of learning and implementing these principles: "When I applied these principles [clarifying outcomes and next actions and tracking them appropriately] it saved my life . . . when I faithfully applied them, it changed my life. This is the vaccination against day-to-day firefighting (the so-called urgent) and an antidote for the imbalance many people bring upon themselves."

Robert Stiller, entrepreneur and C.E.O. of the fast-growing Vermont-based Green Mountain Coffee Roasters, has implemented a company-wide training program to instill these principles. He says: "Particularly exciting and successful for me has been training myself to decide the very next action steps on my projects on the front end. In the past I would list things; and when I'd go to do them, I would have to figure out what to do. I'd often get distracted or lose the energy I had for action. Changing my thought process and categorizing the possible actions appropriately really helps in dealing with the work. By collecting, processing, and organizing the things I have attention on, I'm able to look at the day-to-day flow and go on to the higher level context of the work. With my system working and keeping all the issues, projects, and action steps out of my head and before me, it's easy to sleep, and my sleep can actually help me problem-solve."

MAKING IT HAPPEN

To minimize your work stress:

- Get (and keep) everything out of your head. Whatever you have attention on, write it down. Even the little things.

- Analyze each thing you've collected: does it require action? If not, throw it away or archive it as reference. If it does require action, decide what the next action is and what the successful outcome is that you're committing to. If the action can be done in less than two minutes, do it now. If not, delegate it if you can.
- Organize reminders of the outcomes on a projects list. Organize reminders of work that cannot be delegated, and would take longer than two minutes in lists you can see when you can actually perform the action (for example, be able to see all the calls you have to make when you have a phone and some discretionary time).
- Bring your system current and review everything that represents outstanding outcomes and actions at least once a week.

You don't have to finish something to get it off your mind and sleep well. But stress-free is not free. You do have to stop a distracting thought from rattling in your head by tackling it, clarifying what you're committing to make happen, deciding the next action required to move it forward, and entrusting the results of that thinking to a seamless system.

Getting on top of things that are distracting you requires knowledge work—you must think. You need to discipline your focus to take a minute and answer the key questions—What's the outcome I want here? What's the next action? Then your brain can say, done! There's usually an inverse proportion between the amount of time something is on your mind and the degree to which it's getting done. The more relaxed you are, the more productive you'll be.

David Allen, founder and president of the management consulting and training company, David Allen & Co., was named by *Fast Company* as "one of the world's leading thinkers" in personal productivity. He wrote the bestseller, *Getting Things Done: The Art of Stress-free Productivity* (Viking Penguin, 2001), and his e-newsletter, *David Allen's Productivity Principles,* has thousands of subscribers worldwide. For more information, please refer to the Web site, www.davidco.com.

On Business As a Privilege

Mihaly Csikszentmihalyi

Mihaly Csikszentmihalyi is a professor at the School of Management, Claremont Graduate University, California, where he serves as director of the Quality of Life Research Center. Formerly professor and chairman of the Department of Psychology at the University of Chicago, his research interests include the study of creativity, the evolution of social and cultural systems, and the study of intrinsically rewarding behavior in work and play settings. He is the author of numerous articles and several influential books, including *Flow: The Psychology of Optimal Experience* (HarperCollins, 1991), *The Evolving Self: A Psychology for the Third Millennium* (HarperCollins, 1993, reprint 1994), *Finding Flow: The Psychology of Engagement with Everyday Life* (Basic Books, 1998), *Good Work: When Excellence and Ethics Meet* (with Howard Gardner and William Damon, Basic Books, 2001), and *Good Business: Leadership, Flow, and the Making of Meaning* (forthcoming in 2003 from Viking).

Reflecting on the current environment of uncertainty, I suppose the most profound influence for me was World War II, when I realized how the most advanced and scientifically sophisticated societies can go wrong. You can't take anything for granted, you have to strive constantly to advance. In terms of people, in the field of business, Peter Drucker stands out—his common sense and historical rootedness made me realize that there is a way of looking at business and management from a liberal-arts kind of perspective. To be a good manager, you need to have a good idea of what people are like, to appreciate their essential motivations. In that respect, influencers include Hannah Arendt, many of the existential philosophers (Martin Heidegger and so forth), and many psychologists, including Abraham Maslow, who wrote extensively on management.

If it's true that we are moving more and more into a knowledge economy, then it's clear that you have to learn how to manage people who are more demanding and have a greater aspiration for their lives. You have to learn to provide freedom and self-determination. I believe that's true—provided that we are, in fact, moving toward a knowledge economy.

But I think that, parallel to this movement, many of the trends show an increase in the number of security personnel—more and more watchers and protectors, especially at the bottom levels of the hierarchy. It's true that the top echelon is moving toward the knowledge economy, but it's not clear that there is saturation to the front lines. There is a discrepancy between top management and the rest. That worries me. There are many trends in that direction; for instance, the notorious book, *The Bell Curve* by Richard J. Herrnstein and Charles Murray (Simon & Schuster, 1996)—I wrote a review of that in the *Washington Post* in which I argued that most people had either misunderstood or not read the book. It's not about racial difference. We have become more and more dependent on intelligence (as measured by IQ) as a way of segregating or stratifying people. In earlier times you could be an honest craftworker or respectable farmer, and these values of honesty and perseverance were considered as important as intellectual abilities. But now, unless you have a degree from a respected university, you can't feel respected.

There are two stratifying forces: one is the economic, and the other is this intellectual stratification that is getting out of hand. Making decisions on this basis distorts the complexity of human life, especially when you have a single metric—like money—determining who wins and who loses.

In this context, are there new management questions that we should be asking? For instance, who and what am I ultimately responsible to/for? This is partly what we wrote about in *Good Work*. It's so easy to get caught up in your institution's habits of performance or process. You join a company and "this is how things are done," and you end up doing things that way, instead of asking: What is the ultimate outcome of what I'm getting involved in or getting into? Is this really what I want to do or what society needs? Those shouldn't be new questions!

Meanwhile, the more I learn about the self, the less I can say about it. There are all these people talking about the "protean" self—a jumble of half-digested impulses. I can say that there is at least a constructed self that you *believe* represents who you are. At various times that's not the self that is being enacted in your behavior. Without a constructed self, it's hard to operate with integrity; the less variation there is between your constructed self and your behavior, the better off you are. The notion of what you ultimately take responsibility for should be the same at work and at home. Some of the people we talked to in *Good Business* are very clear about it. One of my favorite examples is Aaron Feuerstein of Malden Mills, the Massachusetts-based manufacturer of Polartec, who vowed to keep the company running after a disastrous fire and more recently strengthened it by wisely filing for bankruptcy. He very much disapproves of people who have one set of values and interests at work, and shift to another mode when they get home. He has an almost biblical view: unless you maintain a consistent set of values, your actions are determined by expediency, and you can't continue to sustain either personal or professional integrity.

What about operating on intuition? Intuition really works best when it's based on experience reflected on. It's at the cutting edge of intellect—where intuition moves just beyond what you can rationally justify. It's kind of unpredictable, a loose cannon. You have to reflect on experience, and then you can afford to go beyond what you can immediately justify intellectually. Trust in your knowledge and your experience instead of passing the buck to others. To promote this marriage between intellect and intuition, when confronted with a problem or issue, you can train yourself to make an intuitive leap to understand what caused the situation, or what could resolve it. Jot down your intuitive understanding in the moment and then try to deal with the situation intellectually, using all the facts. Then match your intuition to what you discovered intellectually. You can also learn to recognize patterns in your intuition, for example, you may tend to blame others, or to be overly pessimistic or optimistic. Recognizing these patterns can help you harness your intuition.

Currently I am fascinated by the notion of business as a privilege. I'm not a historian or sociologist of power, but it's becoming clear that those who have power end up getting more privileges. Take the clergy, for example. Since medieval times they have enjoyed the bounties of wealth, comfort, and a good life. But when people realize that the bishops and abbots are getting bigger and bigger palaces and we still live in the same hovels our grandparents lived in, the bishops and abbots are out. This scenario plays out over and over again. Eventually people get fed up with those who get away with excesses for their own benefit; then there are restrictions, regulations, or even revolutions. In business we are reaching such a turning point now. Will there be enough business leaders who realize that it will be to their advantage to scale down their excessive behavior of getting away with the privileges and impose some forms of internal restrictions and regulations? If not, the pressure will come from the outside. Consider the threat of a players' strike in major league baseball in the summer of 2002: eventually the fans will say, What am I doing to support this behavior? and find cheaper ways to amuse themselves.

Fundamentally, what's true of business is true of other walks of life. I have discovered four simple and essential aims of successful people:

(1) To get to know yourself—good and bad—instead of denying or repressing or deluding yourself, figure out what you really want from life, what you're good at, and what you enjoy doing.

(2) To get to do more and more of what you *like* to do, and at the same time learn to love what you *have* to do and get to the point of saying that you look forward to getting up in the morning and facing the day—this is very important to the people I talk to who are successful in life.

(3) To respect other people, feel that they are worth helping, feel that the human race is not ready for the slag heap—work for the common good, embrace a sense that life as a whole (the environment) is worth preserving, and recognize that it gives meaning and purpose to your life to give meaning to these things.

(4) To be true to yourself—when you have integrity, people will respect you because you try to act in concert with your beliefs.

When I teach MBA students, they're in such a hurry they think that if they don't get their first million by 25, they'll be a failure. They're so impatient and focused that they don't realize they'll be living another 50 years beyond that first million! I started teaching MBA classes in 2000; the difference between that cohort and the one in 2001 was dramatic. In 2000, all of them were sure they would get increasing equity in their firms. That was a hard cohort to teach, because they didn't want to learn anything except how to get into Cisco or Enron. The following year's group, somewhat shell-shocked and not quite sure of anything in the wake of the September 11 attacks, still maintained a remnant of unfounded hope, but were much more interested in traditional business, and even government and nonprofit interests.

One thing that so many of the people I talk to say: If you are looking for a job, look for the best organization in your field and be willing to apprentice yourself to it for a while, even if it means not getting paid. If it's not what you thought it would be, get out of there—cut your losses and move on, and don't settle for less. This is what I mean by being true to yourself.

Whoever Tells the Best Story Wins: The Subjective Side of Business

Annette Simmons

Story is a uniquely powerful way to reveal subjective truths and, in the process, improve collaborative decision making and problem solving. Any task or initiative that involves more than one person is, by its very nature, going to involve participants with different perspectives and interpretations of the situation. In an impasse, for example, facts and analysis often spiral deeper into disagreement. A story, however, can collectively raise perspective to a higher level.

A BRIDGE OVER IMPASSE

I adopted my dog Larry from the racetrack. You don't want to know what happens to the ones that don't get adopted. When Larry first came to live with me, he didn't know how to be a pet. He had never seen a bone before. When I gave him one, he chased it nose down across the back yard until he made the intellectual leap that a well-placed paw could keep it still. One thing he has never learned—and shows no sign of learning—is that when he is on a leash and walks on one side of a telephone pole and I walk on the other, we aren't going anywhere. Larry just looks up at me with his puzzled dog face. I could tell him all day to back up. I could explain the benefits of backing up. I could even pull rank, but he's not going to back up until I back up. Once I back up, he follows. Only then can we disentangle ourselves and move on.

C.E.O.s, senior managers, truck drivers, telemarketers, and nurses alike understand that this story is not really about Larry the dog. With the right delivery and good timing, a story like this can help rescue a group from impasse and prompt introspection, self-awareness, and behavior change. C.E.O.s back off ultimatums. Truck drivers lean forward. Nurses unfold their arms. A more direct approach—"As long as your egos are attached to being right, you'll never reach agreement"—just doesn't work as well as a story.

Tools for crunching numbers and generating facts have improved business immeasurably. Unfortunately, the tools for generating feelings and shifting perspective are way behind. Business success is a function of both facts and feelings. Feelings are subjective, a function of interpreted experience and individual perspective. Remember the buzzword "paradigm shift?" We had the right idea . . . but lousy tools. Good ideas—visions, values, and missions—were reduced to laminated cards, hypocritical meetings, and endless word crafting. Objective tools reduce subjective truths into meaninglessness. Some people did it right, but current cynicism in the workplace is often a result of lousy implementation of subjective ideals—promises that never delivered. Many attempts to make things better only made things worse. Why? Perspective and feelings operate according to different principles than objectivity, logic, and facts.

The Larry story tunnels beneath resistance and shifts perspective to a bigger picture. It prompts introspection without risk. Saving face is a very important (and often neglected) aspect of shifting perspective. All of these factors—resistance, perspective, introspection, and saving face—are highly subjective.

RESPECT IS SUBJECTIVE

A company's new IT system had created a roomful of "winners," who didn't need to change a thing, and "losers," who felt like they had to relearn their jobs from scratch. Implementation fell six months behind, because the people who didn't like the system ignored it completely. Tensions rose. At one point, the group got sidetracked about who said hello in the morning. The energy about who said hello was fierce. Suddenly, one very senior manager showed more feeling than intended when she shouted, "No one ever tells ME hello in the morning!" A hush descended and everyone stared, until one of the IT guys gave some lame explanation about her being so busy no one wanted to bother her. No one believed his explanation. Objective truth was not the issue here. The moment called for someone to say something, and his explanation was as good as any. The real impact was the shift in the group's perspective. People began to see that everyone in the room was feeling neglected (even the dragon lady). Saying hello was a metaphor for respect. People did not want to cooperate with anyone who didn't respect them enough to say hello in the morning.

This particular story articulates a subjective truth lost in objective language. Many work groups are dysfunctional simply because individuals do not feel respected. This story validates respect as a legitimate expectation and simultaneously demonstrates that everyone—the dragon lady included—is feeling neglected. No one ever kneels, whispers *mea culpa*, and begs forgiveness from coworkers—but the shift in perspective alters behavior. Subjective shifts often occur without objectively measurable evidence. Genuine respect is subjective: some days it means saying hello, and some days it means discreetly excusing a coworker from this social convention. Forcing people to provide measurable outcomes for subjective shifts will distort, even destroy, your ability to target subjective issues.

OBJECTIVE IS WHAT?; SUBJECTIVE IS HOW AND WHY?

There are few managers who couldn't improve their leadership with better listening skills. Yet objective, skills-based active-listening courses only seem to teach people how to nod, paraphrase, and hold eye contact—in other words, how to fake listening. I was poking fun at these skills-based courses with a group of consultants in Hungary. One of the women in the group raised her hand and said, "Exactly. Listening is just like sex." I had to know. "How so?" She continued in her Zsa Zsa Gabor accent, "When the desire is there, the skills will follow."

That story is a beautiful example of how objective, what-to-do training courses can miss the subjective essence of *how* and *why*. Story has the power to fill in between the lines, to breathe feelings of human *experience* into outcomes, strategic plans, and objective goals so people can see, hear, and feel enough for it to feel real. Once a goal feels real in their imagination, people are much more likely to do what it takes to make it real in the physical world. They not only understand the what, they have a feeling for the how and the why. Documentation of a best practice in linear form is dry and abstract. Story is reconstituted reality that awakens all the senses and conjures enough emotional glue for an idea to stick. Just as a small-scale model brings a blueprint to life, so does a story bring a list of year-end goals to life.

A story is a narration of events that simulates a visual, sensory, and emotional experience that feels significant for both the listener and the teller. If experience is the best teacher, then story is second-best.

Story takes thinking backward and then forward again through a subjective human experience in a way that prompts new conclusions. Until humans are created with flip-top heads into which you can feed your desired conclusions, the practice of storytelling is the fastest way to prompt people to rethink current practices and reach their own conclusions about how and why they should pursue new initiatives and strategies.

BUSINESS IS OBJECTIVE AND SUBJECTIVE

A so-called merger of equals was not going well; the 30 faces of senior management were a cocktail of anxiety and aggression. They sat around a U-shaped table in a hotel conference room with little faith in this—third—attempt to create a collaborative plan. The C.E.O. had fired the last consulting firm, and when he introduced me as "a young lady from North Carolina," I winced. He clearly saw the dilemma as *us versus them*, and considered me (hired by the chairman of the board) as one of *them*. His sabotage of the process had begun in earnest. Military language like "necessary losses" had placed lines of demarcation and created an impasse. His military training told him that leadership meant clear direction, objective measures, and a firm hand. They hated him. Worse, he didn't care. He was gone in a year.

Many mergers have failed, not because the numbers weren't there, but because the cultures didn't—wouldn't—merge. "Right" answers are useless if people don't accept them. We intuitively know subjective truths have a profound impact on our success. What we *don't* seem to know is what to do about it. One reason is that our business-school training has elevated objective truths over subjective truths for so long that we tend to label time spent making the "right" decision as "real work," and time spent on subjective issues as something less (even irrelevant). When faced with the unreliability of subjective truths we tend to default to objective criteria, or exclude the factor completely. By the rules of objective reality, something is either true or it isn't. So a negative result must mean false, right? Wrong! In the subjective world, something can be true one day (I like this merger) and false the next (I hate this merger).

Story has the capacity to access and influence subjective truths. A story can help you stay connected at a human level—even when you are on opposite sides of the facts. If the C.E.O. had been ready to balance clear directions with subjective stories about feeling conflicted when he fired their much-loved sales manager, or how choosing the system architecture was a gut feeling about what ultimately could only be a shot in the dark (perhaps a story about how he, too, had spent years working on something only to discover it was obsolete when a design decision didn't go his way), it might have made a difference. If he had tools to tend to subjective feelings, he might have survived . . . might even have succeeded.

SUBJECTIVE ISSUES NEED SUBJECTIVE TOOLS

Most of us agree that kittens are cute . . . about 50–70%, since that's how true subjective truths tend to run. So imagine this little white kitten, chasing after a ball of string or hiding behind a chair so he can pounce on his brother. This kind of cute can lure the attention of children from 6 to 60. Suppose we want to use our objective analysis to understand the subjective truth *cute*. That would be like cutting the kitten in half to analyze both sides, understand the components, and then try to recreate cute from what we learned. When we try to analyze subjective truths by breaking them down, we destroy that which we seek to understand.

It's a common mistake in business to tackle subjective problems with rational thinking, root-cause analysis, and cost/benefit studies. Objective tools introduce a terrible gold-into-lead alchemy into subjective issues. For a subjective issue like trust, root-cause analysis translates into placing blame and makes the problem worse, not better. Rather than helping, the increased application of objective tools—like better agendas, more objective measures, and clearer outcomes—sabotages our ability to see and tend to subjective problems/opportunities in organizational life. Subjective tools require that you understand how objective and subjective reality are different. Counterintuitively, trust is better achieved with a self-disclosure story about how you screwed up one day than it is with a résumé of past achievements.

Objective Reality	Subjective Reality
Quality of decision—a decision derived from objective facts, analysis	Quality of acceptance—a decision people like and want to implement
Right/wrong, true/false	It depends—true 50–70% of the time
Root-cause analysis	"Blame game"
Facts	Feelings
Analysis of components = understanding	Kittens
Accuracy (function of rational analysis)	Faith (beyond rational evidence)
Bullet points/charts/statistics	Story and metaphor, laughter, doughnuts
External proof—can prove it is true	Internal experience—you just know

Lightning-fast mental routines that rely too much on objective criteria often cause us to ignore our natural-born wisdom about subjective truths like faith. People don't want more information. They want faith—faith that you know what you're talking about and you mean what you say. Faith is a subjective judgment based on personal experience. Since most people can't experience every aspect of the organization personally, you need to give them a story that inspires faith. Even in a business meeting we are all human beings who have loved and lost, trusted and been betrayed. When you share stories that reveal your humanity, you connect at the level of human experience—the messy, confusing, emotional reality of real people living real lives.

Story is not the only tool to address subjective issues. You probably use many tools you haven't validated as tools. Doughnuts, beer, and pizza, are all very effective subjective tools. Cartoons, jokes, and social time give you access to one of the most powerful tools: laughter, the solvent of negative emotions. As the ambiguity of business and life continues to become more apparent, we will find that our ability to understand subjectivity and to alter subjective feelings will become more important. In other words, whoever tells the best story wins.

———————

Annette Simmons, M.Ed, is president of Group Process Consulting, a firm that helps organizations in the public and private sectors build more collaborative behaviors for bottom-line results. Her books have been translated into nine languages and include: *Territorial Games: Understanding and Ending Turf Wars at Work* (AMACOM, 1998); *A Safe Place for Dangerous Truths: Using Dialogue to Overcome Fear and Distrust at Work* (AMACOM, 1999); and *The Story Factor: Inspiration, Influence, and Persuasion Through the Art of Storytelling* (Perseus, 2002).

Developing Exceptional Problem-solving Skills

Christopher Hoenig

In the digital age, business organizations are being challenged by global competition, as well as technological and social change, to solve bigger, tougher problems faster, better, and cheaper than ever. Improved problem-solving capability is the ultimate competitive advantage, and the best organizations are increasing the sophistication with which they systematize their problem-solving processes. Individuals who wish to lead organizations or build successful careers in the digital age will need to build their understanding of problem-solving as a field in itself.

SOPHISTICATED PROBLEM-SOLVING IS BASED ON SIMPLE ESSENTIALS

Knowing how simple elements generate complex results is the ultimate source of power. Three primary colors blend to make up the paintings and films that capture our imagination. Two binary states are the foundation of the digital processing that underpins the information age.

In the same way, there are six essential skills involved in human problem-solving: generating mindset, acquiring knowledge, building relationships, managing problems, creating solutions, and delivering results. The tougher, larger, and more demanding a problem or opportunity is, and the faster and more competitive your environment is, the more important these skills become.

I am not talking about the "old" problem-solving—traditional cookbook approaches that are small-scale, linear, deficiency-oriented, and tactical. I am talking about a "new," rapidly evolving definition of problem-solving that encompasses large-scale, nonlinear, opportunity-oriented, and strategic work. This is problem-solving in the age of biotech, the Web, smart materials, and the global economy.

We live in an era when information technology is our primary tool, knowledge the strategic asset, and problem-solving the paramount skill. Problem-solving ability is now the most sought-after trait in up-and-coming executives, according to a recent survey of 1,000 executives by Caliper Associates, reported in the *Wall Street Journal* by Hal Lancaster ("Managing Your Career"). To put it bluntly, if you're not a problem-solver, your career potential is limited.

THE PROBLEM-SOLVING JOURNEY

I refer to the problem-solving journey because the mixture of problem-solving and adventure blends two rich sources of knowledge into one. Exactly like an adventure, problem-solving is a journey from a starting point to some distant destination. It is a journey into the unknown—through fear and exhilaration, confidence and disappointment.

Thinking of the solutions to problems (or opportunities) as journeys brings the topic alive. Professional knowledge about problem-solving is, by definition, abstract. But the language, images, ideas, and principles of adventure and exploration make it accessible and invest it with the drama that real problem-solvers experience: the disciplined planning, the long waits, and the moments of crisis and celebration. Moreover, since we have all traveled, this metaphor helps us tap into our own undiscovered sources of wisdom about the principles and practices of problem-solving journeys.

THE DIFFERENCE BETWEEN THE BEST
AND THE WORST PROBLEM-SOLVERS

The difference between the best and the worst problem-solvers is how many of the six essentials they can marshal (by themselves or with others), and how deeply the skills are understood, individually and collectively. Poor problem-solvers understand the skills incompletely and therefore cannot marshal a complete capability. Great problem-solvers know the skills well enough to pull together and manage all six, or exhibit one in great depth as part of a team.

The journey from novice to world-class expert in any field begins by understanding the six essentials, practicing them, mastering them at one level, and then moving on toward the limits of your potential.

At some point in this process, the best problem-solvers rise above their profession in a multidisciplinary fashion. Each of the six essentials represents a bundle of habits, skills, and knowledge that come together in problem-solving "personalities." Each personality draws its strength from a variety of specialties and professions.

The six personalities serve as a convenient way to assess yourself and others. They allow you to determine your own personal mix of strengths and weaknesses and how you can put together a complete problem-solving capability. Great problem-solvers know their strengths and weaknesses, and they build teams to compensate for them, creating wholes that are equal to or greater than the sum of their parts.

THE SIX ESSENTIALS OF PROBLEM-SOLVING

Generate the Mindset (the Innovator). The *innovator* focuses on moving from self-doubt to innovation by developing potent ideas and attitudes, above all through seeking out alternative points of view. The ability to do this improves your effectiveness in moving creatively through a problem-solving effort. An innovator's potent mindset sets the stage for discovery, because the combination of commitment and open-mindedness generates the widest possible field of opportunities to consider.

Leading innovators such as Dee Hock, founder of VISA international, Jeff Bezos of Amazon.com, and John Seely Brown of Xerox PARC epitomize the innovator's mindset. Great companies known for a history of innovation, such as 3M, IDEO, and Procter & Gamble, have made it a pervasive part of their culture.

Know the Territory (the Discoverer). The *discoverer* concentrates on moving from innovation to insight by asking the right questions and getting good, timely information. Better knowledge helps you define problems more effectively, choose the best routes, and identify what's at stake. A discoverer's knowledge of a territory brings understanding and insight, which reveal the most likely problems and opportunities in higher relief. With more investigation, the implications of those problems become more apparent as a foundation for action.

Leading discoverers such as Craig Venter of Celera Genomics, or Nobel Prize winner Dr. Eric Wieschaus, are examples of what outstanding discovery can produce. Great companies and universities that have built a foundation on research and discovery include Bell Labs, MIT, and CalTech.

Build the Relationships (the Communicator).   The *communicator* deals with how to move from insight to community by cultivating quality interaction and so creating an ever-expanding circle of relationships based on service, loyalty, and identity. Communicators develop the support and human context needed to create and implement change effectively. Through their mastery of relationship building, communicators connect potential journeys to their actual implications for real people. They help determine whether a problem-solving effort is worthwhile, for whom, and why. Then they generate a core group that will tackle the journey and a network that will support the effort.

Great communicators like Franklin Roosevelt, or Winston Churchill, demonstrate the power of communication and relationship building in tackling historic problems. Companies that have built worldwide reputations for service because of their attention to communication include L. L. Bean, Hallmark Cards, and Dell.

Manage the Journeys (the Playmaker).   The *playmaker* focuses on moving from building a community to giving that community a sense of direction by choosing destinations and strategies. Fostering an understanding of the stages of any problem-solving journey helps people to set goals, define success, and develop effective plans. Playmakers take the attitude, knowledge, and people brought into play by innovators, discoverers, and communicators, and shape the destinations, direction, and strategies to make the journey a reality.

Playmakers such as Nelson Mandela, Colin Powell, and Jack Welch demonstrate the power of leadership in directing problem-solving efforts. Companies like Kleiner, McKinsey & Company, and American Airlines have institutionalized that leadership in a way that has lasted over decades of business success.

Create the Solutions (the Creator).   The *creator* shows how to move from leadership to power by designing, building, and maintaining optimal solutions. Creators help to bring the best technology, people, and tools together in complete, flexible solutions that will fit the problem you're trying to solve. A creator takes the requirements and goals of a playmaker, which define the journey, and figures out what it will take to get the group where they want to go. When there is more innovation and better knowledge, when there are richer relationships and better-defined problems, then solution design and construction are more focused.

Great creators such as Bill Gates and Paul Allen, Steve Jobs, Steve Wozniak, and Thomas Edison exemplify the passion, talent, and will required to build new solutions. Companies such as Microsoft, Toyota, and General Electric have built corporate systems and cultures that sustain quality creative ability over long periods of time.

Deliver the Results (the Performer). The *performer* concentrates on moving from power to sustainable advantage through intuitive and disciplined implementation, which allows one continually to exceed expectations. Performers can help to conquer complexity, friction, and scale with simplicity, discipline, and a competitive edge. Performers take the goals and strategies of the playmaker and the solutions of the creator, and work to achieve full resolution of the problem. Innovation, knowledge, and well-developed relationships aid in their efforts. When all the other roles are done well, the performer is able to focus completely on achieving full resolution and not on redesign, unplanned maintenance, or changing requirements.

Great performers such as Lou Gerstner in business, Reinhold Messner in mountain climbing, and Isabelle Autissier in sailing, show the character and savvy it takes to deliver great performances. Companies like Federal Express and McDonald's have built empires on the precision and consistency of performance over time.

MAKING IT HAPPEN
To enhance your problem-solving skills:
- Master the six problem-solving essentials and the stages of any problem-solving journey so that you can locate yourself in problem-solving situations and organize your attack on the problem.
- Diagnose yourself, to understand your strengths and weaknesses and how to compensate for them. Do a free diagnostic self-assessment to find out what type of problem solver you are at www.exolve.com.
- Move in the new direction, and fill the gaps in your problem-solving team.

The new professional economy is placing an increasing premium on the mind, body, and soul of the adventurer—the problem-solver—on people who can conceive, organize, and lead expeditions that add value to society, business, and humanity. These problem-solvers have an adventurer's blend of innocence and wisdom, self-reliance and a willingness to collaborate, professional competence and the capacity to scale new peaks, as well as the resilience to persevere through uncharted territory.

And just as in the old economy or the next economy after this one, no amount of buzz, momentum, or technology will cover the lack of problem-solving essentials for long. True problem-solving capability is what drives enduring advantage in any field, at any time, in any place.

Chris Hoenig is founder, chairman and C.E.O. of Exolve Inc., a company providing strategic knowledge about problem-solving concepts, techniques and tools. As director of information technology issues at the General Accounting Office—the investigative arm of Congress—he designed and implemented a reform of technology and information management for the U.S. government, saving several billion dollars to date. He is frequently in the national media and speaks regularly to audiences of corporate and government executives on information and technology management, and how they apply to vital public and private sector issues. He recently wrote *The Problem Solving Journey* (Perseus, 2000).

What's Next? The New Challenges for Business

Eamonn Kelly

Eamonn Kelly is C.E.O. and president of Global Business Network the renowned California-based futures network and consultancy and member of The Monitor Group. In addition to sustaining the company's thought leadership about the future, Kelly has worked at senior levels with dozens of the world's leading corporations in many sectors, as well as with global and national public agencies. He was previously head of strategy for Scottish Enterprise, one of the world's most respected and innovative development agencies. He is coauthor of *What's Next? Exploring the New Terrain for Business* (Perseus, 2002). In this article, Eamonn Kelly highlights the challenging new environment for business created by 2 decades of significant and accelerating change. The solution, he argues, is to learn to anticipate change and to adapt quickly, and this requires organizations to adopt a new set of priorities.

We live in an era of profound transformation. In just a few decades we have witnessed the transition from an industrial, nation-based, resource-orientated economy to a global, networked, knowledge-intensive economy. Corporations have been a powerful catalyst for change: opening markets, promoting privatization, and globalizing goods, services, and production processes. As more parts of the world have adopted market mechanisms to promote wealth creation, millions of people have gained access to new products, as well as technologies, information, and ideas. New economic opportunities have improved the quality of life for many. However, there have also been unintended consequences.

The liberation of markets, driven by the power of corporations, has also created more complex, interconnected economic and social systems that cannot be controlled or predicted. The very forces of globalization, rapid technological advances, increased connectivity, and mounting transparency that businesses have helped to unleash are shaping a new and challenging environment. Global protest movements, demands for greater accountability, increasingly complex geopolitical tensions, wider cultural divides, and rising concerns about environmental and social sustainability, are making the business of business even more complicated. These new realities point to a whole new set of challenges and opportunities for business in the decade ahead.

Foremost among these corporate challenges is a need to move beyond the sole pursuit of competitive advantage to embrace "adaptive advantage" as well. Amidst the economic globalization and deregulation of the past 20 years, companies understandably sought competitive advantage by developing and applying a superior understanding of the marketplace. Using increasingly sophisticated tools and technologies, they analyzed and modeled the economy, finance, industries, customers, competitors, and options. In the next ten years, businesses will continue to improve such tools, but that alone will no longer be sufficient to ensure success. Instead, businesses must also learn to respond more quickly to an increasingly complex environment in which many political, economic, social, cultural, and technological forces are shifting, interacting, and sometimes colliding. This will entail expanding their peripheral vision to encompass a far broader set of concerns and to focus on the development of *adaptive advantage*, based on a deeper understanding of the world as well as the marketplace. Ultimately, adaptive advantage requires significant improvement in two linked areas: the ability to anticipate and sense change, and the capacity to respond quickly and coherently. For companies this will inform a new set of developmental priorities, organized around *thinking differently, learning differently*, and *acting differently*.

THINKING DIFFERENTLY

When it comes to thinking differently, business leaders will have to increase the complexity of their thought to mirror the complexity of their environment. There are three related ways of evolving one's ability to do just that: *outside-in thinking, connective thinking*, and finally, *scenario thinking*.

Outside-in Thinking. Strategic or business development thinking tends to move from the inside out. It typically starts with the organization's purpose and core strengths, then explores its marketplaces and competitive positioning, and finally looks at the broader geopolitical, economic, social, and technological shifts that might matter. Much of the time that trajectory is entirely appropriate, but not when you are seeking to boost your sensitivity to changes in the external business environment. That's because, once you get to the external focus, you have subconsciously introduced so many assumptions about what's important, based on experience, that you only see a small subset of the external world. As a result you can miss the big changes that could be important, such as new security risks or seemingly irrelevant scientific and technological developments that could prove advantageous to you—or your competitors. Conversely, by thinking from the outside in you begin with the external changes that might, over time, profoundly impact your markets and organization. Your filters and assumptions, though still present, are less restrictive. This encourages more open and imaginative thinking about the full range of potential changes that might matter most to your future.

Connective Thinking. Another thinking skill that is becoming more critical is the ability to make creative connections between apparently disparate ideas and trends—connective thinking. This is closely related to systems thinking, but becomes a different creative challenge when applied to the terrain of future possibilities. It is about connecting dots in new ways to discover new patterns of possibility. For example, the seemingly unrelated trends of rising environmental concerns, continued threats of widespread terrorism, the spreading anti-globalization movement, progress toward a hydrogen economy, and manufacturing at the molecular level, together might suggest a possible move toward localized versus global production of goods. Chances are the future will not be determined by one big change but by multiple changes that converge. Adaptive advantage, therefore, will partly come from making quicker, smarter connections across varied domains.

Scenario Thinking. Outside-in and connective thinking inevitably lead you to contemplate "What ifs?" about the future. But to do so productively, organizations can neither deny uncertainty and assume that the future will look pretty much like a projection of the past, or be paralyzed by it—that is, abandon all attempts to take a long view because everything is too complex, too crazy. The well-tested methodology of "scenario thinking" enables us to anticipate the future without the folly of trying to predict it, or the mistake of ignoring it. This "long view" approach involves a process of developing several very different but plausible stories of how the future might unfold in ways that are relevant to organizations. By providing multiple, plausible perspectives on what could happen, scenarios enable you to understand and challenge the organization's dominant assumptions. Scenarios, therefore, help to boost our preparedness for different credible futures, while also providing a context for discovering new opportunities. Above all, scenarios are stories—an ancient and remarkably powerful form of communication that reveals values and beliefs and sustains communities. In a business setting they help to overcome the inertia and denial that can so easily make the future a dangerous place.

LEARNING DIFFERENTLY

Gaining adaptive advantage requires that business leaders not only think differently, but also learn differently. This can be accomplished by identifying key *literacies for the future*, establishing *learning networks*, and getting executives out of the office and onto *learning journeys*.

Literacies for the Future. With so much happening in the world, with so many uncertainties and drivers of change, how can overworked executives identify the limits of their knowledge? Information overload can be channeled productively by creating a specific learning agenda that focuses on a few external developments that may have a low impact on your business today, but could be hugely significant in defining your future. These "literacies for the future" may be very broad, such as emerging geopolitical risks, or bioconvergence—the interactions of bio-, nano-, and info-technologies. Others may focus more narrowly on a specific topic (water resources or China) or technology (quantum computing, carbon sequestration). Similarly, literacies can be explored in a variety of ways: a series of presentations or debates by internal and external experts, brown-bag lunch discussions, white papers, Web-based conversations, even field trips—all designed to achieve familiarity and fluency rather than depth and expertise in a variety of topics and issues.

Learning Networks. Identifying core areas for focused learning is a beginning, not an end. It is equally important to be continually exposed to a broader range of ideas and developments. Learning networks, both internal and external, can serve this function by linking members with a wide variety of expertise and experience. Many networks are organized around a shared interest or expertise to trade information, tools and techniques, and even job opportunities. Learning networks, however, purposely include external experts on a variety of topics—politics and economics, different cultures and religions, science and technology—who provide advance notice of emerging developments in their fields, filter new information, interpret events and issues from different perspectives, and even explore the implications of decisions or actions. Similarly, internal networks can connect people across different business units to leverage expertise, vet options, and facilitate cross-functional teamwork. Some networks are entirely virtual; others periodically come together face-to-face while sustaining their relationships and activities electronically. Networks can also be a powerful force for action as well as learning. For example, the World Trade Organization protests in Seattle and elsewhere were organized by connecting and communicating with networks using the Internet and cell phones. Although networks are not easy to design—indeed, they tend to take on a life and purpose of their own—it is possible to create networks that will provoke, inform, and accelerate learning and community, fulfilling the old adage, "No one is as smart as everyone."

Learning Journeys. John Le Carré once wrote: "A desk is a dangerous place from which to view the world." It is crucial for executives to get out of the office and be exposed to forces that might shape the future—or are already shaping the present in ways that are invisible to most of us. "Learning journeys" around a particular theme (such as the biotech economy, clean technologies, converging and diverging cultures, or customers of the future) can stretch thinking far beyond the obvious and everyday. Unlike fact-finding missions or benchmarking expeditions that tend to substantiate preconceptions or prove hypotheses, learning journeys are truly exploratory: they push the envelope on what is known and redefine the boundaries of what is possible by introducing the participants to striking new experiences, places, people, and ideas. Often the most significant insights are subtle; not the presentation given by the head of R&D at a pioneering technology firm, but the fact that she and her colleagues are such a young, diverse, articulate, and energetic group, especially when compared to the bureaucrats at the shabby government lab down the street. Furthermore, because the learning is visceral—derived from an experience rather than a book or lecture—it tends to be more lasting and actionable.

ACTING DIFFERENTLY

Thinking and learning differently will have little impact in the absence of changed behavior. In fact, both should inform behavior. So the third pillar of adaptive advantage is behaving in ways that will become increasingly important for business success: *acting experimentally, acting inclusively,* and *acting ethically.*

Acting Experimentally. In the coming decade businesses may have to change even more frequently, rapidly, and dramatically than ever before. This requires a critical new capacity: the ability to act *experimentally.* In evolution, nature experiments through speciation, trying out frequent small-scale changes, or genetic variations that iterate and compound over time. Likewise, science is based on experimentation, as hypotheses are tested and revised through small-scale experiments. Most of these experiments will fail, but they are inexpensive and yield valuable learning. Few businesses, however, have mastered the art and practice of experimentation. Most introduce changes through large-scale initiatives that are typically based on a single approach, consume considerable resources, take a long time to implement, and leave little room for course corrections. Indeed, this approach often works against adaptation—it might even be an adaptive *dis*advantage. Instead, business should follow the lead of nature and science: imagine, design, and execute small-scale experiments in new opportunity spaces; systematically extract the learning from both success and failure; and move swiftly on to the next iteration.

Acting Inclusively. A world of growing interconnection and mutual interdependence demands a more holistic and inclusive approach to thinking and acting. For businesses, taking a more inclusive view of the purpose of your business, beyond making a profit and creating shareholder value, reveals new opportunities for alliances or long-term investments that enhance your adaptive advantage. Similarly, adopting a more inclusive definition of your stakeholders and being open to broader opportunities for dialog and collaboration with them could improve your business intelligence, standing, and relationships. Perhaps the most promising and challenging long-term opportunity to create adaptive advantage involves engaging the excluded billions of the world's poor—the two-thirds of the world's population that remain disconnected from the economic mainstream despite globalization. On the one hand, the notion of "B24B," or "business to 4 billion" appeals to direct corporate self-interest since these new markets will allow businesses to sustain high future growth as mature markets evolve toward different patterns of demand. But from a longer-term perspective, businesses need to help create a sustainable business environment by addressing the deep problems found in many parts of the world, laying appropriate foundations for local economic growth, and creating a sense of meaningful opportunity and hope among those currently excluded.

Acting Ethically. In the industrial era, businesses produced widespread economic and quality-of-life improvements through mechanizing, standardizing, automating, and scaling their operations. In most capitalist societies, businesses were considered morally neutral, neither causing deliberate harm nor pursuing a greater social good. Unintended negative consequences of commercial activity, such as environmental degradation, were largely tolerated, even expected. With time, however, there developed a growing disconnect between "economic wisdom"—doing the profitable thing—and "moral wisdom"—doing the right thing. Today, that trend may be reversing as economic and moral wisdom become realigned—enabling and encouraging businesses to "do well by doing good." Many factors are driving this realignment: the sheer scale and reach of market-based business activity, the accumulating evidence of the environmental, social, and cultural consequences of business activity, the unprecedented level of transparency, and a growing sense of public concern regarding the role of corporations and their impact on the world. As we've seen with Enron, Andersen, and WorldCom, it seems inevitable that public scrutiny will grow, leaving fewer places for transgressors to hide or avoid punishment for violating common moral wisdom. Every business could find that its reputation and credibility are constantly in play and at peril. The safest strategy will be to strive for impeccable behavior that over time becomes embedded in your business brand.

This means that business leaders will have to instill a deep ethical consciousness throughout their organization, not merely as an adjunct to business strategy, but as a core organizing principle. Shareholders and other stakeholders will demand it.

However, this will also enhance adaptive advantage because a clear, shared ethical compass will be essential to navigate quickly through the complex terrain of the future business environment. The ability of people at all levels of an organization to develop appropriate options, make rapid decisions, and act swiftly in a changing world will increasingly require a common set of ethical imperatives. Instilling such an ethical consciousness will take more than putting a statement of values on computer mouse pads—the commitment must become embedded in the organization's DNA. Fortunately, promoting ethical behavior does not run counter to the personal instincts of most employees and stakeholders who want to act ethically in their personal and professional lives. By reinforcing and rewarding ethical standards and behavior, ethical consciousness may prove surprisingly easy to achieve. Moreover, those who move early in this direction can expect to attract and retain great people, which in turn fuels adaptive advantage.

Over the last 20 years we have seen businesses large and small, global and local, help create a vibrant, complex, interconnected, and interdependent world, in which wealth and opportunity have spread globally. Looking ahead to the future it is easy to imagine scenarios of increasing complexity, shaped by the interaction of more elaborate technology, more sophisticated products and services, more diverse global markets, more complicated financial instruments, and more demanding collaborative relationships. It is equally easy to imagine businesses rising to the challenges created by such complexity and innovating effectively as they continue to thrive. However, it is all too easy to imagine scenarios in which the increasing complexities and accelerating pace of change that business helped create, actually compound to undermine the economic, social, and physical environment on which we all depend. So in addition to understanding the world better, businesses will need to address the problems of the world more actively. Collectively, the business sector holds too much power to be morally neutral in its activities. We cannot focus solely on profitability and shareholder value. We cannot ignore the plight of billions of people untouched—or worse, harmed—by the economic progress of the last century. We cannot, in short, simply *adapt* to the changing world, in part because the very process of adaptation causes further change. We must exercise long-term responsibility and use our strengths to influence that change for the better. The next stage in the evolution of business is beginning. Having done so much to create a remarkable new world, we now must play a more active part in nurturing and improving it. This may prove to be the most profound source of sustained success in the twenty-first century.

THE
ULTIMATE BUSINESS
LIBRARY

Essential resources for anyone and everyone in business

BUSINESS: THE ULTIMATE RESOURCE
Introduction by Daniel Goleman

"The closest we have to a business bible" *(USA Today), Business: The Ultimate Resource* includes over 100 original best-practice essays from the world's leading thinkers and practitioners, over 300 practical checklists, a world almanac, listings of over 3,000 information resources, and much more.

HARDCOVER
ISBN 0-7382-0242-8

THE ULTIMATE BUSINESS DICTIONARY
Defining the World of Work

Over 6,000 entries. Features a multi-lingual glossary; abbreviations, acronyms, and business slang; world economic data; listings of international stock exchanges and trade organizations; and worked examples of finance and accounting terms.

PAPERBACK
ISBN 0-7382-0821-3

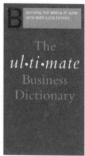

THE BEST BUSINESS BOOKS EVER
The 100 Most Influential Management Books You'll Never Have Time to Read

From the *Art of War* to *Being Digital, The Best Business Books Ever* illuminates the key ideas and contributions of the100 titles that should be in any manager's library.

PAPERBACK
ISBN 0-7382-0849-3
Available July 2003

THE BIG BOOK OF BUSINESS QUOTATIONS
More than 5,000 Indispensible Observations on the World of Commerce, Work, Finance, and Management

A compendium of the most memorable, insightful, and amusing quotes on business, leadership, and the economy.

HARDCOVER
ISBN 0-7382-0848-5
Available July 2003

AVAILABLE AT BOOKSTORES AND ONLINE RETAILERS EVERYWHERE